Demonology and Devil-lore

Volume 1

Demonology and Devil-lore 1
Author: Moncure Daniel Conway

Cover image: *Monster guarding the entrance of the Purgator,* "Compendium rarissimum totius
            Artis Magicae sistematisatae per celeberrimos Artis hujus Magistros"
            - Germany 1775
Lay-out: www.burokd.nl

ISBN 978-94-92355-15-7

© 2016 Revised publication by:

VAMzzz Publishing
P.O. Box 3340
1001 AC Amsterdam
The Netherlands
www.vamzzz.com
contactvamzzz@gmail.com

DEMONOLOGY
and DEVIL-LORE 1

Moncure Daniel Conway

VAMzzz PUBLISHING

Moncure Daniel Conway
Stafford County, March 17, 1832 – Paris, November 15, 1907

contents

Part III The Dragon

Preface

Three Friars, says a legend, hid themselves near the Witch Sabbath orgies that they might count the devils; but the Chief of these, discovering the friars, said—'Reverend Brothers, our army is such that if all the Alps, their rocks and glaciers, were equally divided among us, none would have a pound's weight.' This was in one Alpine valley. Any one who has caught but a glimpse of the world's Walpurgis Night, as revealed in Mythology and Folklore, must agree that this courteous devil did not overstate the case. Any attempt to catalogue the evil spectres which have haunted mankind were like trying to count the shadows cast upon the earth by the rising sun. This conviction has grown upon the author of this work at every step in his studies of the subject.

In 1859 I contributed, as one of the American 'Tracts for the Times,' a pamphlet entitled 'The Natural History of the Devil.' Probably the chief value of that essay was to myself, and this in that its preparation had revealed to me how pregnant with interest and importance was the subject selected. Subsequent researches in the same direction, after I had come to reside in Europe, revealed how slight had been my conception of the vastness of the domain upon which that early venture was made. In 1872, while preparing a series of lectures for the Royal Institution on Demonology, it appeared to me that the best I could do was to print those lectures with some notes and additions; but after they were delivered there still remained with me unused the greater part of materials collected in many countries, and the phantasmal creatures which I had evoked would not permit me to rest from my labours until I had dealt with them more thoroughly.

The fable of Thor's attempt to drink up a small spring, and his failure because it was fed by the ocean, seems aimed at such efforts as mine. But there is another aspect of the case which has yielded me more encouragement. These phantom hosts, however unmanageable as to number, when closely examined, present comparatively few types; they coalesce by hundreds; from being at first overwhelmed by their multiplicity, the classifier finds himself at length beating bushes to start a new variety. Around some single form—the physiognomy, it may be, of Hunger or Disease, of Lust or Cruelty—ignorant imagination has broken up nature into innumerable bits which, like mirrors of various surface, reflect the same in endless sizes and distortions; but they vanish if that central fact be withdrawn.

In trying to conquer, as it were, these imaginary monsters, they have sometimes swarmed and gibbered around me in a mad comedy which travestied their tragic sway over those who believed in their reality. Gargoyles extended their grin over the finest architecture, cornices coiled to serpents, the very words of speakers started out of their conventional sense into images that tripped my attention. Only as what I believed right solutions were given to their problems were my sphinxes laid; but through this psychological experience it appeared that when one was so laid his or her legion disappeared also. Long ago such phantasms ceased to haunt my nerves, because

I discovered their unreality; I am now venturing to believe that their mythologic forms cease to haunt my studies, because I have found out their reality.

Why slay the slain? Such may be the question that will arise in the minds of many who see this book. A Scotch song says, 'The Devil is dead, and buried at Kirkcaldy;' if so, he did not die until he had created a world in his image. The natural world is overlaid by an unnatural religion, breeding bitterness around simplest thoughts, obstructions to science, estrangements not more reasonable than if they resulted from varying notions of lunar figures,—all derived from the Devil-bequeathed dogma that certain beliefs and disbeliefs are of infernal instigation. Dogmas moulded in a fossil demonology make the foundation of institutions which divert wealth, learning, enterprise, to fictitious ends. It has not, therefore, been mere intellectual curiosity which has kept me working at this subject these many years, but an increasing conviction that the sequelæ of such superstitions are exercising a still formidable influence. When Father Delaporte lately published his book on the Devil, his Bishop wrote—'Reverend Father, if every one busied himself with the Devil as you do, the kingdom of God would gain by it.' Identifying the kingdom here spoken of as that of Truth, it has been with a certain concurrence in the Bishop's sentiment that I have busied myself with the work now given to the public.

Part I
Demonolatry

Chapter I
Dualism

Origin of Deism — Evolution from the far to the near — Illustrations from witchcraft — The primitive Pantheism — The dawn of Dualism

A COLLEGE IN the State of Ohio has adopted for its motto the words 'Orient thyself.' This significant admonition to Western youth represents one condition of attaining truth in the science of mythology. Through neglect of it the glowing personifications and metaphors of the East have too generally migrated to the West only to find it a Medusa turning them to stone. Our prosaic literalism changes their ideals to idols. The time has come when we must learn rather to see ourselves in them: out of an age and civilisation where we live in habitual recognition of natural forces we may transport ourselves to a period and region where no sophisticated eye looks upon nature. The sun is a chariot drawn by shining steeds and driven by a refulgent deity; the stars ascend and move by arbitrary power or command; the tree is the bower of a spirit; the fountain leaps from the urn of a naiad. In such gay costumes did the laws of nature hold their carnival until Science struck the hour for unmasking. The costumes and masks have with us become materials for studying the history of the human mind, but to know them we must translate our senses back into that phase of our own early existence, so far as is consistent with carrying our culture with us.

Without conceding too much to Solar mythology, it may be pronounced tolerably clear that the earliest emotion of worship was born out of the wonder with which man looked up to the heavens above him. The splendours of the morning and evening; the azure vault, painted with frescoes of cloud or blackened by the storm; the night, crowned with constellations: these awakened imagination, inspired awe, kindled admiration, and at length adoration, in the being who had reached intervals in which his eye was lifted above the earth. Amid the rapture of Vedic hymns to these sublimities we meet sharp questionings whether there be any such gods as the priests say, and suspicion is sometimes cast on sacrifices. The forms that peopled the celestial spaces may have been those of ancestors, kings, and great men, but anterior to all forms was the poetic enthusiasm which built heavenly mansions for them; and the crude cosmogonies of primitive science were probably caught up by this spirit, and consecrated as slowly as scientific generalisations now are.

Our modern ideas of evolution might suggest the reverse of this—that human worship began with things low and gradually ascended to high objects; that from rude ages, in which adoration was directed to stock and stone, tree and reptile, the human mind climbed by degrees to the contemplation and reverence of celestial grandeurs. But the accord of this view with our ideas of evolution is apparent only. The real progress seems here to have been from the far to the near, from the great to the small. It is, indeed, probably inexact to speak of the worship of stock and stone, weed and wort, insect and reptile, as primitive. There are many indications that such things were by no race considered intrinsically sacred, nor were they really worshipped until the origin of their sanctity was lost; and even now, ages after their oracular or symbolical character has been forgotten, the superstitions that have survived in connection with such insignificant objects point to an original association with the phenomena of the heavens. No religions could, at first glance, seem wider apart than the worship of the serpent and that of the glorious sun; yet many ancient temples are covered with symbols combining sun and snake, and no form is more familiar in Egypt than the solar serpent standing erect upon its tail, with rays around its head.

Nor is this high relationship of the adored reptile found only in regions where it might have been raised up by ethnical combinations as the mere survival of a savage symbol. William Craft, an African who resided for some time in the kingdom of Dahomey, informed me of the following incident which he had witnessed there. The sacred serpents are kept in a grand house, which they sometimes leave to crawl in their neighbouring grounds. One day a negro from some distant region encountered one of these animals and killed it. The people learning that one of their gods had been slain, seized the stranger, and having surrounded him with a circle of brushwood, set it on fire. The poor wretch broke through the circle of fire and ran, pursued by the crowd, who struck him with heavy sticks. Smarting from the flames and blows, he rushed into a river; but no sooner had he entered there than the pursuit ceased, and he was told that, having gone through fire and water, he was purified, and might emerge with safety. Thus, even in that distant and savage region, serpent-worship was associated with fire-worship and river-worship, which have a wide representation in both Aryan and Semitic symbolism. To this day the orthodox Israelites set beside their dead, before burial, the lighted candle and a basin of pure water. These have been associated in rabbinical mythology with the angels Michael (genius of Water) and Gabriel (genius of Fire); but they refer both to the phenomenal glories and the purifying effects of the two elements as reverenced by the Africans in one direction and the Parsees in another.

Not less significant are the facts which were attested at the witch-trials. It was shown that for their pretended divinations they used plants—as rue and vervain—well known in the ancient Northern religions, and often recognised as examples of tree-worship; but it also appeared that around the cauldron a mock zodiacal circle was drawn, and that every herb employed was alleged to have derived its potency from having been gathered at a certain hour of the night or day, a particular quarter of the moon, or from some spot where sun or moon did or did not shine upon it. Ancient planet-worship is, indeed, still reflected in the habit of village herbalists, who gather their simples at certain phases of the moon, or at certain of those holy periods of the year which conform more or less to the pre-christian festivals.

These are a few out of many indications that the small and senseless things which have become almost or quite fetishes were by no means such at first, but were mystically connected with the heavenly elements and splendours, like the animal forms in the zodiac. In one of the earliest hymns of the Rig-Veda it is said—'This earth belongs to Varuna (Οὐρανός) the king, and the wide sky: he is contained also in this drop of water.' As the sky was seen reflected in the shining curve of a dew-drop, even so in the shape or colour of a leaf or flower, the transformation of a chrysalis, or the burial and resurrection of a scarabæus' egg, some sign could be detected making it answer in place of the typical image which could not yet be painted or carved.

The necessities of expression would, of course, operate to invest the primitive conceptions and interpretations of celestial phenomena with those pictorial images drawn from earthly objects of which the early languages are chiefly composed. In many cases that are met in the most ancient hymns, the designations of exalted objects are so little descriptive of them, that we may refer them to a period anterior to the formation of that refined and complex symbolism by which primitive religions have acquired a representation in definite characters. The Vedic comparisons of the various colours of the dawn to horses, or the rain-clouds to cows, denotes a much less mature development of thought than the fine observation implied in the connection of the forked lightning with the forked serpent-tongue and forked mistletoe, or symbolisation of the universe in the concentric folds of an onion. It is the presence of these more mystical and complex ideas in religions which indicate a progress of the human mind from the large and obvious to the more delicate and occult, and the growth of the higher vision which can see small things in their large relationships. Although the exaltation in the Vedas of Varuna as king of heaven, and as contained also in a drop of water, is in one verse, we may well recognise an immense distance in time between the two ideas there embodied. The first represents that primitive pantheism which is the counterpart of ignorance. An unclassified outward universe is the reflection of a mind without form and void: it is while all within is as yet undiscriminating wonder that the religious vesture of nature will be this undefined pantheism. The fruit of the tree of the knowledge of good and evil has not yet been tasted. In some of the earlier hymns of the Rig-Veda, the Maruts, the storm-deities, are praised along with Indra, the sun; Yama, king of Death, is equally adored with the goddess of Dawn. 'No real foe of yours is known in heaven, nor in earth.' 'The storms are thy allies.' Such is the high optimism of sentences found even in sacred books which elsewhere mask the dawn of the Dualism which ultimately superseded the harmony of the elemental Powers. 'I create light and I create darkness, I create good and I create evil.' 'Look unto Yezdan, who causeth the shadow to fall.' But it is easy to see what must be the result when this happy family of sun-god and storm-god and fire-god, and their innumerable co-ordinate divinities, shall be divided by discord. When each shall have become associated with some earthly object or fact, he or she will appear as friend or foe, and their connection with the sources of human pleasure and pain will be reflected in collisions and wars in the heavens. The rebel clouds will be transformed to Titans and Dragons. The adored Maruts will be no longer storm-heroes with unsheathed swords of lightning, marching as the retinue of Indra, but fire-breathing monsters—Vritras and Ahis,—and the morning and evening shadows from faithful watch-dogs become the treacherous hell-hounds, like Orthros and Cerberus. The vehement antagonisms between animals and men and of tribe against tribe, will be expressed in the conception of struggles among gods, who will thus be classified as good or evil deities.

This was precisely what did occur. The primitive pantheism was broken up: in its place the later ages beheld the universe as the arena of a tremendous conflict between good and evil Powers, who severally, in the process of time, marshalled each and everything, from a world to a worm, under their flaming banners.

Chapter II
The Genesis of Demons

THE FIRST PANTHEON of each race was built of intellectual speculations. In a moral sense, each form in it might be described as more
or less demonic; and, indeed, it may almost be affirmed that religion,
considered as a service rendered to superhuman beings, began with
the propitiation of demons, albeit they might be called gods. Man
found that in the earth good things came with difficulty, while thorns
and weeds sprang up everywhere. The evil powers seemed to be
the strongest. The best deity had a touch of the demon in him. The
sun is the most beneficent, yet he bears the sunstroke along with
the sunbeam, and withers the blooms he calls forth. The splendour,
the might, the majesty, the menace, the grandeur and wrath of the
heavens and the elements were blended in these personifications,
and reflected in the trembling adoration paid to them. The flattering
names given to these powers by their worshippers must be interpreted by the costly sacrifices with which men sought to propitiate
them. No sacrifice would have been offered originally to a purely benevolent power. The Furies were called the Eumenides, 'the
well-meaning,' and there arises a temptation to regard the name as

preserving the primitive meaning of the Sanskrit original of Erinyes, namely, *Saranyu*, which signifies the morning light stealing over the sky. But the descriptions of the Erinyes by the Greek poets—especially of Æschylus, who pictures them as black, serpent-locked, with eyes dropping blood, and calls them hounds—show that *Saranyu* as morning light, and thus the revealer of deeds of darkness, had gradually been degraded into a personification of the Curse. And yet, while recognising the name Eumenides as euphemistic, we may admire none the less the growth of that rationalism which ultimately found in the epithet a suggestion of the soul of good in things evil, and almost restored the beneficent sense of Saranyu. 'I have settled in this place,' says Athene in the 'Eumenides' of Æschylus, 'these mighty deities, hard to be appeased; they have obtained by lot to administer all things concerning men. But he who has not found them gentle knows not whence come the ills of life.' But before the dread Erinyes of Homer's age had become the 'venerable goddesses' (σεμναὶ θεαὶ) of popular phrase in Athens, or the Eumenides of the later poet's high insight, piercing their Gorgon form as portrayed by himself, they had passed through all the phases of human terror. Cowering generations had tried to soothe the remorseless avengers by complimentary phrases. The worship of the serpent, originating in the same fear, similarly raised that animal into the region where poets could invest it with many profound and beautiful significances. But these more distinctly terrible deities are found in the shadowy border-land of mythology, from which we may look back into ages when the fear in which worship is born had not yet been separated into its elements of awe and admiration, nor the heaven of supreme forces divided into ranks of benevolent and malevolent beings; and, on the other hand, we may look forward to the ages in which the moral consciousness of man begins to form the distinctions between good and evil, right and wrong, which changes cosmogony into religion, and impresses every deity of the mind's creation to do his or her part in reflecting the physical and moral struggles of mankind.

Fig. 1.—Beelzebub (Calmet)

The intermediate processes by which the good and evil were detached, and advanced to separate personification, cannot always be traced, but the indications of their work are in most cases sufficiently clear. The relationship, for instance, between Baal and Baal-zebub cannot be doubted. The one represents the Sun in his glory as quickener of Nature and painter of its beauty, the other the insect-breeding power of the Sun. Baal-zebub is the Fly-god. Only at a comparatively recent period did the deity of the Philistines, whose oracle was consulted by Ahaziah (2 Kings i.), suffer under the reputation of being 'the Prince of Devils,' his name being changed by a mere pun to Beelzebul (dung-god). It is not impossible that the modern Egyptian mother's hesitation to disturb flies settling on her sleeping child, and the sanctity attributed to various insects, originated in the awe felt for him. The title Fly-god is parallelled by the reverent epithet ἀπόμυιος, applied to Zeus as worshipped at Elis,[1] the *Myiagrus deus* of the Romans,[2] and the *Myiodes* mentioned by Pliny.[3] Our picture is probably from a protecting charm, and evidently by the god's believers. There is a story of a peasant woman in a French church who was found kneeling before a marble group, and was warned by a priest that she was worshipping the wrong figure—namely, Beelzebub. 'Never mind,' she replied, 'it is well enough to have friends on both sides.' The story, though now only *ben trovato*, would represent the actual state of mind in many a Babylonian invoking the protection of the Fly-god against formidable swarms of his venomous subjects.

Not less clear is the illustration supplied by Scandinavian mythology. In Sæmund's Edda the evil-minded Loki says:—

> Odin! dost thou remember
> When we in early days
> Blended our blood together?

The two became detached very slowly; for their separation implied the crumbling away of a great religion, and its distribution into new forms; and a religion requires, relatively, as long to decay as it does to grow, as we who live under a crumbling religion have good reason to know. Protap Chunder Mozoomdar, of the Brahmo-Somaj, in an address in London, said, 'The Indian Pantheon has many millions of deities, and no space is left for the Devil.' He might have added that these deities have distributed between them all the work that the Devil could perform if he were admitted. His remark recalled to me the Eddaic story of Loki's entrance into the assembly of gods in the halls of Oegir. Loki—destined in a later age to be identified with Satan—is angrily received by the deities, but he goes round and mentions incidents in the life of each one which show them to be little if any better than himself. The gods and goddesses, unable to reply, confirm the cynic's criticisms in theologic fashion by tying him up with a serpent for cord.

The late Theodore Parker is said to have replied to a Calvinist who sought to convert him—'The difference between us is simple: your god is my devil.' There can be little question that the Hebrews, from whom the Calvinist inherited his deity, had no devil in their mythology, because the jealous and vindictive Jehovah was quite equal to any work of that kind,—as the hardening of Pharaoh's heart, bringing plagues upon the land, or deceiving a prophet and then destroying him for his false prophecies.[4] The same accommodating relation of the primitive deities to all natural phenomena will account for the absence of distinct representatives of evil of the most primitive religions.

The earliest exceptions to this primeval harmony of the gods, implying moral chaos in man, were trifling enough: the occasional monster seems worthy of mention only to display the valour of the god who slew him. But such were demon-germs, born out of the structural action of the human mind so soon as it began to form some philosophy concerning a universe upon which it had at first looked with simple wonder, and destined to an evolution of vast import when the work of moralising upon them should follow.

Let us take our stand beside our barbarian, but no longer savage, ancestor in the far past. We have watched the rosy morning as it waxed to a blazing noon: then swiftly the sun is blotted out, the tempest rages, it is a sudden night lit only by the forked lightning that strikes tree, house, man, with angry thunder-peal. From an instructed age man can look upon the storm blackening the sky not as an enemy of the sun, but one of its own superlative effects; but some thousands of years ago, when we were all living in Eastern barbarism, we could not conceive that a luminary whose very business it was to give light, could be a party to his own obscuration. We then looked with pity upon the ignorance of our ancestors, who had sung hymns to the storm-dragons, hoping to flatter them into quietness; and we came by irresistible logic to that Dualism which long divided the visible, and still divides the moral, universe into two hostile camps.

This is the mother-principle out of which demons (in the ordinary sense of the term) proceeded. At first few, as distinguished from the host of deities by exceptional harmfulness, they were multiplied with man's growth in the classification of his world. Their principle of existence is capable of indefinite expansion, until it shall include all the realms of darkness, fear, and pain. In the names of demons, and in the fables concerning them, the struggles of man in his ages of weakness with peril, want, and death, are recorded more fully than in any inscriptions on stone. Dualism is a creed which all superficial appearances attest. Side by side the desert and the fruitful land, the sunshine and the frost, sorrow and joy, life and death, sit weaving around every life its vesture of bright and sombre threads, and Science alone can detect how each of these casts the shuttle to the other. Enemies to each other they will appear in every realm which knowledge has not mastered. There is a refrain, gathered from many ages, in William Blake's apostrophe to the tiger:—

Tiger! tiger! burning bright
In the forests of the night;
What immortal hand or eye
Framed thy fearful symmetry?

In what distant deeps or skies
Burned that fire within thine eyes?
On what wings dared he aspire?
What the hand dared seize the fire?

When the stars threw down their spears
And water heaven with their tears,
Did he smile his work to see?
Did he who made the lamb make thee?

That which one of the devoutest men of genius whom England has produced thus asked was silently answered in India by the serpent-worshipper kneeling with his tongue held in his hand; in Egypt, by Osiris seated on a throne of chequer.[5]

It is necessary to distinguish clearly between the Demon and the Devil, though, for some purposes, they must be mentioned together. The world was haunted with demons for many ages before there was any embodiment of their spirit in any central form, much less any conception of a Principle of Evil in the universe. The early demons had no moral character, not any more than the man-eating tiger. There is no outburst of moral indignation mingling with the shout of victory when Indra slays Vritra, and Apollo's face is serene when his dart pierces the Python. It required a much higher development of the moral sentiment to give rise to the conception of a devil. Only that intensest light could cast so black a shadow athwart the world as the belief in a purely malignant spirit. To such a conception—love of evil for its own sake—the word Devil is limited in this work; Demon is applied to beings whose harmfulness is not gratuitous, but incidental to their own satisfactions.

Deity and Demon are from words once interchangeable, and the latter has simply suffered degradation by the conventional use of it to designate the less beneficent powers and qualities, which originally inhered in every deity, after they were detached from these and separately personified. Every bright god had his shadow, so to say; and under the influence of Dualism this shadow attained a distinct existence and personality in the popular imagination. The principle having once been established, that what seemed beneficent and what seemed the reverse must be ascribed to different powers, it is obvious that the evolution of demons must be continuous, and their distribution co-extensive with the ills that flesh is heir to.

NOTES

1 Pausan. v. 14, 2.
2 Solin. Polyhistor, i.
3 Pliny, xxix. 6, 34, init.
4 Ezekiel xiv. 9.
5 As in the Bembine Tablet in the Bodleian Library.

Chapter III
Degradation

THE ATMOSPHERIC CONDITIONS having been prepared in the human mind for the production of demons, the particular shapes or names they would assume would be determined by a variety of circumstances, ethnical, climatic, political, or even accidental. They would, indeed, be rarely accidental; but Professor Max Müller, in his notes to the Rig-Veda, has called attention to a remarkable instance in which the formation of an imposing mythological figure of this kind had its name determined by what, in all probability, was an accident. There appears in the earliest Vedic hymns the name of Aditi, as the holy Mother of many gods, and thrice there is mentioned the female name Diti. But there is reason to believe that Diti is a mere reflex of Aditi, the *a* being dropped originally by a reciter's license. The later reciters, however, regarding every letter in so sacred a book, or even the omission of a letter, as of eternal significance, Diti—this decapitated Aditi—was evolved into a separate and powerful being, and, every niche of beneficence being occupied by its god or goddess, the new form was at once relegated to the newly-defined realm of evil, where she remained as the mother of the enemies of the gods, the

Daityas. Unhappily this accident followed the ancient tendency by which the Furies and Vices have, with scandalous constancy, been described in the feminine gender.

The close resemblance between these two names of Hindu mythology, severally representing the best and the worst, may be thus accidental, and only serve to show how the demon-forming tendency, after it began, was able to press even the most trivial incidents into its service. But generally the names of demons, and for whole races of demons, report far more than this; and in no inquiry more than that before us is it necessary to remember that names are things. The philological facts supply a remarkable confirmation of the statements already made as to the original identity of demon and deity. The word 'demon' itself, as we have said, originally bore a good instead of an evil meaning. The Sanskrit *deva*, 'the shining one,' Zend *daêva*, correspond with the Greek θεος, Latin *deus*, Anglo-Saxon *Tiw*; and remain in 'deity,' 'deuce' (probably; it exists in Armorican, *teuz*, a phantom), 'devel' (the gipsy name for God), and Persian *dīv*, demon. The Demon of Socrates represents the personification of a being still good, but no doubt on the path of decline from pure divinity. Plato declares that good men when they die become 'demons,' and he says 'demons are reporters and carriers between gods and men.' Our familiar word *bogey*, a sort of nickname for an evil spirit, comes from the Slavonic word for God—*bog*. Appearing here in the West as bogey (Welsh *bwg*, a goblin), this word *bog* began, probably, as the 'Baga' of cuneiform inscriptions, a name of the Supreme Being, or possibly the Hindu 'Bhaga,' Lord of Life. In the 'Bishop's Bible' the passage occurs, 'Thou shalt not be afraid of any *bugs* by night:' the word has been altered to 'terror.' When we come to the particular names of demons, we find many of them bearing traces of the splendours from which they have declined. 'Siva,' the Hindu god of destruction, has a meaning ('auspicious') derived from *Svī*, 'thrive'—thus related ideally to Pluto, 'wealth'—and, indeed, in later ages, appears to have gained the greatest elevation. In a story of the Persian poem Masnavi, Ahriman is mentioned with Bahman as a fire-fiend, of which class are the Magian demons and the Jinns generally; which, the sanctity of fire being considered, is an evidence of their high origin. Avicenna says that the genii are ethereal animals. Luci-fer—light-bearing—is the fallen angel of the morning star. Loki—the nearest to an evil power of the Scandinavian personifications—is the German *leucht*, or light. Azazel—a word inaccurately rendered 'scape-goat' in the Bible—appears to have been originally a deity, as the Israelites were originally required to offer up one goat to Jehovah and another to Azazel, a name which appears to signify the 'strength of God.' Gesenius and Ewald regard Azazel as a demon belonging to the pre-Mosaic religion, but it can hardly be doubted that the four arch-demons mentioned by the Rabbins—Samaël, Azazel, Asaël, and Maccathiel—are personifications of the elements as energies of the deity. Samaël would appear to mean the 'left hand of God;' Azazel, his strength; Asaël, his reproductive force; and Maccathiel, his retribu-tive power, but the origin of these names is doubtful..

Although Azazel is now one of the Mussulman names for a devil, it would appear to be nearly related to Al Uzza of the Koran, one of the goddesses of whom the significant tradition exists, that once when Mohammed had read, from the Sura called 'The Star,' the question, 'What think ye of Allat, Al Uzza, and Manah, that other third goddess?' he himself added, 'These are the most high and beauteous damsels, whose intercession is to be hoped for,' the response being afterwards attributed to a suggestion of Satan.[1] Belial is merely a word for godlessness; it has become personified through the mis-understanding of the phrase in the Old Testament by the translators of the Septuagint, and thus passed into christian use, as in 2 Cor. vi. 15, 'What concord hath Christ with Belial?' The word is not used as a proper name in the Old Testament, and the late creation of a demon out of it may be set down to accident.

Even where the names of demons and devils bear no such traces of their degradation from the state of deities, there are apt to be characteristics attributed to them, or myths connected with them, which point in the direction indicated. Such is the case with Satan, of whom much must be said hereafter, whose Hebrew name signifies the adversary, but who, in the Book of Job, appears among the sons of God. The name given to the devil in the Koran—Eblis—is almost certainly *diabolos* Arabicised; and while this Greek word is found in Pindar[2] (5th century B.C.), meaning a slanderer, the fables in the Koran concerning Eblis describe him as a fallen angel of the highest rank.

One of the most striking indications of the fall of demons from heaven is the wide-spread belief that they are lame. Mr. Tylor has pointed out the curious persistence of this idea in various eth-nical lines of development.[3] Hephaistos was lamed by his fall when hurled by Zeus from Olympos; and it is not a little singular that in the English travesty of limping Vulcan, represented in Wayland the

Smith,[4] there should appear the suggestion, remarked by Mr. Cox, of the name 'Vala' (coverer), one of the designations of the dragon destroyed by Indra. 'In Sir Walter Scott's romance,' says Mr. Cox, 'Wayland is a mere impostor, who avails himself of a popular super-stition to keep up an air of mystery about himself and his work, but the character to which he makes pretence belongs to the genuine Teutonic legend.'[5] The Persian demon Aeshma—the Asmodeus of the Book of Tobit—appears with the same characteristic of lameness in the 'Diable Boiteux' of Le Sage. The christian devil's clubbed or cloven foot is notorious.

Even the horns popularly attributed to the devil may possibly have originated with the aureole which indicates the glory of his 'first estate.' Satan is depicted in various relics of early art wearing the aureole, as in a miniature of the tenth century (from Bible No. 6, Bib. Roy.), given by M. Didron.[6] The same author has shown that Pan and the Satyrs, who had so much to do with the shaping of our horned and hoofed devil, originally got their horns from the same high source as Moses in the old Bibles,[7] and in the great statue of him at Rome by Michel Angelo.

It is through this mythologic history that the most powerful demons have been associated in the popular imagination with stars, planets,—Ketu in India, Saturn and Mercury the 'Infortunes,'—com-ets, and other celestial phenomena. The examples of this are so numerous that it is impossible to deal with them here, where I can only hope to offer a few illustrations of the principles affirmed; and in this case it is of less importance for the English reader, because of the interesting volume in which the subject has been specially dealt with.[8] Incidentally, too, the astrological demons and devils must recur from time to time in the process of our inquiry. But it will probably be within the knowledge of some of my readers that the dread of comets and of meteoric showers yet lingers in many parts of Christendom, and that fear of unlucky stars has not passed away with astrologers. There is a Scottish legend told by Hugh Miller of an avenging meteoric demon. A shipmaster who had moored his vessel near Morial's Den, amused himself by watching the lights of the scattered farmhouses. After all the rest had gone out one light lingered for some time. When that light too had disappeared, the shipmaster beheld a large meteor, which, with a hissing noise, moved towards the cottage. A dog howled, an owl whooped; but when the fire-ball had almost reached the roof, a cock crew from within the cottage, and the meteor rose again. Thrice this was repeated, the meteor at the third cock-crow ascending among the stars. On the following day the shipmaster went on shore, purchased the cock, and took it away with him. Returned from his voyage, he looked for the cottage, and found nothing but a few blackened stones. Nearly sixty years ago a human skeleton was found near the spot, doubled up as if the body had been huddled into a hole: this revived the legend, and probably added some of those traits which make it a true bit of mosaic in the mythology of Astræa.[9]

The fabled 'fall of Lucifer' really signifies a process similar to that which has been noticed in the case of Saranyu. The morning star, like the morning light, as revealer of the deeds of darkness, becomes an avenger, and by evolution an instigator of the evil it originally disclosed and punished. It may be remarked also that though we have inherited the phrase 'Demons of Darkness,' it was an ancient rabbinical belief that the demons went abroad in darkness not only because it facilitated their attacks on man, but because being of luminous forms, they could recognise each other better with a background of darkness.

NOTES
1 See Sale's Koran, p. 281.
2 Pindar, Fragm., 270.
3 Tylor's 'Early Hist. of Mankind,' p. 358; 'Prim. Cult.,' vol. ii. p. 230.
4 The Gascons of Labourd call the devil 'Seigneur Voland,' and some revere him as a patron.
5 'Myth. of the Aryan Nations,' vol. ii. p. 327.
6 'Christian Iconography,' Bohn, p. 158.
7 'Videbant faciem egredientis Moysis esse cornutam.'—Vulg. Exod. xxxiv. 35.
8 'Myths and Marvels of Astronomy.' By R. A. Proctor. Chatto & Windus, 1878.
9 'Scenes and Legends,' &c., p. 73.

Chapter IV
The Abgott

The ex-god — Deities demonised by conquest — Theological animosity —
Devil-worship an arrested Deism — Sheik Adi —
Why demons were painted ugly — Survivals of their beauty

THE PHENOMENA OF the transformation of deities into demons meet the student of Demonology at every step. We shall have to consider many examples of a kind similar to those which have been mentioned in the preceding chapter; but it is necessary to present at this stage of our inquiry a sufficient number of examples to establish the fact that in every country forces have been at work to degrade the primitive gods into types of evil, as preliminary to a consideration of the nature of those forces.

We find the history of the phenomena suggested in the German word for idol, Abgott—ex-god. Then we have 'pagan,' villager, and 'heathen,' of the heath, denoting those who stood by their old gods after others had transferred their faith to the new. These words bring us to consider the influence upon religious conceptions of the struggles which have occurred between races and nations, and consequently between their religions. It must be borne in mind that by the time any tribes had gathered to the consistency of a nation, one of the strongest forces of its coherence would be its priesthood. So soon as it became a general belief that there were in the universe good and evil Powers, there must arise a popular demand for the means of obtaining their favour; and this demand has never failed to obtain a supply of priesthoods claiming to bind or influence the præternatural beings. These priesthoods represent the strongest motives and fears of a people, and they were gradually intrenched in great institutions involving powerful interests. Every invasion or collision or mingling of races thus brought their respective religions into contact and rivalry; and as no priesthood has been known to consent peaceably to its own downfall and the degradation of its own deities, we need not wonder that there have been perpetual wars for religious ascendency. It is not unusual to hear sects among ourselves accusing each other of idolatry. In earlier times the rule was for each religion to denounce its opponent's gods as devils. Gregory the Great wrote to his missionary in Britain, the Abbot Mellitus, second Bishop of Canterbury, that 'whereas the people were accustomed to sacrifice many oxen in honour of demons, let them celebrate a religious and solemn festival, and not slay the animals to the devil (diabolo), but to be eaten by themselves to the glory of God.' Thus the devotion of meats to those deities of our ancestors which the Pope pronounces demons, which took place chiefly at Yule-tide, has survived in our more comfortable Christmas banquets. This was the fate of all the deities which Christianity undertook to suppress. But it had been the habit of religions for many ages before. They never denied the actual existence of the deities they were engaged in suppressing. That would have been too great an outrage upon popular beliefs, and might have caused a reaction; and, besides, each new religion had an interest of its own in preserving the basis of belief in these invisible beings. Disbelief in the very existence of the old gods might be followed by a sceptical spirit that might endanger the new. So the propagandists maintained the existence of native gods, but called them devils. Sometimes wars or intercourse between tribes led to their fusion; the battle between opposing religions was drawn, in which case there would be a compromise by which several deities of different origin might continue together in the same race and receive equal homage. The differing degrees of importance ascribed to the separate persons of the Hindu triad in various localities of India, suggest it as quite probable that Brahma, Vishnu, and Siva signalled in their union the political unity of certain districts in that country.[1] The blending of the names of Confucius and Buddha, in many Chinese and Japanese temples, may show us an analogous process now going on, and, indeed, the various ethnical ideas combined in the christian Trinity render the fact stated one of easy interpretation. But the religious difficulty was sometimes not susceptible of compromise. The most powerful priesthood carried the day, and they used every ingenuity to degrade the gods of their opponents. Agathodemons were turned into kakodemons. The serpent, worshipped in many lands, might be adopted as the support of sleeping Vishnu in India, might be associated with the rainbow ('the heavenly serpent') in Persia, but elsewhere was cursed as the very genius of evil.

The operation of this force in the degradation of deities, is particularly revealed in the Sacred Books of Persia. In that country the great religions of the East would appear to have contended against each other with especial fury, and their struggles were probably instrumental in causing one or more of the early migrations into Western Europe. The great celestial war between Ormuzd and Ahriman—Light and Darkness—corresponded with a violent theological conflict, one result of which is that the word *deva*, meaning 'deity' to Brahmans, means 'devil' to Parsees. The following extract from the Zend-Avesta will serve as an example of the spirit in which the war was waged:—

'All your devas are only manifold children of the Evil Mind—and the great one who worships the Saoma of lies and deceits; besides the treacherous acts for which you are notorious throughout the seven regions of the earth.

'You have invented all the evil which men speak and do, which is indeed pleasant to the Devas, but is devoid of all goodness, and therefore perishes before the insight of the truth of the wise.

'Thus you defraud men of their good minds and of their immortality by your evil minds—as well through those of the Devas as that of the Evil Spirit—through evil deeds and evil words, whereby the power of liars grows.'[2]

That is to say—Ours is the true god: your god is a devil.

The Zoroastrian conversion of *deva* (deus) into *devil* does not alone represent the work of this *odium theologicum*. In the early hymns of India the appellation *asuras* is given to the gods. Asura means a spirit. But in the process of time *asura*, like dæmon, came to have a sinister meaning: the gods were called *suras*, the demons *asuras*, and these were said to contend together. But in Persia the *asuras*—demonised in India—retained their divinity, and gave the name *ahura* to the supreme deity, Ormuzd (Ahura-mazda). On the other hand, as Mr. Muir supposes, *Varenya*, applied to evil spirits of darkness in the Zendavesta, is cognate with Varuna (Heaven); and the Vedic Indra, king of the gods—the Sun—is named in the Zoroastrian religion as one of the chief councillors of that Prince of Darkness.

But in every country conquered by a new religion, there will always be found some, as we have seen, who will hold on to the old deity under all his changed fortunes. These will be called 'bigots,' but still they will adhere to the ancient belief and practise the old rites. Sometimes even after they have had to yield to the popular terminology, and call the old god a devil, they will find some reason for continuing the transmitted forms. It is probable that to this cause was originally due the religions which have been developed into what is now termed Devil-worship. The distinct and avowed worship of the evil Power in preference to the good is a rather startling phenomenon when presented baldly; as, for example, in a prayer of the Madagascans to Nyang, author of evil, quoted by Dr. Réville:—'O Zamhor! to thee we offer no prayers. The good god needs no asking. But we must pray to Nyang. Nyang must be appeased. O Nyang, bad and strong spirit, let not the thunder roar over our heads! Tell the sea to keep within its bounds! Spare, O Nyang, the ripening fruit, and dry not up the blossoming rice! Let not our women bring forth children on the accursed days. Thou reignest, and this thou knowest, over the wicked; and great is their number, O Nyang. Torment not, then, any longer the good folk!'[3]

This is natural, and suggestive of the criminal under sentence of death, who, when asked if he was not afraid to meet his God, replied, 'Not in the least; it's that other party I'm afraid of.' Yet it is hardly doubtful that the worship of Nyang began in an era when he was by no means considered morally baser than Zamhor. How the theory of Dualism, when attained, might produce the phenomenon called Devil-worship, is illustrated in the case of the Yezedis, now so notorious for that species of religion. Their theory is usually supposed to be entirely represented by the expression uttered by one of them, 'Will not Satan, then, reward the poor Izedis, who alone have never spoken ill of him, and have suffered so much for him?'[4] But these words are significant, no doubt, of the underlying fact: they 'have never spoken ill of' the Satan they worship. The Mussulman calls the Yezedi a Satan-worshipper only as the early Zoroastrian held the worshipper of a *deva* to be the same. The chief object of worship among the Yezedis is the figure of the bird *Taous*, a half-mythical peacock. Professor King of Cambridge traces the *Taous* of this Assyrian sect to the "sacred bird called a phœnix," whose picture, as seen by Herodotus (ii. 73) in Egypt, is described by him as 'very like an eagle in outline and in size, but with plumage partly gold-coloured, partly crimson,' and which was said to return to Heliopolis every five hundred years, there to burn itself on the altar of the Sun, that another might rise from its ashes.[5] Now the name Yezedis is simply Izeds, genii; and we are thus pointed to Arabia, where we find the belief in genii is strongest, and also associated with the mythical bird *Rokh* of its folklore. There we find Mohammed rebuking the popular belief in a certain bird called Hamâh, which was said to take form from the blood near the brain of a dead person and fly away, to return, however, at the end of every hundred years to visit that person's sepulchre. But this is by no means Devil-worship, nor can we find any trace of that in the most sacred scripture of the Yezedis, the 'Eulogy of Sheikh Adi.' This Sheikh inherited from his father, Moosafir, the sanctity of an incarnation of the divine essence, of which he (Adi) speaks as 'the All-merciful.'

> By his light he hath lighted the lamp of the morning.
> I am he that placed Adam in my Paradise.
> I am he that made Nimrod a hot burning fire.
> I am he that guided Ahmet mine elect,
> I gifted him with my way and guidance.
> Mine are all existences together,
> They are my gift and under my direction.
> I am he that possesseth all majesty,
> And beneficence and charity are from my grace,
> I am he that entereth the heart in my zeal;
> And I shine through the power of my awfulness and majesty.
> I am he to whom the lion of the desert came:
> I rebuked him and he became like stone.
> I am he to whom the serpent came,
> And by my will I made him like dust.
> I am he that shook the rock and made it tremble,
> And sweet water flowed therefrom from every side.[6]

The reverence shown in these sacred sentences for Hebrew names and traditions—as of Adam in Paradise, Marah, and the smitten rock—and for Ahmet (Mohammed), appears to have had its only requital in the odious designation of the worshippers of *Taous* as Devil-worshippers, a label which the Yezedis perhaps accepted as the Wesleyans and Friends accepted such names as 'Methodist' and 'Quaker.'

46

Mohammed has expiated the many deities he degraded to devils by being himself turned to an idol (mawmet), a term of contempt all the more popular for its resemblance to 'mummery.' Despite his denunciations of idolatry, it is certain that this earlier religion represented by the Yezedis has never been entirely suppressed even among his own followers. In Dr. Leitner's interesting collection there is a lamp, which he obtained from a mosque, made in the shape of a peacock, and this is but one of many similar relics of primitive or alien symbolism found among the Mussulman tribes.

The evolution of demons and devils out of deities was made real to the popular imagination in every country where the new religion found art existing, and by alliance with it was enabled to shape the ideas of the people. The theoretical degradation of deities of previously fair association could only be completed where they were presented to the eye in repulsive forms. It will readily occur to every one that a rationally conceived demon or devil would not be repulsive. If it were a demon that man wished to represent, mere euphemism would prevent its being rendered odious. The main characteristic of a demon—that which distinguishes it from a devil—is, as we have seen, that it has a real and human-like motive for whatever evil it causes. If it afflict or consume man, it is not from mere malignancy, but because impelled by the pangs of hunger, lust, or other suffering, like the famished wolf or shark. And if sacrifices of food were offered to satisfy its need, equally we might expect that no unnecessary insult would be offered in the attempt to portray it. But if it were a devil—a being actuated by simple malevolence—one of its essential functions, temptation, would be destroyed by hideousness.

Fig. 2.—HANDLE OF HINDU CHALICE

For the work of seduction we might expect a devil to wear the form
of an angel of light, but by no means to approach his intended victim
in any horrible shape, such as would repel every mortal. The great
representations of evil, whether imagined by the speculative or the

religious sense, have never been, originally, ugly. The gods might be described as falling swiftly like lightning out of heaven, but in the popular imagination they retained for a long time much of their splendour. The very ingenuity with which they were afterwards invested with ugliness in religious art, attests that there were certain popular sentiments about them which had to be distinctly reversed. It was because they were thought beautiful that they must be painted ugly; it was because they were—even among converts to the new religion—still secretly believed to be kind and helpful, that there was employed such elaboration of hideous designs to deform them. The pictorial representations of demons and devils will come under a more detailed examination hereafter: it is for the present sufficient to point out that the traditional blackness or ugliness of demons and devils, as now thought of, by no means militates against the fact that they were once the popular deities. The contrast, for instance, between the horrible physiognomy given to Satan in ordinary christian art, and the theological representation of him as the Tempter, is obvious. Had the design of Art been to represent the theological theory, Satan would have been portrayed in a fascinating form. But the design was not that; it was to arouse horror and antipathy for the native deities to which the ignorant clung tenaciously. It was to train children to think of the still secretly-worshipped idols as frightful and bestial beings. It is important, therefore, that we should guard against confusing the speculative or moral attempts of mankind to personify pain and evil with the ugly and brutal demons and devils of artificial superstition, oftenest pictured on church walls. Sometimes they are set to support water-spouts, often the brackets that hold their foes, the saints. It is a very ancient device. Our figure 2 is from the handle of a chalice in possession of Sir James Hooker, meant probably to hold the holy water of Ganges. These are not genuine demons or devils, but carefully caricatured deities. Who that looks upon the grinning bestial forms carved about the roof of any old church—as those on Melrose Abbey and York Cathedral7—which, there is reason to believe, represent the primitive deities driven from the interior by potency of holy water, and chained to the uncongenial service of supporting the roof-gutter—can see in these gargoyles (Fr. *gargouille*, dragon), anything but carved imprecations? Was it to such ugly beings, guardians of their streams, hills, and forests, that our ancestors consecrated the holly and mistletoe, or with such that they associated their flowers, fruits, and homes? They were caricatures inspired by missionaries, made to repel and disgust, as the images of saints beside them were carved in beauty to attract. If the pagans had been the artists, the good looks would have been on the other side. And indeed there was an art of which those pagans were the unconscious possessors, through which the true characters of the imaginary beings they adored have been transmitted to us. In the fables of their folklore we find the Fairies that represent the spirit of the gods and goddesses to which they are easily traceable. That goddess who in christian times was pictured as a hag riding on a broom-stick was Frigga, the Earth-mother, associated with the first sacred affections clustering around the hearth; or Freya, whose very name was consecrated in *frau*, woman and wife. The mantle of Bertha did not cover more tenderness when it fell to the shoulders of Mary. The German child's name for the pre-christian Madonna was Mother Rose: distaff in hand, she watched over the industrious at their household work: she hovered near the cottage, perhaps to find there some weeping Cinderella and give her beauty for ashes.

NOTES

1   'Any Orientalist will appreciate the wonderful hotchpot of Hindu and Arabic language and religion in the following details, noted down among rude tribes of the Malay Peninsula. We hear of Jin Bumi, the earth-god (Arabic jin = demon, Sanskrit bhümi = earth); incense is burnt to Jewajewa (Sanskrit dewa = god), who intercedes with Pirman, the supreme invisible deity above the sky (Brahma?); the Moslem Allah Táala, with his wife Nabi Mahamad (Prophet Mohammed), appear in the Hinduised characters of creator and destroyer of all things; and while the spirits worshipped in stones are called by the Hindu term of 'dewa' or deity, Moslem conversion has so far influenced the mind of the stone-worshipper that he will give to his sacred boulder the name of Prophet Mohammed.'—Tylor's 'Primitive Culture,' vol. ii. p. 230.

2   Yaçna, 32.

3   'The Devil,' &c., from the French of the Rev. A. Réville, p. 5.

4   Tylor's 'Primitive Culture,' vol. ii. p. 299.

5   'The Gnostics,' &c., by C. W. King, M.A., p. 153.

6   Those who wish to examine this matter further will do well to refer to Badger, 'Nestorians and their Rituals,' in which the whole of the 'Eulogy' is translated; and to Layard, 'Ninevah and Babylon,' in which there is a translation of the same by Hormuzd Rassam, the King of Abyssinia's late prisoner.

7   The significance of the gargoyles on the churches built on the foundations of pagan temples may be especially observed at York, where the forms of various animals well known to Indo-Germanic mythology appear. They are probably copies of earlier designs, surviving from the days when the plan of Gregory for the conversion of temples prevailed. 'The temples of the idols in that nation,' wrote the Pope, A.C. 601, 'ought not to be destroyed; but let the idols that are in them be destroyed; let holy water be made and sprinkled in the said temples, let altars be erected and relics placed. For if those temples are well built, it is requisite that they be converted from the worship of devils to the service of the true God.'—Bede, Eccl. Hist. ch. 30.

Chapter V
Classification

THE STATEMENTS MADE concerning the fair names of the chief
demons and devils which have haunted the imagination of mankind,
heighten the contrast between their celestial origin and the functions
attributed to them in their degraded forms. The theory of Dualism,
representing a necessary stage in the mental development of every
race, called for a supply of demons, and the supply came from the innumerable dethroned, outlawed, and fallen deities and angels which
had followed the subjugation of races and their religions. But though
their celestial origin might linger around them in some slight legend
or characteristic as well as in their names, the evil phenomenon to
which each was attached as an explanation assigned the real form
and work with which he or she was associated in popular superstition. We therefore find in the demons in which men have believed
a complete catalogue of the obstacles with which they have had to
contend in the long struggle for existence. In the devils we discover equally the history of the moral and religious struggles through
which priesthoods and churches have had to pass. And the relative
extent of this or that particular class of demons or devils, and the

intensity of belief in any class as shown in the number of survivals from it, will be found to reflect pretty faithfully the degree to which the special evil represented by it afflicted primitive man, as attested by other branches of pre-historic investigation.

As to function, the demons we shall have to consider are those representing—

1. Hunger;
2. Excessive Heat;
3. Excessive Cold;
4. Destructive elements and physical convulsions;
5. Destructive animals;
6. Human enemies;
7. The Barrenness of the Earth, as rock and desert;
8. Obstacles, as the river or mountain;
9. Illusion, seductive, invisible, and mysterious agents, causing delusions;
10. Darkness (especially when unusual), Dreams, Nightmare;
11. Disease;
12. Death.

These classes are selected, in obedience to necessary limitations, as representing the twelve chief labours of man which have given shape to the majority of his haunting demons, as distinguished from his devils. Of course all classifications of this character must be understood as made for convenience, and the divisions are not to be too sharply taken. What Plotinus said of the gods, that each contained all the rest, is equally true of both demons and devils. The demons of Hunger are closely related to the demons of Fire: Agni devoured his parents (two sticks consumed by the flame they produce); and from them we pass easily to elemental demons, like the lightning, or demons of fever. And similarly we find a relationship between other destructive forces. Nevertheless, the distinctions drawn are not fanciful, but exist in clear and unmistakable beliefs as to the special dispositions and employments of demons; and as we are not engaged in dealing with natural phenomena, but with superstitions concerning them, the only necessity of this classification is that it shall not be arbitrary, but shall really simplify the immense mass of facts which the student of Demonology has to encounter.

But there are several points which require especial attention as preliminary to a consideration of these various classes of demons.

First, it is to be borne in mind that a single demonic form will often appear in various functions, and that these must not be confused. The serpent may represent the lightning, or the coil of the whirlwind, or fatal venom; the earthquake may represent a swallowing Hunger-demon, or the rage of a chained giant. The separate functions must not be lost sight of because sometimes traceable to a single form, nor their practical character suffer disguise through their fair euphemistic or mythological names.

Secondly, the same form appears repeatedly in a diabolic as well as a demonic function, and here a clear distinction must be maintained in the reader's mind. The distinction already taken between a demon and a devil is not arbitrary: the word demon is related to deity; the word devil, though sometimes connected with the Sanskrit *deva*, has really no relation to it, but has a bad sense as 'calumniator:' but even if there were no such etymological identity and difference, it would be necessary to distinguish such widely separate offices as those representing the afflictive forces of nature where attributed to humanly appreciable motives on the one hand, and evils ascribed to pure malignancy or a principle of evil on the other. The Devil may, indeed, represent a further evolution in the line on which the Demon has appeared; Ahriman the Bad in conflict with Ormuzd the Good may be a spiritualisation of the conflict between Light and Darkness, Sun and Cloud, as represented in the Vedic Indra and Vritra; but the two phases represent different classes of ideas, indeed different worlds, and the apprehension of both requires that they shall be carefully distinguished even when associated with the same forms and names.

Thirdly, there is an important class of demons which the reader may expect to find fully treated of in the part of my work more particularly devoted to Demonology, which must be deferred, or further traced in that portion relating to the Devil; they are forms which in their original conception were largely beneficent, and have become of evil repute mainly through the anathema of theology. The chequer-board on which Osiris sat had its development in hosts of primitive shapes of light opposing shapes of darkness. The evil of some of these is ideal; others are morally amphibious: Teraphim, Lares, genii, were ancestors of the guardian angels and patron saints of the present

day; they were oftenest in the shapes of dogs and cats and aged human ancestors, supposed to keep watch and ward about the house,
like the friendly Domovoi respected in Russia; the evil disposition
and harmfulness ascribed to them are partly natural but partly also
theological, and due to the difficulty of superseding them with patron
saints and angels. The degradation of beneficent beings, already
described in relation to large demonic and diabolic forms, must be
understood as constantly acting in the smallest details of household
superstition, with what strange reaction and momentous result will
appear when we come to consider the phenomena of Witchcraft.

Finally, it must be remarked that the nature of our inquiry renders
the consideration of the origin of myths—whether 'solar' or other—of
secondary importance. Such origin it will be necessary to point out
and discuss incidentally, but our main point will always be the forms
in which the myths have become incarnate, and their modifications
in various places and times, these being the result of those actual
experiences with which Demonology is chiefly concerned. A myth, as
many able writers have pointed out, is, in its origin, an explanation by
the uncivilised mind of some natural phenomenon—not an allegory,
not an esoteric conceit. For this reason it possesses fluidity, and
takes on manifold shapes. The apparent sleep of the sun in winter
may be represented in a vast range of myths, from the Seven Sleepers to the Man in the Moon of our nursery rhyme; but the variations
all have relation to facts and circumstances. Comparative Mythology
is mainly concerned with the one thread running through them, and
binding them all to the original myth; the task of Demonology is rath-

er to discover the agencies which have given their several shapes. If it be shown that Orthros and Cerberus were primarily the morning and evening twilight or howling winds, either interpretation is here secondary to their personification as dogs. Demonology would ask, Why dogs? why not bulls? Its answer in each case detaches from the anterior myth its mode, and shows this as the determining force of further myths.

Part ll
The Demon

Chapter I
Hunger

Hunger-demons — Kephn — Miru — Kagura — Ráhu the Hindu sun-devourer
— The earth monster at Pelsall — A Franconian custom — Sheitan as moon-
devourer — Hindu offerings to the dead — Ghoul — Goblin — Vampyres —
Leanness of demons — Old Scotch custom — The origin of sacrifices

IN EVERY PART of the earth man's first struggle was for his daily food. With only a rude implement of stone or bone he had to get fish from the sea, bird from the air, beast from the forest. For ages, with such poor equipment, he had to wring a precarious livelihood from nature. He saw, too, every living form around him similarly trying to satisfy its hunger. There seemed to be a Spirit of Hunger abroad. And, at the same time, there was such a resistance to man's satisfaction of his need—the bird and fish so hard to get, the stingy earth so ready to give him a stone when he asked for bread—that he came to the conclusion that there must be invisible voracious beings who wanted all good things for themselves. So the ancient world was haunted by a vast brood of Hunger-demons. There is an African tribe, the Karens, whose representation of the Devil (Kephn) is a huge stomach floating through the air; and this repulsive image may be regarded as the type of nearly half the demons which have haunted the human imagination. This, too, is the terrible Miru, with her daughters and slave, haunting the South Sea Islander. 'The esoteric doctrine of the priests was, that souls leave the body ere breath has quite gone, and travel to the edge of a cliff facing the setting sun (Rā). A large wave now approaches the base of the cliff, and a gigantic *bua* tree, covered with fragrant blossoms, springs up from Avaiki (nether world) to receive on its far-reaching branches human spirits, who are mysteriously impelled to cluster on its limbs. When at length the mystic tree is covered with human spirits, it goes down with its living freight to the nether world. Akaanga, the slave of fearful Miru, mistress of the invisible world, infallibly catches all these unhappy spirits in his net and laves them to and fro in a lake. In these waters the captive ghosts exhaust themselves by wriggling about like fishes, in the vain hope of escape. The net is pulled up, and the half-drowned spirits enter into the presence of dread Miru, who is ugliness personified. The secret of Miru's power over her intended victims is the 'kava' root (*Piper mythisticum*). A bowl of this drink is prepared for each visitor to the shades by her four lovely daughters. Stupefied with the draught, the unresisting victims are borne off to a mighty oven and cooked. Miru, her peerless daughters, her dance-loving son, and the attendants, subsist exclusively on human spirits decoyed to the nether world and then cooked. The drinking-cups of Miru are the skulls of her victims. She is called in song 'Miru-the-ruddy,' because her cheeks ever glow with the heat of the oven where her captives are cooked. As the surest way to Miru's oven is to die a natural death, one need not marvel that the Rev. Mr. Gill, who made these statements before the Anthropological Institute in London (February 8, 1876), had heard 'many anecdotes of aged warriors, scarcely able to hold a spear, insisting on being led to the field of battle in the hope of gaining the house of the brave.' As the

South Sea paradise seems to consist in an eternal war-dance, or, in one island, in an eternal chewing of sugar-cane, it is not unlikely that the aged seek violent death chiefly to avoid the oven. We have here a remarkable illustration of the distinguishing characteristic of the demon. Fearful as Miru is, it may be noted that there is not one gratuitous element of cruelty in her procedure. On the contrary, she even provides her victims with an anæsthetic draught. Her prey is simply netted, washed, and cooked, as for man are his animal inferiors. In one of the islands (Aitutaki), Miru is believed to resort to a device which is certainly terrible—namely, the contrivance that each soul entering the nether world shall drink a bowl of living centipedes; but this is simply with the one end in view of appeasing her own pangs of hunger, for the object and effect of the draught is to cause the souls to drown themselves, it being apparently only after entire death that they can be cooked and devoured by Miru and her household.

Fortunately for the islanders, Miru is limited in her tortures to a transmundane sphere, and room is left for many a slip between her dreadful cup and the human lip. The floating stomach Kephn is, however, not other-worldly. We see, however, a softened form of him in some other tribes. The Greenlanders, Finns, Laps, conceived the idea that there is a large paunch-demon which people could invoke to go and suck the cows or consume the herds of their enemies; and the Icelanders have a superstition that some people can construct such a demon out of bones and skins, and send him forth to transmute the milk or flesh of cattle into a supply of flesh and blood. A form of this kind is represented in the Japanese Kagura (figure 3), the favourite mask of January dancers and drum-beaters seeking money. The

Kagura is in precise contrast with the Pretas (Siam), which, though twelve miles in height, are too thin to be seen, their mouths being so small as to render it impossible to satisfy their fearful hunger.

The pot-bellies given to demons in Travancore and other districts of India, and the blood-sacrifices by which the natives propitiate them—concerning which a missionary naively remarks, that even these heathen recognise, though in corrupted form, 'the great truth that without shedding of blood there is no remission of sins'—refer to the Hunger-demon. They are the brood of Kali, girt round with human skulls.

Fig. 3—A Swallower

The expedition which went out to India to observe the last solar eclipse was incidentally the means of calling attention to a remarkable survival of the Hunger-demon in connection with astronomic phenomena. While the English observers were arranging their apparatus, the natives prepared a pile of brushwood, and, so soon as the eclipse began, they set fire to this pile and began to shout and yell as they danced around it. Not less significant were the popular observances generally. There was a semi-holiday in honour of the eclipse. The ghauts were crowded with pious worshippers. No Hindu, it is thought, ought to do any work whatever during an eclipse, and there was a general tendency to prolong the holiday a little beyond the exact time when the shadow disappears, and indeed to prolong it throughout the day. All earthenware vessels used for cooking were broken, and all cooked food in the houses at the time of the eclipse was thrown out. It is regarded as a time of peculiar blessings if taken in the right way, and of dread consequences to persons inclined to heterodoxy or neglect of the proper observances. Between nine and ten in the evening two shocks of an earthquake occurred, the latter a rather unpleasant one, shaking the tables and doors in an uncomfortable fashion for several seconds. To the natives it was no surprise—they believe firmly in the connection of eclipses and earthquakes.[2]

Especially notable is the breaking of their culinary utensils by the Hindus during an eclipse. In Copenhagen there is a collection of the votive weapons of ancient Norsemen, every one broken as it was offered up to the god of their victory in token of good faith, lest they should be suspected of any intention to use again what they had given away. For the same reason the cup was offered—broken—with the libation. The Northman felt himself in the presence of the Jötunn (giants), whose name Grimm identifies as the Eaters.

For the Hindu of to-day the ceremonies appropriate at an eclipse, however important, have probably as little rational meaning as the occasional Belfire that lights up certain dark corners of Europe has for those who build it. But the traditional observances have come up from the childhood of the world, when the eclipse represented a demon devouring the sun, who was to have his attention called by outcries and prayers to the fact that if it was fire he needed there was plenty on earth; and if food, he might have all in their houses, provided he would consent to satisfy his appetite with articles of food less important than the luminaries of heaven.

Such is the shape now taken in India of the ancient myth of the eclipse. When at the churning of the ocean to find the nectar of immortality, a demon with dragon-tail was tasting that nectar, the sun and moon told on him, but not until his head had become immortal; and it is this head of Ráhu which seeks now to devour the informers—the Sun and Moon.[3] Mythologically, too, this Ráhu has been divided; for we shall hereafter trace the dragon-tail of him to the garden of Eden and in the christian devil, whereas in India he has been improved from a vindictive to a merely voracious demon.

The fires kindled by the Hindus to frighten Ráhu on his latest appearance might have defeated the purpose of the expedition by the smoke it was sending up, had not two officers leaped upon the fire and scattered its fuel; but just about the time when these coura-geous gentlemen were trampling out the fires of superstition whose smoke would obscure the vision of science, an event occurred in England which must be traced to the same ancient belief—the belief, namely, that when anything is apparently swallowed up, as the sun and moon by an eclipse, or a village by earthquake or flood, it is the work of a hungry dragon, earthworm, or other monster. The Pelsall mine was flooded, and a large number of miners drowned. When the accident became known in the village, the women went out with the families of the unfortunate men, and sat beside the mouth of the flooded pit, at the bottom of which the dead bodies yet remained. These women then yelled down the pit with voices very different from ordinary lamentation. They also refused unanimously to taste food of any kind, saying, when pressed to do so, that so long as they could refrain from eating, their husbands might still be spared to them. When, finally, one poor woman, driven by the pangs of hunger, was observed to eat a crust of bread, the cries ceased, and the women, renouncing all hope, proceeded in silent procession to their homes in Pelsall.

The Hindu people casting their food out of the window during an eclipse, the Pelsall wives refusing to eat when the mine is flooded, are acting by force of immemorial tradition, and so are doing unconsciously what the African woman does consciously when she surrounds the bed of her sick husband with rice and meat, and beseeches the demon to devour them instead of the man. To the same class of notions belong the old custom of trying to discover the body of one drowned by means of a loaf of bread with a candle stuck in it, which it was said would pause above the body, and the body might be made to appear by firing a gun over it—that is, the demon holding it would be frightened off. A variant, too, is the Persian custom of protecting a woman in parturition by spreading a table, with a lamp at each corner, with seven kinds of fruits and seven different aromatic seeds upon it.

In 1769, when Pennant made his 'Scottish Tour,' he found fully observed in the Highlands the ceremony of making the Beltane Cake on the first of May, and dedicating its distributed fragments to birds and beasts of prey, with invocation to the dread being of whom they were the supposed agents to spare the herds. Demons especially love milk: the Lambton Worm required nine cows' milk daily; and Jerome mentions a diabolical baby which exhausted six nurses.

The Devil nominally inherits, among the peasantry of Christendom, the attributes of the demons which preceded him; but it must be understood that in every case where mere voracity is ascribed to the Devil, a primitive demon is meant, and of this fact the superstitious peasant is dimly conscious. In Franconia, when a baker is about to put dough biscuits into an oven to be baked, he will first throw half-a-dozen of them into the fire, saying, 'There, poor devil! those are for you.' If pressed for an explanation, he will admit his fear that but for this offering his biscuits are in danger of coming out burnt; but that the 'poor devil' is not bad-hearted, only driven by his hunger to make mischief. The being he fears is, therefore, clearly not the Devil at all—whose distinction is a love of wickedness for its own sake—but the half-starved gobbling ghosts of whom, in Christian countries, 'Devil' has become the generic name. Of their sacrifices, Grace before meat is a remnant. In Moslem countries, however, 'Sheitan' combines the demonic and the malignant voracities. During the late lunar eclipse, the inhabitants of Pera and Constantinople fired guns over their houses to drive 'Sheitan' (Satan) away from the moon, for, whoever the foe, the Turk trusts in gunpowder. But superstitions representing Satan as a devourer are becoming rare. In the church of Nôtre Dame at Hal, Belgium, the lectern shows a dragon attempting to swallow the Bible, which is supported on the back of an eagle.

There is another and much more formidable form in which the Hunger-demon appears in Demonology. The fondness for blood, so characteristic of supreme gods, was distributed as a special thirst through a large class of demons. In the legend of Ishtar descending to Hades[4] to seek some beloved one, she threatens if the door be not opened—

> I will raise the dead to be devourers of the living!
> Upon the living shall the dead prey!

This menace shows that the Chaldæan and Babylonian belief in the vampyre, called Akhkharu in Assyrian, was fully developed at a very early date. Although the Hunger-demon was very fully developed in India, it does not appear to have been at any time so cannibalistic, possibly because the natives were not great flesh-eaters. In some cases, indeed, we meet with the vampyre superstition; as in the story of Vikram and the Vampyre, and in the Tamil drama of Harichándra, where the frenzied Sandramáti says to the king, 'I belong to the race of elves, and I have killed thy child in order that I might feed on its delicate flesh.' Such expressions are rare enough to warrant suspicion of their being importations. The Vetala's appetite is chiefly for corpses. The poor hungry demons of India—such as the Bhút, a dismal, ravenous ghost, dreaded at the moon-wane of the month Katik (Oct.-Nov.)—was not supposed to devour man, but only man's food. The Hindu demons of this class may be explained by reference to the sráddha, or oblation to ancestors, concerning which we read directions in the Manu Code. 'The ancestors of men are satisfied a whole month with *tila*, rice, &c.; two months with fish, &c. The Manes say, Oh, may that man be born in our line who may give us milky food, with honey and pure butter, both on the thirteenth of the moon and when the shadow of an elephant falls to the east!' The bloodthirsty demons of India have pretty generally been caught up like Kali into a higher symbolism, and their voracity systematised and satisfied in sacrificial commutations. The popular belief in the southern part of that country is indicated by Professor Monier Williams, in a letter written from Southern India, wherein he remarks that the devils alone require propitiation. It is generally a simple procedure, performed by offerings of food or other articles supposed to be acceptable to disembodied beings. For example, when a certain European, once a terror to the district in which he lived, died in the South of India, the natives were in the constant habit of depositing brandy and cigars on his tomb to propitiate his spirit, supposed to roam about the neighbourhood in a restless manner, and with evil proclivities. The very same was done to secure the good offices of the philanthropic spirit of a great European sportsman, who, when he was alive, delivered his district from the ravages of tigers. Indeed all evil spirits are thought to be opposed by good ones, who, if duly propitiated, make it their business to guard the inhabitants of particular places from demonic intruders. Each district, and even every village, has its guardian genius, often called its Mother.[5]

Such ideas as these are represented in Europe in some varieties of the Kobold and the Goblin (Gk. κόβαλος). Though the goblin must, according to folk-philosophy, be fed with nice food, it is not a deadly being; on the contrary, it is said the Gobelin tapestry derives its name because the secret of its colours was gained from these ghosts. Though St. Taurin expelled one from Evreux, he found it so polite that he would not send it to hell, and it still haunts the credulous there and at Caen, without being thought very formidable.

The demon that 'lurks in graveyards' is universal, and may have suggested cremation. In the East it is represented mainly by such forms as the repulsive *ghoul*, which preys on dead bodies; but it has been developed in some strange way to the Slavonic phantom called Vampyre, whose peculiar fearfulness is that it represents the form in which any deceased person may reappear, not ghoul-like to batten on the dead, but to suck the blood of the living. This is perhaps the most formidable survival of demonic superstition now existing in the world.

A people who still have in their dictionary such a word as 'miscreant' (misbeliever) can hardly wonder that the priests of the Eastern Church fostered the popular belief that heretics at death changed into drinkers of the blood of the living. The Slavonic vampyres have declined in England and America to be the 'Ogres,' who 'smell the blood of an Englishman,' but are rarely supposed to enjoy it; but it exposes the real ugliness of the pious superstitions sometimes deemed pretty, that, in proportion to the intensity of belief in supernaturalism, the people live in terror of the demons that go about seeking whom they may devour. In Russia the watcher beside a corpse is armed with holy charms against attack from it at midnight.

A vampyre may be the soul of any outcast from the Church, or one over whose corpse, before burial, a cat has leaped or a bird flown. It may be discovered in a graveyard by leading a black colt through; the animal will refuse to tread on the vampyre's grave, and the body is taken out and a stake driven through it, always by a single blow. A related class of demons are the 'heart-devourers.' They touch their victim with an aspen or other magical twig; the heart falls out, and is, perhaps, replaced by some baser one. Mr. Ralston mentions a Mazovian story in which a hero awakes with the heart of a hare, and remains a coward ever after;[6] and in another case a quiet peasant received a cock's heart and was always crowing. The Werewolf, in some respects closely related to the vampyre, also pursues his ravages among the priest-ridden peasantry of the South and East.

In Germany, though the more horrible forms of the superstition are rare, the 'Nachzehrer' is much dreaded. Even in various Protestant regions it is thought safest that a cross should be set beside every grave to impede any demonic propensities that may take possession of the person interred; and where food is not still buried with the corpse to assuage any pangs of hunger that may arise, a few grains of corn or rice are scattered upon it in reminiscence of the old custom. In Diesdorf it is believed that if money is not placed in the dead person's mouth at burial, or his name not cut from his shirt, he is likely to become a Nachzehrer, and that the ghost will come forth in the form of a pig. It is considered a sure preventative of such a result to break the neck of the dead body. On one occasion, it is there related, several persons of one family having died, the suspected corpse was exhumed, and found to have eaten up its own grave-clothes.

Dr. Dyer, an eminent physician of Chicago, Illinois, told me (1875) that a case occurred in that city within his personal knowledge, where the body of a woman who had died of consumption was taken out of the grave and the lungs burned, under a belief that she was drawing after her into the grave some of her surviving relatives. In 1874, according to the *Providence Journal*, in the village of Peacedale, Rhode Island, U.S., Mr. William Rose dug up the body of his own daughter, and burned her heart, under the belief that she was wasting away the lives of other members of his family.

The characteristics of modern 'Spiritualism' appear to indicate that the superstitious have outgrown this ancient fear of ghostly malevolence where surrounded by civilisation. It is very rare in the ancient world or in barbarous regions to find any invocations for the return of the spirits of the dead. Mr. Tylor has quoted a beautiful dirge used by the Ho tribe of India, beginning—

> We never scolded you, never wronged you;
> Come to us back!

But generally funereal customs are very significant of the fear that spirits may return, and their dirges more in the vein of the Bodo of North-East India: 'Take and eat: heretofore you have eaten and drunk with us, you can do so no more: you were one of us, you can be so no longer: we come no more to you, come you not to us.' 'Even,' says Mr. Tylor, 'in the lowest culture we find flesh holding its own against spirit, and at higher stages the householder rids himself with little scruple of an unwelcome inmate. The Greenlanders would carry the dead out by the window, not by the door, while an old woman, waving a firebrand behind, cried 'Piklerrukpok!' *i.e.*, 'There is nothing more to be had here!' the Hottentots removed the dead from the hut by an opening broken out on purpose, to prevent him from finding the way back; the Siamese, with the same intention, break an opening through the house wall to carry the coffin through, and then hurry it at full speed thrice round the house; the Siberian Chuwashes fling a red-hot stone after the corpse is carried out, for an obstacle to bar the soul from coming back; so Brandenburg peasants pour out a pail of water at the door after the coffin to prevent the ghost from walking; and Pomeranian mourners returning from the churchyard leave behind the straw from the hearse, that the wandering soul may rest there, and not come back so far as home.'[7]

It may be remarked, in this connection, that in nearly all the pictures of demons and devils, they are represented as very lean. The exceptions will be found generally in certain Southern and tropical demons which represent cloud or storm—Typhon, for instance—and present a swollen or bloated appearance. No Northern devil is fat. Shakespeare ascribes to Cæsar a suspicion of leanness—

Yond' Cassius hath a lean and hungry look:

He thinks too much: such men are dangerous.

When Antony defends Cassius, Cæsar only replies, 'Would he were fatter!' This mistrust of leanness is a reflection from all the Hunger-demons; it interprets the old sayings that a devil, however fair in front, may be detected by hollowness of the back, and that he is usually so thin as to cast no shadow.[8]

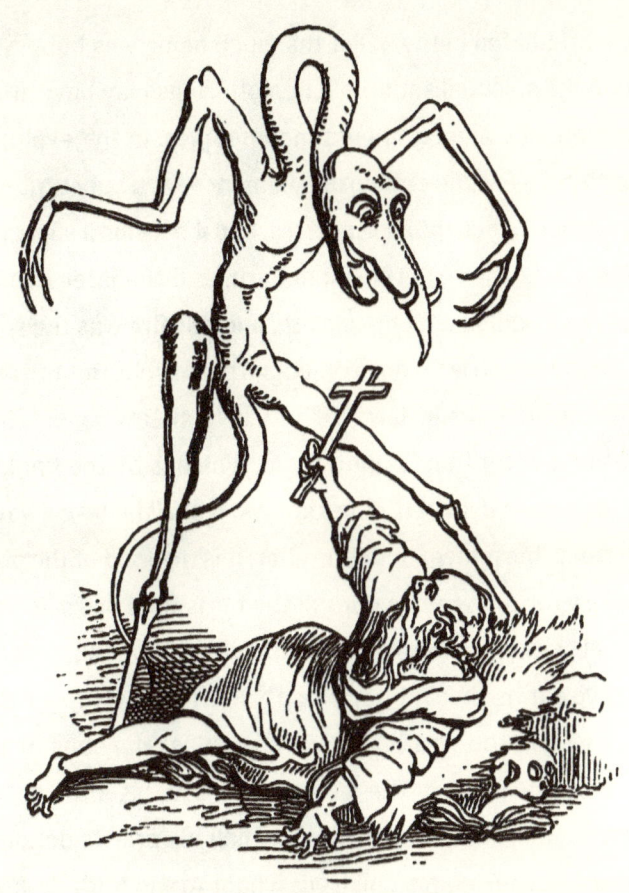

Fig. 4.—St. Anthony's Lean Persecutor (Salvator Rosa)

Illustrations of the Hunger-demon and its survivals might be greatly multiplied, were it necessary. It need only, however, be mentioned that it is to this early and most universal conception of præternatural danger that the idea of sacrifice as well as of fasting must be ascribed. It is, indeed, too obvious to require extended demonstration that the notion of offering fruits and meat to an invisible being could only have originated in the belief that such being was hungry, however much the spiritualisation of such offerings may have attended their continuance among enlightened peoples. In the evolution of purer deities, Fire—'the devouring element'—was substituted for a coarser method of accepting sacrifices, and it became a sign of baser beings—such as the Assyrian Akhkharu, and the later Lamia—to consume dead bodies with their teeth; and this fire was the spiritual element in the idolatries whose objects were visible. But the original accent of sacrifice never left it. The Levitical Law says: 'The two kidneys, and the fat that is upon them, which is by the flanks, and the caul above the liver, with the kidneys, it shall he take away. And the priest shall burn them upon the altar: it is the food of the offering made by fire for a sweet savour: all the fat is the Lord's. It shall be a perpetual statute for your generations throughout all your dwellings, that ye eat neither fat nor blood.'[9] We find the Hunger-demon shown as well in the wrath of Jehovah against the sons of Eli for eating the choice parts of the meats offered on his altar, as in that offering of tender infants to Moloch which his priests denounced, or in Saturn devouring his children, whom Aryan faith dethroned; and they all reappear as phantoms thinly veiled above the spotless Lamb offered up on Calvary, the sacrificed Macaria ('Blessed'), the pierced heart of Mary. The beautiful boy Menœceus must be sacrificed to save Thebes; the gods will not have aged and tough Creon, though a king, in his place. Iphigenia, though herself saved from the refined palate of Artemis, through the huntress's fondness for kid's blood, becomes the priestess of human sacrifices. The human offering deemed half-divine could alone at last satisfy the Deity, gathered in his side this sheaf of sacrificial knives, whetted in many lands and ages, and in his self-sacrifice the Hunger-demon himself was made the victim. Theologians have been glad to rescue the First Person of their Trinity from association with the bloodthirsty demons of barbarous ages by describing the sacrifice of Jesus as God himself becoming the victim of an eternal law. But, whatever may be said of this complex device, it is sufficient evidence that man's primitive demon which personified his hunger has ended with being consumed on his own altar. For though fasting is a survival of the same savage notion that man may secure benefits from invisible beings by leaving them the food, it is a practice which survives rather through the desire of imitating ascetic saints than because of any understood principle. The strange yet natural consummation adds depth of meaning to the legend of Odin being himself sacrificed in his disguise on the Holy Tree at Upsala, where human victims were hung as offerings to him; and to his rune in the Havamal—

> I know that I hung
> On a wind-rocked tree
> Nine whole nights,
> With a spear wounded,
> And to Odin offered
> Myself to myself.

NOTES

1 'The Land of Charity,' by Rev. Samuel Mateer, p. 214.
2 London 'Times' Calcutta correspondence.
3 The Persian poet Sádi uses the phrase, 'The whale swallowed Jonah,' as a familiar expression for sunset; which is in curious coincidence with a Mimac (Nova Scotian) myth that the holy hero Glooscap was carried to the happy Sunset Land in a whale. The story of Jonah has indeed had interesting variants, one of them being that legend of Oannes, the fish-god, emerging from the Red Sea to teach Babylonians the arts (a saga of Dagon); but the phrase in the Book of Jonah—'the belly of Hell'—had a prosaic significance for the christian mind, and, in connection with speculations concerning Behemoth and Leviathan, gave us the mediæval Mouth of Hell.
4 Tablet K 162 in the British Museum. See 'Records of the Past,' i. 141.
5 London 'Times,' July 11, 1877.
6 'Songs of the Russian People,' p. 409.
7 'Primitive Culture.'
8 Cæsarius D'Heisterbach, Miracul. iii.
9 Lev. iii. 15.

Chapter II
Heat

Demons of Fire — Agni — Asmodeus — Prometheus — Feast of fire —
Moloch — Tophet — Genii of the lamp — Bel-fires — Hallowe'en —
Negro superstitions — Chinese fire-god — Volcanic and incendiary demons —
Mangaian fire-demon — Demons' fear of water

FIRE WAS OF old the element of fiends. No doubt this was in part due to the fact that it also was a devouring element. Sacrifices were burnt; the demon visibly consumed them. But the great flame-demons represent chiefly the destructive and painful action of intense heat. They originate in regions of burning desert, of sunstroke, and drouth.

Agni, the Hindu god of fire, was adored in Vedic hymns as the twin of Indra.

'Thy appearance is fair to behold, thou bright-faced Agni, when like gold thou shinest at hand; thy brightness comes like the lightning of heaven; thou showest splendour like the splendour of the bright sun.

'Adorable and excellent Agni, emit the moving and graceful smoke.

'The flames of Agni are luminous, powerful, fearful, and not to be trusted.

'I extol the greatness of that showerer of rain, whom men celebrate as the slayer of Vritra: the Agni, Vaiswanara, slew the stealer of the waters.'

The slaying of Vritra, the monster, being the chief exploit of Indra, Agni could only share in it as being the flame that darted with Indra's weapon, the disc (of the sun).

'Thou (Agni) art laid hold off with difficulty, like the young of tortuously twining snakes, thou who art a consumer of many forests as a beast is of fodder.'

Petrifaction awaits all these glowing metaphors of early time. Verbal inspiration will make Agni a literally tortuous serpent and consuming fire. His smoke, called Kali (black), is now the name of Siva's terrible bride.

Much is said in Vedic hymns of the method of producing the sacred flame symbolising Agni; namely, the rubbing together of two sticks. 'He it is whom the two sticks have engendered, like a new-born babe.' It is a curious coincidence that a similar phrase should describe 'the devil on two sticks,' who has come by way of Persia into European romance. Asmodeus was a lame demon, and his 'two sticks' as 'Diable Boiteux' are crutches; but his lameness may be referable to the attenuated extremities suggested by spires of flame—'tortuously twining snakes,'—rather than to the rabbinical myth that he broke his leg on his way to meet Solomon. Benfey identified Asmodeus as Zend Aêshma-daêva, demon of lust. His goat-feet and fire-coal eyes are described by Le Sage, and the demon says he was lamed by falling from the air, like Vulcan, when contending with Pillardoc. It is not difficult to imagine how flame engendered by the rubbing of sticks might have attained personification as sensual passion, especially among Zoroastrians, who would detach from the adorable Fire all associations of evil. It would harmonise well with the Persian tendency to diabolise Indian gods, that they should note the lustful character occasionally ascribed to Agni in the Vedas. 'Him alone, the ever-youthful Agni, men groom like a horse in the evening and at dawn; they bed him as a stranger in his couch; the light of Agni, the worshipped male, is lighted.' Agni was the Indian 'Brulefer' or love-charmer, and patron of marriage; the fire-god Hephaistos was the husband of Aphrodite; the day of the Norse thunder-and-lightning god Thor (Thursday), is in Scandinavian regions considered the luckiest for marriages.

The process of obtaining fire by friction is represented by a nobler class of myths than that referred to. In the *Mahábhárata* the gods and demons together churn the ocean for the nectar of immortality; and they use for their churning-stick the mountain Manthara. This word appears in *pramantha,* which means a fire-drill, and from it comes the great name of Prometheus, who stole fire from heaven, and conferred on mankind a boon which rendered them so powerful that the jealousy and wrath of Zeus were excited. This fable is generally read in its highly rationalised and mystical form, and on this account belongs to another part of our general subject; but it may be remarked here that the Titan so terribly tortured by Zeus could hardly have been regarded, originally, as the friend of man. At the time when Zeus was a god genuinely worshipped—when he first stood forth as the supplanter of the malign devourer Saturn—it could have been no friend of man who was seen chained on the rock for ever to be the vulture's prey. It was fire in some destructive form which must have been then associated with Prometheus, and not that power by which later myths represented his animating with a divine spark the man of clay. The Hindu myth of churning the ocean for the immortal draught, even if it be proved that the ocean is heaven and the draught lightning, does not help us much. The traditional association of Prometheus with the Arts might almost lead one to imagine that the early use of fire by some primitive inventor had brought upon him the wrath of his mates, and that Zeus' thunderbolts represented some early 'strike' against machinery.

It is not quite certain that it may not have been through some euphemistic process that Fire-worship arose in Persia. Not only does fire occupy a prominent place in the tortures inflicted by Ahriman in the primitive Parsee Inferno, but it was one of the weapons by which he attempted to destroy the heavenly child Zoroaster. The evil magicians kindled a fire in the desert and threw the child on it; but his mother, Dogdo, found him sleeping tranquilly on the flames, which were as a pleasant bath, and his face shining like Zohore and Moschteri (Jupiter and Mercury).[1] The Zoroastrians also held that the earth would ultimately be destroyed by fire; its metals and minerals, ignited by a comet, would form streams which all souls would have to pass through: they would be pleasant to the righteous, but terrible to the sinful,—who, however, would come through, purified, into paradise, the last to arrive being Ahriman himself.

The combustible nature of many minerals under the surface of the earth,—which was all the realm of Hades (invisible),—would assist the notion of a fiery abode for the infernal gods. Our phrase 'plutonic rock' would then have a very prosaic sense. Pliny says that in his time sulphur was used to keep off evil spirits, and it is not impossible that it first came to be used as a medicine by this route.[2]

Fire-festivals still exist in India, where the ancient raiment of Agni has been divided up and distributed among many deities. At the popular annual festival in honour of Dharma Rajah, called the Feast of Fire, the devotees walk barefoot over a glowing fire extending forty feet. It lasts eighteen days, during which time those that make a vow to keep it must fast, abstain from women, lie on the bare ground, and walk on a brisk fire. The eighteenth day they assemble on the sound of instruments, their heads crowned with flowers, their bodies daubed with saffron, and follow the figures of Dharma Rajah and Draupadi his wife in procession. When they come to the fire, they stir it to animate its activity, and take a little of the ashes, with which they rub their foreheads; and when the gods have been carried three times round it they walk over a hot fire, about forty feet. Some carry their children in their arms, and others lances, sabres, and standards. After the ceremony the people press to collect the ashes to rub their foreheads with, and obtain from devotees the flowers with which they were adorned, and which they carefully preserve.[3]

The passion of Agni reappears in Draupadi purified by fire for her five husbands, and especially her union with Dharma Rajah, son of Yama, is celebrated in this unorthodox passion-feast. It has been so much the fashion for travellers to look upon all 'idolatry' with biblical eyes, that we cannot feel certain with Sonnerat that there was anything more significant in the carrying of children by the devotees, than the supposition that what was good for the parent was equally beneficial to the child. But the identification of Moloch with an Aryan deity is not important; the Indian Feast of Fire and the rites of Moloch are derived by a very simple mental process from the most obvious aspects of the Sun as the quickening and the consuming power in nature. The child offered to Moloch was offered to the god by whom he was generated, and as the most precious of all the fruits of the earth for which his genial aid was implored and his destructive intensity deprecated. Moloch, a word that means 'king,' was a name almost synonymous with human sacrifice. It was in all probability at first only a local (Ammonite) personification growing out of an ancient shrine of Baal. The Midianite Baal accompanied the Israelites into the wilderness, and that worship was never thoroughly eradicated. In the Egyptian Confession of Faith, which the initiated took even into their graves inscribed upon a scroll, the name of God is not mentioned, but is expressed only by the words *Nuk pu Nuk*, 'I am he who I am.'[4] The flames of the burning bush, from which these same words came to Moses, were kindled from Baal, the Sun; and we need not wonder that while the more enlightened chiefs of Israel preserved the higher ideas and symbols of the countries they abandoned, the ignorant would still cling to Apis (the Golden Calf), to Ashtaroth, and to Moloch. Amos (v. 26), and after him Stephen the martyr (Acts vii. 43), reproach the Hebrews with having carried into the wilderness the tabernacle of their god Moloch. And though the passing of children through the fire to Moloch was, by the Mosaic Law, made a capital crime, the superstition and the corresponding practice retained such strength that we find Solomon building a temple to Moloch on the Mount of Olives (1 Kings xi. 7), and, long after, Manasseh making his son pass through the fire in honour of the same god.

It is certain from the denunciations of the prophets[5] that the destruction of children in these flames was actual. From Jeremiah xix. 6, as well as other sources, we know that the burnings took place in the Valley of Tophet or Hinnom (Gehenna). The idol Moloch was of brass, and its throne of brass; its head was that of a calf, and wore a royal crown; its stomach was a furnace, and when the children were placed in its arms they were consumed by the fierce heat,— their cries being drowned by the beating of drums; from which, *toph* meaning a 'drum,' the place was also called Tophet. In the fierce war waged against alien superstitions by Josiah, he defiled Gehenna, filling it with ordure and dead men's bones to make it odious, 'that no man might make his son or his daughter to pass through the fire to Moloch' (2 Kings xxiii. 10), and a perpetual fire was kept there to consume the filth of Jerusalem.

From this horrible Gehenna, with its perpetual fire, its loathsome worm, its cruelties, has been derived the picture of a never-ending Hell prepared for the majority of human beings by One who, while they live on earth, sends the rain and sunshine alike on the evil and the good. Wo Chang, a Chinaman in London, has written to a journal[6] his surprise that our religious teachers should be seized with such concern for the victims of Turkish atrocities in Bulgaria, while they are so calm in view of the millions burning, and destined to burn endlessly, in the flames of hell. Our Oriental brothers will learn a great deal from our missionaries; among other things, that the theological god of Christendom is still Moloch.

The Ammonites, of whom Moloch was the special demon, appear to have gradually blended with the Arabians. These received from many sources their mongrel superstitions, but among them were always prominent the planet-gods and fire-gods, whom their growing monotheism (to use the word still in a loose sense) transformed to powerful angels and genii. The genii of Arabia are slaves of the lamp; they are evoked by burning tufts of hair; they ascend as clouds of smoke. Though, as subordinate agents of the Fire-fiend, they may be consumed by flames, yet those who so fight them are apt to suffer a like fate, as in the case of the Lady of Beauty in the Arabian Nights' Entertainments. Many stories of this kind preceded the declarations of the Old Testament, that Jehovah breathes fire and brimstone, his breath kindling Tophet; and also the passages of the Koran, and of the New Testament describing Satan as a fiery fiend.

Various superstitions connecting infernal powers with fire survive among the Jews of some remote districts of Europe. The Passover is kept a week by the Jewish inhabitants in the villages on the Vosges mountains and on the banks of the Rhine. The time of *omer* is the interval between the Passover and Pentecost, the seven weeks elapsing from the departure from Egypt and the giving of the law, marked in former days by the offering of an omer of barley daily at the temple. It is considered a fearful time, during which every Jew is particularly exposed to the evil influence of evil spirits. There is something dangerous and fatal in the air; every one should be on the watch, and not tempt the *schedim*(demons) in any way. Have a strict eye upon your cattle, say the Jews, for the sorceress will get into your stables, mount your cows and goats, bring diseases upon them, and turn their milk sour. In the latter case, try to lay your hand upon the suspected person; shut her up in a room with a basin of sour milk, and beat the milk with a hazel-wand, pronouncing God's name three times. Whilst you are doing this, the sorceress will make great lamentation, for the blows are falling upon her. Only stop when you see blue flames dancing on the surface of the milk, for then the charm is broken. If at nightfall a beggar comes to ask for a little charcoal to light his fire, be very careful not to give it, and do not let him go without drawing him three times by his coat-tail; and without losing time, throw some large handfuls of salt on the fire. In all of which we may trace traditions of parched wildernesses and fiery serpents, as well as of Abraham's long warfare with the Fire-worshippers, until, according to the tradition, he was thrown into the flames he refused to worship.

It is probable that in all the popular superstitions which now connect devils and future punishments with fire are blended both the apotheosis and the degradation of demons. The first and most universal of deities being the Sun, whose earthly representative is fire, the student of Comparative Mythology has to pick his way very carefully in tracing by any ethnological path the innumerable superstitions of European folklore in which Fire-worship is apparently reflected. The collection of facts and records contained in a work so accessible to all who care to pursue the subject as that of Brand and his editors,[7] renders it unnecessary that I should go into the curious facts to any great extent here. The uniformity of the traditions by which the midsummer fires of Northern Europe have been called Baal-fires or Bel-fires warrant the belief that they are actually descended from the ancient rites of Baal, even apart from the notorious fact that they have so generally been accompanied by the superstition that it is a benefit to children to leap over or be passed through such fires. That this practice still survives in out-of-the way places of the British Empire appears from such communications as the following (from the *Times*), which are occasionally addressed to the London journals:—'LERWICK (Shetland), *July 7, 1871.*—SIR,—It may interest some of your readers to know that last night (being St. John's Eve, old style) I observed, within a mile or so of this town, seven bonfires blazing, in accordance with the immemorial custom of celebrating the Midsummer solstice. These fires were kindled on various heights around the ancient hamlet of Sound, and the children leaped over them, and 'passed through the fire to Moloch,' just as their ancestors would have done a thousand years ago on the same heights, and their still remoter progenitors in Eastern lands many thousand years ago. This persistent adherence to mystic rites in this scientific epoch seems to me worth taking note of.—A. J.'

To this may be added the following recent extract from a Scotch journal:—

'Hallowe'en was celebrated at Balmoral Castle with unusual ceremony, in the presence of her Majesty, the Princess Beatrice, the ladies and gentlemen of the royal household, and a large gathering of the tenantry. The leading features of the celebration were a torchlight procession, the lighting of large bonfires, and the burning in effigy of witches and warlocks. Upwards of 150 torch-bearers assembled at the castle as dark set in, and separated into two parties, one band proceeding to Invergelder, and the other remaining at Balmoral. The torches were lighted at a quarter before six o'clock, and shortly after the Queen and Princess Beatrice drove to Invergelder, followed by the Balmoral party of torchbearers. The two parties then united and returned in procession to the front of Balmoral Castle, where refreshments were served to all, and dancing was engaged in round a huge bonfire. Suddenly there appeared from the rear of the Castle a grotesque apparition representing a witch with a train of followers dressed like sprites, who danced and gesticulated in all fashions. Then followed a warlock of demoniac shape, who was succeeded by another warlock drawing a car, on which was seated the figure of a witch, surrounded by other figures in the garb of demons. The unearthly visitors having marched several times round the burning pile, the principal figure was taken from the car and tossed into the flames amid the burning of blue lights and a display of crackers and fireworks. The health of her Majesty the Queen was then pledged, and drunk with Highland honours by the assembled hundreds. Dancing was then resumed, and was carried on till a late hour at night.'

The Sixth Council of Constantinople (an. 680), by its sixty-fifth canon, forbids these fires in the following terms:—'Those bonefires that are kindled by certain people before their shops and houses, over which also they use ridiculously to leap, by a certain ancient custom, we command them from henceforth to cease. Whoever, therefore, shall do any such thing, if he be a clergyman, let him be deposed; if he be a layman, let him be excommunicated. For in the

Fourth Book of the Kings it is thus written: And Manasseh built an altar to all the host of heaven, in the two courts of the Lord's house, and made his children to pass through the fire.' There is a charming naïveté in this denunciation. It is no longer doubtful that this 'bonefire' over which people leaped came from the same source as that Gehenna from which the Church derived the orthodox theory of hell, as we have already seen. When Shakespeare speaks (Macbeth) of 'the primrose way to the everlasting bonfire,'[8] he is, with his wonted felicity, assigning the flames of hell and the fires of Moloch and Baal their right archæological relation.

In my boyhood I have often leaped over a bonfire in a part of the State of Virginia mainly settled by Scotch families, with whom probably the custom migrated thither. In the superstitions of the negroes of that and other Southern States fire plays a large part, but it is hardly possible now to determine whether they have drifted there from Africa or England. Sometimes there are queer coincidences between their notions and some of the early legends of Britain. Thus, the tradition of the shepherd guided by a distant fire to the entrance of King Arthur's subterranean hall, where a flame fed by no fuel coming through the floor reveals the slumbering monarch and his court, resembles somewhat stories I have heard from negroes of their being led by distant fires to lucky—others say unlucky—or at any rate enchanted spots. A negro belonging to my father told me that once, as he was walking on a country road, he saw a great fire in the distance; he supposed it must be a house on fire, and hastened towards it, meantime much puzzled, since he knew of no house in that direction. As he went on his way he turned into a small wood near which the fire seemed to be, but when he emerged, all he found was a single fire-coal burning in the path. There were no other traces whatever of fire, but just then a large dog leaped past him with a loud bark and disappeared.

In a letter on 'Voudouism in Virginia,' which appeared in the *New York Tribune*, dated Richmond, September 17, 1875, occurs an account of a class of superstitions generally kept close from the whites, as I have always believed because of their purely African origin. As will be seen, fire represents an important element in the superstitious practices.

'If an ignorant negro is smitten with a disease which he cannot comprehend, he often imagines himself the victim of witchcraft, and having no faith in 'white folks' physic' for such ailments, must apply to one of these quacks. A physician residing near this city was invited by such a one to witness his mode of procedure with a dropsical patient for whom the physician in question had occasionally charitably prescribed. Curiosity led him to attend the seance, having previously informed the quack that since the case was in such hands he relinquished all connection with it. On the coverlet of the bed on which the sick man lay was spread a quantity of bones, feathers, and other trash. The charlatan went through with a series of so-called conjurations, burned feathers, hair, and tiny fragments of wood in a charcoal furnace, and mumbled gibberish past the physician's comprehension. He then proceeded to rip open the pillows and bolsters, and took from them some queer conglomerations of feathers. These he said had caused all the trouble. Sprinkling a whitish powder over them, he burnt them in his furnace. A black offensive smoke was produced, and he announced triumphantly that the evil influence was destroyed and that the patient would surely get well. He died not many days later, believing, in common with all his friends and relatives, that the conjurations of the 'trick doctor' had failed to save him only because resorted to too late.'

The following account of a spell from which his wife was rescued, was given me by a negro in Virginia:—

'The wizard,' to quote the exact words of my informant, 'threw a stick on a chest; the stick bounded like a trapball three times; then he opened the chest, took out something looking like dust or clay, and put it into a cup with water over a fire; then he poured it over a board (after chopping it three times), which he then put up beneath the shingles of the house. Returning to the chest he took a piece of old chain, near the length of my hand, took a hoe and buried the chain near the sill of the door of my wife's house where she would pass; then he went away. I saw my wife coming and called to her not to pass, and to go for a hoe and dig up the place. She did this, and I took up the chain, which burned the ends of all my fingers clean off. The same night the conjuror came back: my wife took two half dollars and a quarter in silver and threw them on the ground before him. The man seemed as if he was shocked, and then offered her his hand, which she refused to take, as I had bid her not to let him touch her. He left and never came to the house again. The spell was broken.'

I am convinced that this is a pure Voudou procedure, and it

is interesting in several regards. The introduction of the chain may have been the result of the excitement of the time, for it was during the war when negroes were breaking their chains. The fire and water show how wide-spread in Africa is that double ordeal which, as we have seen, is well known in the kingdom of Dahomey.[9] But the mingling of 'something like dust' with the water held in a cup over the fire, is strongly suggestive of the Jewish method of preparing holy water, 'the water of separation.' 'For an unclean person they shall take of the dust of the burnt heifer of purification for sin, and running water shall be put thereto in a vessel.'[10] The fiery element of the mixture was in this case imported with the ashes of the red heifer. As for this sacrifice of the red heifer itself[11] it was plainly the propitiation of a fiery demon. In Egypt red hair and red animals of all kinds were considered infernal, and all the details of this sacrifice show that the colour of this selected heifer was typical. The heifer was not a usual sacrifice: a red one was obviously by its colour marked for the genii of fire—the terrible Seven—and not to be denied them. Its blood was sprinkled seven times before the tabernacle, and the rest was utterly consumed—including the hide, which is particularly mentioned—and the ashes taken to make the 'water of separation.' Calmet notes, in this connection, that the Apis of India was red-coloured.

The following interesting story of the Chinese Fire-god was supplied to Mr. Dennys[12] by Mr. Playfair of H.M. Consulate, to whom it was related in Peking:—

'The temples of the God of Fire are numerous in Peking, as is natural in a city built for the most part of very combustible materials. The idols representing the god are, with one exception, decked with red beards, typifying by their colour the element under his control. The exceptional god has a white beard, and 'thereby hangs a tale.'

'A hundred years ago the Chinese imperial revenue was in much better case than it is now. At that time they had not yet come into collision with Western Powers, and the word 'indemnity' had not, so far, found a place in their vocabulary; internal rebellions were checked as soon as they broke out, and, in one word, Kien Lung was in less embarrassed circumstances than Kwang Hsu; he had more money to spend, and did lay out a good deal in the way of palaces. His favourite building, and one on which no expense had been spared, was the 'Hall of Contemplation.' This hall was of very large dimensions; the rafters and the pillars which supported the roof were of a size such as no trees in China furnish now-a-days. They were not improbably originally sent as an offering by the tributary monarch of some tropical country, such as Burmah or Siam. Two men could barely join hands round the pillars; they were cased in lustrous jet-black lacquer, which, while adding to the beauty of their appearance, was also supposed to make them less liable to combustion. Indeed, every care was taken that no fire should approach the building; no lighted lamp was allowed in the precincts, and to have smoked a pipe inside those walls would have been punished with death. The floor of the hall was of different-coloured marbles, in a mosaic of flowers and mystic Chinese characters, always kept polished like a mirror. The sides of the room were lined with rare books and precious manuscripts. It was, in short, the finest palace in the imperial city, and it was the pride of Kien Lung.

'Alas for the vanity of human wishes! In spite of every precaution, one night a fire broke out, and the Hall of Contemplation was in danger. The Chinese of a century ago were not without fire-engines, and though miserably inefficient as compared with those of our London fire brigade, they were better than nothing, and a hundred of them were soon working round the burning building. The Emperor himself came out to superintend their efforts and encourage them to renewed exertions. But the hall was doomed; a more than earthly power was directing the flames, and mortal efforts were of no avail. For on one of the burning rafters Kien Lung saw the figure of a little old man, with a long white beard, standing in a triumphant attitude. 'It is the God of Fire,' said the Emperor, 'we can do nothing;' so the building was allowed to blaze in peace. Next day Kien Lung appointed a commission to go the round of the Peking temples in order to discover in which of them there was a Fire-god with a white beard, that he might worship him, and appease the offended deity. The search was fruitless; all the Fire-gods had red beards. But the commission had done its work badly; being highly respectable mandarins of genteel families, they had confined their search to such temples as were in good repair and of creditable exterior. Outside the north gate of the imperial city was one old, dilapidated, disreputable shrine which they had overlooked. It had been crumbling away for years, and even the dread figure of the God of Fire, which sat above the altar, had not escaped desecration. 'Time had thinned his flowing locks,' and the beard had fallen away altogether. One day some water-carriers who frequented the locality thought, either in charity or by way of a joke, that the face would look the better for a new beard. So they unravelled some cord, and with the frayed-out hemp adorned the beardless chin. An official passing the temple one day peeped in out of curiosity, and saw the hempen beard. 'Just the thing the Emperor was inquiring about,' said he to himself, and he took the news to the palace without delay. Next day there was a state visit to the dilapidated temple, and Kien Lung made obeisance and vowed a vow.

'O Fire-god,' said he, 'thou hast been wroth with me in that I have built me palaces, and left thy shrine unhonoured and in ruins. Here do I vow to build thee a temple surpassed by none other of the Fire-gods in Peking; but I shall expect thee in future not to meddle with my palaces.'

'The Emperor was as good as his word. The new temple is on the site of the old one, and the Fire-god has a flowing beard of fine white hair.'

In the San Francisco *Bulletin*, I recently read a description of the celebration by the Chinese in that city of their Feast for the Dead, in which there are some significant features. The chief attention was paid, says the reporter, to a figure 'representing what answers in their theology to our devil, and whom they evidently think it necessary to propitiate before proceeding with their worship over individual graves.' This figure is on the west side of their temple; before and around it candles and joss-sticks were kept burning. On the east side was the better-looking figure, to which they paid comparatively little attention.

It was of course but natural that the demons of fire should gradually be dispelled from that element in its normal aspects, as its uses became more important through human invention, and its evil possibilities were mastered. Such demons became gradually located in the region of especially dangerous fires, as volcanoes and boiling springs. The Titan whom the ancients believed struggling beneath Ætna remained there as the Devil in the christian age. St. Agatha is said to have prevented his vomiting fire for a century by her prayers. St. Philip ascended the same mountain, and with book and candle pronounced a prayer of exorcism, at which three devils came out like fiery flying stones, crying, 'Woe is us! we are still hunted by Peter through Philip the Elder!' The volcanoes originated the belief that hell is at the earth's centre, and their busy Vulcans of classic ages have been easily transformed into sulphurous lords of the christian Hell. Such is the mediæval Haborym, demon of arson, with his three heads—man, cat, and serpent—who rides through the air mounted on a serpent, and bears in his hand a flaming torch. The astrologers assigned him command of twenty-six legions of demons in hell, and the superstitious often saw him laughing on the roofs of burning houses.[13] But still more dignified is Raum, who commands thirty legions, and who destroys villages; hence, also, concerned in the destructions of war, he became the demon who awards dignities; and although this made his usual form of apparition on the right bank of the Rhine that of the Odinistic raven, on the left bank he may be detected in the little red man who was reported as the familiar of Napoleon I. during his career.

Among Mr. Gill's South Pacific myths is one of a Prometheus,

Maui, who by assistance of a red pigeon gets from the subterranean fire-demon the secret of producing fire (by rubbing sticks), the demon (Mauike) being then consumed with his realm, and fire being brought to the upper world to remain the friend of man. In Vedic legend, when the world was enveloped in darkness, the gods prayed to Agni, who suddenly burst out as Tvashtri—pure fire, the Vedic Vulcan—to the dismay of the universe. In Eddaic sagas, Loki was deemed the most voracious of beings until defeated in an eating match with Logi (devouring fire).

Survivals of belief in the fiery nature of demons are very numerous. Thus it is a very common belief that the Devil cannot touch or cross water, and may therefore be escaped by leaping a stream. This has sometimes been supposed to have something to do with the purifying character of water; but there are many instances in Christian folklore where the Devil is shown quite independent of even holy water if it is not sprinkled on him or does not wet his feet. Thus in the Norfolk legend concerning St. Godric, the Devil is said to have thrown the vessel with its holy water at the saint's head out of anger at his singing a canticle which the Virgin taught him. But when the Devil attacked him in various ferocious animal shapes, St. Godric escaped by running into the Wear, where he sometimes stood all night in water up to his neck.

The Kobolds get the red jackets they are said to wear from their fiery nature. Originally the *lar familiaris* of Germany, the Kobold became of many varieties; but in one line he has been developed from the house-spirit, whose good or evil temper was recognised in the comforts or dangers of fire, to a special Stone-demon. The hell-dog in Faust's room takes refuge from the spell of 'Solomon's Key' behind the stone, and is there transformed to human shape. The German maidens read many pretty oracles in the behaviour of the fire, and the like in that of its fellow Wahrsager the house-dog. It is indeed a widespread notion that imps and witches lurk about the fireside, obviously in cat and dog, and ride through the air on implements that usually stand about the fire,—shovel, tongs, or broom. In Paris it was formerly the custom to throw twenty-four cats into the fire on St. John's night, the animals being, according to M. De Plancy, emblems of the devil. So was replaced the holocaust of human witches, until at last civilisation rang out its curfew for all such fires as that.

NOTES

1 Du Perron, 'Vie de Zoroastre.'
2 The principle similia similibus curantur is a very ancient one; but though it may have originated in a euphemistic or propitiatory aim, the homoeopathist may claim that it could hardly have lived unless it had been found to have some practical advantages.
3 Sonnerat's 'Travels,' ii. 38.
4 Deutsch, 'Literary Remains,' p. 178.
5 Isa. lvii. 5; Ezek. xvi. 20; Jer. xix. 5.
6 The 'Jewish World.'
7 'Observations on Popular Antiquities,' &c., by John Brand. With the additions of Sir Henry Ellis. An entirely new and revised edition. Chatto & Windus, 1877. See especially the chapter on 'Summer Solstice,' p. 165.
8 'Pyra, a bonefire, wherein men's bodyes were burned.'—Cooper's Thesaurus. Probably from Fr. bon; Wedgewood gives Dan. baun, beacon.
9 See Chapter i. Compare Numbers xxxi. 23.
10 Numbers xix. 17.
11 Ibid. xix. 2, seq.
12 'Folklore of China,' p. 121.
13 In Russia the pigeon, from being anciently consecrated to the thunder god, has become emblem of the Holy Ghost, or celestial fire, and as such the foe of earthly fire. Pigeons are trusted as insurers against fire, and the flight of one through a house is regarded as a kindly warning of conflagration.

Chapter III
Cold

Descent of Ishtar into Hades — Bardism — Baldur — Hercules — Christ —
Survivals of the Frost Giant in Slavonic and other countries — The Clavie —
The Frozen Hell — The Northern abode of demons — North side of churches

EVEN ACROSS IMMEMORIAL generations it is impossible to read
without emotion the legend of the Descent of Ishtar into Hades.[1]
Through seven gates the goddess of Love passes in search of her beloved, and at each some of her ornaments and clothing are removed
by the dread guardian. Ishtar enters naked into the presence of the
Queen of Death. But gods, men, and herds languish in her absence,
and the wonder-working Hea, the Saviour, so charms the Infernal
Queen, that she bids the Judge of her realm, Annunak, absolve Ishtar
from his golden throne.

> 'He poured out for Ishtar the waters of life and let her go.
> Then the first gate let her forth, and restored to her the first
> garment of her body.
> The second gate let her forth, and restored to her the diamonds of
> her hands and feet.
> The third gate let her forth, and restored to her the central girdle
> of her waist.
> The fourth gate let her forth, and restored to her the small lovely
> gems of her forehead.
> The fifth gate let her forth, and restored to her the precious
> stones of her head.

The sixth gate let her forth, and restored to her the earrings of her ears.
The seventh gate let her forth, and restored to her the great crown on her head.'

This old miracle-play of Nature—the return of summer flower by flower—is deciphered from an ancient Assyrian tablet in a town within only a few hours of another, where a circle of worshippers repeat the same at every solstice! Myfyr Morganwg, the Arch-Druid, adores still Hea by name as his Saviour, and at the winter solstice assembles his brethren to celebrate his coming to bruise the head of the Serpent of Hades (Annwn, nearly the same as in the tablet), that seedtime and harvest shall not fail.[2]

Is this a survival? No doubt; but there is no cult in the world which, if 'scratched,' as the proverb says, will not reveal beneath it the same conception. However it may be spiritualised, every 'plan of salvation' is cast in the mould of Winter conquered by the Sun, the Descent of Love to the Under World, the delivery of the imprisoned germs of Life.

It is very instructive to compare with the myth of Ishtar that of Hermödr, seeking the release of Baldur the Beautiful from Helheim.

The deadly powers of Winter are represented in the Eddaic account of the death of Baldur, soft summer Light, the Norse Baal. His blind brother Hödr is Darkness; the demon who directed his arrow is Loki, subterranean fire; the arrow itself is of mistletoe, which, fostered by Winter, owes no duty to Baldur; and the realm to which he is borne is that of Hel, the frozen zone. Hermödr, having arrived, assured Hel that the gods were in despair for the loss of Baldur. The

Queen replied that it should now be tried whether Baldur was so beloved. 'If, therefore, all things in the world, both living and lifeless, weep for him, he shall return to the Æsir.' In the end all wept but the old hag Thokk (Darkness), who from her cavern sang—

> Thokk will wail
> With dry eyes
> Baldur's bale-fire.
> Nought quick or dead
> For Carl's son care I.
> Let Hel hold her own.

So Baldur remained in Helheim. The myth very closely resembles that of Ishtar's Descent. In similar accent the messenger of the Southern gods weeps and lacerates himself as he relates the grief of the upper world, and all men and animals 'since the time that mother Ishtar descended into Hades.' But in the latter the messenger is successful, in the North he is unsuccessful. In the corresponding myths of warm and sunny climes the effort at release is more or less successful, in proportion to the extent of winter. In Adonis released from Hades for four months every year, and another four if he chose to abandon Persephone for Aphrodite, we have a reflection of a variable year. That, and the similar myth of Persephone, varied in the time specified for their passing in the upper and under worlds, probably in accordance with the climatic averages of the regions in which they were told. But in the tropics it was easy to believe the release complete, as in the myth of Ishtar. In Mangaian myths the hero, Maui, escapes from a nether world of fire, aided by a red pigeon.

When this contest between Winter's Death and Spring's Life

became humanised, it was as Hercules vanquishing Death and completely releasing Alcestis. When it became spiritualised it was as Christ conquering Death and Hell, and releasing the spirits from prison. The wintry desolation had to be artificially imitated in a forty days' fast and Lent, closing with a thrust from the spear (the mistletoe arrow) amid darkness (blind Hödr). But the myth of a swift resurrection had to be artificially preserved in the far North. The legend of a full triumph over Death and Hell could never have originated among our Norse ancestors. Their only story resembling it, that of Iduna, related how her recovery from the Giants brought back health to the gods, not men. But it was from the South that men had to hear tidings of a rescue for the earth and man.

We cannot realise now what glad tidings were they which told this new gospel to peoples sitting in regions of ice and gloom, after it had been imposed on them against their reluctant fears. In manifold forms the old combat was renewed in their festivals, and peoples who had long been prostrate and helpless before the terrible powers of nature were never weary of the Southern fables of heroic triumphs over them, long interpreted in the simple physical sense.

The great Demon of the Northern World is still Winter, and the hereditary hatred of him is such that he is still cursed, scourged, killed, and buried or drowned under various names and disguises. In every Slavonic country, says Mr. Ralston, there are to be found, about carnival time, traces of ancient rites, intended to typify the death of Winter and the birth of Spring or Summer. In Poland a puppet made of hemp or straw is flung into a pond or swamp with the words, 'The Devil take thee!' Then the participators in the deed scamper home, and if one of them stumbles and falls it is believed he will die within the year. In Upper Lausatia a similar figure is fastened on a pole to be pelted, then taken to the village boundary and thrown across it or cast into the water, its bearers returning with green boughs. Sometimes the figure is shrouded in white, representing snow, and bears in its hands a broom (the sweeping storm) and a sickle (the fatal reaper). In Russia the 'Straw Mujik' is burned, and also in Bulgaria; in the latter the bonfire is accompanied by the firing of guns, and by dances and songs to Lado, goddess of Spring. This reminiscence of Leto, on whose account Apollo slew the Python, is rendered yet more striking by the week of archery which accompanies it, recalling the sunbeam darts of the god. In Spain and Italy the demon puppet is scourged under the name of Judas, as indeed is the case in the annual Good Friday performance of Portuguese sailors in the London Docks. Mr. Tylor found in Mexico a similar custom, the Judas being a regular horned and hoofed devil. In Scotland the pre-christian accessories of a corresponding custom are more pronounced both in the time selected (the last day of the year, old style) and the place. 'The Clavie,' as the custom of burning the puppet of Winter is mysteriously called, occurred on January 12 of this year (1878) at Burghead, a fishing village near Forres, where stands an old Roman altar locally named the 'Douro.' A tar-barrel was set on fire and carried by a fisherman round the town, while the people shouted and hallooed. (If the man who carries the barrel falls it is an evil omen.) The lighted barrel, having gone round the town, was carried to the top of the hill and placed on the Douro. More fuel was added. The sparks as they fly upwards are supposed to be witches and evil spirits leaving the town; the people therefore shout at and curse them as they disappear in vacancy. When the burning tar-barrel falls in pieces, the fishwomen rush in and endeavour to get a lighted bit of wood from its remains; with this light the fire on the cottage hearth is at once kindled, and it is considered lucky to keep this flame alive all the rest of the year. The charcoal of the Clavie is collected and put in bits up the chimney to prevent the witches and evil spirits coming into the house. The Douro is covered with a thick layer of tar from the fires that are annually lighted upon it. Close to it is a very ancient Roman well.

It is an instance of the irony of etymology that the word 'Hell' means a place of fireless darkness. Nor is the fact that the name of the Scandinavian demoness Hel, phonetically corresponding with Kali, 'the Black One' (Goth. Halja), whose abode was an icy hole, has her name preserved as a place of fiery torment, without significance. In regions where cold was known to an uncomfortable extent as well as heat, we usually find it represented in the ideas of future punishment. The realm called Hades, meaning just the same as Hell, suggests cold. Tertullian and Jerome say that Christ's own phrases 'outer darkness' and the 'gnashing (chattering) of teeth' suggest a place of extreme cold alternating with the excessive heat. Traces of similar speculations are found with the Rabbins. Thus Rabbi Joseph says Gehenna had both water and fire. Noah saw the angel of death approaching and hid from him twelve months. Why twelve? Because (explains Rabbi Jehuda) such is the trial of sinners,—six in water, six in fire. Dante (following Virgil) has frigid as well as burning hells;

and the idea was refined by some scholiasts to a statement which would seem to make the alternations of future punishment amount to a severe ague and fever. Milton (Paradise Lost, ii.) has blended the rabbinical notions with those of Virgil (Æn. vi.) in his terrible picture of the frozen continent, where

> The parching air
> Burns frore, and cold performs th' effect of fire:
> Thither by harpy-footed Furies haled
> At certain revolutions all the damn'd
> Are brought; and feel by turns the bitter change
> Of fierce extremes, extremes by change more fierce,
> From beds of raging fire to starve in ice
> Their soft etherial warmth, and there to pine
> Immovable, infix'd, and frozen round.

With which may be compared Shakespeare's lines in 'Measure for Measure'—

> The de-lighted spirit
> To bathe in fiery floods, or to reside
> In thrilling region of thick-ribbed ice.

In Thibet hell is believed to have sixteen circles, eight burning, eight frozen, which M. Delepierre attributes to the rapid changes of their climate between the extremes of heat and cold.[3] Plutarch, relating the vision of Thespesius in Hades, speaks of the frozen region there. Denys le Chartreux (De Pœnis Inferni) says the severest of infernal torments is freezing. In the 'Kalendar of Shepherds' (1506) a legend runs:—'Lazarus sayde, 'I sawe a flode of frosone yce in the whiche envyous men and women were plonged unto the navyll, and then sodynly came a colde wynde ryght great that blewe and dyd depe downe all the envyous into the colde water that nothynge was seen of them.' Such, too, is Persian Ardá Viráf's vision.

The Demon of Cold has a habitat, naturally, in every Northern region. He is the Ke-mung of China, who—man-shaped, dragon-headed—haunts the Chang river, and causes rain-storms.[4] In Greenland it is Erleursortok, who suffers perpetual agues, and leaps on souls at death to satisfy his hunger. The Chenoos (demons) of the Mimacs of Nova Scotia present certain features of the race-demons, but are fearfully cold. The Chenoo weapon is a dragon's horn, his yell is fatal to the hearer, his heart is a block of ice. This heart must be destroyed if the demon is to be slain, but it can only be done by melting in the fire: the chief precaution required is that one is not drowned in the flood so caused. The icy demon survived long in Scotland. Sir James Melville, in his 'Memoirs,' says 'the spirit or devil that helped the Scottish witches to raise a storm in the sea of Norway was cold as ice and his body hard as iron; his face was terrible, his nose like the beak of an eagle, great burning eyes, his hands and legs hairy, with claws on his nails like a griffin.' Dr. Fian was burnt for raising this demon to oppose James I. on his stormy passage from Denmark.

This type of demon haunted people's minds in Scandinavia, where, though traditions of a flame demon (Loki) and the end of the world by fire were imported, the popular belief seems to have been mainly occupied with Frost giants, and the formidable Oegir, god of the bleak sea east winds, preserved in our word awe (Anglo-Saxon *ege*), and more directly in the name of our familiar demon, the Ogre, so often slain in the child's Gladsheim. Loki (fire) was, indeed, speedily relegated by the Æsir (gods) to a hidden subterraneous realm, where his existence could only be known by the earthquakes, geysers, and Hecla eruptions which he occasioned. Yet he was to come forth at Ragnarök, the Twilight of the Gods. We can see a singular blending of tropical and frigid zones—the one traditional, the other native—in the Prose Edda. Thus:—'What will remain,' said Gangler, 'after heaven and earth and the whole universe shall be consumed, and after all the gods and the homes of Valhalla and all mankind shall have perished?' 'There will be many abodes,' replied Thridi, 'some good, some bad. The best place of all to be in will be Gimil, in heaven; and all who delight in quaffing good drink will find a great store in the hall called Brimir, which is also in heaven in the region Okolni. There is also a fair hall of ruddy gold, (for) Sindri, which stands on the mountains of Nida. In those halls righteous and well-minded men shall abide. In Ná-strönd there is a vast and direful structure with doors that face the north. It is formed entirely of the backs of serpents, wattled together like wicker-work. But the serpents' heads are turned towards the inside of the hall, and continually vomit forth floods of venom, in which wade all those who commit murder or who forswear themselves. As it is said in the Völuspá:—

> She saw a hall
> Far from the sun
> In Náströnd standing,
> Northward the doors look,
> And venom-drops
> Fall in through loopholes.
> Formed is that hall
> Of wreathed serpents.
> There saw she wade

Through heavy streams
Men forsworn
And murderers.

These names for the heavenly regions and their occupants indicate sunshine and fire. Gimil means fire (*gimr*): Brimir (*brimi*, flame), the giant, and Sindri (*cinder*), the dwarf, jeweller of the gods, are raised to halls of gold. Nothing is said of a garden, or walking therein 'in the cool of the day.' On the other hand, Ná-strönd means Strand of the Dead, in that region whose 'doors face the north, far from the sun,' we behold an inferno of extreme cold. Christianity has not availed to give the Icelanders any demonic name suggestive of fire. They speak of 'Skratti' (the roarer, perhaps our Old Scratch), and 'Kolski' (the coal black one), but promise nothing so luminous and comfortable as fire or fire-fiend to the evil-doer.

In the great Epic of the *Nibelungen Lied* we have probably the shape in which the Northman's dream of Paradise finally cohered,—a Rose-garden in the South, guarded by a huge Worm (water-snake, or glittering glacial sea intervening), whose glowing charms, with Beauty (Chriemhild) for their queen, could be won only by a brave dragon-slaying Siegfried. In passing by the pretty lakeside home of Richard Wagner, on my way to witness the Ammergau version of another dragon-binding and paradise-regaining legend, I noted that the old name of the (Starnberg) lake was *Wurmsee*, from the dragon that once haunted it, while from the composer's window might be seen its 'Isle of Roses,' which the dragon guarded. Since then the myth of many forms has had its musical apotheosis at Bayreuth under his wand.

England, partly perhaps on account of its harsh climate, once had the reputation of being the chief abode of demons. A demoness leaving her lover on the Continent says, 'My mother is calling me in England.'[5] But England assigned them still higher latitudes; in christianising Ireland, Iona, and other islands far north, it was preliminary to expel the demons. 'The Clavie,' the 'Deis-iuil' of Lewis and other Hebrides islands—fire carried round cattle to defend them from demons, and around mothers not yet churched, to keep the babes from being 'changed'—show that the expulsion still goes on, though in such regions Norse and christian notions have become so jumbled that it is 'fighting the devil with fire.' So in the Havamal men are warned to invoke 'fire for distempers;' and Gudrun sings—

> Raise, ye Jarls, an oaken pile;
> Let it under heaven the lightest be.
> May it burn a breast full of woes!
> The fire round my heart its sorrows melt.

The last line is in contrast with the Hindu saying, 'the flame of her husband's pyre cools the widow's breast.'

The characters of the Northern Heaven and Hell survive in the English custom of burying the dead on the southern side of a church. How widely this usage prevailed in Brand's time may be seen by reference to his chapter on churchyards. The north side of the graveyard was set apart for unbaptized infants and executed criminals, and it was permitted the people to dance or play tennis in that part. Dr. Lee says that in the churchyard at Morwenstow the southern portion only contains graves, the north part being untenanted; as the Cornish believe (following old traditions) that the north is the region of demons. In some parishes of Cornwall when a baptism occurs the north door of the nave opposite the font is thrown open, so that the devil cast out may retire to his own region, the north.[6] This accords with the saying in Martin's 'Month's Mind'—*ab aquilone omne malum.*

Indeed, it is not improbable that the fact noted by White, in his 'History of Selborne,' that 'the usual approach to most country churches is by the south,' indicated a belief that the sacred edifice should turn its back on the region of demons. It is a singular instance of survival which has brought about the fact that people who listen devoutly to sermons describing the fiery character of Satan and his abode should surround the very churches in which those sermons are heard with evidences of their lingering faith that the devil belongs to the region of ice, and that their dead must be buried in the direction of the happy abodes of Brimir and Sindri,—Fire and Cinders!

M. François Lenormant has written an extremely instructive chapter in comparison of the Accadian and the Finnish mythologies. He there shows that they are as one and the same tree, adapted to antagonistic climates.[7] With similar triad, runes, charms, and even names in some cases, their regard for the fire worshipped by both varies in a way that seems at first glance somewhat anomalous. The Accadians in their fire-worship exhausted the resources of praise in ascription of glory and power to the flames; the Finns in their cold home celebrated the fire festival at the winter solstice, uttered invocations over the fire, and the mother of the family, with her domestic libation, said: 'Always rise so high, O my flame, but burn not larger nor more ardent!' This diminution of enthusiasm in the Northern fire-worshipper, as compared with the Southern, may only be the result of euphemism in the latter; or perhaps while the formidable character of the fire-god among the primitive Assyrians is indicated in the utter prostration before him characteristic of their litanies and invocations, in the case of the Finns the perpetual presence of the more potent cold led to the less excessive adoration. These ventured to recognise the faults of fire.

The true nature of this anomaly becomes visible when we consider that the great demon, dreaded by the two countries drawing their cult from a common source, represented the excess of the power most dreaded. The demon in each case was a wind; among the Finns the north wind, among the Accadians the south-west (the most fiery) wind. The Finnish demon was Hiisi, speeding on his pale horse through the air, with a terrible train of monster dogs, cats, furies, scattering pain, disease, and death.[8] The Accadian demon, of which the bronze image is in the Louvre, is the body of a dog, erect on eagle's feet, its arms pointed with lion's paws; it has the tail of a scorpion and the head of a skeleton, half stripped of flesh, preserving the eyes, and mounted with the horns of a goat. It has four outspread wings. On the back of this ingeniously horrible image is an inscription in the Accadian language, apprising us that it is the demon of the south-west wind, made to be placed at the door or window, to avert its hostile action.

As we observe such figures as these on the one hand, and on the other the fair beings imagined to be antagonistic to them; as we note in runes and incantations how intensely the ancients felt themselves to be surrounded by these good and evil powers, and, reading nature so, learned to see in the seasons successively conquering and conquered by each other, and alternation of longer days and longer nights, the changing fortunes of a never-ending battle; we may better realise the meaning of solstitial festivals, the customs that gathered around Yuletide and New Year, and the manifold survivals from them which annually masquerade in Christian costume and names. To our sun-worshipping ancestor the new year meant the first faint advantage of the warmer time over winter, as nearly as he could fix it. The hovering of day between superiority of light and darkness is now named after doubting Thomas. At Yuletide the dawning victory of the sun is seen as a holy infant in a manger amid beasts of the stall. The old nature-worship has bequeathed to christian belief a close-fitting mantle. But the old idea of a war between the wintry and the warm powers still haunts the period of the New Year; and the twelve days and nights, once believed to be the period of a fiercely-contested battle between good and evil demons, are still regarded by many as a period for especial watchfulness and prayer. New Year's Eve, in the north of England still 'Hogmanay,'—probably O. N. *höku-nött*, midwinter-night, when the sacrifices of Thor were prepared,—formerly had many observances which reflected the belief that good and evil ghosts were contending for every man and woman: the air was believed to be swarming with them, and watch must be kept to see that the protecting fire did not go out in any household; that no strange man, woman, or animal approached,—possibly a demon in disguise. Sacred plants were set in doors and windows to prevent the entrance of any malevolent being from the multitudes filling the air. John Wesley, whose noble heart was allied with a mind strangely open to stories of hobgoblins, led the way of churches and sects back into this ancient atmosphere. Nevertheless, the rationalism of the age has influenced St. Wesley's Feast—Watchnight. It can hardly recognise its brother in the Boar's Head Banquet of Queen's College, Oxford, which celebrated victory over tusky winter, the decapitated demon whose bristles were once icicles fallen beneath the sylvan spirits of holly and rosemary. Yet what the Watchnight really signifies in the antiquarian sense is just that old culminating combat between the powers of fire and frost, once believed to determine human fates. In White Russia, on New Year's Day, when the annual elemental battle has been decided, the killed and wounded on one hand, and the fortunate on the other, are told by carrying from house to house the rich and the poor Kolyadas. These are two children, one dressed in fine attire, and crowned with a wreath of full ears of grain, the other ragged, and wearing a wreath of threshed straw. These having been closely covered, each householder is called in, and chooses one. If his choice chances upon the 'poor Kolyada,' the attending chorus chant a mournful strain, in which he is warned to expect a bad harvest, poverty, and perhaps death; if he selects the 'rich Kolyada,' a cheerful song is sung promising him harvest, health, and wealth.

The natives of certain districts of Dardistan assign political and social significance to their Feast of Fire, which is celebrated in the month preceding winter, at new moon, just after their meat provision for the season is laid in to dry. Their legend is, that it was then their national hero slew their ancient tyrant and introduced good government. This legend, related elsewhere, is of a tyrant slain through the discovery that his heart was made of snow. He was slain by the warmth of torches. In the celebrations all the men of the villages go forth with torches, which they swing round their heads, and throw in the direction of Ghilgit, where the snow-hearted tyrant so long held his castle. When the husbands return home from their torch-throwing a little drama is rehearsed. The wives refuse them entrance till they have entreated, recounting the benefits they have brought them; after admission the husband affects sulkiness, and must be brought round with caresses to join in the banquet. The wife leads him forward with this song:—'Thou hast made me glad, thou favourite of the Rajah! Thou hast rejoiced me, oh bold horse-man! I am pleased with thee who so well usest the gun and sword! Thou hast delighted me, oh thou invested with a mantle of honours! Oh great happiness, I will buy it by giving pleasure's price! Oh thou nourishment to us, heap of corn, store of ghee—delighted will I buy it all by giving pleasure's price!'

NOTES
1 Tablet K 162 in Brit. Mus. Tr. by H. F. Talbot in 'Records of the Past.'
2 The Western Mail, March 12, 1874, contains a remarkable letter by the Arch-Druid, in which he maintains that 'Jesus' is a derivation from Hea or Hu, Light, and the Christian system a corruption of Bardism.
3 'L'Enfer,' p. 5.
4 Dennys' 'Folklore of China,' p. 98.
5 Procopius, 'De Bello Gothico,' iv. 20.
6 'Memorials of the Rev. R. S. Hawkes'.
7 'La Magie chez les Chaldéens,' iii.
8 Lönnrot, 'Abhandlung über die Magische Medicin der Finnen.'

Chapter IV
Elements

A Scottish Munasa — Rudra — Siva's lightning eye — The flaming sword —
Limping demons — Demons of the storm — Helios, Elias, Perun — Thor arrows
— The Bob-tailed Dragon — Whirlwind — Japanese thunder god — Christian
survivals — Jinni — Inundations — Noah — Nik, Nicholas, Old Nick — Nixies —
Hydras — Demons of the Danube — Tides — Survivals in Russia and England

DURING SOME RECENT years curious advertisements have appeared in a journal of Edinburgh, calling for pious persons to occupy
certain hours of the night with holy exercises. It would appear that
they refer to a band of prayerful persons who provide that there shall
be an unbroken round of prayers during every moment of the day
and night. Their theory is, that it is the usual cessation of christian
prayers at night which causes so many disasters. The devils being
then less restrained, raise storms and all elemental perils. The praying circle, which hopes to bind these demons by an uninterrupted
chain of prayers, originated, as I am informed, in the pious enthusiasm of a lady whose kindly solicitude in some pre-existent sister was
no doubt personified in the Hindu Munasa, who, while all gods slept,
sat in the shape of a serpent on a branch of Euphorbia to preserve
mankind from the venom of snakes. It is to be feared, however, that
it is hardly the wisdom of the serpent which is on prayerful watch
at Edinburgh, but rather a vigilance of that perilous kind which was
exercised by 'Meggie o' the Shore,' anno 1785, as related by Hugh
Miller.[1] On a boisterous night, when two young girls had taken ref-

uge in her cottage, they all heard about midnight cries of distress mingling with the roar of the sea, 'Raise the window curtain and look out,' said Meggie. The terrified girls did so, and said, 'There is a bright light in the middle of the Bay of Udall. It hangs over the water about the height of a ship's mast, and we can see something below it like a boat riding at anchor, with the white sea raging around her.' 'Now drop the curtain,' said Meggie; 'I am no stranger, my lasses, to sights and noises like these—sights and noises of another world; but I have been taught that God is nearer to me than any spirit can be; and so have learned not to be afraid.' Afterwards it is not wonderful that a Cromarty yawl was discovered to have foundered, and all on board to have been drowned; though Meggie's neighbours seemed to have preserved the legend after her faith, and made the scene described a premonition of what actually occurred. It was in a region where mariners when becalmed invoke the wind by whistling; and both the whistling and the praying, though their prospects in the future may be slender, have had a long career in the past.

In the 'Rig-Veda' there is a remarkable hymn to Rudra (the Roarer), which may be properly quoted here:—

1. Sire of the storm gods, let thy favour extend to us; shut us not out from the sight of the sun; may our hero be successful in the onslaught. O Rudra, may we wax mighty in our offspring.
2. Through the assuaging remedies conferred by thee, O Rudra, may we reach a hundred winters; drive away far from us hatred, distress, and all-pervading diseases.
3. Thou, O Rudra, art the most excellent of beings in glory, the strongest of the strong, O wielder of the bolt; bear us safely through evil to the further shore; ward off all the assaults of sin.

4. May we not provoke thee to anger, O Rudra, by our adorations, neither through faultiness in praises, nor through wantonness in invocations; lift up our heroes by thy remedies; thou art, I hear, the chief physician among physicians.

5. May I propitiate with hymns this Rudra who is worshipped with invocations and oblations; may the tender-hearted, easily-entreated, tawny-haired, beautiful-chinned god not deliver us up to the plotter of evil [literally, to the mind meditating 'I kill'].

6. The bounteous giver, escorted by the storm-gods, hath gladdened me, his suppliant, with most invigorating food; as one distressed by heat seeketh the shade, may I, free from harm, find shelter in the good-will of Rudra.

7. Where, O Rudra, is that gracious hand of thine, which is healing and comforting? Do thou, removing the evil which cometh from the gods, O bounteous giver, have mercy upon me.

8. To the tawny, the fair-complexioned dispenser of bounties, I send forth a great and beautiful song of praise; adore the radiant god with prostrations; we hymn the illustrious name of Rudra.

9. Sturdy-limbed, many-shaped, fierce, tawny, he hath decked himself with brilliant ornaments of gold; truly strength is inseparable from Rudra, the sovereign of this vast world.

10. Worthy of worship, thou bearest the arrows and the bow; worthy of worship, thou wearest a resplendent necklace of many forms; worthy of worship, thou rulest over this immense universe; there is none, O Rudra, mightier than thou.

11. Celebrate the renowned and ever-youthful god who is seated on a chariot, who is, like a wild beast, terrible, fierce, and destructive; have mercy upon the singer, O Rudra, when thou art praised; may thy hosts strike down another than us.

12. As a boy saluteth his father who approacheth and speaketh to him, so, O Rudra, I greet thee, the giver of much, the lord of the good; grant us remedies when thou art praised.

13. Your remedies, O storm-gods, which are pure and helping, O bounteous givers, which are joy-conferring, which our father Manu chose, these and the blessing and succour of Rudra I crave.

14. May the dart of Rudra be turned aside from us, may the great malevolence of the flaming-god be averted; unbend thy strong

bow from those who are liberal with their wealth; O generous god, have mercy upon our offspring and our posterity (*i.e.*, our children and children's children).

15. Thus, O tawny Rudra, wise giver of gifts, listen to our cry, give heed to us here, that thou mayest not be angry with us, O god, nor slay us; may we, rich in heroic sons, utter great praise at the sacrifice.[2]

In other hymns the malevolent character of Rudra is made still more prominent:—

7. Slay not our strong man nor our little child, neither him who is growing nor him who is grown, neither our father nor our mother; hurt not, O Rudra, our dear selves.

8. Harm us not in our children and children's children, nor in our men, nor in our kine, nor in our horses. Smite not our heroes in thy wrath; we wait upon thee perpetually with offerings.[3]

In this hymn (verse 1) Rudra is described as 'having braided hair;' and in the 'Yajur-veda' and the 'Atharva-veda' other attributes of Siva are ascribed to him, such as the epithet *nîla-grîva*, or blue-necked. In the 'Rig-veda' Siva occurs frequently as an epithet, and means *auspicious*. It was used as a euphemistic epithet to appease Rudra, the lord of tempests; and finally, the epithet developed into a distinct god.

The parentage of Siva is further indicated in the legends that his glance destroyed the head of the youthful deity Ganesa, who now wears the elephant head, with which it was replaced; and that the gods persuaded him to keep his eyes perpetually winking (like sheet-lightning), lest his concentrated look (the thunderbolt) should reduce the universe to ashes. With the latter legend the gaze of the evil eye in India might naturally be associated, though in the majority of countries this was rather associated with the malign influences ascribed to certain planets, especially Saturn; the charms against the evil eye being marked over with zodiacal signs. The very myth of Siva's eye survives in the Russian demon Magarko ('Winker') and the Servian Vii, whose glance is said to have power to reduce men, and even cities, to ashes.

The terrible Rudra is represented in a vast number of beliefs, some of them perhaps survivals; in the rough sea and east-wind demon Oegir of the northern world, and Typhon in the south; and in Luther's faith that 'devils do house in the dense black clouds, and send storms, hail, thunder and lightning, and poison the air with their infernal stench,' a doctrine which Burton, the Anatomist of Melancholy, too, maintained against the meteorologists of his time.

Among the ancient Aryans lightning seems to have been the supreme type of divine destructiveness. Rudra's dart, Siva's eye, reappear with the Singhalese prince of demons Wessamonny, described as wielding a golden sword, which, when he is angry, flies out of his hand, to which it spontaneously returns, after cutting off a thousand heads.[4] A wonderful spear was borne by Odin, and was possibly the original Excalibur. The four-faced Sviatevit of Russia, whose mantle has fallen to St. George, whose statue was found at Zbrucz in 1851, bore a horn of wine (rain) and a sword (lightning).

In Greece similar swords were wielded by Zeus, and also by the god of war. Through Zeus and Ares, the original wielders of the lightning—Indra and Siva—became types of many gods and semi-divine heroes. The evil eye of Siva glared from the forehead of the Cyclopes, forgers of thunderbolts; and the saving disc of Indra flashed in the swords and arrows of famous dragon-slayers—Perseus, Pegasus, Hercules, and St. George. The same sword defended the Tree of Life in Eden, and was borne in the hand of Death on the Pale Horse (a white horse was sacrificed to Sviatevit in Russia within christian times). And, finally, we have the wonderful sword which obeys the command 'Heads off!' delighting all nurseries by the service it does to the King of the Golden Mountain.

'I beheld Satan as lightning falling out of heaven.' To the Greeks this falling of rebellious deities out of heaven accounted, as we have seen explained, for their lameness. But a universal phenomenon can alone account for the many demons with crooked or crippled legs (like 'Diable Boiteux')[5] all around the world. The Namaquas of South Africa have a 'deity' whose occupation it is to cause pain and death; his name is Tsui'knap, that is 'wounded knee.'[6] Livingstone says of the Bakwains, another people of South Africa, 'It is curious that in all their pretended dreams or visions of their god he has always a crooked leg, like the Egyptian Thau.'[7] In Mainas, South America, they believe in a treacherous demon, Uchuella-chaqui, or Lame-foot, who in dark forests puts on a friendly shape to lure Indians to destruction; but the huntsmen say they can never be deceived if they examine this demon's foot-track, because of the unequal size of the two feet.[8] The native Australians believed in a demon named Biam; he is black and deformed in his lower extremities; they attributed to him many of their songs and dances, but also a sort of small-pox to which they were liable.[9] We have no evidence that these superstitions migrated from a common centre; and there can be little doubt that many of these crooked legs are traceable to the crooked lightning.[10] At the same time this is by no means inconsistent with what has been already said of the fall of Titans and angels from heaven as often accounting for their lameness in popular myths. But in such details it is hard to reach certainty, since so many of the facts bear a suspicious resemblance to each other. A wild boar with 'distorted legs' attacked St. Godric, and the temptation is strong to generalise on the story, but the legs probably mean only to certify that it was the devil.

Dr. Schliemann has unearthed among his other treasures the remarkable fact that a temple of Helios (the sun) once stood near the site of the present Church of Elias, at Mycenæ, which has from time immemorial been the place to which people repair to pray for rain.[11] When the storm-breeding Sun was succeeded by the Prophet whose prayer evoked the cloud, even the name of the latter did not need to be changed. The discovery is the more interesting because it has always been a part of the christian folklore of that region that, when a storm with lightning occurs, it is 'Elias in his chariot of fire.' A similar phrase is used in some part of every Aryan country, with variation of the name: it is Woden, or King Waldemar, or the Grand Veneur, or sometimes God, who is said to be going forth in his chariot.

These storm-demons in their chariots have their forerunner in Vata or Vayu, the subject of one of the most beautiful Vedic hymns. 'I celebrate the glory of Vata's chariot; its noise comes rending and resounding. Touching the sky he moves onward, making all things ruddy; and he comes propelling the dust of the earth.

'Soul of the gods, source of the universe, this deity moves as he lists. His sounds have been heard, but his form is not seen; this Vata let us worship with an oblation.'[12]

This last verse, as Mr. Muir has pointed out, bears a startling resemblance to the passage in John, 'The Wind bloweth where it listeth, and thou canst not tell whence it cometh or whither it goeth; so is every one that is born of the Wind.'[13]

But an equally striking development of the Vedic idea is represented in the Siamese legend of Buddha, and in this case the Vedic Wind-god Vayu reappears by name for the Angels of Tempests, or Loka Phayu. The first portent which preceded the descent of Buddha from the Tushita heavens was 'when the Angels of the Tempest, clothed in red garments, and with streaming hair, travel among the abodes of mankind crying, 'Attend all ye who are near to death; repent and be not heedless! The end of the world approaches, but one hundred thousand years more and it will be destroyed. Exert yourselves, then, exert yourselves to acquire merit. Above all things be charitable; abstain from doing evil; meditate with love to all beings, and listen to the teachings of holiness. For we are all in the mouth of the king of death. Strive then earnestly for meritorious fruits, and seek that which is good.'[14]

Not less remarkable is the Targum of Jonathan Ben Uzziel to 1 Kings xix., where around Elias on the mountain gather 'a host of angels of the wind, cleaving the mountain and breaking the rocks before the Lord;' and after these, 'angels of commotion,' and next 'of fire,' and, finally, 'voices singing in silence' preceded the descent of Jehovah. It can hardly be wondered that a prophet of whom this story was told, and that of the storm evoked from a small cloud, should be caught up into that chariot of the Vedic Vayu which has rolled on through all the ages of mythology.

Mythologic streams seem to keep their channels almost as steadfastly as rivers, but as even these change at last or blend, so do the old traditions. Thus we find that while Thor and Odin remain as separate in survivals as Vayu and Parjanya in India, in Russia Elias has inherited not the mantle of the wind-god or storm-breeding sun, but of the Slavonic Thunderer Perun. There is little doubt that this is Parjanya, described in the 'Rig-Veda' as 'the thunderer, the showerer, the bountiful,'[15] who 'strikes down trees' and 'the wicked.' 'The people of Novgorod,' says Herberstein, 'formerly offered their chief worship and adoration to a certain idol named Perun. When subsequently they received baptism they removed it from its place, and threw it into the river Volchov; and the story goes that it swam against the stream, and that near the bridge a voice was heard saying, 'This for you, O inhabitants of Novgorod, in memory of me;' and at the same time a certain rope was thrown upon the bridge. Even now it happens from time to time on certain days of the year that this voice of Perun may be heard, and on these occasions the citizens run together and lash each other with ropes, and such a tumult arises therefrom that all the efforts of the governor can scarcely assuage it.'[16] The statue of Perun in Kief, says Mr. Ralston, had a trunk of wood, while the head was of silver, with moustaches of gold, and among its weapons was a mace. Afanasief states that in White-Russian traditions Perun is tall and well-shaped, with black hair and a long golden beard. This beard relates him to Barbarossa, and, perhaps, though distantly, with the wood-demon Barbatos, the Wild Archer, who divined by the songs of birds.[17] Perun also has a bow which is 'sometimes identified with the rainbow, an idea which is known also to the Finns. From it, according to the White Russians, are shot burning arrows, which set on fire all things that they touch. In many parts of Russia (as well as of Germany) it is supposed that these bolts sink deep into the soil, but that at the end of three or seven years they return to the surface in the shape of longish stones of a black or dark grey colour—probably belemnites, or masses of fused sand—which are called thunderbolts, and considered as excellent preservations against lightning and conflagrations. The Finns call them Ukonkiwi—the stone of thunder-god Ukko, and in Courland their name is Perkuhnsteine, which explains itself. In some cases the flaming dart of Perun became, in the imagination of the people, a golden key. With it he unlocked the earth, and brought to light its concealed treasures, its restrained waters, its captive founts of light. With it also he locked away in safety fugitives who wished to be put out of the power of malignant conjurors, and performed various other good offices. Appeals to him to exercise these functions still exist in the spells used by the peasants, but his name has given way to that of some christian personage. In one of them, for instance, the Archangel Michael is called upon to secure the invoker behind an iron door fastened by twenty-seven locks, the keys of which are given to the angels to be carried to heaven. In another, John the Baptist is represented as standing upon a stone in the Holy Sea [*i.e.*, in heaven], resting upon an iron crook or staff, and is called upon to stay the flow of blood from a wound, locking the invoker's veins 'with his heavenly key.' In this case the myth has passed into a rite. In order to stay a violent bleeding from the nose, a locked padlock is brought, and the blood is allowed to drop through its aperture, or the sufferer grasps a key in each hand, either plan being expected to prove efficacious. As far as the key is concerned, the belief seems to be still maintained among ourselves.'[18]

Fig. 5.

The Key has a holy sense in various religions, and consequently an infernal key is its natural counterpart. The Vedic hymns, which say so much about the shutting and opening, imprisoning and releasing, of heavenly rains and earthly fruits by demons and deities, interpret many phenomena of nature, and the same ideas have arisen in many lands. We cannot be certain, therefore, that Calmet is right in assigning an Indian origin to the subjoined Figure 5, an ancient Persian medal. The signs of the zodiac on its body show it to be one of those celestial demons believed able to bind the beneficent or loose the formidable powers of nature. The Key is of especial import in Hebrew faith. It was the high-priest Eliakim's symbol of office, as being also prefect in the king's house. 'The key of the house of David will I lay upon his shoulder: he shall open and none shall shut; he shall shut and none shall open.'[19] The Rabbins had a saying that God reserves to himself four keys, which he will intrust not even to the angels: the key of rain, the key of the grave, the key of fruitfulness, and the key of barrenness. It was the sign of one set above angels when Christ was seen with the keys of Hell and Death, or when he delivered the keys of heaven to Peter,[20]—still thrust down the backs of protestant children to cure nose-bleed.

The ubiquitous superstition which attributes the flint arrows of pre-historic races to gods, shot by them as lightning, and, as some said, from a rainbow, is too childlike a theory to call for elaborate treatment. We need not, ethnographically, connect our 'Thor arrows' and 'Elf shots' with the stones hurled at mortals by the Thunder-Duke (Lui-tsz) of China. The ancient Parthians, who used to reply to the thunderstorm by shooting arrows at it, and the Turks, who attack an eclipse with guns, fairly represent the infancy of the human race, though perhaps with more than its average pluck. Dr. Macgowan relates, concerning the Lei-chau (Thunder District) of China, various myths which resemble those which surround the world. After thunderstorms, black stones, it is believed, may be found which emit light and peculiar sounds on being struck. In a temple consecrated to the Thunder Duke the people annually place a drum for that stormy demon to beat. The drum was formerly left on a mountain-top with a little boy as a sacrifice.[21] Mr. Dennys[22] speaks of the belief in the same country that violent winds and typhoons are caused by the passage through the air of the 'Bob-tailed Dragon,' and also of the rain-god Yü-Shüh. A storm-god connected with the 'Eagre,' or bore of the river Tsien-tang, presents a coincidence of name with the Scandinavian Oegir, which would be hardly noticeable were it not for the very close resemblance between the folklore concerning the 'Bob-tailed Dragon' and the storm-dragons of several Aryan races. Generally, in both China and Japan the Dragon is regarded with a veneration equal to the horror with which the serpent is visited. Of this phenomenon and its analogies in Britain I shall have an explanation to submit when we come to consider Dragon-myths more particularly. To this general rule the 'Bob-tailed Dragon' of China is a partial exception. His fidelity as a friend led to the ill return of an attack by which his tail was amputated, and ever since his soured temper has shown itself in raising storms. When a violent tempest arises the Cantonese say, 'The Bob-tailed Dragon is passing,' in the same proverbial way as the Aryan peasantries attribute the same phenomenon to their storm-gods.

The notion is widely prevalent in some districts of France that all whirlwinds, however slight, are caused by wizards or witches, who are in them, careering through the air; and it is stated by the

Melusine that in the department of the Orne storms are attributed to the clergy, who are supposed to be circling in them. The same excellent journal states that some years ago, in that department, a parishioner who saw his crops threatened by a hail-storm fired into the cloud. The next day he heard that the parish priest had broken his leg by a fall for which he could not account.

The following examples are given by Kuhn. Near Stangenhagen is a treasure hid in a mountain which Lord von Thümen tried to seek, but was caught up with his horse by a whirlwind and deposited at home again. The Devil is believed to be seated at the centre of every whirlwind. At Biesenthal it is said a noble lady became the Wind's bride. She was in her time a famous rider and huntress, who rode recklessly over farmers' fields and gardens; now she is herself hunted by snakes and dragons, and may be heard howling in every storm.

I suspect that the bristling hair so frequently portrayed in the Japanese Oni, Devils, refers to their frequent residence at the centre of a gale of wind. Their demon of the storm is generally pictured throned upon a flower of flames, his upraised and extended fingers emitting the most terrific lightnings, which fall upon his victims and envelop them in flames. Sometimes, however, the Japanese artists poke fun at their thunder-god, and show him sprawling on the ground from the recoil of his own lightnings. The following extract from *The Christian Herald* (London, April 12, 1877) will show how far the dread of this Japanese Oni extends: 'A pious father writes, 'A few days ago there was a severe thunderstorm, which seemed to gather very heavily in the direction where my son lived; and I had a feeling that I must go and pray that he might be protected, and not be killed by the lightning. The impression seemed to say, 'There is no time to be lost.' I obeyed, and went and knelt down and prayed that the Lord would spare his life. I believe he heard my prayer. My son called on me afterwards, and, speaking of the shower, said, 'The lightning came downwards and struck the very hoe in my hands, and numbed me.' I said, 'Perhaps you would have been killed if some one had not been praying for you.' Since then he has been converted, and, I trust, will be saved in God's everlasting kingdom."

Such paragraphs may now strike even many christians as 'survivals.' But it is not so very long since some eminent clergymen looked upon Benjamin Franklin as the heaven-defying Ajax of Christendom, because he undertook to show people how they might divert the lightnings from their habitations. In those days Franklin personally visited a church at Streatham, whose steeple had been struck by lightning, and, after observing the region, gave an opinion that if the steeple were again erected without a lightning-rod, it would again be struck. The audacious man who 'snatched sceptres from tyrants and lightnings from heaven,' as the proverb ran, was not listened to: the steeple was rebuilt, and again demolished by lightning.

The supreme god of the Quichuas (American), Viracocha ('sea foam'), rises out of Lake Titicaca, and journeys with lightnings for all opposers, to disappear in the Western Ocean. The Quichua is mentally brother of the Arab camel-driver. 'The sea,' it is said in the 'Arabian Nights,'—'the sea became troubled before them, and there arose from it a black pillar, ascending towards the sky, and approaching the meadow,' and 'behold it was a Jinn[23] of gigantic stature.' The Jinn is sometimes helpful as it is formidable; it repays the fisherman who unseals it from the casket fished up from the sea, as fruitfulness comes out of the cloud no larger than a man's hand evoked by Elijah. The perilous Jinn described in the above extract is the waterspout. Waterspouts are attributed in China to the battles of dragons in the air, and the same country recognises a demon of high tides. The newest goddess in China is a canonised protectress against the shipwrecking storm-demons of the coast, an exaltation recently proclaimed by the Government of the empire in obedience, as the edict stated, to the belief prevailing among sailors. In this the Chinese are a long way behind the mariners and fishermen of the French coast, who have for centuries, by a pious philology, connected 'Maria' with 'La Marée' and 'La Mer;' and whenever they have been saved from storms, bring their votive offerings to sea-side shrines of the Star of the Sea.

The old Jewish theology, in its eagerness to claim for Jehovah the absolutism which would make him 'Lord of lords,' instituted his responsibility for many doubtful performances, the burthen of which is now escaped by the device of saying that he 'permitted' them. In this way the Elohim who brought on the Deluge have been identified with Jehovah. None the less must we see in the biblical account of the Flood the action of tempestuous water-demons. What power a christian would recognise in such an event were it related in the sacred books of another religion may be seen in the vision of the Apocalypse—'The Serpent cast out of his mouth a flood of water after the woman, that he might cause her to be carried away with the flood; and the earth helped the woman and opened its mouth and swallowed up the flood.' This Demon of Inundation meets the explorer of Egyptian and Accadian inscriptions at every turn. The terrible Seven, whom even the God of Fire cannot control, 'break down the banks of the Abyss of Waters.'[24] The God of the Tigris, Tourtak (Tartak of the Bible), is 'the great destroyer.'[25] Leviathan 'maketh the deep to boil like a pot:' 'when he raises up himself the mighty are afraid; by reason of breakings they purify themselves.'[26]

In the Astronomical Tablets, which Professor Sayce dates about B.C. 1600, we have the continual association of eclipse and flood: 'On the fifteenth day an eclipse takes place. The king dies; and rains in the heaven, floods in the channels are.' 'In the month of Elul (August), the fourteenth day, an eclipse takes place.... Northward ... its shadow is seen; and to the King of Mullias a crown is given. To the king the crown is an omen; and over the king the eclipse passes. Rains in heaven, floods in the channels flow. A famine is in the country. Men their sons for silver sell.' 'After a year the Air-god inundates.'[27]

In the Chaldæo-Babylonian cosmogony the three zones of the universe were ruled over by a Triad as follows: the Heaven by Anu; the surface of the earth, including the atmosphere, by Bel; the under-world by Nouah.[28] This same Nouah is the Assyrian Hea or Saviour; and it is Noah of the Bible. The name means a rest or resi-dence,—the place where man may dwell. When Tiamat the Dragon, or the Leviathan, opens 'the fountains of the great deep,' and Anu 'the windows of Heaven,' it is Hea or Noah who saves the life of man. M. François Lenormant has shown this to be the probable sense of one of the most ancient Accadian fragments in the British Museum. In it allusion is made to 'the serpent of seven heads ... that beats the sea.'[29] Hea, however, appears to be more clearly indicated in a fragment which Professor Sayce appends to this:—

Below in the abyss the forceful multitudes may they sacrifice.
The overwhelming fear of Anu in the midst of Heaven encircles his path.
The spirits of earth, the mighty gods, withstand him not.
The king like a lightning-flash opened.
Adar, the striker of the fortresses of the rebel band, opened.
Like the streams in the circle of heaven I besprinkled the seed of men.
His marching in the fealty of Bel to the temple I directed,
(He is) the hero of the gods, the protector of mankind, far (and) near....
O my lord, life of Nebo (breathe thy inspiration), incline thine ear.
O Adar, hero, crown of light, (breathe) thy inspiration, (incline) thine ear.
The overwhelming fear of thee may the sea know....
Thy setting (is) the herald of his rest from marching,
In thy marching Merodach (is) at rest [30]....
Thy father on his throne thou dost not smite.
Bel on his throne thou dost not smite.
The spirits of earth on their throne may he consume.
May thy father into the hands of thy valour cause (them) to go forth.
May Bel into the hands of thy valour cause (them) to go forth.
(The king, the proclaimed) of Anu, the firstborn of the gods.
He that stands before Bel, the heart of the life of the House of the Beloved.[31]
The hero of the mountain (for those that) die in multitudes.... the one god, he will not urge.[32]

In this primitive fragment we find the hero of the mountain (Noah), invoking both Bel and Nebo, aerial and infernal Intelligences, and Adar the Chaldæan Hercules, for their 'inspiration'—that breath which, in the biblical story, goes forth in the form of the Dove ('the herald of his rest' in the Accadian fragment), and in the 'wind' by which the waters were assuaged (in the fragment 'the spirits of the earth' which are given into the hand of the violent 'hero of the mountain,' whom alone the gods 'will not urge').

The Hydra may be taken as a type of the destructive water-demon in a double sense, for its heads remain in many mythical forms. The Syrian Dagon and Atergatis, fish-deities, have bequeathed but their element to our Undines of romance. Some nymphs have so long been detached from aqueous associations as to have made their names puzzling, and their place in demonology more so. To the Nixy (νήχω) of Germany, now merely mischievous like the British Pixy, many philologists trace the common phrase for the Devil,—'Old Nick.' I believe, however, that this phrase owes its popularity to St. Nicholas rather than to the Norse water-god whose place he was assigned after the christian accession. This saintly Poseidon, who, from being the patron of fishermen, gradually became associated with that demon whom, Sir Walter Scott said, 'the British sailor feared when he feared nothing else,' was also of old the patron of pirates; and robbers were called 'St. Nicholas' clerks.'[33] In Norway and the Netherlands the ancient belief in the demon Nikke was strong; he was a kind of Wild Huntsman of the Sea, and has left many legends, of which 'The Flying Dutchman' is one. But my belief is that, through his legendary relation to boys, St. Nicholas gave the name Old Nick its modern moral accent. Because of his reputation for having restored to life three murdered children St. Nicholas was made their patron, and on his day, December 6, it was the old custom to consecrate a Boy-Bishop, who held office until the 28th of the month. By this means he became the moral appendage of the old Wodan god of the Germanic races, who was believed in winter time to find shelter in and shower benefits from evergreens, especially firs, on his favourite children who happened to wander beneath them. 'Bartel,' 'Klaubauf,' or whatever he might be called, was reduced to be the servant of St. Nicholas, whose name is now jumbled into 'Santaclaus.' According to the old custom he appeared attended by his Knecht Klaubauf—personated by those who knew all about the children—bringing a sort of doomsday. The gifts having been bestowed on the good children, St. Nicholas then ordered Klaubauf to put the naughty ones into his pannier and carry them off for punishment. The terror and shrieks thus caused have created vast misery among children, and in Munich and some other places the authorities have very properly made such tragedies illegal. But for many centuries it was the custom of nurses and mothers to threaten refractory children with being carried off at the end of the year by Nicholas; and in this way each year closed, in the young apprehension, with a Judgment Day, a Weighing of Souls, and a Devil or Old Nick as agent of retribution.

Nick has long since lost his aquatic character, and we find his name in the Far West (America) turning up as 'The Nick of the Woods,'—the wild legend of a settler who, following a vow of vengeance for his wrongs, used to kill the red men while they slept, and was supposed to be a demon. The Japanese have a water-dragon—Kappa—of a retributive and moral kind, whose office it is to swallow bad boys who go to swim in disobedience to their parents' commands, or at improper times and places. It is not improbable that such dangers to the young originated some of the water-demons,—probably such as are thought of as diminutive and mischievous,—*e.g.*, Nixies. The Nixa was for a long time on the Baltic coast the female 'Old Nick,' and much feared by fishermen. Her malign disposition is represented in the Kelpie of Scotland,—a water-horse, believed to carry away the unwary by sudden floods to devour them. In Germany there was a river-goddess whose temple stood at Magdeburg, whence its name. A legend exists of her having appeared in the market there in christian costume, but she was detected by a continual dripping of water from the corner of her apron. In Germany the Nixies generally played the part of the naiads of ancient times.[34] In Russia similar beings, called Rusalkas, are much more formidable.

In many regions of Christendom it is related that these demons, relatives of the Swan-maidens, considered in another chapter, have been converted into friendly or even pious creatures, and baptized into saintly names. Sometimes there are legends which reveal this transition. Thus it is related that in the year 1440, the dikes of Holland being broken down by a violent tempest, the sea overflowed the meadows; and some maidens of the town of Edam, in West Friesland, going in a boat to milk their cows, espied a mermaid embarrassed in the mud, the waters being very shallow. They took it into their boat and brought it to Edam, and dressed it in women's apparel, and taught it to spin. It ate as they did, but could not be brought to speak. It was carried to Haarlem, where it lived for some years, though showing an inclination to water. Parival, who tells the story, relates that they had conveyed to it some notions of the existence of a deity, and it made its reverences devoutly whenever it passed a crucifix.

Another creature of the same species was in the year 1531 caught in the Baltic, and sent as a present to Sigismund, King of Poland. It was seen by all the persons about the court, but only lived three days.

Fig. 6.—Hercules and the Hydra (Louvre)

The Hydra—the torrent which, cut off in one direction, makes many headways in others—has its survivals in the many diabolical names assigned to boiling springs and to torrents that become dangerously swollen. In California the boiling springs called 'Devil's Tea-kettle' and 'Devil's Mush-pot' repeat the 'Devil's Punch-bowls' of Europe, and the innumerable Devil's Dikes and Ditches. St. Gerard's Hill, near Pesth, on which the saint suffered martyrdom, is believed to be crowded with devils whenever an inundation threatens the city; they indulge in fiendish laughter, and play with the telescopes of the observatory, so that they who look through them afterwards see only devils' and witches' dances![35] At Buda, across the river from Pesth, is the famous 'Devil's Ditch,' which the inhabitants use as a sewer while it is dry, making it a Gehenna to poison them with stenches, but which often becomes a devastating torrent when thaw comes on the Blocksberg. In 1874 the inhabitants vaulted it over to keep away the normal stench, but the Hydra-head so lopped off grew again, and in July 1875 swallowed up a hundred people.[36]

The once perilous Strudel and Wirbel of the Danube are haunted by diabolical legends. From Dr. William Beattie's admirable work on 'The Danube' I quote the following passages:—'After descending the Greinerschwall, or rapids of Grein above mentioned, the river rolls on for a considerable space, in a deep and almost tranquil volume, which, by contrast with the approaching turmoil, gives increased effect to its wild, stormy, and romantic features. At first a hollow, subdued roar, like that of distant thunder, strikes the ear and rouses the traveller's attention. This increases every second, and the stir and activity which now prevail among the hands on board show that additional force, vigilance, and caution are to be employed in the use of the helm and oars. The water is now changed in its colour—chafed into foam, and agitated like a seething cauldron. In front, and in the centre of the channel, rises an abrupt, isolated, and colossal rock, fringed with wood, and crested with a mouldering tower, on the summit of which is planted a lofty cross, to which in the moment of danger the ancient boatmen were wont to address their prayers for deliverance. The first sight of this used to create no little excitement and apprehension on board; the master ordered strict silence to be observed, the steersman grasped the helm with a firmer hand, the passengers moved aside, so as to leave free space for the boatmen, while the women and children were hurried into the cabin, there to await, with feelings of no little anxiety, the result of the enterprise. Every boatman, with his head uncovered, muttered a prayer to his patron saint; and away dashed the barge through the tumbling breakers, that seemed as if hurrying it on to inevitable destruction. All these preparations, joined by the wildness of the adjacent scenery, the terrific aspect of the rocks, and the tempestuous state of the water, were sufficient to produce a powerful sensation on the minds even of those who had been all their lives familiar with dangers; while the shadowy phantoms with which superstition had peopled it threw a deeper gloom over the whole scene.'

Concerning the whirlpool called Wirbel, and the surrounding ruins, the same author writes: 'Each of these mouldering fortresses was the subject of some miraculous tradition, which circulated at every hearth. The sombre and mysterious aspect of the place, its wild scenery, and the frequent accidents which occurred in the passage, invested it with awe and terror; but above all, the superstitions of the time, a belief in the marvellous, and the credulity of the boatmen, made the navigation of the Strudel and the Wirbel a theme of the wildest romance. At night, sounds that were heard far above the roar of the Danube issued from every ruin. Magical lights flashed through their loopholes and casements, festivals were held in the long-deserted halls, maskers glided from room to room, the waltzers maddened to the strains of an infernal orchestra, armed sentinels paraded the battlements, while at intervals the clash of arms, the neighing of steeds, and the shrieks of unearthly combatants smote fitfully on the boatmen's ear. But the tower on which these scenes were most fearfully enacted was that on the Longstone, commonly called the 'Devil's Tower,' as it well deserved to be—for here, in close communion with his master, resided the 'Black Monk,' whose office it was to exhibit false lights and landmarks along the gulf, so as to decoy the vessels into the whirlpool, or dash them against the rocks. He was considerably annoyed in his quarters, however, on the arrival of the great Soliman in these regions; for to repel the turbaned host, or at least to check their triumphant progress to the Upper Danube, the inhabitants were summoned to join the national standard, and each to defend his own hearth. Fortifications were suddenly thrown up, even churches and other religious edifices were placed in a state of military defence; women and children, the aged and the sick, as already mentioned in our notice of Schaumburg, were lodged in fortresses, and thus secured from the violence of the approaching Moslem. Among the other points at which the greatest efforts were made to check the enemy, the passage of the Strudel and Wirbel was rendered as impregnable as the time and circumstances of the case would allow. To supply materials for the work, patriotism for a time got the better of superstition, and the said Devil's Tower was demolished and converted into a strong breastwork. Thus forcibly dislodged, the Black Monk is said to have pronounced a malediction on the intruders, and to have chosen a new haunt among the recesses of the Harz mountains.'

When the glaciers send down their torrents and flood the Rhone, it is the immemorial belief that the Devil may be sometimes seen swimming in it, with a sword in one hand and a golden globe in the other. Since it is contrary to all orthodox folklore that the Devil should be so friendly with water, the name must be regarded as a modern substitute for the earlier Rhone demon. We probably get closer to the original form of the superstition in the Swiss Oberland, which interprets the noises of the Furka Glacier, which feeds the Rhone, as the groans of wicked souls condemned for ever to labour there in directing the river's course; their mistress being a demoness who sometimes appears just before the floods, floating on a raft, and ordering the river to rise.

There is a tidal demonolatry also. The author of 'Rambles in Northumberland' gives a tradition concerning the river Wansbeck: 'This river discharges itself into the sea at a place called Cambois, about nine miles to the eastward, and the tide flows to within five miles of Morpeth. Tradition reports that Michael Scott, whose fame as a wizard is not confined to Scotland, would have brought the tide to the town had not the courage of the person failed upon whom the execution of this project depended. This agent of Michael, after his principal had performed certain spells, was to run from the neighbourhood of Cambois to Morpeth without looking behind, and the tide would follow him. After having advanced a certain distance he became alarmed at the roaring of the waters behind him, and forgetting the injunction, gave a glance over his shoulder to see if the danger was imminent, when the advancing tide immediately stopped, and the burgesses of Morpeth thus lost the chance of having the Wansbeck navigable between their town and the sea. It is also said that Michael intended to confer a similar favour on the inhabitants of Durham, by making the Wear navigable to their city; but his good intentions, which were to be carried into effect in the same manner, were also frustrated by the cowardice of the person who had to guide the tide.'

The gentle and just king Æolus, who taught his islanders navigation, in his mythologic transfiguration had to share the wayward dispositions of the winds he was said to rule; but though he wrecked the Trojan fleet and many a ship, his old human heart remained to be trusted on the appearance of Halcyon. His unhappy daughter of that name cast herself into the sea after the shipwreck of her husband (Cëyx), and the two were changed into birds. It was believed that for seven days before and seven after the shortest day of the year, when the halcyon is breeding, Æolus restrains his winds, and the sea is calm. The accent of this fable has been transmitted to some variants of the folklore of swans. In Russia the Tsar Morskoi or Water Demon's beautiful daughters (swans) may naturally be supposed to influence the tides which the fair bathers of our time are reduced to obey. In various regions the tides are believed to have some relation to swans, and to respect them. I have met with a notion of this kind in England. On the day of Livingstone's funeral there was an extraordinary tide in the Thames, which had been predicted and provided for. The crowds which had gathered at the Abbey on that occasion repaired after the funeral to Westminster Bridge to observe the tide, and among them was a venerable disbeliever in science, who announced to a group that there would be no high tide, 'because the swans were nesting.' This sceptic was speedily put to confusion by the result, and perhaps one superstition the less remained in the circle that seemed to regard him as an oracle.

The Russian peasantry live in much fear of the Rusalkas and Vodyanuie, water-spirits who, of course, have for their chief the surly Neptune Tsar Morskoi. In deprecation of this tribe, the peasant is careful not to bathe without a cross round the neck, nor to ford a stream on horseback without signing a cross on the water with a scythe or knife. In the Ukrain these water-demons are supposed to be the transformed souls of Pharaoh and his host when they were drowned, and they are increased by people who drown themselves. In Bohemia fishermen are known sometimes to refuse aid to one drowning, for fear the Vodyany will be offended and prevent the fish, over which he holds rule, from entering their nets. The wrath of such beings is indicated by the upheavals of water and foam; and they are supposed especially mischievous in the spring, when torrents and floods are pouring from melted snow. Those undefined monsters which Beowulf slew, Grendel and his mother, are interpreted by Simrock as personifications of the untamed sea and stormy floods invading the low flat shores, whose devastations so filled Faust with horror (ll. iv.), and in combating which his own hitherto desolating powers found their task.

> The Sea sweeps on in thousand quarters flowing,
> Itself unfruitful, barrenness bestowing;
> It breaks, and swells, and rolls, and overwhelms
> The desert stretch of desolated realms....
> Let that high joy be mine for evermore,
> To shut the lordly Ocean from the shore,
> The watery waste to limit and to bar,
> And push it back upon itself afar!

In such brave work Faust had many forerunners, whose art and courage have their monument in the fairer fables of all these elemental powers in which fear saw demons. Pavana, in India, messenger of the gods, rides upon the winds, and in his forty-nine forms, corresponding with the points of the Hindu compass, guards the earth. Solomon, too, journeyed on a magic carpet woven of the winds, which still serves the purposes of the Wise. From the churned ocean rose Lakshmí (after the solar origin was lost to the myth), Hindu goddess of prosperity; and from the sea-foam rose Aphrodite, Beauty. These fair forms had their true worshipper in the Northman, who left on mastered wind and wave his song as Emerson found it—

> The gale that wrecked you on the sand,
> It helped my rowers to row;
> The storm is my best galley hand,
> And drives me where I go.

NOTES
1   'Scenes and Legends of the North of Scotland.' Nimmo, 1876.
2   'Rig-Veda,' ii. 33. Tr. by Professor Evans of Michigan.
3   'Rig-Veda,' i. 114.
4   'Jour. Ceylon R. A. Soc.,' 1865–66.
5   Welcker, 'Griechische Götterlehre,' vol. i. p. 661.
6   Moffat, p. 257.
7   Livingstone, p. 124.
8   Pöppig, 'Reise in Chile,' vol. ii. p. 358.
9   Eyre, vol. ii. p. 362.
10 Tylor, 'Early Hist.,' p. 359.
11 So confirming the conjecture of Wachsmuth, in 'Das alte Griechenland im neuen,' p. 23. Elias might also easily be associated with the name Æolus.
12 'Rig-Veda,' x. (Muir).
13 John iii. 8.
14 'The Wheel of the Law,' by Henry Alabaster, Trübner & Co.
15 'Rig-Veda,' v. 83 (Wilson).
16 'Major's Tr.,' ii. 26.
17 Wierus' 'Pseudomonarchia Dæmon.'
18 'Songs of the Russian People,' by W. R. S. Ralston, M.A.
19 Isa. xxii. 22. It is remarkable that (according to Callimachus) Ceres bore a key on her shoulder. She kept the granary of the earth.
20 Rev. i. 18.; Matt. xvi. 19.
21 'Journal N. C. B. R. A. S.,' 1853.
22 'Folklore of China,' p. 124. The drum held by the imp in Fig. 3 shows his relation to the thunder-god. In Japan the thunder-god is represented as having five drums strung together. The wind-god has a large bag of compressed air between his shoulders; and he has steel claws, representing the keen and piercing wind. The Tartars in Siberia believe that a potent demon may be evoked by beating a drum; their sorcerers provide a tame bear, who starts upon the scene, and from whom they pretend to get answers to questions. In Nova Scotian superstition we find demons charmed by drums into quietude. In India the temple-drum preserved such solemn associations even for the new theistic sect, the Brahmo-Somaj, that it is said to be still beaten as accompaniment to the organ sent to their chief church by their English friends.
23 Although the Koran and other authorities, as already stated, have associated the Jinn with etherial fire, Arabic folklore is nearer the meaning of the word in assigning the name to all demons. The learned Arabic lexicographer of Beirut, P. Bustani, says 'The Jinn is the opposite of mankind, or it is whatever is veiled from the sense, whether angel or devil.'
24 'Cuneiform Ins.,' iv. 15.
25 Ib. ii. 27.
26 Job xli.
27 'Records of the Past,' i.
28 Lenormant, 'La Magie.'
29 'Records of the Past,' iii. 129.
30 The god of the Euphrates.
31 The Assyrian has 'of the high places.'
32 'Records of the Past,' iii. 129, 130.
33 'Henry IV.,' Part 1st, Act 2. 'Heart of Mid-Lothian,' xxv. An interesting paper on this subject by Mr. Alexander Wilder appeared in The Evolution, New York, December 16, 1877.

34 De Plancy.

35 An individual by this means saw his wife among the witches, so detecting her unhallowed nature, which gave rise to a saying there that husbands must not be star-gazing on St. Gerard's Eve.

36 London 'Times,' July 8, 1875.

Chapter V
Animals

THE ANIMAL DEMONS—those whose evil repute is the result of something in their nature which may be inimical to man—should be distinguished from the forms which have been diabolised by association with mythological personages or ideas. The lion, tiger, and wolf are examples of the one class; the stag, horse, owl, and raven of the other. But there are circumstances which render it very difficult to observe this distinction. The line has to be drawn, if at all, between the measureless forces of degradation on the one side, discovering some evil in animals which, but for their bad associations, would not have been much thought of; and of euphemism on the other, transforming harmful beasts to benignant agents by dwelling upon some minor characteristic.

There are a few obviously dangerous animals, such as the serpent, where it is easy to pick our way; we can recognise the fear that flatters it to an agathodemon and the diminished fear that pronounces it accurst.[1] But what shall be said of the Goat? Was there really anything in its smell or in its flesh when first eaten, its butting, or injury to plants, which originally classed it among the unclean animals? or was it merely demonised because of its uncanny and shaggy appearance? What explanation can be given of the evil repute of our household friend the Cat? Is it derived by inheritance from its fierce ancestors of the jungle? Was it first suggested by its horrible human-like sleep-murdering caterwaulings at night? or has it simply suffered from a theological curse on the cats said to draw the chariots of the goddesses of Beauty? The demonic Dog is, if anything, a still more complex subject. The student of mythology and folklore speedily becomes familiar with the trivial sources from which vast streams of superstition often issue. The cock's challenge to the all-detecting sun no doubt originated his ominous career from the Code of Manu to the cock-headed devils frescoed in the cathedrals of Russia. The fleshy, forked roots of a soporific plant issued in that vast Mandrake Mythology which has been the subject of many volumes, without being even yet fully explored. The Italians have a saying that 'One knavery of the hedgehog is worth more than many of the fox;' yet the nocturnal and hibernating habits and general quaintness of the humble hedgehog, rather than his furtive propensity to prey on eggs and chickens, must have raised him to the honours of demonhood. In various popular fables this little animal proves more than a match for the wolf and the serpent. It was in the form of a hedgehog that the Devil is said to have made the attempt to let in the sea through the Brighton Downs, which was prevented by a light being brought, though the seriousness of the scheme is still attested in the Devil's Dyke. There is an ancient tradition that when the Devil had smuggled himself into Noah's Ark, he tried to sink it by boring a hole; but this scheme was defeated, and the human race saved, by the hedgehog stuffing himself into the hole. In the Brighton story the Devil would appear to have remembered his former failure in drowning people, and to have appropriated the form which defeated him.

Fig. 7.—Japanese Demon

The Fox, as incarnation of cunning, holds in the primitive belief of the Japanese almost the same position as the Serpent in the nations that have worshipped, until bold enough to curse it. In many of the early pictures of Japanese demons one may generally detect amid their human, wolfish, or other characters some traits of the *kitsune* (fox). He is always the soul of the three-eyed demon of Japan (fig. 7). He is the sagacious 'Vizier,' as the Persian Desatir calls him, and is practically the Japanese scape-goat. If a fox has appeared in any neighbourhood, the next trouble is attributed to his visit; and on such occasions the sufferers and their friends repair to some ancient gnarled tree in which the fox is theoretically resident and propitiate him, just as would be done to a serpent in other regions. In Japan the fox is not regarded as always harmful, but generally so. He is not to be killed on any account. Being thus spared through superstition, the foxes increase sufficiently to supply abundant material for the continuance of its demonic character. 'Take us the foxes, the little foxes that spoil the vines,'[2] is an admonition reversed in Japan. The correspondence between the cunning respected in this animal and that of the serpent, reverenced elsewhere, is confirmed by Mr. Fitz Cunliffe Owen, who observed, as he informs me, that the Japanese will not kill even the poisonous snakes which crawl freely amid the decaying Buddhist temples of Nikko, one of the most sacred places in Japan, where once as many as eight thousand monastic Buddhists were harboured. It is the red fox that abounds in Japan, and its human-like cry at night near human habitations is such as might easily encourage these superstitions. But, furthermore, mythology supplies many illustrations of a creditable tendency among rude tribes to mark out for special veneration or fear any force in nature finer than mere strength. Emerson says, 'Foxes are so cunning because they are not strong.' In our Japanese demon, whose three eyes alone connect it with the præternatural vision ascribed by that race to the fox, the harelip is very pronounced. That little animal, the Hare, is associated with a large mythology, perhaps because out of its weakness proceeds its main forces of survival—timidity, vigilance, and swiftness. The superstition concerning the hare is found in Africa. The same animal is the much-venerated good genius of the Calmucs, who call him Sákya-muni (Buddha), and say that on earth he submitted himself to be eaten by a starving man, for which gracious deed he was raised to dominion over the moon, where they profess to see him. The legend is probably traceable back to the Sanskrit word *sasin*, moon, which means literally 'the hare-marked.' *Sasa* means 'hare.' Pausanias relates the story of the moon-goddess instructing exiles to build their city where they shall see a hare take refuge in a myrtle-grove.[3] In the demonic fauna of Japan another cunning animal figures—the Weasel. The name of this demon is 'the sickle weasel,' and it also seems to occupy the position of a scape-goat. In the language of a Japanese report, 'When a person's clogs slip from under his feet, and he falls and cuts his face on the gravel, or when a person, who is out at night when he ought to have been at home, presents himself to his family with a freshly-scarred face, the wound is referred to the agency of the malignant invisible weasel and his sharp sickle.' In an aboriginal legend of America, also, two sister demons commonly take the form of weasels.

The popular feeling which underlay much of the animal-worship in ancient times was probably that which is reflected in the Japanese notions of to-day, as told in the subjoined sketch from an amusing book.

'One of these visitors was an old man, who himself was at the time a victim of a popular superstition that the departed revisit the scenes of their life in this world in shapes of different animals. We noticed that he was not in his usual spirits, and pressed him to unburden his mind to us. He said he had lost his little son Chiosin, but that was not so much the cause of his grief as the absurd way in which his wife, backed up by a whole conclave of old women who had taken up their abode in his house to comfort her, was going on. 'What do they all do?' we asked sympathetically. 'Why,' he replied, 'every beastly animal that comes to my house, there is a cry amongst them all, 'Chiosin, Chiosin has come back!' and the whole house swarms with cats and dogs and bats—for they say they are not quite sure which is Chiosin, and that they had better be kind to the lot than run the chance of treating him badly; the consequence is, all these brutes are fed on my rice and meat, and now I am driven out of doors and called an unnatural parent because I killed a mosquito which bit me!'[4]

The strange and inexplicable behaviour of animals in cases of fear, panic, or pain has been generally attributed by ignorant races to their possession by demons. Of this nature is the story of the devil entering the herd of swine and carrying them into the sea, related in the New Testament. It is said that even yet in some parts of Scotland the milkmaid carries a switch of the magical rowan to expel the demon that sometimes enters the cow. Professor Monier Williams writes from Southern India—'When my fellow-travellers and myself were nearly dashed to pieces over a precipice the other day by some restive horses on a ghat near Poona, we were told that the road at this particular point was haunted by devils who often caused similar accidents, and we were given to understand that we should have done well to conciliate Ganesa, son of the god Siva, and all his troops of evil spirits, before starting.' The same writer also tells us that the guardian spirits or 'mothers' who haunt most regions of the Peninsula are believed to ride about on horses, and if they are angry, scatter blight and disease. Hence the traveller just arrived from Europe is startled and puzzled by apparitions of rudely-formed terra-cotta horses, often as large as life, placed by the peasantry round shrines in the middle of fields as acceptable propitiatory offerings, or in the fulfilment of vows in periods of sickness.[5]

This was the belief of the Corinthians in the Taraxippos, or shade of Glaucus, who, having been torn in pieces by the horses with which he had been racing, and which he had fed on human flesh to make more spirited, remained to haunt the Isthmus and frighten horses during the races.

There is a modern legend in the Far West (America) of a horse called 'The White Devil,' which, in revenge for some harm to its comrades, slew men by biting and trampling them, and was itself slain after defying many attempts at its capture; but among the many ancient legends of demon-horses there are few which suggest anything about that animal hostile to man. His occasional evil character is simply derived from his association with man, and is therefore postponed. For a similar reason the Goat also must be dealt with hereafter, and as a symbolical animal. A few myths are met with which relate to its unpleasant characteristics. In South Guinea the odour of goats is accounted for by the Saga that their ancestor having had the presumption to ask a goddess for her aromatic ointment, she angrily rubbed him with ointment of a reverse kind. It has also been said that it was regarded as a demon by the worshippers of Bacchus, because it cropped the vines; and that it thus originated the Trageluphoi, or goat-stag monsters mentioned by Plato,[6] and gave us also the word *tragedy*.[7] But such traits of the Goat can have very little to do with its important relations to Mythology and Demonology. To the list of animals demonised by association must also be added the Stag. No doubt the anxious mothers, wives, or sweethearts of rash young huntsmen utilised the old fables of beautiful hinds which in the deep forests changed to demons and devoured their pursuers,[8] for admonition; but the fact that such stags had to transform themselves for evil work is a sufficient certificate of character to prevent their being included among the animal demons proper, that is, such as have in whole or part supplied in their disposition to harm man the basis of a demonic representation.

It will not be deemed wonderful that Rats bear a venerable rank in Demonology. The shudder which some nervous persons feel at sight of even a harmless mouse is a survival from the time when it was believed that in this form unshriven souls or unbaptized children haunted their former homes; and probably it would be difficult to estimate the number of ghost-stories which have originated in their nocturnal scamperings. Many legends report the departure of unhallowed souls from human mouths in the shape of a Mouse. During the earlier Napoleonic wars mice were used in Southern Germany as diviners, by being set with inked feet on the map of Europe to show where the fatal Frenchmen would march. They gained this sanctity by a series of associations with force stretching back to the Hindu fable of a mouse delivering the elephant and the lion by gnawing the cords that bound them. The battle of the Frogs and Mice is ascribed to Homer. Mice are said to have foretold the first civil war in Rome by gnawing the gold in the temple. Rats appear in various legends as avengers. The uncles of King Popelus II., murdered by him and his wife and thrown into a lake, reappear as rats and gnaw the king and queen to death. The same fate overtakes Miskilaus of Poland, through the transformed widows and orphans he had wronged. Mouse Tower, standing in the middle of the Rhine, is the haunted monument of cruel Archbishop Hatto, of Mainz, who (anno 970) bade the famine-stricken people repair to his barn, wherein he shut them fast and burned them. But next morning an army of rats, having eaten all the corn in his granaries, darkened the roads to the palace. The prelate sought refuge from them in the Tower, but they swam after, gnawed through the walls and devoured him.[9]

St. Gertrude, wearing the funereal mantle of Holda, commands an army of mice. In this respect she succeeds to the Pied Piper of Hamelin, who also leads off children; and my ingenious friend Mr. John Fiske suggests that this may be the reason why Irish servant-maids often show such frantic terror at sight of a mouse.[10] The care of children is often intrusted to them, and the appearance of mice prognosticated of old the appearance of the præternatural rat-catcher and psychopomp. Pliny says that in his time it was considered fortunate to meet a white rat. The people of Bassorah always bow to these revered animals when seen, no doubt to propitiate them.

The Lion is a symbol of majesty and of the sun in his glory (reached in the zodiacal Leo), though here and there his original demonic character appears,—as in the combats of Indra, Samson, and Herakles with terrible lions. Euphemism, in one sense, fulfils the conditions of Samson's riddle—Sweetness coming out of the Strong—and has brought honey out of the Lion. His cruel character has subtly fallen to Sirius the Dog-star, to whom are ascribed the drought and malaria of 'dog-days' (when the sun is in Leo); but the primitive fact is intimated in several fables like that of Aristæus, who, born after his mother had been rescued from the Lybian lion, was worshipped in Ceos as a saviour from both droughts and lions. The Lion couching at the feet of beautiful Doorga in India, reappears drawing the chariot of Aphrodite, and typifies the potency of beauty rather than, as Emerson interprets, that beauty depends on strength. The chariot of the Norse Venus, Freyja, was drawn by Cats, diminished forms of her Southern sister's steeds. It was partly by these routes the Cat came to play the sometimes beneficent rôle in Russian, and to some extent in German, French, and English folklore,—*e.g.*, Puss in Boots, Whittington and his Cat, and Madame D'Aulnoy's *La Chatte Blanche*. The demonic characteristics of the destructive cats have been inherited by the black,—or, as in Macbeth, the brindled,—cat. In Germany the approach of a cat to a sick-bed announces death; to dream of one is an evil omen. In Hungary it is said every black cat becomes a witch at the age of seven. It is the witch's favourite riding-horse, but may sometimes be saved from such servitude by incision of the sign of the cross. A scratch from a black cat is thought to be the beginning of a fatal spell.

De Gubernatis[11] has a very curious speculation concerning the origin of our familiar fable the Kilkenny Cats, which he traces to the German superstition which dreads the combat between cats as presaging death to one who witnesses it; and this belief he finds reflected in the Tuscan child's 'game of souls,' in which the devil and angel are supposed to contend for the soul. The author thinks this may be one outcome of the contest between Night and Twilight in Mythology; but, if the connection can be traced, it would probably prove to be derived from the struggle between the two angels of Death, one variation of which is associated with the legend of the strife for the body of Moses. The Book of Enoch says that Gabriel was sent, before the Flood, to excite the man-devouring giants to destroy one another. In an ancient Persian picture in my possession, animal monsters are shown devouring each other, while their proffered victim, like Daniel, is unharmed. The idea is a natural one, and hardly requires comparative tracing.

Dr. Dennys tells us that in China there exists precisely the same superstition as in Scotland as to the evil omen of a cat (or dog) passing over a corpse. Brand and Pennant both mention this, the latter stating that the cat or dog that has so done is killed without mercy. This fact would seem to show that the fear is for the living, lest the soul of the deceased should enter the animal and become one of the innumerable werewolf or vampyre class of demons. But the origin of the superstition is no doubt told in the Slavonic belief that if a cat leap over a corpse the deceased person will become a vampyre.

In Russia the cat enjoys a somewhat better reputation than it does in most other countries. Several peasants in the neighbourhood of Moscow assured me that while they would never be willing to remain in a church where a dog had entered, they would esteem it a good sign if a cat came to church. One aged woman near Moscow told me that when the Devil once tried to creep into Paradise he took the form of a mouse: the Dog and Cat were on guard at the gates, and the Dog allowed the evil one to pass, but the Cat pounced on him, and so defeated another treacherous attempt against human felicity.

The Cat superstition has always been strong in Great Britain. It is, indeed, in one sense true, as old Howell wrote (1647)—'We need not cross the sea for examples of this kind, we have too many (God wot) at home: King James a great while was loath to believe there were witches; but that which happened to my Lord Francis of Rutland's children convinced him, who were bewitched by an old woman that was a servant of Belvoir Castle, but, being displeased, she contracted with the Devil, who conversed with her in the form of a Cat, whom she called Rutterkin, to make away those children out of mere malignity and thirst of revenge.' It is to be feared that many a poor woman has been burned as a witch against whom her cherished cat was the chief witness. It would be a curious psychological study to trace how far the superstition owns a survival in even scientific minds,—as in Buffon's vituperation of the cat, and in the astonishing story, told by Mr. Wood, of a cat which saw a ghost (anno 1877)!

The Dog, so long the faithful friend of man, and even, possibly, because of the degree to which he has caught his master's manners, has a large demonic history. In the Semitic stories there are many that indicate the path by which 'dog' became the Mussulman synonym of infidel; and the one dog Katmir who in Arabic legend was admitted to Paradise for his faithful watching three hundred and nine years before the cave of the Seven Sleepers,[12] must have drifted among the Moslems from India as the Ephesian Sleepers did from the christian world. In the beautiful episode of the 'Mahábhárata,' Yudhisthira having journeyed to the door of heaven, refuses to enter into that happy abode unless his faithful dog is admitted also. He is told by Indra, 'My heaven hath no place for dogs; they steal away our offerings on earth;' and again, 'If a dog but behold a sacrifice, men esteem it unholy and void.' This difficulty was solved by the Dog—Yama in disguise—revealing himself and praising his friend's fidelity. It is tolerably clear that it is to his connection with Yama, god of Death, and under the evolution of that dualism which divided the universe into upper and nether, that the Dog was degraded among our Aryan ancestors; at the same time his sometimes wolfish disposition and some other natural characters supplied the basis of his demonic character. He was at once a dangerous and a corruptible guard.

In the early Vedic Mythology it is the abode of the gods that is guarded by the two dogs, identified by solar mythologists as the morning and evening twilight: a later phase shows them in the service of Yama, and they reappear in the guardian of the Greek Hades, Cerberus, and Orthros. The first of these has been traced to the Vedic Sarvara, the latter to the monster Vritra. 'Orthros' is the phonetical equivalent of Vritra. The bitch Sarama, mother of the two Vedic dogs, proved a treacherous guard, and was slain by Indra.

Fig. 8.—Cerberus (Calmet)

Hence the Russian peasant comes fairly by another version of how the Dog, while on guard, admitted the Devil into heaven on being thrown a bone. But the two watch-dogs of the Hindu myth do not seem to bear an evil character. In a funeral hymn of the 'Rig-Veda' (x. 14), addressed to Yama, King of Death, we read:—'By an auspicious path do thou hasten past the two four-eyed brindled dogs, the offspring of Sarama; then approach the beautiful Pitris who rejoice together with Yama. Intrust him, O Yama, to thy two watch-dogs, four-eyed, road-guarding, and man-observing. The two brown messengers of Yama, broad of nostril and insatiable, wander about among men; may they give us again to-day the auspicious breath of life that we may see the sun!'

And now thousands of years after this was said we find the

Dog still regarded as the seer of ghosts, and watcher at the gates of death, of whose opening his howl forewarns. The howling of a dog on the night of December 9, 1871, at Sandringham, where the Prince of Wales lay ill, was thought important enough for newspapers to report to a shuddering country. I read lately of a dog in a German village which was supposed to have announced so many deaths that he became an object of general terror, and was put to death. In that country belief in the demonic character of the dog seems to have been strong enough to transmit an influence even to the powerful brain of Goethe.

In Goethe's poem, it was when Faust was walking with the student Wagner that the black Dog appeared, rushing around them in spiral curves—spreading, as Faust said, 'a magic coil as a snare around them;'[13] that after this dog had followed Faust into his study, it assumed a monstrous shape, until changed to a mist, from which Mephistopheles steps forth—'the kernel of the brute'—in guise of a travelling scholar. This is in notable coincidence with the archaic symbolism of the Dog as the most frequent form of the 'Lares' (fig. 9), or household genii, originally because of its vigilance. The form here presented is nearly identical with the Cynocephalus, whom the learned author of 'Mankind: their Origin and Destiny,' identifies as the Adamic being set as a watch and instructor in Eden (Gen. xvi. 15), an example of which, holding pen and tablet (as described by Horapollo), is given in that work from Philæ. Chrysippus says that these were afterwards represented as young men clothed with dog-skins. Remnants of the tutelary character of the dog are scattered through German folklore: he is regarded as oracle, ghost-seer, and gifted with second sight; in Bohemia he is sometimes made to lick an infant's face that it may see well.

Fig. 9.—Canine Lar (Herculaneum)

The passage in 'Faust' has been traced to Goethe's antipathy to dogs, as expressed in his conversation with Falk at the time of Wieland's death. 'Annihilation is utterly out of the question; but the possibility of being caught on the way by some more powerful and yet baser monas, and subordinated to it; this is unquestionably a very serious consideration; and I, for my part, have never been able entirely to divest myself of the fear of it, in the way of a mere observation of nature.' At this moment, says Falk, a dog was heard repeatedly barking in the street. Goethe, sprang hastily to the window and called to it: 'Take what form you will, vile larva, you shall not subjugate me!' After some pause, he resumed with the remark:

'This rabble of creation is extremely offensive. It is a perfect pack of monades with which we are thrown together in this planetary nook; their company will do us little honour with the inhabitants of other planets, if they happen to hear anything about them.'

In visiting the house where Goethe once resided in Weimar, I was startled to find as the chief ornament of the hall a large bronze dog, of full size, and very dark, looking proudly forth, as if he possessed the Goethean monas after all. However, it is not probable that the poet's real dislike of dogs arose solely from that speculation about monades. It is more probable that in observing the old wall-picture in Auerbach's cellar, wherein a dog stands beside Mephistopheles, Goethe was led to consider carefully the causes of that intimacy. Unfortunately, and notwithstanding the fables and the sentiment which invest that animal, there are some very repulsive things about him, such as his tendency to madness and the infliction on man of a frightful death. The Greek Mania's 'fleet hounds' (Bacchæ 977) have spread terrors far and wide.

Those who carefully peruse the account given by Mr. Lewes of the quarrel between Karl August and Goethe, on account of the opposition of the latter to the introduction of a performing dog on the Weimar stage—an incident which led to his resignation of his position of intendant of the theatre—may detect this aversion mingling with his disgust as an artist; and it may be also suspected that it was not the mere noise which caused the tortures he described himself as having once endured at Göttingen from the barking of dogs.

It is, however, not improbable that in the wild notion of Goethe, joined with his cynophobia, we find a survival of the belief of the

Parsees of Surat, who venerate the Dog above all other animals, and who, when one is dying, place a dog's muzzle near his mouth, and make it bark twice, so that it may catch the departing soul, and bear it to the waiting angel.

The devil-worshippers of Travancore to this day declare that the evil power approaches them in the form of a Dog, as Mephistopheles approached Faust. But before the superstition reached Goethe's poem it had undergone many modifications; and especially its keen scent had influenced the Norse imagination to ascribe to it præternatural wisdom. Thus we read in the Saga of Hakon the Good, that when Eystein the Bad had conquered Drontheim, he offered the people choice of his slave Thorer or his dog Sauer to be their king. They chose the Dog. 'Now the dog was by witchcraft gifted with three men's wisdom; and when he barked he spoke one word and barked two.' This Dog wore a collar of gold, and sat on a throne, but, for all his wisdom and power, seems to have been a dog still; for when some wolves invaded the cattle, he attacked and was torn to pieces by them.

Among the negroes of the Southern States in America I have found the belief that the most frequent form of a diabolical apparition is that of a large Dog with fiery eyes, which may be among them an original superstition attributable to their horror of the bloodhound, by which, in some regions, they were pursued when attempting to escape. Among the whites of the same region I have never been able to find any instance of the same belief, though belief in the presage of the howling dog is frequent; and it is possible that this is a survival from some region in Africa, where the Dog has an evil name of the same kind as the scape-goat. Among some tribes in Fazogl there is an annual carnival at which every one does as he likes. The king is then seated in the open air, a dog tied to the leg of his chair, and the animal is then stoned to death.

Mark Twain[14] records the folklore of a village of Missouri, where we find lads quaking with fear at the howling of a 'stray dog' in the night, but indifferent to the howling of a dog they recognise, which may be a form of the common English belief that it is unlucky to be followed by a 'strange' dog. From the same book it appears also that the dog will always have his head in the direction of the person whose doom is signified: the lads are entirely relieved when they find the howling animal has his back turned to them.

It is remarkable that these fragments of European superstition should meet in the Far West a plentiful crop of their like which has sprung up among the aborigines, as the following extract from Mr. Brinton's work, 'Myths of the New World,' will show: 'Dogs were supposed to stand in some peculiar relation to the moon, probably because they howl at it and run at night, uncanny practices which have cost them dear in reputation. The custom prevailed among tribes so widely asunder as Peruvians, Tupis, Creeks, Iroquois, Algonquins, and Greenland Eskimos to thrash the curs most soundly during an eclipse. The Creeks explained this by saying that the big Dog was swallowing the sun, and that by whipping the little ones they could make him desist. What the big Dog was they were not prepared to say. We know. It was the night goddess, represented by the Dog, who was thus shrouding the world at mid-day. In a better sense, they represented the more agreeable characteristics of the lunar goddess. Xochiquetzal, most fecund of Aztec divinities, patroness of love, of sexual pleasure, and of child-birth, was likewise called*Itzcuinan*, which, literally translated, is 'bitch-mother.' This strange and to us so repugnant title for a goddess was not without parallel elsewhere. When in his wars the Inca Pachacutec carried his arms into the province of Huanca, he found its inhabitants had installed in their temples the figure of a Dog as their highest deity.... This canine canonisation explains why in some parts of Peru a priest was called, by way of honour, *allco*, Dog!... Many tribes on the Pacific coast united in the adoration of a wild species, the coyote, the *Canis latrans* of naturalists.' Of the Dog-demon Chantico the legend of the Nahuas was, 'that he made a sacrifice to the gods without observing a preparatory fast, for which he was punished by being changed into a Dog. He then invoked the god of death to deliver him, which attempt to evade a just punishment so enraged the divinities that they immersed the world in water.'

The common phrase 'hell-hounds' has come to us by various routes. Diana being degraded to Hecate, the dogs of Hades, Orthros and Cerberus, multiplied into a pack of hounds for her chase, were degraded with her into infernal howlers and hunters. A like degradation of Odin's hunt took place at a later date. The Wild Huntsman, being a diabolical character, is considered elsewhere. Concerning the Dog, it may be further said here, that there are probably various characteristics of that animal reflected in his demonic character. His liability to become rabid, and to afflict human beings with hydrophobia, appears to have had some part in it. Spinoza alludes to the custom in his time of destroying persons suffering from this canine rabies by suffocation; and his English biographer and editor, Dr. Willis, tells me that in his boyhood in Scotland he always heard this spoken of as the old custom. That such treatment could have prevailed can hardly be ascribed to anything but a belief in the demonic character of the rabid dog, cognate with the unconscious superstition which still causes rural magistrates to order a dog which has bitten any one to be slain. The notion is, that if the dog goes mad thereafter, the man will also. Of course it would be rational to preserve the dog's life carefully, in order that, if it continues healthy, the bitten may feel reassured, as he cannot be if it be dead.

But the degradation of the dog had a cause even in his fidelity as a watch. For this, as we have just seen, made him a common form among Lares or domestic demons. The teraphim also were often in this shape. Christianity had therefore a special reason for ascribing an infernal character to these little idols, which interfered with the popular dependence on the saints. It will thus be seen that there were many causes operating to create that formidable class of demons which were called in the Middle Ages Cynocephaloi. The ancient holy pictures of Russia especially abound in these dog-headed devils; in the sixteenth century they were frequently represented rending souls in hell; and sometimes the dragon of the Apocalypse is represented with seven horrible canine heads.

M. Toussenel, in his transcendental interpretations, has identified the Wolf as the bandit and outlaw.[15] The proverbial mediæval phrase for an outlaw—one who wears a *teste læve, caput lupinum, wulfesheofod*, which the ingenious author perhaps remembered—is of good antiquity. The wolf is called robber in the 'Rig-Veda,' and he is there also demonised, since we find him fleeing before a devotee. (In the Zend 'Vendidad' the souls of the pious fear to meet the wolf on the way to heaven.) The god Pushan is invoked against the evil wolf, the malignant spirit.[16] Cardano says that to dream of a wolf announces a robber. There is in the wolf, at the same time, that always attractive love of liberty which, in the well-known fable, makes him prefer leanness to the comfort of the collar-wearing dog, which makes him among demonic animals sometimes the same as the mighty huntsmen Nimrod and shaggy Esau among humanised demons. One is not surprised to find occasionally good stories about the wolf. Thus the Nez Perces tribe in America trace the origin of the human race to a wolf. They say that originally, when there were nothing but animals, there was a huge monster which devoured them whole and alive. This monster swallowed a wolf, who, when he entered its belly, found the animals therein snarling at and biting one another as they had done on the earth outside. The wolf exhorted them that their common sufferings should teach them friendliness, and finally he induced them to a system of co-operation by which they made their way out through the side of the monster, which instantly perished. The animals so released were at once transformed to men, how and why the advocates of co-operation will readily understand, and founded the Nez Perces Indians. The myths of Asia and Europe are unhappily antipodal to this in spirit and form, telling of human beings transformed to wolves. In the Norse Mythology, however, there stands a demon wolf whose story bears a touch of feeling, though perhaps it was originally the mere expression for physical law. This is the wolf

Fenris, which, from being at first the pet of the gods and lapdog of the goddesses, became so huge and formidable that Asgard itself was endangered. All the skill and power of the gods could not forge chains which might chain him; he snapped them like straws and toppled over the mountains to which he was fastened. But the little Elves working underground made that chain so fine that none could see or feel it,—fashioned it out of the beards of women, the breath of fish, noise of the cat's footfall, spittle of birds, sinews of bears, roots of stones,—by which are meant things non-existent. This held him. Fenris is chained till the final destruction, when he shall break loose and devour Odin. The fine chain that binds ferocity,—is it the love that can tame all creatures? Is it the sunbeam that defines to the strongest creature its habitat?

The two monsters formed when Ráhu was cloven in twain, in Hindu Mythology, reappear in Eddaic fable as the wolves Sköll and Hati, who pursue the sun and moon. As it is said in the Völuspá:—

> Eastward in the Iron-wood
> The old one sitteth,
> And there bringeth forth
> Fenrir's fell kindred.
> Of these one, the mightiest,
> The moon's devourer,
> In form most fiend-like,
> And filled with the life-blood
> Of the dead and the dying,
> Reddens with ruddy gore
> The seats of the high gods.

Euphemism attending propitiation of such monsters may partly explain the many good things told of wolves in popular legend.

169

The stories of the she-wolf nourishing children, as Romulus and Remus, are found in many lands. They must, indeed, have had some prestige, to have been so largely adopted in saintly tradition. Like the bears that Elisha called to devour the children, the wolves do not lose their natural ferocity by becoming pious. They devour heretics and sacrilegious people. One guarded the head of St. Edmund the Martyr of England; another escorted St. Oddo, Abbot of Cluny, as his ancestors did the priests of Cluny. The skin of the wolf appears in folklore as a charm against hydrophobia; its teeth are best for cutting children's gums, and its bite, if survived, is an assurance against any future wound or pain.

Fig. 10.—The Wolf as Confessor (probably Dutch)

The tragedy which is so foolishly sprung upon the nerves of children, Little Red Riding-Hood, shows the wolf as a crafty animal. There are many legends of a like character which have made it a favourite figure in which to represent pious impostors. In our figure 10, the wolf appears as the 'dangerous confessor;' it was intended, as Mr. Wright thought, for Mary of Modena, Queen of James II., and Father Petre. At the top of the original are the words '*Converte Angliam*' and beneath, 'It is a foolish sheep that makes the wolf her confessor.' The craft of the wolf is represented in a partly political partly social turn given by an American fabulist to one of Æsop's fables. The wolf having accused the lamb he means to devour of fouling the stream, and receiving answer that the lamb was drinking farther down the current, alters the charge and says, 'You opposed my candidature at the caucus two years ago.' 'I was not then born,' replies the lamb. The wolf then says, 'Any one hearing my accusations would testify that I am insane and not responsible for my actions,' and thereupon devours the lamb with full faith in a jury of his countrymen. M. Toussenel says the wolf is a terrible strategist, albeit the less observant have found little in his character to warrant this attribute of craft, his physiognomy and habits showing him a rather transparent highwayman. It is probable that the fables of this character have derived that trait from his association with demons and devils supposed to take on his shape.

In a beautiful hymn to the Earth in the 'Atharva Veda' it is said, 'The Earth, which endureth the burden of the oppressor, beareth up the abode of the lofty and of the lowly, suffereth the hog, and giveth entrance to the wild boar.' Boar-hounds in Brittany and some other regions are still kept at Government expense. There are many indications of this kind that in early times men had to defend themselves vigorously against the ravages of the wild boar, and, as De Gubernatis remarks,[17] its character is generally demoniacal. The contests of Hercules with the Erymanthian, and of Meleager with the Calydonian, Boar, are enough to show that it was through its dangerous character that he became sacred to the gods of war, Mars and Odin. But it is also to be remembered that the third incarnation of Vishnu was as a Wild Boar; and as the fearless exterminator of snakes the pig merited this association with the Preserver. Provided with a thick coat of fat, no venom can harm him unless it be on the lip. It may be this ability to defy the snake-ordeal which, after its uncleanliness had excepted the hog from human voracity in some regions, assigned it a diabolical character. In rabbinical fable the hog and rat were created by Noah to clear the Ark of filth; but the rats becoming a nuisance, he evoked a cat from the lion's nose.

It is clear that our Asiatic and Norse ancestors never had such a ferocious beast to encounter as the Grisly Bear (*Ursus horribilis*) of America, else the appearances of this animal in Demonology could never have been so respectable. The comparatively timid Asiatic Bear (*U. labiatus*), the small and almost harmless Thibetan species (*U. Thibetanus*), would appear to have preponderated over the fiercer but rarer Bears of the North in giving us the Indo-Germanic fables, in which this animal is, on the whole, a favourite. Emerson finds in the fondness of the English for their national legend of 'Beauty and the Beast' a sign of the Englishman's own nature. 'He is a bear with a soft place in his heart; he says No, and helps you.' The old legend found place in the heart of a particularly representative American also—Theodore Parker, who loved to call his dearest friend 'Bear,' and who, on arriving in Europe, went to Berne to see his favourites, from which its name is derived. The fondness of the Bear for honey— whence its Russian name, *medv-jed*, 'honey-eater'—had probably something to do with its dainty taste for roses and its admiration for female beauty, as told in many myths. In his comparative treat- ment of the mythology of the Bear, De Gubernatis[18] mentions the transformation of King Trisankus into a bear, and connects this with the constellation of the Great Bear; but it may with equal probabil- ity be related to the many fables of princes who remain under the form of a bear until the spell is broken by the kiss of some maiden. It is worthy of note that in the Russian legends the Bear is by no means so amiable as in those of our Western folklore. In one, the Bear-prince lurking in his fountain holds by the beard the king who, while hunting, tries to quench his thirst, and releases him only after a promise to deliver up whatever he has at home without his knowl- edge; the twins, Ivan and Maria, born during his absence, are thus doomed—are concealed, but discovered by the bear, who carries them away. They are saved by help of the bull. When escaping the bear Ivan throws down a comb, which becomes a tangled forest, which, however, the bear penetrates; but the spread-out towel which becomes a lake of fire sends the bear back.[19] It is thus the ferocious Arctic Bear which gives the story its sombre character. Such also is the Russian tale of the Bear with iron hairs, which devastates the kingdom, devouring the inhabitants until Ivan and Helena alone remain; after the two in various ways try to escape, their success is secured by the Bull, which, more kindly than Elisha, blinds the Bear with his horns.[20] (The Bear retires in winter.) In Norwegian story the Bear becomes milder,—a beautiful youth by night, whose wife loses him because she wishes to see him by lamplight: her place is taken by a long-nosed princess, until, by aid of the golden apple and the rose, she recovers her husband. In the Pentameron,[21] Pretiosa, to escape the persecutions of her father, goes into the forest disguised as a she-bear; she nurses and cures the prince, who is enamoured of her, and at his kiss becomes a beautiful maid. The Bear thus has a twofold development in folklore. He used to be killed (13th century) at the end of the Carnival in Rome, as the Devil.[22] The Siberians, if they have killed a bear, hang his skin on a tree and apologise humbly to it, declaring that they did not forge the metal that pierced it, and they meant the arrow for a bird; from which it is plain that they rely more on its stupidity than its good heart. In Canada, when the hunters kill a bear, one of them approaches it and places between his teeth the stem of his pipe, breathes in the bowl, and thus, filling with smoke the animal's mouth, conjures its soul not to be offended at his death. As the bear's ghost makes no reply, the huntsman, in order to know if his prayer is granted, cuts the thread under the bear's tongue, and keeps it until the end of the hunt, when a large fire is kindled, and all the band solemnly throw in it what threads of this kind they have; if these sparkle and vanish, as is natural, it is a sign that the bears are appeased.[23] In Greenland the great demon, at once feared and invoked, especially by fishermen, is Torngarsuk, a huge Bear with a human arm. He is invisible to all except his priests, the Anguekkoks, who are the only physicians of that people.

The extreme point of demonic power has always been held by the Serpent. So much, however, will have to be said of the destructiveness and other characteristics of this animal when we come to consider at length its unique position in Mythology, that I content myself here with a pictorial representation of the Singhalese Demon of Serpents. If any one find himself shuddering at sight of a snake, even in a country where they are few and comparatively harmless, perhaps this figure (11) may suggest the final cause of the shudder.

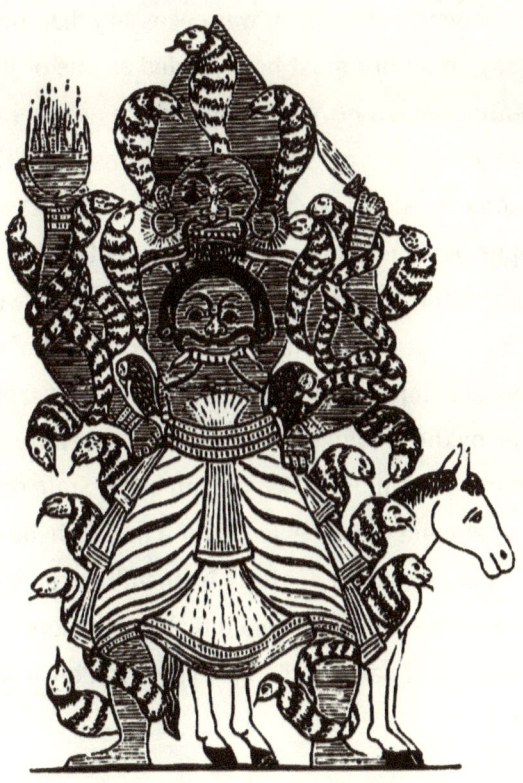

Fig. 11.—Singhalese Demon of Serpents

In conclusion, it may be said that not only every animal feroc-ity, but every force which can be exerted injuriously, has had its demonic representations. Every claw, fang, sting, hoof, horn, has been as certain to be catalogued and labelled in demonology as in physical science. It is remarkable also how superstition rationalises. Thus the horn in the animal world, though sometimes dangerous to man, was more dangerous to animals, which, as foes of the horned animals, were foes to man's interests. The early herdsman knew the value of the horn as a defence against dog and wolf, besides its other utilities. Consequently, although it was necessary that the horn-prin-ciple, so to say, in nature must be regarded as one of its retractile and cruel features, man never demonised the animals whose butt was most dangerous, but for such purpose transferred the horns to the head of some nondescript creature. The horn has thus become a natural weapon of man-demons. The same evolution has taken place in America; for, although among its aboriginal legends we may meet with an occasional demon-buffalo, such are rare and of apocryphal antiquity. The accompanying American figure (12) is from a photo-graph sent me by the President of Vanderbilt University, Tennessee, who found it in an old mound (Red Indian) in the State of Georgia. It is probably as ancient as any example of a human head with horns in the world; and as it could not have been influenced by European notions, it supplies striking evidence that the demonisation of the forces and dangers of nature belongs to the structural action of the human mind.

Fig. 12.—American Indian Demon

NOTES

1 This Protean type of both demon and devil must accompany us so continually through this volume that but little need be said of it in this chapter.
2 Canticles ii. 15.
3 De Gubernatis, II. viii.
4 'Our Life in Japan' (Jephson and Elmhirst, 9th Regiment), Chapman & Hall, 1869.
5 London 'Times,' June 11, 1877.
6 Rep. 488.
7 Literally, goat-song. More probably it has an astrological sense.
8 E.g., the demon Huorco in the 'Pentamerone.'
9 See De Gubernatis' 'Zoological Mythology,' which contains further curious details on this subject.
10 'Myths and Myth-makers.' Boston: Osgood & Co.
11 'Zoological Mythology,' p. 64.
12 Koran, xviii.
13 Wagner. Behold him stop—upon his belly crawl....
   The clever scholar of the students, he!
14 'The Adventures of Tom Sawyer.' London: Chatto & Windus.
15 'Spirit of the Beasts of France,' ch. i.
16 'Rigv.' i. 105, 18, 42, 2; 'Vendidad,' xix. 108. Quoted by De Gubernatis ('Zoolog. Mythology,' ii. 142), to whose invaluable work I am largely indebted in this chapter.
17 'Zoolog. Myth.,' ii. 7. Trübner & Co.
18 'Zoolog. Myth.,' ii. 108 seq.
19 Afanasief, v. 28.
20 Ibid., v. 27.
21 ii. 6 (De Gubernatis, ii. 117).
22 Rather the devil of lust than of cruelty, according to Du Cange: "Occidunt ursum, occiditur diabolus, id est, temptator nostræ carnis."
23 De Plancy (Dict. Inf.), who also relates an amusing legend of the bear who came to a German choir, as seen by a sleepy chorister as he awoke; the naïve narrator of which adds, that this was the devil sent to hold the singers to their duty! The Lives of the Saints abound with legends of pious bears, such as that commemorated along with St. Sergius in Troitska Lavra, near Moscow; and that which St. Gallus was ungracious enough to banish from Switzerland after it had brought him firewood in proof of its conversion.

Chapter VI
Enemies

Aryas, Dasyus, Nagas — Yakkhos — Lycians — Ethiopians — Hirpini —Polites
— Sosipolis — Were-wolves — Goths and Scythians — Giants and Dwarfs —
Berserkers — Britons — Iceland — Mimacs — Gog and Magog

WE PAINT THE DEVIL black, says George Herbert. On the other hand the negro paints him white, with reason enough. The name of the Devil at Mozambique is Muzungu Maya, or Wicked White Man. Of this demon they make little images of extreme hideousness, which are kept by people on the coast, and occasionally displayed, in the belief that if the White Devil is lurking near them he will vanish out of sheer disgust with a glimpse of his own ugliness. The hereditary horror of the kidnapper displayed in this droll superstition may possibly have been assisted by the familiarity with all things infernal represented in the language of the white sailors visiting the coast. Captain Basil Hall, on visiting Mozambique about fifty years ago, found that the native dignitaries had appropriated the titles of English noblemen, and a dumpy little Duke of Devonshire met him with his whole vocabulary of English,—'How do you do, sir. Very glad see you. Damn your eyes. Johanna man like English very much. God damn. That very good? Eh? Devilish hot, sir. What news? Hope your ship stay too long while very. Damn my eye. Very fine day.'

In most parts of India Siva also is painted white, which would indicate that there too was found reason to associate diabolism with the white face. It is said the Thugs spared Englishmen because their white faces suggested relationship to Siva. In some of the ancient Indian books the monster whom Indra slew, Vritra, is called Dasyu (enemy), a name which in the Vedas designates the Aborigines as contrasted with the Aryans of the North. 'In the old Sanskrit, in the hymns of the Veda, ârya occurs frequently as a national name and as a name of honour, comprising the worshippers of the gods of the Brahmans, as opposed to their enemies, who are called in the Veda Dasyus. Thus one of the gods, Indra, who in some respects answers to the Greek Zeus, is invoked in the following words (Rigveda, i. 57, 8):—'Know thou the Aryas, O Indra, and those who are Dasyus; punish the lawless, and deliver them unto thy servant! Be thou the mighty helper of the worshippers, and I will praise all these thy deeds at the festivals.'[1]

Naglok (snakeland) was at an early period a Hindu name for hell. But the Nagas were not real snakes,—in that case they might have fared better,—but an aboriginal tribe in Ceylon, believed by the Hindus to be of serpent origin,—'naga' being an epithet for 'native.'[2] The Singhalese, on the other hand, have adapted the popular name for demons in India, 'Rakshasa,' in their *Rakseyo*, a tribe of invisible cannibals without supernatural powers (except invisibility), who no doubt merely embody the traditions of some early race. The dreaded powers were from another tribe designated Yakkhos (demons), and believed to have the power of rendering themselves invisible. Buddha's victories over these demonic beings are related in the 'Mahawanso.' 'It was known (by inspiration) by the vanquishers that in Lanka, filled by yakkhos, ... would be the place where his religion would be glorified. In like manner, knowing that in the centre of Lanka, on the delightful bank of a river, ... in the agreeable Mahanaga garden, ... there was a great assembly of the principal yakkhos, ... the deity of happy advent, approaching that great congregation, ... immediately over their heads hovering in the air, ... struck terror into them by rains, tempests, and darkness. The yakkhos, overwhelmed with awe, supplicated of the vanquisher to be released from their terror.... The consoling vanquisher thus replied: 'I will release ye yakkhos from this your terror and affliction: give ye unto me here by unanimous consent a place for me to alight on.' All these yakkhos replied: 'Lord, we confer on thee the whole of Lanka, grant thou comfort to us.' The vanquisher thereupon dispelling their terror and cold shivering, and spreading his carpet of skin on the spot bestowed on him, he there seated himself. He then caused the aforesaid carpet, refulgent with a fringe of flames, to extend itself on all sides: they, scorched by the flames, (receding) stood around on the shores (of the island) terrified. The Saviour then caused the delightful isle of Giri to approach for them. As soon as they transferred themselves thereto (to escape the conflagration), he restored it to its former position.'[3]

This legend, which reminds one irresistibly of the expulsion of reptiles by saints from Ireland, and other Western regions, is the more interesting if it be considered that these Yakkhos are the Sanskrit Yakshas, attendants on Kuvera, the god of wealth, employed in the care of his garden and treasures. They are regarded as generally inoffensive. The transfer by English authorities of the Tasmanians from their native island to another, with the result of their extermination, may suggest the possible origin of the story of Giri.

Buddha's dealings with the serpent-men or nagas is related as follows in the same volume:—

'The vanquisher (*i.e.*, of the five deadly sins), ... in the fifth year of his buddhahood, while residing at the garden of (the prince) Jeto, observing that, on account of a disputed claim for a gem-set throne between the naga Mahodaro and a similar Chalodaro, a maternal uncle and nephew, a conflict was at hand, ... taking with him his sacred dish and robes, out of compassion to the nagas, visited Nagadipo.... These mountain nagas were, moreover, gifted with supernatural powers.... The Saviour and dispeller of the darkness of sin, poising himself in the air over the centre of the assembly, caused a terrifying darkness to these nagas. Attending to the prayer of the dismayed nagas, he again called forth the light of day. They, overjoyed at having seen the deity of felicitous advent, bowed down at the feet of the divine teacher. To them the vanquisher preached a sermon of reconciliation. Both parties rejoicing thereat, made an offering of the gem-throne to the divine sage. The divine teacher, alighting on the earth, seated himself on the throne, and was served by the naga kings with celestial food and beverage. The lord of the universe procured for eighty kotis of nagas, dwelling on land and in the waters, the salvation of the faith and the state of piety.'

At every step in the conversion of the native Singhalese,—the demons and serpent-men,—Buddha and his apostles are represented as being attended by the *devas*,—the deities of India,—who are spoken of as if glad to become menials of the new religion. But we find Zoroaster using this term in a demonic sense, and describing alien worshippers as children of the Devas (a Semite would say, Sons of Belial). And in the conventional Persian pictures of the Last Judgment (moslem), the archfiend has the Hindu complexion. A similar phenomenon may be observed in various regions. In the mediæval frescoes of Moscow, representing infernal tortures, it is not very difficult to pick out devils representing the physical characteristics of most of the races with which the Muscovite has struggled in early times. There are also black Ethiopians among them, which may be a result of devils being considered the brood of Tchernibog, god of Darkness; but may also, not impossibly, have come of such apocryphal narratives as that ascribed to St. Augustine. 'I was already Bishop of Hippo when I went into Ethiopia with some servants of Christ, there to preach the gospel. In this country we saw many men and women without heads, who had two great eyes in their breasts; and in countries still more southerly we saw a people who had but one eye in their foreheads.'[4]

In considering animal demons, the primitive demonisation of the Wolf has been discussed. But it is mainly as a transformation of man and a type of savage foes that this animal has been a prominent figure in Mythology.

Professor Max Müller has made it tolerably clear that Bellerophon means Slayer of the Hairy; and that Belleros is the transliteration of Sanskrit *varvara*, a term applied to the dark Aborigines by their Aryan invaders, equivalent to barbarians.[5] This points us for the origin of the title rather to Bellerophon's conquest of the Lycians, or Wolf-men, than to his victory over the Chimæra. The story of Lycaon and his sons—barbarians defying the gods and devouring human flesh—turned into wolves by Zeus, connects itself with the Lycians (hairy, wolfish barbarians), whom Bellerophon conquered.

It was not always, however, the deity that conquered in such encounters. In the myth of Soracte, the Wolf is seen able to hold his own against the gods. Soranus, worshipped on Mount Soracte, was at Rome the god of Light, and is identified with Apollo by Virgil.[6] A legend states that he became associated with the infernal gods, though called Diespiter, because of the sulphurous exhalations from the side of Mount Soracte. It is said that once when some shepherds were performing a sacrifice, some wolves seized the flesh; the shepherds, following them, were killed by the poisonous vapours of the mountain to which the wolves retreated. An oracle gave out that this was a punishment for their pursuing the sacred animals; and a general pestilence also having followed, it was declared that it could only cease if the people were all changed to wolves and lived by prey. Hence the Hirpini, from the Sabine '*hirpus*,' a wolf. The story is a variant of that of the Hirpinian Samnites, who were said to have received their name from their ancestors having followed a sacred wolf when seeking their new home. The Wolf ceremonies were, like the Roman Lupercalia, for purposes of purification. The worshippers ran naked through blazing fires. The annual festival, which Strabo describes as occurring in the grove of Feronia, goddess of Nature, became at last a sort of fair. Its history, however, is very significant of the formidable character of the Hirpini, or Wolf-tribe, which could alone have given rise to such euphemistic celebrations of the wolf.

It is interesting to note that in some regions this wolf of super-stition was domesticated into a dog. Pierius says there was a temple of Vulcan in Mount Ætna, in whose grove were dogs that fawned on the pious, but rent the polluted worshippers. It will be seen by the left form of Fig. 13 that the wolf had a diminution, in pictorial representation similar to that which the canine Lares underwent (p. 135). This picture is referred by John Beaumont[7] to Cartarius' work on 'The Images of the Gods of the Ancients;' the form wearing a wolf's skin and head is that of the demon Polites, who infested Temesa in Italy, according to a story related by Pausanias. Ulysses, in his wanderings, having come to this town, one of his companions was stoned to death for having ravished a virgin; after which his ghost appeared in form of this demon, which had to be appeased, by the direction of the oracle of Apollo, by the annual sacrifice to him of the most beautiful virgin in the place. Euthymus, enamoured of a virgin about to be so offered, gave battle to this demon, and, having expelled him from the country, married the virgin. However, since the infernal powers cannot be deprived of their rights without sub-stitution, this saviour of Temesa disappeared in the river Cæcinus.

Fig. 13.—Italian and Roman Genii

The form on the right in Fig. 13 represents the genius of the city of Rome, and is found on some of Hadrian's coins; he holds the cornucopia and the sacrificial dish. The child and the serpent in the same picture represent the origin of the demonic character attributed to the Eleans by the Arcadians. This child-and-serpent symbol, which bears resemblance to certain variants of Bel and the Dragon, no doubt was brought to Elea, or Velia in Italy, by the Phocæans, when they abandoned their Ionian homes rather than submit to Cyrus, and founded that town, B.C.544. The two forms were jointly worshipped with annual sacrifices in the temple of Lucina, under the name Sosipolis. The legend of this title is related by

Pausanias. When the Arcadians invaded the Eleans, a woman came to the Elean commander with an infant at her breast, and said that she had been admonished in a dream to place her child in front of the army. This was done; as the Arcadians approached the child was changed to a serpent, and, astounded at the prodigy, they fled without giving battle. The child was represented by the Eleans decorated with stars, and holding the cornucopia; by the Arcadians, no doubt, in a less celestial way. It is not uncommon in Mythology to find the most dangerous demons represented under some guise of weakness, as, for instance, among the South Africans, some of whom recently informed English officers that the Galeikas were led against them by a terrible sorcerer in the form of a hare. The most fearful traditional demon ever slain by hero in Japan was Shuden Dozi—the Child-faced Drinker. In Ceylon the apparition of a demon is said to be frequently under the form of a woman with a child in her arms.

Many animal demons are mere fables for the ferocity of human tribes. The Were-wolf superstition, which exists still in Russia, where the transformed monster is called *volkodlák* (*volk*, a wolf, and *dlak*, hair), might even have originated in the costume of Norse barbarians and huntsmen. The belief was always more or less rationalised, resembling that held by Verstegan three hundred years ago, and which may be regarded as prevalent among both the English and Flemish people of his day. 'These Were-wolves,' he says, 'are certain sorcerers, who, having anointed their bodies with an ointment they make by the instinct of the devil, and putting on a certain enchanted girdle, do not only unto the view of others seem as wolves, but to their own thinking have both the nature and shape of wolves so long as they wear the said girdle; and they do dispose themselves as very wolves, in worrying and killing, and waste of human creatures.' During the Franco-German war of 1870–71, a family of ladies on the German side of the Rhine, sitting up all night in apprehension, related to me such stories of the 'Turcos' that I have since found no difficulty in understanding the belief in weird and præternatural wolves which once filled Europe with horror. The facility with which the old Lycian wolf-girdle, so to say, was caught up and worn in so many countries where race-wars were chronic for many ages, renders it nearly certain that this superstition (Lycanthropy), however it may have originated, was continued through the custom of ascribing demonic characteristics to hostile and fierce races. It has been, indeed, a general opinion that the theoretical belief originated in the Pythagorean doctrine of metempsychosis. Thus Shakspere:—

> Thou almost makest me waver in my faith,
> To hold opinion with Pythagoras,
> That souls of animals infuse themselves
> Into the trunks of men: thy currish spirit
> Governed a wolf, who, hanged for human slaughter,
> Even from the gallows did his fell soul fleet,
> And whilst thou layest in thy unhallowed dam
> Infused itself in thee; for thy desires
> Are wolfish, bloody, starved, and ravenous.

But the superstition is much older than Pythagoras, who, no doubt, tried to turn it into a moral theory of retributions,—as indeed did Plato in his story of the Vision of Er the Armenian.

Professor Weber and others have adduced evidence indicating

that although belief in the transformation of men into beasts was not developed in the Vedic age of India, the matrix of it was there. But of our main fact—the association of demonic characters with certain tribes—India has presented many examples. In the mountains of Travancore there are tribes which are still generally believed to be on terms of especial familiarity with the devils of that region; and the dwellers on the plains relate that on these mountains gigantic demons, sixteen or seventeen feet high, may sometimes be seen hurling firebrands at each other.

Professor Monier Williams contributes an interesting note concerning this general phase of South-Indian demonology. 'Furthermore, it must not be forgotten that although a belief in devils and homage to bhutas, or spirits, of all kinds is common all over India, yet what is called devil-worship is far more systematically practised in the South of India and Ceylon than in the North. And the reason may be that as the invading Aryans advanced towards Southern India, they found portions of it peopled by wild aboriginal savages, whose behaviour and aspect appeared to them to resemble that of devils. The Aryan mind, therefore, naturally pictured to itself the regions of the South as the chief resort and stronghold of the demon race, and the dread of demonical agency became more deeply rooted in Southern India than in the North. Curiously enough, too, it is commonly believed in Southern India that every wicked man contributes by his death to swell the ever-increasing ranks of devil legions. His evil passions do not die with him; they are intensified, concentrated, and perpetuated in the form of a malignant and mischievous spirit.'[8]

It is obvious that this principle may be extended from individuals to entire tribes. The Cimmerians were regarded as dwelling in a land allied with hell. In the legend of the Alhambra, as told by Washington Irving, the astrologer warns the Moorish king that the beautiful damsel is no doubt one of those Gothic sorceresses of whom they have heard so much. Although, as we have seen, England was regarded on the Continent as an island of demons because of its northern latitude, probably some of its tribes were of a character dangerous enough to prolong the superstition. The nightmare elves were believed to come from England, and to hurry away through the keyholes at daybreak, saying 'The bells are calling in England.'[9] Visigoth probably left us our word *bigot*; and 'Goths and Vandals' sometimes designate English roughs, as 'Turks' those of Constantinople. Herodotus says the Scythians of the Black Sea regarded the Neurians as wizards, who transformed themselves into wolves for a few days annually; but the Scythians themselves are said by Herodotus to have sprung from a monster, half-woman half-serpent; and possibly the association of the Scotch with the Scythians by the Germans, who called them both *Scutten*, had something to do with the uncanny character ascribed to the British Isles. Sir Walter Raleigh described the Red Men of America as gigantic monsters. 'Red Devils' is still the pioneer's epithet for them in the Far West. The hairy Dukes of Esau were connected with the goat, and demonised as Edom; and Ishmael was not believed much better by the more peaceful Semitic tribes. Such notions are akin to those which many now have of the Thugs and Bashi-Bazouks, and are too uniform and natural to tax much the ingenuity of Comparative Mythology.

Underlying many of the legends of giants and dwarfs may be found a similar demonologic formation. A principle of natural selection would explain the existence of tribes, which, though of small stature, are able to hold their own against the larger and more powerful by their superior cunning. That such equalisation of apparently unequal forces has been known in pre-historic ages may be gathered from many fables. Before Bali, the monarch already mentioned, whose power alarmed the gods themselves, Vishnu appeared as a dwarf, asking only so much land as he could measure with three steps; the apparently ridiculous request granted, the god strode over the whole earth with two steps and brought his third on the head of Bali. In Scandinavian fable we have the young giantess coming to her mother with the plough and ploughman in her apron, which she had picked up in the field. To her child's inquiry, 'What sort of beetle is this I found wriggling in the sand?' the giantess replies, 'Go put it back in the place where thou hast found it. We must be gone out of this land, for these little people will dwell in it.'

The Sagas contain many stories which, while written in glorification of the 'giant' race, relate the destruction of their chiefs by the magical powers of the dwarfs. I must limit myself to a few notes on the Ynglinga Saga. 'In Swithiod,' we are told, 'are many great domains, and many wonderful races of men, and many kinds of languages. There are giants, and there are dwarfs, and there are also blue men. There are wild beasts, and dreadfully large dragons.' We learn that in Asaland was a great chief, Odin, who went out to conquer Vanaland. The Vanalanders are declared to have magic arts,—such as are ascribed to Finns and Lapps to this day by the more ignorant of their neighbours. But that the people of Asaland learned their magic charms. 'Odin was the cleverest of them all, and from him all the others learned their magic arts.' 'Odin could make his enemies in battle blind, or deaf, or terror-struck, and their weapons so blunt that they could no more cut than a willow twig; on the other hand, his men rushed forward without armour, were as mad as dogs or wolves, bit their shields, and were as strong as bears or wild bulls, and killed people at a blow, and neither fire nor iron told upon them. These were called Berserkers.' (From *ber*, bear, and *serkr*, sark or coat; the word being probably, as Maurer says, a survival of an earlier belief in the transformation of men into bears.) But the successors of Odin did not preserve his occult power. Svegdir, for instance, saw a large stone and a dwarf at the door entering in it. The dwarf called him to come in and he should see Odin. 'Swedger ran into the stone, which instantly closed behind him, and Swedger never came back.' The witchcraft of the Finn people is said to have led Vanlandi (Svegdir's son) to his death by Mara (night-mare). Vanlandi's son too, Visbur, fell a victim to sorcery. Such legends as these, and many others which may be found in Sturleson's Heimskringla, have influenced our popular stories whose interest turns on the skill with which some little Jack or Thumbling overcomes his adversary by superior cunning.

Superstitions concerning dwarf-powers are especially rife in Northumberland, where they used to be called *Duergar*, and they were thought to abound on the hills between Rothbury and Elsdon.

They mislead with torches. One story relates that a traveller, beguiled at night into a hut where a dwarf prepared a comfortable fire for him, found himself when daylight returned sitting upon the edge of a deep rugged precipice, where the slightest movement had caused him to be dashed to pieces.[10] The Northumbrian stories generally, however, do not bear the emphasis of having grown out of aboriginal conditions, or even of having been borrowed for such. The legends of Scotland, and of the South-West of England, appear to me much more suggestive of original struggles between large races and small. They are recalled by the superstitions which still linger in Norway concerning the Lapps, who are said to carry on unholy dealings with gnomes.

In the last century the 'Brownie' was commonly spoken of in Scotland as appearing in shape of 'a tall man,' and the name seems to refer to the *brown* complexion of that bogey, and its long brown hair, hardly Scottish.[11] It is generally the case that Second Sight, which once attained the dignity of being called 'Deuteroscopia,' sees a doomed man or woman shrink to the size of a dwarf. The 'tall man' is not far off in such cases. 'In some age of the world more remote than even that of Alypos,' says Hugh Miller, 'the whole of Britain was peopled by giants—a fact amply supported by early English historians and the traditions of the North of Scotland. Diocletian, king of Syria, say the historians, had thirty-three daughters, who, like the daughters of Danaus, killed their husbands on their wedding night. The king, their father, in abhorrence of the crime, crowded them all into a ship, which he abandoned to the mercy of the waves, and which was drifted by tides and winds till it arrived on the coast of

Britain, then an uninhabited island. There they lived solitary, sub-sisting on roots and berries, the natural produce of the soil, until an order of demons, becoming enamoured of them, took them for their wives; and a tribe of giants, who must be regarded as the true abo-rigines of the country, if indeed the demons have not a prior claim, were the fruit of these marriages. Less fortunate, however, than even their prototypes the Cyclops, the whole tribe was extirpated a few ages after by Brutus the parricide, who, with a valour to which mere bulk could offer no effectual resistance, overthrew Gog-Magog and Termagol, and a whole host of others with names equally terrible. Tradition is less explicit than the historians in what relates to the origin and extinction of the race, but its narratives of their prowess are more minute. There is a large and ponderous stone in the parish of Edderston which a giantess of the tribe is said to have flung from the point of a spindle across the Dornoch Firth; and another, within a few miles of Dingwall, still larger and more ponderous, which was thrown by a person of the same family, and which still bears the marks of a gigantic finger and thumb.'[12]

Perhaps we may find the mythological descendants of these Titans, and also of the Druids, in the so-called 'Great Men' once dreaded by Highlanders. The natives of South Uist believed that a valley, called Glenslyte, situated between two mountains on the east side of the island, was haunted by these Great Men, and that if any one entered the valley without formally resigning themselves to the conduct of those beings, they would infallibly become mad. Martin, having remonstrated with the people against this superstition, was told of a woman's having come out of the valley a lunatic because she had not uttered the spell of three sentences. They also told him of voices heard in the air. The Brownie ('a tall man with very long brown hair'), who has cow's milk poured out for him on a hill in the same region, probably of this giant tribe, might easily have been demonised at the time when the Druids were giving St. Columba so much trouble, and trying to retain their influence over the people by professing supernatural powers.[13]

The man of the smaller stature, making up for his inferiority by invention, perhaps first forged the sword, the coat of mail, and the shield, and so confronted the giant with success. The god with the Hammer might thus supersede the god of the Flint Spear. Magic art seemed to have rendered invulnerable the man from whom the arrow rebounded.

It would appear from King Olaf Tryggvason's Saga that nine hundred years ago the Icelanders and the Danes reciprocally regarded each other as giants and dwarfs. The Icelanders indited lampoons against the Danes which allude to their diminutive size:—

> The gallant Harald in the field
> Between his legs lets drop his shield,
> Into a pony he was changed, &c.

On the other hand, the Danes had by no means a contemptuous idea of their Icelandic enemies, as the following narrative from Heimskringla proves. 'King Harald told a warlock to hie to Iceland in some altered shape, and to try what he could learn there to tell him: and he set out in the shape of a whale. And when he came near to the land he went to the west side of Iceland, north around the land, when he saw all the mountains and hills full of land-serpents, some great, some small. When he came to Vapnafiord he went in towards the land, intending to go on shore; but a huge dragon rushed down the dale against him, with a train of serpents, paddocks, and toads, that blew poison towards him. Then he turned to go westward around the land as far as Eyafiord, and he went into the fiord. Then a bird flew against him, which was so great that its wings stretched over the mountains on either side of the fiord, and many birds, great and small, with it. Then he swam further west, and then south into Breidafiord. When he came into the fiord a large grey bull ran against him, wading into the sea, and bellowing fearfully, and he was followed by a crowd of land-serpents. From thence he went round by Reikaness and wanted to land at Vikarsted, but there came down a hill-giant against him with an iron staff in his hands. He was a head higher than the mountains, and many other giants followed him.' The most seductive Hesperian gardens of the South and East do not appear to have been so thoroughly guarded or defended as Iceland, and one can hardly call it cowardice when (after the wizard-whale brought back the log of its voyage) it is recorded: 'Then the Danish king turned about with his fleet and sailed back to Denmark.'

It is a sufficiently curious fact that the Mimacs, aborigines of Nova Scotia,[14] were found with a whale-story, already referred to (p. 46), so much like this. They also have the legend of an ancient warrior named Booin, who possessed the præternatural powers especially ascribed to Odin, those of raising storms, causing excessive cold, increasing or diminishing his size, and assuming any shape. Besides the fearful race of gigantic ice-demons dreaded by this tribe, as elsewhere stated (p. 84), they dread also a yellow-horned dragon called Cheepichealm, (whose form the great Booin sometimes assumes). They make offerings to the new moon. They believe in pixies, calling them Wigguladum-moochkik, 'very little people.' They anciently believed in two great spirits, good and evil, both called Manitoos; since their contact with christians only the evil one has been so called.

The entire *motif* of the Mimac Demonology is, to my mind, that of early conflicts with some formidable races. It is to be hoped that travellers will pay more attention to this unique race before it has ceased to exist. The Chinese theory of genii is almost exactly that of the Mimacs. The Chinese genii are now small as a moth, now fill the world; can assume any form; they command demons; they never die, but, at the end of some centuries, ride to heaven on a dragon's back.[15] Ordinarily the Chinese genii use the yellow heron as an aerial courser. The Mimacs believe in a large præternatural water-bird, Culloo, which devours ordinary people, but bears on its back those who can tame it by magic.

Mr. Mayers, in his 'Chinese Reader's Manual,' suggests that the designation of Formosa as 'Isles of the Genii' (San Shén Shan) by the Chinese, has some reference to their early attempts at colonisation in Japan. Su Fuh, a necromancer, who lived B.C. 219, is said to have announced their discovery, and at the head of a troop of young men and maidens, voyaged with an expedition towards them, but, when within sight of the magic islands, were driven back by contrary winds.

Gog and Magog stand in London Guildhall, though much diminished in stature, to suit the English muscles that had to bear them in processions, monuments of the præternatural size attributed to the enemies which the Aryan race encountered in its great westward migrations. Even to-day, when the progress of civilisation is harassed by untamed Scythian hordes, how strangely fall upon our ears the ancient legends and prophecies concerning them!

> Thus saith the Lord Jehovah:
> Behold I am against thee, O Gog,
> Prince of Rosh, of Meshech, and of Tubul:
> And I will turn thee back, and leave but the sixth part of thee;
> And I will cause thee to come up from the north parts,
> And will bring thee upon the mountains of Israel:
> And I will smite thy bow out of thy left hand,
> And will cause thine arrows to fall from thy right hand.
> Thou shalt fall upon the mountains of Israel,
> Thou and all thy bands.[16]

In the Koran it is related of Dhulkarnein:—'He journeyed from south to north until he came between the two mountains, beneath which he found a people who could scarce understand what was said. And they said, O Dhulkarnein, verily Gog and Magog waste the land; shall we, therefore, pay thee tribute, on condition that thou build a rampart between us and them? He answered, The power wherewith my Lord hath strengthened me is better than your tribute; but assist me strenuously and I will set a strong wall between you and them.... Wherefore when this wall was finished, Gog and Magog could not scale it, neither could they dig through it. And Dhulkarnein said, This is a mercy from my Lord; but when the prediction of my Lord shall come to be fulfilled, he will reduce the wall to dust.'

The terror inspired by these barbarians is reflected in the prophecies of their certain irruption from their supernaturally-built fastnesses; as in Ezekiel:—

> Thou shalt ascend and come like a storm,
> Thou shalt be like a cloud to cover the land,
> Thou and all thy bands,
> And many people with thee;

and in the Koran, 'Gog and Magog shall have a passage open for them, and they shall hasten from every high hill;' and in the Apocalypse, 'Satan shall be loosed out of his prison, and shall go out to deceive the nations which are in the four quarters of the earth, Gog and Magog, to gather them in battle: the number of whom is as the sand of the sea.' Five centuries ago Sir John Maundeville was telling in England the legend he had heard in the East. 'In that same regioun ben the mountaynes of Caspye, that men clepen Uber in the contree. Betwene the mountaynes the Jews of 10 lynages ben enclosed, that men clepen Gothe and Magothe: and they mowe not gon out on no syde. There weren enclosed 22 kynges, with hire peple, that dwelleden betwene the mountayns of Sythe. There King Alisandre chacede hem betwene the mountaynes, and there he thought for to enclose hem thorghe work of his men. But when he saughe that he might not doon it, ne bringe it to an ende, he preyed to God of Nature, that he wolde performe that that he had begoune. And all were it so, that he was a Payneme, and not worthi to ben herd, zit God of his grace closed the mountaynes to gydre: so that thei dwellen there, all fast ylokked and enclosed with highe mountaynes all aboute, saf only on o syde; and on that syde is the See of Caspye.'

NOTES

1   Max Müller, 'Science of Language,' i. 275.
2   The term is now used very vaguely. Mr. Talboys Wheeler, speaking of the 'Scythic Nagas' (Hist. of India, i. 147), says: 'In process of time these Nagas became identified with serpents, and the result has been a strange confusion between serpents and human beings.' In the 'Padma Purana' we read of 'serpent-like men.' (See my 'Sacred Anthology,' p. 263.)
3   'Mahawanso' (Turnour), pp. 3, 6.
4   Ser. xxxiii. Hardly consistent with De Civ. Dei, xvi. 8.
5   'Chips,' ii.
6   'Sancti custos Soractis Apollo.'—Æn. xi. 785.
7   'Treatise of Spirits,' by John Beaumont, Gent., London, 1705.
8   London 'Times,' June 11, 1877.
9   Wuttke, 'Volksaberglaube,' 402. Pliny (iv. 16) says: 'Albion insula sic dicta ab albis rupibus quas mare alluit.' This etymon of Albion from the white cliffs is very questionable; but, since Alb and Elf are generally related, it might have suggested the notion about English demons. Heine identifies the 'White Island,' or Pluto's realm of Continental folklore, as England.
10 Richardson's 'Borderer's Fable-Book,' vi. 97.
11 Martin, Appendix to Report on 'Ossian,' p. 310.
12 'Scenes and Legends,' p. 13.
13 Dr. James Browne's 'History of the Highlands,' p. 113.
14 'North American Review,' January 1871.
15 Dennys, p. 81 et seq.
16 Ezekiel xxxix.

Chapter VII
Barrenness

IN THEIR ADORATION of rain-giving Indra as also a solar majesty, the ancient Hindus seem to have been fully aware of his inconsistent habits. 'Thy inebriety is most intense,' exclaims the eulogist, and soothingly adds, 'Thou desirest that both thy inebriety and thy benef-icence should be the means of destroying enemies and distributing riches.'[1] Against famine is invoked the thunderbolt of Indra, and it is likened to the terrible Tvashtri, in whose fearful shape (pure fire) Agni once appeared to the terror of gods and men.[2] This Tvashtri was not an evil being himself, but, as we have seen, an artificer for the gods similar to Vulcan; he was, however, father of a three-headed monster who has been identified with Vritra. Though these early worshippers recognised that their chief trouble was connected with 'glaring heat' (which Tvashtri seems to mean in the passage just referred to), Indra's celebrants beheld him superseding his father Dyaus, and reigning in the day's splendour as well as in the cloud's bounty. This monopolist of parts in their theogony anticipated Jupiter Pluvius. Vedic mythology is pervaded with stories of the demons that arrested the rain and stole the cloud-cows of Indra—shutting them away in caves,—and the god is endlessly praised for dealing death to such. He slays Vritra, the 'rain-arresting,' and Dribhika, Bala, Urana, Arbuda, 'devouring Swasna,' 'unabsorbable Súshna,' Pipru, Namuchi, Rudhikrá, Varchin and his hundred thousand descendants;[3] the deadly strangling serpent Ahi, especial type of Drouth as it dries up rivers; and through all these combats with the alleged authors of the recurring Barrenness and Famine, as most of these monsters were, the seat of the evil was the Sun-god's adorable self!

Almost pathetic does the long and vast history appear just now, when competent men of science are giving us good reason to believe that right knowledge of the sun, and the relation of its spots to the rainfall, might have covered India with ways and means which would have adapted the entire realm to its environment, and wrested from Indra his hostile thunderbolt—the sunstroke of famine. The Hindus have covered their lands with temples raised to propitiate and deprecate the demons, and to invoke the deities against such sources of drouth and famine. Had they concluded that famine was the result of inexactly quartered sun-dials, the land would have been covered with perfect sun-dials; but the famine would have been more destructive, because of the increasing withdrawal of mind and energy from the true cause, and its implied answer. Even so were conflagrations in London attributed to inexact city clocks; the clocks would become perfect, the conflagrations more numerous, through misdirection of vigilance. But how much wiser are we of Christendom than the Hindus? They have adapted their country perfectly for propitiation of famine-demons that do not exist, at a cost which would long ago have rendered them secure from the famine-forces that do exist. We have similarly covered Christendom with a complete system of securities against hells and devils and wrathful deities that do not exist, while around our churches, chapels, cathedrals, are the actually-existent seething hells of pauperism, shame, and crime.

'Nothing can advance art in any district of this accursed machine-and-devil-driven England until she changes her mind in many things.' So wrote John Ruskin recently. Of course, so long as the machine toils and earns wealth and other power which still goes to support and further social and ecclesiastical forms, constituted with reference to salvation from a devil or demons no longer believed in, the phrase 'machine-and-devil-driven' is true. Until the invention and enterprise of the nation are administered in the interest of right ideas, we may still sigh, like John Sterling, for 'a dozen men to stand up for ideas as Cobden and his friends do for machinery.' But it still remains as true that all the machinery and wealth of England devoted to man might make its every home happy, and educate every inhabitant, as that every idolatrous temple in India might be commuted into a shield against famine.

Our astronomers and economists have enabled us to see clearly how the case is with the country whose temples offer no obstruction to christian vision. The facts point to the conclusion that the sun-spots reach their maximum and minimum of intensity at intervals of eleven years, and that their high activity is attended with frequent fluctuations of the magnetic needle, and increased rainfall. In 1811, and since then, famines in India have, with one exception, followed years of minimum sun-spots.[4] These facts are sufficiently well attested to warrant the belief that English science and skill will be able to realise in India the provision which Joseph is said to have made for the seven lean years of which Pharaoh dreamed.

Until that happy era shall arrive, the poor Hindus will only go on alternately adoring and propitiating the sun, as its benign or its cruel influences shall fall upon them. The artist Turner said, 'The sun is God.' The superb effects of light in Turner's pictures could hardly have come from any but a sun-worshipper dwelling amid fogs. Unfamiliarity often breeds reverence. There are few countries in which the sun, when it does shine, is so likely to be greeted with enthusiasm, and observed in all its variations of splendour, as one in which its appearance is rare. Yet the superstition inherited from regions where the sun is equally a desolation was strong enough to blot out its glory in the mind of a writer famous in his time, Tobias Swinden, M.A., who wrote a work to prove the sun to be the abode of the damned.[5] The speculation may now appear only curious, but, probably, it is no more curious than a hundred years from now will seem to all the vulgar notion of future fiery torments for mankind, the scriptural necessity of which led the fanciful rector to his gro-tesque conclusion. These two extremes—the Sun-worship of Turner, the Sun-horror of Swinden,—survivals in England, represent the two antagonistic aspects of the sun, which were of overwhelming import to those who dwelt beneath its greatest potency. His ill-humour, or his hunger and thirst, in any year transformed the earth to a desert, and dealt death to thousands.

In countries where drouth, barrenness, and consequent fam-ine were occasional, as in India, it would be an inevitable result that they would represent the varying moods of a powerful will, and in such regions we naturally find the most extensive appliances for propitiation. The preponderant number of fat years would tell powerfully on the popular imagination in favour of priestly intercession, and the advantage of sacrifices to the great Hunger-demon who sometimes consumed the seeds of the earth. But in countries where barrenness was an ever-present, visible, unvarying fact, the Demon of the Desert would represent Necessity, a power not to be coaxed or changed. People dwelling in distant lands might invent theoretical myths to account for the desert. It might be an accident resulting from the Sun-god having given up his chariot one day to an inexperienced driver who came too close to the earth. But to those who lived beside the desert it could only seem an infernal realm, quite irrecoverable. The ancient civilisation of Egypt, so full of grandeur, might, in good part, have been due to the lesson taught them by the desert, that they could not change the conditions around them by any entreaties, but must make the best of what was left. If such, indeed, was the force that built the ancient civilisation whose monuments remain so magnificent in their ruins, its decay might be equally accounted for when that primitive faith passed into a theological phase. For as Necessity is the mother of invention, Fate is fatal to the same. Belief in facts, and laws fixed in the organic nature of things, stimulates man to study them and constitute his life with reference to them; but belief that things are fixed by the arbitrary decree of an individual power is the final sentence of enterprise. Fate might thus steadily bring to ruin the grandest achievements of Necessity.

Had we only the true history of the Sphinx—the Binder—we

might find it a landmark between the rise and decline of Egyptian civilisation. When the great Limitation surrounding the powers of man was first personified with that mystical grandeur, it would stand in the desert not as the riddle but its solution. No such monument was ever raised by Doubt. But once personified and outwardly shaped, the external Binder must bind thought as well; nay, will throttle thought if it cannot pierce through the stone and discover the meaning of it. 'How true is that old fable of the Sphinx who sat by the wayside propounding her riddle to the passengers, which if they could not answer she destroyed them! Such a Sphinx is this Life of ours to all men and societies of men. Nature, like the Sphinx, is of womanly celestial loveliness and tenderness; the face and bosom of a goddess, but ending in claws and the body of a lioness. There is in her a celestial beauty,—which means celestial order, pliancy to wisdom; but there is also a darkness, a ferocity, fatality, which are infernal. She is a goddess, but one not yet disimprisoned; one still half-imprisoned,—the articulate, lovely still encased in the inarticulate, chaotic. How true! And does she not propound her riddles to us? Of each man she asks daily, in mild voice, yet with a terrible significance, 'Knowest thou the meaning of this Day? What thou canst do To-day, wisely attempt to do.' Nature, Universe, Destiny, Existence, howsoever we name this grand unnameable Fact, in the midst of which we live and struggle, is as a heavenly bride and con-quest to the wise and brave, to them who can discern her behests and do them; a destroying fiend to them who cannot. Answer her riddle, it is well with thee. Answer it not, pass on regarding it not, it will answer itself; the solution for thee is a thing of teeth and claws;

Nature to thee is a dumb lioness, deaf to thy pleadings, fiercely devouring. Thou art not now her victorious bridegroom; thou art her mangled victim, scattered on the precipices, as a slave found treacherous, recreant, ought to be, and must.'[6]

On the verge of the Desert, Prime Minister to the Necropolis at whose gateway it stands, the Sphinx reposes amid the silence of science and the centuries. Who built it? None can answer, so far as the human artist, or the king under whom he worked, is concerned. But the ideas and natural forces which built the Sphinx surround even now the archæologist who tries to discover its history and chronology. As fittest appendage to Carlyle's interpretation, let us read some passages from Lepsius.

'The Oedipus for this king of the Sphinxes is yet wanting. Whoever would drain the immeasurable sand-flood which buries the tombs themselves, and lay open the base of the Sphinx, the ancient temple-path, and the surrounding hills, could easily decide it. But with the enigmas of history there are joined many riddles and wonders of nature, which I must not leave quite unnoticed. The newest of all, at least, I must describe.

'I had descended with Abeken into a mummy-pit, to open some newly discovered sarcophagi, and was not a little astonished, upon descending, to find myself in a regular snow-drift of locusts, which, almost darkening the heavens, flew over our heads from the south-west from the desert in hundreds of thousands to the valley. I took it for a single flight, and called my companions from the tombs, where they were busy, that they might see this Egyptian wonder ere it was over. But the flight continued; indeed the work-people said it had begun an hour before. Then we first observed that the whole region, near and far, was covered with locusts. I sent an attendant into the desert to discover the breadth of the flock. He ran for the distance of a quarter of an hour, then returned and told us that, as far as he could see, there was no end to them. I rode home in the midst of the locust shower. At the edge of the fruitful plain they fell down in showers; and so it went on the whole day until the evening, and so the next day from morning till evening, and the third; in short to the sixth day, indeed in weaker flights much longer. Yesterday it did seem that a storm of rain in the desert had knocked down and destroyed the last of them. The Arabs are now lighting great smoke-fires in the fields, and clattering and making loud noises all day long to preserve their crops from the unexpected invasion. It will, however, do little good. Like a new animated vegetation, these millions of winged spoilers cover even the neighbouring sand-hills, so that scarcely anything is to be seen of the ground; and when they rise from one place they immediately fall down somewhere in the neighbourhood; they are tired with their long journey, and seem to have lost all fear of their natural enemies, men, animals, smoke, and noise, in their furious wish to fill their stomachs, and in the feeding of their immense number. The most wonderful thing, in my estimation, is their flight over the naked wilderness, and the instinct which has guided them from some oasis over the inhospitable desert to the fat soil of the Nile vale. Fourteen years ago, it seems, this Egyptian plague last visited Egypt with the same force. The popular idea is that they are sent by the comet which we have observed for twelve days in the South-west, and which, as it is now no longer obscured by the rays of the moon, stretches forth its stately tail across the heavens in the hours of the night. The Zodiacal light, too, so seldom seen in the north, has lately been visible for several nights in succession.'

Other plagues of Egypt are described by Lepsius:—

'Suddenly the storm grew to a tremendous hurricane, such as I have never seen in Europe, and hail fell upon us in such masses as almost to turn day into night.... Our tents lie in a valley, whither the plateau of the pyramids inclines, and are sheltered from the worst winds from the north and west. Presently I saw a dashing mountain flood hurrying down upon our prostrate and sand-covered tents, like a giant serpent upon its certain prey. The principal stream rolled on to the great tent; another arm threatened mine without reaching it. But everything that had been washed from our tents by the shower was torn away by the two streams, which joined behind the tents, and carried into a pool behind the Sphinx, where a great lake immediately formed, which fortunately had no outlet. Just picture this scene to yourself! Our tents, dashed down by the storm and heavy rain, lying between two mountain torrents, thrusting themselves in several places to the depth of six feet in the sand, and depositing our books, drawings, sketches, shirts, and instruments—yes, even our levers and iron crow-bars; in short, everything they could seize, in the dark foaming mud-ocean. Besides this, ourselves wet to the skin, without hats, fastening up the weightier things, rushing after the lighter ones, wading into the lake to the waist to fish out what the sand had not yet swallowed; and all this was the work of a quarter of an hour, at the end of which the sun shone radiantly again, and announced the end of this flood by a bright and glorious rainbow.

'Now comes the plague of mice, with which we were not formerly acquainted; in my tent they grow, play, and whistle, as if they had been at home here all their lives, and quite regardless of my presence. At night they have already run across my bed and face, and yesterday I started terrified from my slumbers, as I suddenly felt the sharp tooth of such a daring guest at my foot.

'Above me a canopy of gauze is spread, in order to keep off the flies, these most shameless of the plagues of Egypt, during the day, and the mosquitos at night.... Scorpions and serpents have not bitten us yet, but there are very malicious wasps, which have often stung us.

'The dale (in the Desert) was wild and monotonous, nothing but sandstone rock, the surfaces of which were burned as black as coals, but turned into burning golden yellow at every crack, and every ravine, whence a number of sand-rivulets, like fire-streams from black dross, ran and filled the valleys. No tree, no tuft of grass had we yet seen, also no animals, except a few vultures and crows feeding on the carcase of the latest fallen camel.... Over a wild and broken path, and cutting stones, we came deeper and deeper into the gorge. The first wide basins were empty, we therefore left the camels and donkeys behind, climbed up the smooth granite wall, and thus proceeded amidst these grand rocks from one basin to another; they were all empty. Behind there, in the farthest ravine, the guide said there must be water, for it was never empty; but there proved to be not a single drop. We were obliged to return dry.... We saw the most beautiful *mirages* very early in the day; they most minutely resemble seas and lakes, in which mountains, rocks, and everything in their vicinity, are reflected as in the clearest water. They form a remarkable contrast with the staring dry desert, and have probably deceived many a poor wanderer, as the legend goes. If one be not aware that no water is there, it is quite impossible to distinguish the appearance from the reality. A few days ago I felt quite sure that I perceived an overflowing of the Nile, or a branch near El Mechêref, and rode towards it, but only found Bahr Sheitan, Satan's water, as the Arabs call it.'[7]

Amid such scenery the Sphinx arose. Egypt was able to recognise the problem of blended barrenness and beauty—alternation of Nature's flowing breast and leonine claw—but could she return the right answer? The primitive Egyptian answer may, indeed, as I have guessed, be the great monuments of her civilisation, but her historic solution has been another world. This world a desert, with here and there a momentary oasis, where man may dance and feast a little, stimulated by the corpse borne round the banquet, ere he passes to paradise. So thought they and were deceived; from generation to generation have they been destroyed, even unto this day. How destroyed, Lepsius may again be our witness.

'The Sheîkh of the Saadîch-derwishes rides to the chief Sheîkh of all the derwishes of Egypt, El Bekri. On the way thither, a great number of these holy folk, and others, too, who fancy themselves not a whit behind-hand in piety, throw themselves flat on the ground, with their faces downward, and so that the feet of one lie close to the head of the next; over this living carpet the sheîkh rides on his horse, which is led on each side by an attendant, in order to compel the animal to the unnatural march. Each body receives two treads of the horse; most of them jump up again without hurt, but whoever suffers serious, or as it occasionally happens, mortal injury, has the additional ignominy to bear of not having pronounced, or not being able to pronounce, the proper prayers and magical charms that alone could save him.'

'What a fearful barbarous worship' (the Sikr, in which the derwishes dance until exhausted, howling 'No God but Allah') 'which the astounded multitude, great and small, gentle and simple, gaze upon seriously, and with stupid respect, and in which it not unfrequently takes a part! The invoked deity is manifestly much less an object of reverence than the fanatic saints who invoke him; for mad, idiotic, or other psychologically-diseased persons are very generally looked upon as holy by the Mohammedans, and treated with great respect. It is the demoniacal, incomprehensibly-acting, and therefore fearfully-observed, power of nature that the natural man always reveres when he perceives it, because he is sensible of some connection between it and his intellectual power, without being able to command it; first in the mighty elements, then in the wondrous but obscure law-governed instincts of animals, and at last in the yet more overpowering ecstatical or generally abnormal mental condition of his own race.'

The right answer to the enigma of the Sphinx is Man. But this creature prostrating himself under the Sheîkh's horse, or under the invisible Sheîkh called Allah, and ascribing sanctity to the half-witted, is not Man at all. Those hard-worked slaves who escaped into the wilderness, and set up for worship an anthropomorphic Supreme Will, and sought their promised milk and honey in this world alone, carried with them the only force that could rightly answer the Sphinx. *Their* Allah or Elohim they heard say,—'Why howlest thou to me? Go forward.' Somewhat more significant than his usual jests was that cartoon of *Punch* which represented the Sphinx with relaxed face smiling recognition on the most eminent of contemporary Israelites returning to the land of his race's ancient bondage, to buy the Suez Canal. The Suez Canal half answers the Sphinx; when man has subdued the Great Desert to a sea, the solution will be complete, and the Sphinx may cast herself into it.

Far and wide through the Southern world have swarmed the locusts described by Lepsius, and with them have migrated many superstitions. The writer of this well remembers the visit of the so-called 'Seventeen-year locusts,' to the region of Virginia where he was born, and across many years can hear the terrible never-ceasing roar coming up from the woods, uttering, as all agreed, the ominous word 'Pharaoh.' On each wing every eye could see the letter W, signifying War. With that modern bit of ancient Egypt in my memory, I find the old Locust-mythology sufficiently impressive.

By an old tradition the Egyptians, as described by Lepsius, connected the locusts with the comet. In the Apocalypse (ix.) a falling star is the token of the descent of the Locust-demon to unlock the pit that his swarms may issue forth for their work of destruction. Their king Abaddon, in Greek Apollyon,—Destroyer,—has had an evolution from being the angel of the two (rabbinical) divisions of Hades to the successive Chiefs of Saracenic hordes. It is interesting to compare the graphic description of a locust-storm in Joel, with its adaptation to an army of human destroyers in the Apocalypse. And again the curious description of these hosts of Abaddon in the latter book, partly repeat the strange notions of the Bedouins concerning the locust,—one of whom, says Niebuhr, 'compared the head of the locust to that of the horse; its breast to that of a lion; its feet to those of a camel; its body to that of the serpent; its tail to that of the scorpion; its horns (antennæ) to the locks of hair of a virgin.' The present generation has little reason to deny the appropriateness of the biblical descriptions of Scythian hordes as locusts. 'The land is as the garden of Eden before them, and behind them a desolate wilderness.'

The ancient seeming contest between apparent Good and Evil in Egypt, was represented in the wars of Ra and Set. It is said (Gen. iv. 26), 'And to Seth, to him also was born a son; and he called his name Enos; then began men to call upon the name of the Lord.' Aquila reads this—'Then Seth began to be called by the name of the Lord.' Mr. Baring-Gould remarks on this that Seth was at first regarded by the Egyptians as the deity of light and civilisation, but that they afterwards identified as Typhon, because he was the chief god of the Hyksos or shepherd kings; and in their hatred of these oppressors the name of Seth was everywhere obliterated from their monuments, and he was represented as an ass, or with an ass's head.[8] But the earliest date assigned to the Hyksos dominion in Egypt, B.C. 2000, coincides with that of the Egyptian planisphere in Kircher,[9] where Seth is found identified with Sirius, or the dog-headed Mercury, in Capricorn. This is the Sothiac Period, or Cycle of the Dog-star. He was thus associated with the goat and the winter solstice, to which (B.C. 2000) Capricorn was adjacent. That Seth or Set became the name for the demon of disorder and violence among the Egyptians is, indeed, probably due to his being a chief god, among some tribes Baal himself, among the Asiatics, before the time of the Hyksos. It was already an old story to put their neighbours' Light for their own Darkness. The Ass's ears they gave him referred not to his stupidity, but to his hearing everything, as in the case of the Ass of Apuleius, and the ass Nicon of Plutarch, or, indeed, the many examples of the same kind which preceeded the appearance of this much misunderstood animal as the steed of Christ's triumphal entry into Jerusalem. In Egyptian symbolism those long ears were as much dreaded as devils' horns. From the eyes of Ra all beneficent things, from the eyes of Set all noxious things, were produced. Amen-Ra, as the former was called, slew the son of Set, the great serpent Naka, which in one hymn is perhaps tauntingly said to have 'saved his *feet.*' Amen-Ra becomes Horus and Set becomes Typhon. The Typhonian myth is very complex, and includes the conflict between the Nile and all its enemies—the crocodiles that lurk in it, the sea that swallows it, the drouth that dries it, the burning heat that brings malaria from it, the floods that render it destructive—and Set was through it evolved to a point where he became identified with Saturn, Sheitan, or Satan. Plutarch, identifying Set with Typho, says that those powers of the universal Soul, which are subject to the influences of passions, and in the material system whatever is noxious, as bad air, irregular seasons, eclipses of the sun and moon, are ascribed to Typho. The name Set, according to him, means 'violent' and 'hostile;' and he was described as 'double-headed,' 'he who has two countenances,' and 'the Lord of the World.' Not the least significant fact, in a moral sense, is that Set or Typho is represented as the brother of Osiris whom he slew.

Without here going into the question of relationship between Typhaon and Typhoeus, we may feel tolerably certain that the fire-breathing hurricane-monster Typhaon of Homer, and the hundred-headed, fierce-eyed roarer Typhoeus—son of Tartarus, father of Winds and Harpies—represent the same ferocities of Nature. No fitter place was ever assigned him than the African desert, and the story of the gods and goddesses fleeing before Typhon into Egypt, and there transforming themselves into animals, from terror, is a transparent tribute to the dominion over the wilderness of sand exercised by the typhoon in its many moods. The vulture-harpy tearing the dead is his child. He is many-headed; now hot, stifling, tainted; now tempestuous; here sciroc, there hurricane, and often tornado. It may be indeed that as at once coiled in the whirlwind and blistering, he is the fiery serpent to appease whom Moses lifted the brasen serpent for the worship of Israel. I have often seen snakes hung up by negroes in Virginia, to bring rain in time of drouth. Typhon, as may easily be seen by the accompanying figure (14), is a hungry and thirsty demon. His tongue is lolling out with thirst.[10] His later connection with the underworld is shown in various myths, one of which seems to suggest a popular belief that Typhon is not pleased with the mummies withheld from him, and that he can enjoy his human viands only through burials of the dead. In Egypt, after the Coptic Easter Monday—called Shemmen-Nesseem (smelling the zephyr)—come the fifty-days' hot wind, called Khamseen or Cain wind. After slaying Abel, Cain wandered amid such a wind, tortured with fever and thirst. Then he saw two birds fight in the air; one having killed the other scratched a hole in the desert sand and buried it. Cain then did the like by his brother's body, when a zephyr sprang up and cooled his fever. But still, say the Alexandrians, the fifty-days' hot Cain wind return annually.

Fig. 14.—TYPHON (Wilkinson)

In pictures of the mirage, or in cloud-shapes faintly illumined by the afterglow, the dwellers beside the plains of sand saw, as in phantasmagoria, the gorgeous palaces, the air-castles, and mysterious cities, which make the romance of the desert. Unwilling to believe that such realms of barrenness had ever been created by any good god, they beheld in dreams, which answer to nature's own mirage-dreaming, visions of dynasties passed away, of magnificent palaces and monarchs on whose pomp and heaven-defying pride the fatal sand-storm had fallen, and buried their glories in the dust for ever. The desert became the emblem of immeasurable all-devouring Time. In many of these legends there are intimations of a belief that Eden itself lay where now all is unbroken desert. In the beautiful legend in the Midrash of Solomon's voyage on the Wind, the monarch alighted near a lofty palace of gold, 'and the scent there was like the scent of the garden of Eden.' The dust had so surrounded this palace that Solomon and his companions only learned that there had been an entrance from an eagle in it thirteen centuries old, which had heard from its father the tradition of an entrance on the western side. The obedient Wind having cleared away the sand, a door was found on whose lock was written, 'Be it known to you, ye sons of men, that we dwelt in this palace in prosperity and delight many years. When the famine came upon us we ground pearls in the mill instead of wheat, but it profited us nothing.' Amid marvellous splendours, from chamber to chamber garnished with ruby, topaz, emerald, Solomon passed to a mansion on whose three gates were written admonitions of the transitory nature of all things but—Death. 'Let not fortune deceive thee.' 'The world is given from one to another.' On the third gate was written, 'Take provision for thy journey, and make ready food for thyself while it is yet day; for thou shalt not be left on the earth, and thou knowest not the day of thy Death.' This gate Solomon opened and saw within a life-like image seated: as the monarch approached, this image cried with a loud voice, 'Come hither, ye children of Satan; see! King Solomon is come to destroy you.' Then fire and smoke issued from the nostrils of the image; and there were loud and bitter cries, with earthquake and thunder. But Solomon uttered against them the Ineffable Name, and all the images fell on their faces, and the sons of Satan fled and cast themselves into the sea, that they might not fall into the hands of Solomon. The king then took from the neck of the image a silver tablet, with an inscription which he could not read, until the Almighty sent a youth to assist him. It said:—'I, Sheddad, son of Ad, reigned over a thousand thousand provinces, and rode on a thousand thousand horses; a thousand thousand kings were subject to me, and a thousand thousand warriors I slew. Yet in the hour that the Angel of Death came against me, I could not withstand him. Whoso shall read this writing let him not trouble himself greatly about this world, for the end of all men is to die, and nothing remains to man but a good name.'[11]

Azazel—'of doubtful meaning'—is the biblical name of the Demon of the Desert (Lev. xvi.). 'Aaron shall cast lots upon the two goats: one lot for Jehovah, and the other for Azazel. And Aaron shall bring the goat upon which the lot for Jehovah fell, and offer him for a sin-offering: But the goat, on which the lot for Azazel fell, shall be presented alive before Jehovah, to make an atonement with him, to let him go to Azazel in the wilderness.... And Aaron shall lay both his hands upon the head of the live goat, and confess over him all the iniquities of the children of Israel, and all their transgressions in all their sins, putting them upon the head of the goat, and send him away by the hand of a fit man into the desert. And the goat shall bear upon him all their iniquities unto a land not inhabited; and he shall let go the goat in the desert.' Of the moral elements here involved much will have to be said hereafter. This demon ultimately turned to a devil; and persisting through both forms is the familiar principle that it is 'well enough to have friends on both sides' so plainly at work in the levitical custom; but it is particularly interesting to observe that the same animal should be used as offerings to the antagonistic deities. In Egyptian Mythology we find that the goat had precisely this two-fold consecration. It was sacred to Chem, the Egyptian Pan, god of orchards and of all fruitful lands; and it became also sacred to Mendes, the 'Destroyer,' or 'Avenging Power' of Ra. It will thus be seen that the same principle which from the sun detached the fructifying from the desert-making power, and made Typhon and Osiris hostile brothers, prevailed to send the same animal to Azazel in the Desert and Jehovah of the milk and honey land. Originally the goat was supreme. The Samaritan Pentateuch, according to Aben Ezra (Preface to Esther), opens, 'In the beginning Ashima created the heaven and the earth.' In the Hebrew culture-myth of Cain and Abel, also brothers, there may be represented, as Goldziher supposes, the victory of the agriculturist over the nomad or shepherd; but there is also traceable in it the supremacy of the Goat, Mendez or Azima.

'Abel brought the firstling of the goats.'

Very striking is the American (Iroquois) myth of the conflict between Joskeha and Tawiscara,—the White One and the Dark One. They were twins, born of a virgin who died in giving them life. Their grandmother was the moon (Ataensic, *she who bathes*). These brothers fought, Joskeha using as weapon the horns of a stag, Tawiscara the wild-rose. The latter fled sorely wounded, and the blood gushing from him turned to flint-stones. The victor, who used the stag-horns (the same weapon that Frey uses against Beli, in the Prose Edda, and denoting perhaps a primitive bone-age art), destroyed a monster frog which swallowed all the waters, and guided the torrents into smooth streams and lakes. He stocked the woods with game, invented fire, watched and watered crops, and without him, says the old missionary Brebeuf, 'they think they could not boil a pot.' The use by the desert-demon Tawiscara of a wild rose as his weapon is a beautiful touch in this myth. So much loveliness grew even amid the hard flints. One is reminded of the closing scene in the second part of Goethe's *Faust*. There, when Faust has realised the perfect hour to which he can say, 'Stay, thou art fair!' by causing by his labour a wilderness to blossom as a rose, he lies down in happy death; and when the demons come for his soul, angels pelt them with roses, which sting them like flames. Not wild roses were these, such as gave the Dark One such poor succour. The defence of Faust is the roses he has evoked from briars.

NOTES

1 'Rig-Veda,' iv. 175, 5 (Wilson).
2 Ibid., i. 133, 6.
3 'Rig-Veda,' vi. 14.
4 'The Nineteenth Century,' November 1877. Article: 'Sun-Spots and Famines,' by Norman Lockyer and W. W. Hunter.
5 'An Inquiry into the Nature and Place of Hell,' by Tobias Swinden, M.A., late Rector of Cuxton-in-Kent. 1727.
6 Carlyle, 'Past and Present,' i. 2.
7 'Discoveries in Egypt,' &c. (Bentley.) 1852.
8 'Legends of Old Testament Characters,' i. p. 83.
9 Œdip., 1. II. ii. See 'Mankind: their Origin and Destiny,' p. 699.
10 Compare Kali, Fig. 18.
11 Soc. of Heb. Literature's Publications. 2d Series. 'Legends from the Midrash,' by Thomas Chenery (Trübner & Co.). The same legend is referred to in the story of the Astrologer in Washington Irving's 'Alhambra.'

Chapter VIII
Obstacles

RELATED TO THE DEMONS of Barrenness, and to the hostile human demons, but still possessing characteristics of their own, are the demons supposed to haunt gorges, mountain ranges, ridges of rocks, streams which cannot be forded and are yet unbridged, rocks that wreck the raft or boat. Each and every obstruction that stood in the way of man's plough, or of his first frail ship, or his migration, has been assigned its demon. The reader of Goethe's page has only to turn to the opening lines of Walpurgisnacht in *Faust* to behold the real pandemonium of the Northern man, as in Milton he may find that of the dweller amid fiery deserts and volcanoes. That labyrinth of vales, crossed with wild crag and furious torrent, is the natural scenery to surround the orgies of the phantoms which flit from the uncultured brain to uncultured nature. Elsewhere in Goethe's great poem, Mephistopheles pits against the philosophers the popular theory of the rugged remnants of chaos in nature, and the obstacles before which man is powerless.

Faust. For me this mountain mass rests nobly dumb;
I ask not whence it is, nor why 'tis come?
Herself when Nature in herself did found
This globe of earth, she then did purely round;
The summit and abyss her pleasure made,
Mountain to mountain, rock to rock she laid;
The hillocks down she neatly fashion'd then,
To valleys soften'd them with gentle train.
Then all grew green and bloom'd, and in her joy
She needs no foolish spoutings to employ.

Mephistopheles. So say ye! It seems clear as noon to ye,
Yet he knows who was there the contrary.
I was hard by below, when seething flame
Swelled the abyss, and streaming fire forth came;
When Moloch's hammer forging rock to rock,
Far flew the fragment-cliffs beneath the shock:
Of masses strange and huge the land was full;
Who clears away such piles of hurl'd misrule?
Philosophers the reason cannot see;
There lies the rock, and they must let it be.
We have reflected till ashamed we've grown;
The common folk can thus conceive alone,
And in conception no disturbance know,
Their wisdom ripen'd has long while ago:
A miracle it is, they Satan honour show.
My wanderer on faith's crutches hobbles on
Towards the devil's bridge and devil's stone.[1]

**The great American poet made his pilgrimage to the mountain so
beautiful in the distance, thinking to find there the men of equal
elevation. Did not Milton describe Freedom as 'a mountain nymph?'**

To myself I oft recount
The tale of many a famous mount,—
Wales, Scotland, Uri, Hungary's dells;
Roys, and Scanderbergs, and Tells.
Here Nature shall condense her powers,

Her music, and her meteors,
And lifting man to the blue deep
Where stars their perfect courses keep,
Like wise preceptor, lure his eye.
To sound the science of the sky.

But instead of finding there the man using those crags as a fastness to fight pollution of the mind, he

searched the region round
And in low hut my monarch found:
He was no eagle, and no earl;—
Alas! my foundling was a churl,
With heart of cat and eyes of bug,
Dull victim of his pipe and mug.[2]

Ruskin has the same gloomy report to make of the mountaineers of Europe. 'The wild goats that leap along those rocks have as much passion of joy in all that fair work of God as the men that toil among them. Perhaps more.' 'Is it not strange to reflect that hardly an evening passes in London or Paris but one of those cottages is painted for the better amusement of the fair and idle, and shaded with pasteboard pines by the scene-shifter; and that good and kind people,—poetically minded,—delight themselves in imagining the happy life led by peasants who dwell by Alpine fountains, and kneel to crosses upon peaks of rock? that nightly we lay down our gold to fashion forth simulacra of peasants, in gay ribbons and white bodices, singing sweet songs and bowing gracefully to the picturesque crosses; and all the while the veritable peasants are kneeling, songlessly, to veritable crosses in another temper than the kind and fair audiences dream of, and assuredly with another kind of answer than is got out of the opera catastrophe.'[3]

The writer remembers well the emphasis with which a poor woman at whose cottage he asked the path to the Natural Bridge in Virginia said, 'I don't know why so many people come to these rocks; for my part, give me a level country.' Many ages lay between that aged crone and Emerson or Ruskin, and they were ages of heavy war with the fortresses of nature. The fabled ordeals of water and fire through which the human race passed were associated with Ararat and Sinai, because to migrating or farming man the mountain was always an ordeal, irrespective even of its torrents or its occasional lava-streams. A terrible vista is opened by the cry of Lot, 'I cannot escape to the mountain lest some evil take me!' Not even the fire consuming Sodom in the plains could nerve him to dare cope with the demons of the steep places. As time went on, devotees proved to the awe-stricken peasantries their sanctity and authority by combating those mountain demons, and erecting their altars in the 'high places.' So many summits became sacred. But this very sanctity was the means of bringing on successive demoniac hordes to haunt them; for every new religion saw in those altars in 'high places' not victories over demons, but demon-shrines. And thus mountains became the very battlefields between rival deities, each demon to his or her rival; and the conflict lasts from the cursing of the 'high places' by the priests of Israel [4] to the Devil's Pulpits of the Alps and Apennines. Among the beautiful frescoes at Baden is that of the Angel's and the Devil's Pulpit, by Götzenberger. Near Gernsbach, appropriately at the point where the cultivable valley meets the unconquerable crests of rock, stand the two pulpits from which Satan and an Angel contended, when the first Christian missionaries had failed to convert the rude foresters. When, by the Angel's eloquence, all were won from the Devil's side except a few witches and usurers, the fiend tore up great masses of rock and built the 'Devil's Mill' on the mountain-top; and he was hurled down by the Almighty on the rocks near 'Lord's Meadow,' where the marks of his claws may still be seen, and where, by a diminishing number of undiminished ears, his groans are still heard when a storm rages through the valley.

Such conflicts as these have been in some degree associated with every mountain of holy or unholy fame. Each was in its time a prosaic Hill Difficulty, with lions by no means chained, to affright the hearts of Mistrust and Timorous, till Dervish or Christian impressed there his holy footprint, visible from Adam's Peak to Olivet, or built there his convents, discernible from Meru and Olympus to Pontyprydd and St. Catharine's Hill. By necessary truces the demons and deities repair gradually to their respective summits,—Seir and Sinai hold each their own. But the Holy Hills have never equalled the number of Dark Mountains [5] dreaded by man. These obstructive demons made the mountains Moul-ge and Nin-ge, names for the King and Queen of the Accadian Hell; they made the Finnish Mount Kippumaki the abode of all Pests. They have identified their name (Elf) with the Alps, given nearly every tarn an evil fame, and indeed created a special class of demons, 'Montagnards,' much dreaded by mediæval miners, whose faces they sometimes twisted so that they must look backward physically, as they were much in the habit of doing mentally, for ever afterward. Gervais of Tilbury, in his Chronicle, declares that on the top of Mount Canigon in France, which has a very inaccessible summit, there is a black lake of unknown depth, at whose bottom the demons have a palace, and that if any one drops a stone into that water, the wrath of the mountain demons is shown in sudden and frightful tempests. From a like tarn in Cornwall, as Cornish Folklore claims, on an accessible but very tedious hill, came up the hand which received the brand Escalibore when its master could wield it no more,—as told in the Morte D'Arthur, with, however, clear reference to the sea.

I cannot forbear enlivening my page with the following sketch of a visit of English officers to the realm of Ten-jo, the long-nosed Mountain-demon of Japan, which is very suggestive of the mental atmosphere amid which such spectres exist. The mountains and forests of Japan are, say these writers, inhabited as thickly by good and evil spirits as the Hartz and Black Forest, and chief among them, in horrible sanctity, is O-yama,—the word echoes the Hindu Yama, Japanese Amma, kings of Hades,—whose demon is Ten-jo. 'Abdul and Mulney once started, on three days' leave, with the intention of climbing to the summit—not of Ten-jo's nose, but of the mountain; their principal reason for so doing being simply that they were told by every one that they had better not. They first tried the ascent on the most accessible side, but fierce two-sworded yakomins jealously guarded it; and they were obliged to make the attempt on the other, which was almost inaccessible, and was Ten-jo's region. The villagers at the base of the mountain begged them to give up the project; and one old man, a species of patriarch, reasoned with them. 'What are you going to do when you get to the top?' he asked. Our two friends were forced to admit that their course, then, would be very similar to that of the king of France and his men—come down again.

The old man laughed pityingly, and said, 'Well, go if you like; but, take my word for it, Ten-jo will do you an injury.'

They asked who Ten-jo was.

'Why Ten-jo,' said the old man, 'is an evil spirit, with a long nose, who will dislocate your limbs if you persist in going up the mountain on this side.'

'How do you know he has got a long nose?' they asked, 'Have you ever seen him?'

'Because all evil spirits have long noses'—here Mulney hung his head,—'and,' continued the old man, not noticing how dreadfully personal he was becoming to one of the party, 'Ten-jo has the longest of the lot. Did you ever know a man with a long nose who was good?'

'Come on,' said Mulney hurriedly to Abdul, 'or the old fool will make me out an evil spirit.'

'Syonara,' said the old man as they walked away, 'but look out for Ten-jo!'

After climbing hard for some hours, and not meeting a single human being,—not even the wood-cutter could be tempted by the fine timber to encroach on Ten-jo's precincts,—they reached the top, and enjoyed a magnificent view. After a rest they started on their descent, the worst part of which they had accomplished, when, as they were walking quietly along a good path, Abdul's ankle turned under him, and he went down as if he had been shot, with his leg broken in two places. With difficulty Mulney managed to get him to the village they had started from, and the news ran like wild-fire that

Ten-jo had broken the leg of one of the adventurous tojins.

'I told you how it would be,' exclaimed the old man, 'but you would go. Ah, Ten-jo is a dreadful fellow!'

All the villagers, clustering round, took up the cry, and shook their heads. Ten-jo's reputation had increased wonderfully by this accident. Poor Abdul was on his back for eleven weeks, and numbers of Japanese—for he was a general favourite amongst them—went to see him, and to express their regret and horror at Ten-jo's behaviour.[6]

It is obvious that to a demon dwelling in a high mountain a long nose would be variously useful to poke into the affairs of people dwelling in the plains, and also to enjoy the scent of their sacrifices offered at a respectful distance. That feature of the face which Napoleon I. regarded as of martial importance, and which is prominent in the warriors marked on the Mycenæ pottery, has generally been a physiognomical characteristic of European ogres, who are blood-smellers. That the significance of Ten-jo's long nose is this, appears probable when we compare him with the Calmuck demon Erlik, whose long nose is for smelling out the dying. The Cossacks believed that the protector of the earth was a many-headed elephant. The snouted demon (figure 15) is from a picture of Christ delivering Adam and Eve from hell, by Lucas Van Leyden, 1521.

Fig. 15.—Snouted Demon

The Chinese Mountains also have their demons. The demon of the mountain T'ai-shan, in Shantung, is believed to regulate the punishments of men in this world and the next. Four other demon princes rule over the principal mountain chains of the Empire. Mr. Dennys remarks that mountainous localities are so regularly the homes of fairies in Chinese superstition that some connection between the fact and the relation of 'Elf' to 'Alp' in Europe is suggested.[7] But this coincidence is by no means so remarkable as the appearance among these Chinese mountain sprites of the magical 'Sesame,' so familiar to us in Arabian legend. The celebrated mountain Ku'en Lun (usually identified with the Hindoo Kush) is said to be peopled with fairies, who cultivate upon its terraces the 'fields of sesamum and gardens of coriander seeds,' which are eaten as ordinary food by those who possess the gift of longevity.

In the superstitions of the American Aborigines we find gigantic demons who with their hands piled up mountain-chains as their castles, from whose peak-towers they hurled stones on their enemies in the plains, and slung them to the four corners of the earth.[8] Such was the terrible Apocatequil, whose statue was erected on the mountains, with that of his mother on the one hand and his brother on the other. He was Prince of Evil and the chief god of the Peruvians. From Quito to Cuzco every Indian would give all he possessed to conciliate him. Five priests, two stewards, and a crowd of slaves served his image. His principal temple was surrounded by a considerable village, whose inhabitants had no other occupation than to wait on him.[9]

The plaudits which welcomed the first railway train that sped beneath the Alps, echoing amid their crags and gorges, struck with death the old phantasms which had so long held sway in the imagination of the Southern peasantry. The great tunnel was hewn straight through the stony hearts of giants whom Christianity had tried to slay, and, failing that, baptised and adopted. It is in the Tyrol that we find the clearest survivals of the old demons of obstruction, the mountain monarchs. Such is Jordan the Giant of Kohlhütte chasm, near Ungarkopf, whose story, along with others, is so prettily told by the Countess Von Gunther. This giant is something of a Ten-jo as to nose, for he smells 'human meat' where his pursued victims are hidden, and his snort makes things tremble as before a tempest; but he has not the intelligence ascribed to large noses, for the boys ultimately persuade him that the way to cross a stream is to tie a stone around his neck, and he is drowned. One of the giants of Albach could carry a rock weighing 10,000 pounds, and his comrades, while carrying others of 700 pounds, could leap from stone to stone across rivers, and stoop to catch the trout with their hands as they leaped. The ferocious Orco, the mountain-ghost who never ages, fulfils the tradition of his classic name by often appearing as a monstrous black dog, from whose side stones rebound, and fills the air with a bad smell (like Mephisto). His employment is hurling wayfarers down precipices. In her story of the 'Unholdenhof'—or 'monster farm' in the Stubeithal—the Countess Von Gunther describes the natural character of the mountain demons.

'It was on this self-same spot that the forester and his son took up their abode, and they became the dread and abomination of the whole surrounding country, for they practised, partly openly and partly in secret, the most manifold iniquities, so that their nature and bearing grew into something demoniacal. As quarrellers very strong, and as enemies dreadfully revengeful, they showed their diabolical nature by the most inhuman deeds, which brought down injury not only on those against whom their wrath was directed, but also upon their families for centuries. In the heights of the mountains they turned the beds of the torrents, and devastated by this means the most flourishing tracts of land; on other places the Unholde set on fire whole mountain forests, to allow free room for the avalanches to rush down and overwhelm the farms. Through certain means they cut holes and fissures in the rocks, in which, during the summer, quantities of water collected, which froze in the winter, and then in the spring the thawing ice split the rocks, which then rolled down into the valleys, destroying everything before them.... But at last Heaven's vengeance reached them. An earthquake threw the forester's house into ruins, wild torrents tore over it, and thunderbolts set all around it in a blaze; and by fire and water, with which they had sinned, father and son perished, and were condemned to everlasting torments. Up to the present day they are to be seen at nightfall on the mountain in the form of two fiery boars."[10]

Some of these giants, as has been intimated, were converted. Such was the case with Heimo, who owned and devastated a vast tract of country on the river Inn, which, however, he bridged—whence Innsbruck—when he became a christian and a monk. This conversion was a terrible disappointment to the devil, who sent a huge dragon to stop the building of the monastery; but Heimo attacked the dragon, killed him, and cut out his tongue. With this tongue, a yard and a half long, in his hand, he is represented in his statue, and the tongue is still preserved in the cloister. Heimo became a monk at Wilten, lived a pious life, and on his death was buried near the monastery. The stone coffin in which the gigantic bones repose is shown there, and measures over twenty-eight feet.

Of nearly the same character as the Mountain Demons, and possessing even more features of the Demons of Barrenness, are the monsters guarding rocky passes. They are distributed through land, sea, and rivers. The famous rocks between Italy and Sicily bore the names of dangerous monsters, Scylla and Charybdis, which have now become proverbial expressions for alternative perils besetting any enterprise. According to Homer, Scylla was a kind of canine monster with six long necks, the mouths paved each with three rows of sharp teeth; while Charybdis, sitting under her fig-tree, daily swallowed the waters and vomited them up again."[11] Distantly related to these fabulous monsters, probably, are many of the old notions of ordeals undergone between rocks standing close together, or sometimes through holes in rocks, of which examples are found in Great Britain. An ordeal of this kind exists at Pera, where the holy well is reached through a narrow slit. Visitors going there recently on New Year's Day were warned by the dervish in charge—'Look through it at the water if you please, but do not essay to enter unless your consciences are completely free from sin, for as sure as you try to pass through with a taint upon your soul, you will be gripped by the rock and held there for ever.'[12] The 'Bocca della Verità'—a great stone face like a huge millstone—stands in the portico of the church S. Maria in Cosmedin at Rome, and its legend is that a suspected person was required to place his hand through the open mouth; if he swore falsely it would bite off the hand—the explanation now given being that a swordsman was concealed behind to make good the judicial shrewdness of the stone in case the oath were displeasing to the authorities.

The myth of Scylla, which relates that she was a beautiful maiden, beloved by Glaucus, whom Circe through jealousy trans- formed to a monster by throwing magic herbs into the well where she was wont to bathe, is recalled by various European legends. In Thuringia, on the road to Oberhof, stands the Red Stone, with its rosebush, and a stream issuing from beneath it, where a beautiful maid is imprisoned. Every seven years she may be seen bathing in the stream. On one occasion a peasant passing by heard a sneeze in the rock, and called out, 'God help thee!' The sneeze and the bene- diction were repeated, until at the seventh time the man cried, 'Oh, thou cursed witch, deceive not honest people!' As he then walked off, a wailing voice came out of the stone, 'Oh, hadst thou but only wished the last time that God would help me.He would have helped me, and thou wouldst have delivered me; now I must tarry till the Day of Judgment!' The voice once cried out to a wedding procession passing by the stone, 'To-day wed, next year dead;' and the bride having died a year after, wedding processions dread the spot.

The legends of giants and giantesses, so numerous in Great Britain, are equally associated with rocky mountain-passes, or the boulders they were supposed to have tossed thence when sportively stoning each other. They are the Tor of the South and Ben of the North. The hills of Ross-shire in Scotland are mythological monuments of *Cailliachmore,* great woman, who, while carrying a pannier filled with earth and stones on her back, paused for a moment on a level spot, now the site of Ben-Vaishard, when the bottom of the pannier gave way, forming the hills. The recurrence of the names Gog and Magog in Scotland suggests that in mountainous regions the demons were especially derived from the hordes of robbers and savages, among whom, in their uncultivable hills, the ploughshare could never conquer the spear and club. Richard Doyle enriched the first Exhibition of the Grosvenor Gallery in London, 1877, with many beautiful pictures inspired by European Folklore. They were a pretty garniture for the cemetery of dead religions. The witch once seen on her broom departing from the high crags of Cuhillan, cheered by her faithful dwarf, is no longer unlovely as in the days when she was burned by proxy in some poor human hag; obedient to art—a more potent wand than her own—she reascends to the clouds from which she was borne, and is hardly distinguishable from them. Slowly man came to learn with the poet—

> It was the mountain streams that fed
> The fair green plain's amenities.[13]

Then the giants became fairies, and not a few of these wore at last the mantles of saints. A similar process has been undergone by another subject, which finds its pretty epitaph in the artist's treatment. We saw in two pictures the Dame Blanche of Normandy, lurking in the ravine beside a stream under the dusk, awaiting yon rustic wood-cutter who is presently horizontal in the air in that mad dance, after which he will be found exhausted. As her mountain-sister is faintly shaped out of the clouds that cap Cuhillan, this one is an imaginative outgrowth of the twilight shadows, the silvery glintings of moving clouds mirrored in pools, and her tresses are long luxuriant grasses. She is of a sisterhood which passes by hardly perceptible gradations into others, elsewhere described—the creations of Illusion and Night. She is not altogether one of these, however, but a type of more direct danger—the peril of fords, torrents, thickets, marshes, and treacherous pools, which may seem shallow, but are deep.

The water-demons have been already described in their obvious aspects, but it is necessary to mention here the simple obstructive river-demons haunting fords and burns, and hating bridges. Many tragedies, and many personifications of the forces which caused them, preceded the sanctity of the title *Pontifex*. The torrent that roared across man's path seemed the vomit of a demon: the sacred power was he who could bridge it. In one of the most beautiful celebrations of Indra it is said: 'He tranquillised this great river so that it might be crossed; he conveyed across it in safety the sages who had been unable to pass over it, and who, having crossed, proceeded to realise the wealth they sought; in the exhilaration of the *soma,* Indra has done these deeds.'[14] In Ceylon, the demon Tota still casts malignant spells about fords and ferries.

Many are the legends of the opposition offered by demons to bridge-building, and of the sacrifices which had to be made to them before such works could be accomplished. A few specimens must suffice us. Mr. Dennys relates a very interesting one of the 'Loh-family bridge' at Shanghai. Difficulty having been found in laying the foundations, the builder vowed to Heaven two thousand children if the stones could be placed properly. The goddess addressed said she would not require their lives, but that the number named would be attacked by small-pox, which took place, and half the number died. A Chinese author says, 'If bridges are not placed in proper positions, such as the laws of geomancy indicate, they may endanger the lives of thousands, by bringing about a visitation of small-pox or sore eyes.' At Hang-Chow a tea-merchant cast himself into the river Tsien-tang as a sacrifice to the Spirit of the dikes, which were constantly being washed away.

The 'Devil's Bridges,' to which Mephistopheles alludes so proudly, are frequent in Germany, and most of them, whether natural or artificial, have diabolical associations. The oldest structures often have legends in which are reflected the conditions exacted by evil powers, of those who spanned the fords in which men had often been drowned. Of this class is the Montafon Bridge in the Tyrol, and another is the bridge at Ratisbon. The legend of the latter is a fair specimen of those which generally haunt these ancient structures. Its architect was apprentice to a master who was building the cathedral, and laid a wager that he would bridge the Danube before the other laid the coping-stone of the sacred edifice. But the work of bridging the river was hard, and after repeated failures the apprentice began to swear, and wished the devil had charge of the business! Whereupon he of the cloven foot appeared in guise of a friar, and agreed to build the fifteen arches—for a consideration. The fee was to be the first three that crossed the bridge. The cunning apprentice contrived that these three should not be human, but a dog, a cock, and a hen. The devil, in wrath at the fraud, tore the animals to pieces and disappeared; a procession of monks passed over the bridge and made it safe; and thereon are carved figures of the three animals. In most of the stories it is a goat which is sent over and mangled, that poor animal having preserved its character as scape-goat in a great deal of the Folklore of Christendom. The Danube was of old regarded as under the special guardianship of the Prince of Darkness, who used to make great efforts to obstruct the Crusaders voyaging down it to rescue the Holy Land from pagans. On one occasion, near the confluence of the Vilz and Danube, he began hurling huge rocks into the river-bed from the cliffs; the holy warriors resisted successfully by signing the cross and singing an anthem, but the huge stone first thrown caused a whirl and swell in that part of the river, which were very dangerous until it was removed by engineers.

It is obvious, especially to the English, who have so long found a defensive advantage in the silver streak of sea that separates them from the Continent, that an obstacle, whether of mountain-range or sea, would, at a certain point in the formation of a nation, become as valuable as at another it might be obstructive. Euphemism is credited with having given the friendly name 'Euxine' to the rough 'Axine' Sea,—'terrible to foreigners.' But this is not so certain. Many a tribe has found the Black Sea a protection and a friend. In the case of mountains, their protective advantages would account at once for Milton's celebration of Freedom as a mountain nymph, and for the stupidity of the people that dwell amid them, so often remarked; the very means of their independence would also be the cause of their insulation and barbarity. It is for those who go to and fro that knowledge is increased. The curious and inquiring are most apt to migrate; the enterprising will not submit to be shut away behind rocks and mountains; by their departure there would be instituted, behind the barriers of rock and hill, a survival of the stupidest. These might ultimately come to worship their chains and cover their craggy prison-walls with convents and crosses. The demons of aliens would be their gods. The climbing Hannibals would be their devils. It might have been expected, after the passages quoted from Mr. Ruskin concerning the bovine condition of Alpine peasantries, that he would salute the tunnel through Mont Cenis. The peasantries who would see in the sub-alpine engine a demon are extinct. Admiration of the genii of obstruction, and horror of the demons that vanquished them, are discoverable only in folk-tales distant enough to be pretty, such as the interesting Serbian story of 'Satan's jugglings and God's might,' in which fairies hiding in successively opened nuts vainly try to oppose with fire and flood a she-demon pursuing a prince and his bride, to whose aid at last comes a flash of lightning which strikes the fiend dead.

One of the beautiful 'Contes d'une Grand'mère,' by George Sand, *Le géant Yéous*, has in it the sense of many fables born of man's struggle with obstructive nature. With her wonted felicity she places the scene of this true human drama near the mountain Yéous, in the Pyrenees, whose name is a far-off echo of Zeus. The summit bore an enormous rock which, seen from a distance, appeared somewhat like a statue. The peasant Miquelon, who had his little farm at the mountain's base, whenever he passed made the sign of the cross and taught his little son Miquel to do the same, telling him that the great form was that of a pagan god, an enemy of the human race. An avalanche fell upon the home and garden of Miquelon; the poor man himself was disabled for life, his house and farm turned in a moment into a wild mass of stones. Miquel looked up to the summit of Yéous; the giant had disappeared; henceforth it was the mighty form of an organic monster which the boy saw stretched over what had once been their happy home and smiling acres. The family went about begging, Miquelon repeating his strange appeal, 'Le géant s'est couché sur moi.' But when at last the old man dies, the son resolves to fulfil the silent dream of his life; he will encounter the giant Yéous still in possession of his paternal acres. With eyes of the young world this boy sees starting up here and there amid the vast debris, the head of the demon he wishes to crush. He hurls stones hither and thither where some fearful feature or limb appears. He is filled with rage; his dreams are filled with attacks on the giant, in which the colossal head tumbles only to reappear on the shoulders; every broken limb has the self-repairing power. There is no progress. But as the boy grows, and the contest grows, and need comes, there gathers in Miquel a desire to clear the ground. When he begins to think, it is no longer the passion to avenge his father on the stony giant which possesses him, but to recover their lost garden. Thus, indeed, the giant himself could alone be conquered. The huge rocks are split by gunpowder, some fragments are made into fences, others into a comfortable mansion for Miquel's mother and sisters. When the garden smiles again, and all are happy the demon form is no longer discoverable.[15]

This little tale interprets with fine insight the demonology of barrenness and obstruction. The boy's wrath against the unconscious cause of his troubles is the rage often observed in children who retaliate upon the table or chair on which they have been bruised, and it repeats embryologically the rage of the world's boyhood inspired by ascription of personal motives to inanimate obstructions. Possibly such wrath might have added something to the force with which man entered upon his combat with nature; but George Sand's tale reminds us that whatever was gained in force was lost in its misdirection. Success came in the proportion that fury was replaced by the youth's growing recognition that he was dealing with facts that could not be raged out of existence. It is crowned when he makes friends with the unconquerable remnant of the giant, and sees that he is not altogether evil.

It is at this stage that the higher Art, conversant with Beauty, enters to relieve man of many moral wounds received in the struggle. Clothed with moss and clematis, Yéous appears not so hideous after all. Further invested by the genius of a Turner, he would be beautiful. Yéous is a fair giant after all, only he needed finish. He is a type of nature.

The boyhood of the world has not passed away with Miquel. We find a fictitious dualism cherished by the lovers of nature in their belief or feeling that nature exerts upon man some spiritual influence. Ruskin has said that in looking from the Campanile at Venice to the circle of snow which crowns the Adriatic, and then to the buildings which contain the works of Titian and Tintoret, he has felt unable to answer the question of his own heart, By which of these—the nature or the manhood—has God given mightier evidence of Himself? So nature may teach the already taught. While Ruskin looks from the Campanile, the peasant is fighting the mountain and calling its rocky grandeurs by the devil's name; before the pictures he kneels. Untaught by art and science, the mind can derive no elevation from nature, can find no sympathy in it. It is a false notion that there is any compensation for the ignorant, denied access to art-galleries, in ability to pass their Sundays amid natural scenery. Health that may bring them, but mentally they are still inside the prison-walls from which look the stony eyes of Fates and Furies. Natural sublimities cannot refine minds crude as themselves; they must pass through thought before they can feed thought; it is nature transfigured in art that changes the snow-clad mountain from a heartless giant to a saviour in snow-pure raiment.

NOTES

1 Faust, ii. Act 4 (Hayward's Translation).
2 'Emerson's Poems. Monadnoc.'
3 'Modern Painters,' Part V. 19.
4 Bel's mountain, 'House of the Beloved,' is called 'high place' in Assyrian, and would be included in these curses ('Records of the Past,' iii. 129).
5 Jer. xiii. 16.
6 'Our Life in Japan.' By Jephson and Elmhirst.
7 Another derivation of Elf (Alf) is to connect it with Sanskrit Alpa = little; so that the Elves are the Little Folk. Professor Buslaef of Moscow suggests connection with the Greek Alphito, a spectre. See pp. 160n. and 223.
8 Brinton, p. 85.
9 Ibid., p. 166.
10 'Tales and Legends of the Tyrol.' (Chapman and Hall, 1874.)
11 Od. xii. 73; 235, &c.
12 London Daily Telegraph Correspondence.
13 John Sterling.
14 'Rig-Veda,' ii. 15, 5. Wilson. 1854.
15 'Du monstre qui m'avait tant ennuyé, il n'était plus question; il était pour jamais réduit au silence. Il n'avait plus forme de géant. Déjà en partie couvert de verdure, de mousse et de clématites qui avaient grimpé sur la partie où j'avais cessé de passer, il n'était plus laid; bientôt on ne le verrait plus du tout. Je me sentais si heureux que je voulus lui pardonner, et, me tournant vers lui:—A present, lui dis-je, tu dormiras tous tes jours et tous tes nuits sans que je te dérange. Le mauvais esprit qui était en toi est vaincu, je lui defends de revenir. Je t'en ai délivré en te forçant à devenir utile à quelque chose; que la foudre t'épargne et que la neige te soit légère! Il me sembla passer, le long de l'escarpement, comme un grand soupir de résignation qui se perdit dans les hauteurs. Ce fut la dernière fois que je l'entendais, et je ne l'ai jamais revu autre qu'il n'est maintenant.'

Chapter IX
Illusion

MOST BEAUTIFUL OF all the goddesses of India is Maya, Illusion. In
Hindu iconography she is portrayed in drapery of beautiful colours,
with decoration of richest gems and broidery of flowers. From above
her crown falls a veil which, curving above her knees, returns on
the other side, making, as it were, also an apron in which are held
fair animal forms—prototypes of the creation over which she has
dominion. The youthful yet serious beauty of her face and head is
surrounded with a semi-aureole, fringed with soft lightning, striated
with luminous sparks; and these are background for a cruciform
nimbus made of three clusters of rays. Maya presses her full breasts,
from which flow fountains of milk which fall in graceful streams to
mingle with the sea on which she stands.

So to our Aryan ancestors appeared the spirit that paints the
universe, flushing with tints so strangely impartial fruits forbidden
and unforbidden for man and beast. Mankind are slandered by the
priest's creed, *Populus vult decipi;* they are justly vindicated in Plato's aphorism, 'Unwillingly is the soul deprived of truth;' but still they
are deceived. Large numbers are truly described by Swedenborg,

who found hells whose occupants believed themselves in heaven and sang praises therefor. Such praises we may hear in the loud laughter proceeding from dens where paradise has been gained by the cheap charm of a glass of gin or a prostitute's caress. Serpent finds its ideal in serpent. In heaven, says Swedenborg, we shall see things as they are. But it is the adage of those who have lost their paradise, and eat still the dry dust of reality not raised by science; the general world has not felt that divine curse, or it has been wiped away so that the most sensual fool may rejoice in feeling himself God's darling, and pities the paganism of Plato. Man and beast are certain that they do see things as they are. Maya's milk is tinctured from the poppies of her robe; untold millions of misgivings have been put to sleep by her tender bounty; the waters that sustain her are those of Lethe.

But beneath every illusive heaven Nature stretches also an illusive hell. The poppies lose their force at last, and under the scourge of necessity man wakes to find all his paradise of roses turned to briars. Maya's breast-fountains pass deeper than the surface—from one flows soft Lethe, the other issues at last in Phlegethon. Fear is even a more potent painter than Hope, and out of the manifold menaces of Nature can at last overlay the fairest illusions. It is a pathetic fact, that so soon as man begins to think his first theory infers a will at work wherever he sees no cause; his second, to suppose that it will harm him!

Harriet Martineau's account of her childish terror caused by seeing some prismatic colours dancing on the wall of a vacant room she was entering—'imps' that had no worse origin than a tremulous candelabrum, but which haunted her nerves through life—is an experience which may be traced in the haunted childhood of every nation. There are other phenomena besides these prismatic colours, which have had an evil name in popular superstition, despite their beauty. Strange it might seem to a Buddhist that yon exquisite tree with its blood-red buds should be called the Judas-tree, as to us that the graceful swan which might be the natural emblem of purity should be associated with witchcraft! But the student of mythology will at every moment be impressed by the fact that myths oftener represent a primitive science than mere fancies and conceits. The sinuous neck of the swan, its passionate jealousy, and the uncanny whistle, or else dumbness, found where, from so snowy an outside, melody might have been looked for, may have made this animal the type of a double nature. The treacherous brilliants of the serpent, or honey protected by stings, or the bright blossoms of poisons, would have trained the instinct which apprehends evil under the apparition of beauty. This, as we shall have occasion to see, has had a controlling influence upon the ethical constitution of our nature. But it is at present necessary to observe that the primitive science generally reversed the induction of our later philosophy; for where an evil or pain was discovered in anything, it concluded that such was its *raison d'être*, and its attractive qualities were simply a demon's treacherous bait. However, here are the first stimulants to self-control in the lessons that taught distrust of appearances.

Because many a pilgrim perished through a confidence in the lake-pictures of the mirage which led to carelessness about economising his skin of water, the mirage gained its present name—

Bahr Sheitan, or Devil's Water. The 'Will o' wisp,' which appeared to promise the night-wanderer warmth or guidance, but led him into a bog, had its excellent directions as to the place to avoid perverted by an unhappy misunderstanding into a wilful falsehood, and has been branded *ignis fatuus*. Most of the mimicries in nature gradually became as suspicious to the primitive observer as *aliases* to a magistrate. The thing that seemed to be fire, or water, but was not; the insect or animal which took its hue or form from some other, from the leaf-spotted or stem-striped cats to that innocent insect whose vegetal disguise has gained for it the familiar name of 'Devil's Walking-stick;' the humanlike hiss, laugh, or cry of animals; the vibratory sound or movement which so often is felt as if near when it really is far; the sand which seems hard but sinks; the sward which proves a bog;—all these have their representation in the demonology of delusion. The Coroados of Brazil says that the Evil One 'sometimes transforms (himself) into a swamp, &c., leads him astray, vexes him, brings him into danger, and even kills him.'[1] It is like an echo of Burton's account. 'Terrestrial devils are those lares, genii, faunes, satyrs, wood-nymphs, foliots, fairies, Robin Good-fellows, trulli, &c., which, as they are most conversant with men, so they do them most harm. These are they that dance on heaths and greens, as Lavater thinks with Trithemius, and, as Olaus Magnus adds, leave that green circle which we commonly find in plain fields. They are sometimes seen by old women and children. Hieron. Pauli, in his description of the city of Bercino, Spain, relates how they have been familiarly seen near that town, about fountains and hills. 'Sometimes,' saith Trithemius, 'they lead simple people into the recesses of mountains and show them wonderful sights,' &c. Giraldus Cambrensis gives an instance of a monk of Wales that was so deluded. Paracelsus reckons up many places in Germany where they do usually walk about in little coats, some two feet long.[2] Real dangers beset the woods and mountain passes, the swamp and quicksand; in such forms did they haunt the untamed jungles of imagination!

Over that sea on which Maya stands extends the silvery wand of Glamour. It descended to the immortal Old Man of the Sea, favourite of the nymphs, oracle of the coasts, patron of fishermen, friend of Proteus, who could see through all the sea's depths and assume all shapes. How many witcheries could proceed from the many-tinted sea to affect the eyes and enable them to see Triton with his wreathed horn, and mermaids combing their hair, and marine monsters, and Aphrodite poised on the white foam! Glaucoma it may be to the physicians; but Glaucus it is in the scheme of Maya, who has never left land or sea without her witness. Beside the Polar Sea a Samoyed sailor, asked by Castrén 'where is Num' (*i.e.*, Jumala, his god), pointed to the dark distant sea, and said, *He is there*.

To the ancients there were two seas,—the azure above, and that beneath. The imaginative child in its development passes all those dreamy coasts; sees in clouds mountains of snow on the horizon, and in the sunset luminous seas laving golden isles. When as yet to the young world the shining sun was Berchta, the white fleecy clouds were her swans. When she descended to the sea, as a thousand stories related, it was to repeat the course of the sun for all tribes looking on a westward sea. No one who has read that charming little book, 'The Gods in Exile,'[3] will wonder at the happy instinct of learning shown in Heine's little poem, 'Sonnenuntergang,'[4] wherein we see shining solar Beauty compelled to become the spinning housewife, or reluctant spouse of Poseidon:—

A lovely dame whom the old ocean-god
For convenience once had married;
And in the day-time she wanders gaily
Through the high heaven, purple-arrayed,
And all in diamonds gleaming,
And all beloved, and all amazing
To every worldly being,
And every worldly being rejoicing
With warmth and splendour from her glances.
Alas! at evening, sad and unwilling,
Back must she bend her slow steps
To the dripping house, to the barren embrace
Of grisly old age.

This of course is Heinesque, and has no relation to any legend of Bertha, but is a fair specimen of mythology in the making, and is quite in the spirit of many of the myths that have flitted around sunset on the sea. Whatever the explanation of their descent, the Shining One and her fleecy retinue were transformed. When to sea or lake came Berchta (or Perchta), it was as Bertha of the Large Foot (*i.e.*, webbed), or of the Long Nose (beak), and her troop were Swan-maidens. Their celestial character was changed with that of their mistress. They became familiars of sorcerers and sorceresses. To 'wear yellow slippers' became the designation of a witch.

How did these fleecy white cloud-phantoms become demonised? What connection is there between them and the enticing Lorelei and the dangerous Rhine-daughters watching over golden treasures, once, perhaps, metaphors of moonlight ripples? They who have listened to the wild laughter of these in Wagner's opera, *Das Rheingold,* and their weird 'Heiayaheia!' can hardly fail to suspect that they became associated with the real human nymphs whom the summer sun still finds freely sporting in the bright streams of Russia, Hungary, Austria, and East Germany, naked and not ashamed. Many a warning voice against these careless Phrynes, who may have left tattered raiment on the shore to be transfigured in the silvery waves, must have gone forth from priests and anxious mothers. Nor would there be wanting traditions enough to impress such warnings. Few regions have been without such stories as those which the travel-ler Hiouen-Thsang (7th century) found in Buddhist chronicles of the Rakshasis of Ceylon. 'They waylay the merchants who land in the isle, and, changing themselves to women of great beauty, come before them with fragrant flowers and music; attracting them with kind words to the town of Iron, they offer them a feast, and give themselves up to pleasure with them; then shut them in an iron prison, and eat them one after the other.'

There is a strong accent of human nature in the usual plot of the Swan-maiden legend, her garments stolen while she bathes, and her willingness to pay wondrous prices for them—since they are her feathers and her swanhood, without which she must re-main for ever captive of the thief. The stories are told in regions so widely sundered, and their minor details are so different, that we may at any rate be certain that they are not all traceable solely to fleecy clouds. Sometimes the garments of the demoness—and these beings are always feminine—are not feathery, as in the German stories, but seal-skins, or of nondescript red tissue. Thus, the Envoy Li Ting-yuan (1801) records a Chinese legend of a man named Ming-ling-tzu, a poor and worthy farmer without family, who, on going to draw water from a spring near his house, saw a woman bathing in it. She had hung her clothes on a pine tree, and, in punishment for her 'shameless ways' and for her fouling the well, he carried off the dress. The clothing was unlike the familiar Lewchewan in style, and 'of a ruddy sunset colour.' The woman, having finished her bath, cried out in great anger, 'What thief has been here in broad day? Bring back my clothes, quick.' She then perceived Ming-ling-tzu, and threw herself on the ground before him. He began to scold her, and asked why she came and fouled his water; to which she replied that both the pine tree and the well were made by the Creator for the use of all. The farmer entered into conversation with her, and pointed out that fate evidently intended her to be his wife, as he absolutely refused to give up her clothes, while without them she could not get away. The result was that they were married. She lived with him for ten years, and bore him a son and a daughter. At the end of that time her fate was fulfilled: she ascended a tree during the absence of her husband, and having bidden his children farewell, glided off on a cloud and disappeared.[5]

In South Africa a parallel myth, in its demonological aspect, bears no trace of a cloud origin. In this case a Hottentot, travelling with a Bushwoman and her child, met a troop of wild horses. They were all hungry; and the woman, taking off a petticoat made of human skin, was instantly changed into a lioness. She struck down a horse, and lapped its blood; then, at the request of the Hottentot, who in his terror had climbed a tree, she resumed her petticoat and womanhood, and the friends, after a meal of horseflesh, resumed their journey.[6] Among the Minussinian Tartars these demons partake of the nature of the Greek Harpies; they are bloodthirsty vampy-re-demons who drink the blood of men slain in battle, darken the air in their flight, and house themselves in one great black fiend.[7] As we go East the portrait of the Swan-maiden becomes less dark, and she is not associated with the sea or the under-world. Such is one among the Malays, related by Mr. Tylor. In the island of Celebes it is said that seven nymphs came down from the sky to bathe, and were seen by Kasimbaha, who at first thought them white doves, but in the bath perceived they were women. He stole the robe of one of them, Utahagi, and as she could not fly without it, she became his wife and bare him a son. She was called Utahagi because of a single magic white hair she had; this her husband pulled out, when immediately a storm arose, and she flew to heaven. The child was in great grief, and the husband cast about how he should follow her up into the sky.

The Swan-maiden appears somewhat in the character of a Nemesis in a Siberian myth told by Mr. Baring-Gould. A certain Samoyed who had stolen a Swan-maiden's robe, refused to return it unless she secured for him the heart of seven demon robbers, one of whom had killed the Samoyed's mother. The robbers were in the hab-it of hanging up their hearts on pegs in their tent. The Swan-maiden procured them. The Samoyed smashed six of the hearts; made the seventh robber resuscitate his mother, whose soul, kept in a purse, had only to be shaken over the old woman's grave for that feat to be accomplished, and the Swan-maiden got back her plumage and flew away rejoicing.[8]

In Slavonic Folklore the Swan-maiden is generally of a dangerous character, and if a swan is killed they are careful not to show it to children for fear they will die. When they appear as ducks, geese, and other water-fowl, they are apt to be more mischievous than when they come as pigeons; and it is deemed perilous to kill a pigeon, as among sailors it was once held to kill an albatross. Afanasief relates a legend which shows that, even when associated with the water-king, the Tsar Morskoi or Slavonic Neptune, the pigeon preserves its beneficent character. A king out hunting lies down to drink from a lake (as in the story related on p. 146), when Tsar Morskoi seizes him by the beard, and will not release him until he agrees to give him his infant son. The infant prince, deserted on the edge of the fatal lake, by advice of a sorceress hides in some bushes, whence he presently sees twelve pigeons arrive, which, having thrown off their feathers, disport themselves in the lake. At length a thirteenth, more beautiful than the rest, arrives, and her *sorochka* (shift) Ivan seizes. To recover it she agrees to be his wife, and, having told him he will find her beneath the waters, resumes her pigeon-shape and flies away. Beneath the lake he finds a beautiful realm, and though the Tsar Morskoi treats him roughly and imposes heavy tasks on him, the pigeon-maiden (Vassilissa) assists him, and they dwell together happily.[9]

In Norse Mythology the vesture of the uncanny maid is oftenest a seal-skin, and a vein of pathos enters the legends. Of the many legends of this kind, still believed in Sweden and Norway, one has been pleasantly versified by Miss Eliza Keary. A fisherman having found a pretty white seal-skin, took it home with him. At night there was a wailing at his door; the maid enters, becomes his wife, and bears him three children. But after seven years she finds the skin, and with it ran to the shore. The eldest child tells the story to the father on his return home.

> Then we three, Daddy,
> Ran after, crying, 'Take us to the sea!
> Wait for us, Mammy, we are coming too!
> Here's Alice, Willie can't keep up with you!
> Mammy, stop—just for a minute or two!'
> At last we came to where the hill
> Slopes straight down to the beach,
> And there we stood all breathless, still
> Fast clinging each to each.
> We saw her sitting upon a stone,
> Putting the little seal-skin on.
> O Mammy! Mammy!
> She never said goodbye, Daddy,
> She didn't kiss us three;
> She just put the little seal-skin on
> And slipt into the sea!

Some of the legends of this character are nearly as realistic as Mr. Swinburne's 'Morality' of David and Bathsheba. To imagine the scarcity of wives in regions to which the primitive Aryan race migrated, we have only to remember the *ben trovato* story of Californians holding a ball in honour of a bonnet, in the days before women had followed them in migration. To steal Bathsheba's clothes, and so capture her, might at one period have been sufficiently common in Europe to require all the terrors contained in the armoury of tradition concerning the demonesses that might so be taken in, and might so tempt men to take them in. In the end they might disappear, carrying off treasures in the most prosaic fashion, or perhaps they might bring to one's doors a small Trojan war. It is probable that the sentiment of modesty, so far as it is represented in the shame of nudity, was the result of prudential agencies. Though the dread of nudity has become in some regions a superstition in the female mind strong enough to have its martyrs—as was seen at the sinking of the *Northfleet* and the burning hotel in St. Louis—it is one that has been fostered by men in distrust of their own animalism. In barbarous regions, where civilisation introduces clothes, the women are generally the last to adopt them; and though Mr. Herbert Spencer attributes this to female conservatism, it appears more probable that it is because the men are the first to lose their innocence and the women last to receive anything expensive. It is noticeable how generally the Swan-maidens are said in the myths to be captured by violence or stratagem. At the same time the most unconscious temptress might be the means of breaking up homes and misleading workmen, and thus become invested with all the wild legends told of the illusory phenomena of nature in popular mythology.

It is marvellous to observe how all the insinuations of the bane were followed by equal dexterities in the antedote. The fair tempters might disguise their intent in an appeal to the wayfarer's humanity; and, behold, there were a thousand well-attested narratives ready for the lips of wife and mother showing the demoness appealing for succour to be fatalest of all!

There is a stone on the Müggelsberger, in Altmark, which is said to cover a treasure; this stone is sometimes called 'Devil's Altar,' and sometimes it is said a fire is seen there which disappears when approached. It lies on the verge of Teufelsee,—a lake dark and small, and believed to be fathomless. Where the stone lies a castle once stood which sank into the ground with its fair princess. But from the underground castle there is a subterranean avenue to a neighbouring hill, and from this hill of an evening sometimes comes an old woman, bent over her staff. Next day there will be seen a most beautiful lady combing her long golden hair. To all who pass she makes her entreaties that they will set her free, her pathetic appeals being backed by offer of a jewelled casket which she holds. The only means of liberating her is, she announces, that some one shall bear her on his shoulders three times round Teufelsee church without looking back. The experiment has several times been made. One villager at his first round saw a large hay-waggon drawn past him by four mice, and following it with his eyes received blows on the ears. Another saw a waggon drawn by four coal-black fire-breathing horses coming straight against him, started back, and all disappeared with the cry 'Lost again for ever!' A third tried and almost got through. He was found senseless, and on recovering related that when he took the princess on his shoulders she was light as a feather, but she grew heavier and heavier as he bore her round. Snakes, toads, and all horrible animals with fiery eyes surrounded him; dwarfs hurled blocks of wood and stones at him; yet he did not look back, and had nearly completed the third round, when he saw his village burst into flames; then he looked behind—a blow felled him—and he seems to have only lived long enough to tell this story. The youth of Köpernick are warned to steel their hearts against any fair maid combing her hair near Teufelsee. But the folklore of the same neighbourhood admits that it is by no means so dangerous for dames to listen to appeals of this kind. In the Gohlitzsee, for example, a midwife was induced to plunge in response to a call for aid; having aided a little Merwoman in travail, she was given an apronful of dust, which appeared odd until on shore it proved to be many thalers.

In countries where the popular imagination, instead of being scientific, is trained to be religiously retrospective, it relapses at the slightest touch into the infantine speculations of the human race. Not long ago, standing at a shop-window in Ostend where a 'Japanese Siren' was on view, the clever imposture interested me less than the comments of the passing and pausing observers. The most frequent wonders seriously expressed were, whether she sang, or combed her hair, or was under a doom, or had a soul to be saved. Every question related to Circe, Ulysses and the Sirens, and other conceptions of antiquity. The Japanese artists rightly concluded they could float their Siren in any intellectual waters where Jonah in his whale could pass, or a fish appear with its penny. Nay, even in their primitive form the Sirens find their kith and kin still haunting all the coasts of northern Europe. A type of the Irish and Scottish Siren may be found in the very complete legend of one seen by John Reid, shipmaster of Cromarty. With long flowing yellow hair she sat half on a rock, half in water, nude and beautiful, half woman half fish, and John managed to catch and hold her tight till she had promised to fulfil three wishes; then, released, she sprang into the sea. The wishes were all fulfilled, and to one of them (though John would never reveal it) the good-luck of the Reids was for a century after ascribed.[10]

The scene of this legend is the 'Dropping Cave,' and significantly near the Lover's Leap. One of John's wishes included the success of his courtship. These Caves run parallel with that of Venusberg, where the minstrel Tannhäuser is tempted by Venus and her nymphs. Heine finishes off his description of this Frau Venus by saying he fancied he met her one day in the Place Bréda. 'What do you take this lady to be?' asked he of Balzac, who was with him. 'She is a mistress,' replied Balzac. 'A duchess rather,' returned Heine. But the friends found on further explanation that they were both quite right. Venus' doves, soiled for a time, were spiritualised at last and made white, while the snowy swan grew darker. An old German word for swan, *elbiz*, originally denoting its whiteness (*albus*), furthered its connection with all 'elfish' beings—*elf* being from the same word, meaning white; but, as in Goethe's 'Erl König,' often disguising a dark character. The Swan and the Pigeon meet (with some modifications) as symbols of the Good and Evil powers in the legend of Lohengrin. The witch transforms the boy into a Swan, which, however, draws to save his sister, falsely accused of his murder, the Knight of the Sangreal, who, when the mystery of his holy name is inquired into by his too curious bride, is borne away by white doves. These legends all bear in them, however faintly, the accent of the early conflict of religion with the wild passions of mankind. Their religious bearings bring us to inquiries which must be considered at a later phase of our work. But apart from purely moral considerations, it is evident that there must have been practical dangers surrounding the early social chaos amid which the first immigrants in Europe found themselves.

Although the legend of Lady Godiva includes elements of another origin, it is probable that in the fate of Peeping Tom there is a distant reflection of the punishment sometimes said to overtake those who gazed too curiously upon the Swan-maiden without her feathers. The devotion of the nude lady of Coventry would not be out of keeping with one class of these mermaiden myths. There is a superstition, now particularly strong in Iceland, that all fairies are children of Eve, whom she hid away on an occasion when the Lord came to visit her, because they were not washed and presentable. So he condemned them to be for ever invisible. This superstition seems to be related to an old debate whether these præternatural beings are the children of Adam and Eve or not. A Scotch story bears against that conclusion. A beautiful nymph, with a slight robe of green, came from the sea and approached a fisherman while he was reading his Bible. She asked him if it contained any promise of mercy for her. He replied that it contained an offer of salvation to 'all the children of Adam;' whereupon with a loud shriek she dashed into the sea again. Euphemism would co-operate with natural compassion in saying a good word for 'the good little people,' whether hiding in earth or sea. In Altmark, 'Will-o'-wisps' are believed to be the souls of unbaptized children—sometimes of lunatics—unable to rest in their graves; they are called 'Light-men,' and it is said that though they may sometimes mislead they often guide rightly, especially if a small coin be thrown them,—this being also an African plan of breaking a sorcerer's spell. Christianity long after its advent in Germany had to contend seriously with customs and beliefs found in some lakeside villages where the fishermen regarded themselves as in friendly relations with the præternatural guardians of the waters, and unto this day speak of their presiding sea-maiden as a Holy Fräulein. They hear her bells chiming up from the depths in holy seasons to mingle with those whose sounds are wafted from church towers; and it seems to have required many fables, told by prints of fishermen found sitting lifeless on their boats while listening to them, to gradually transfer reverence to the new christian fairy.

It may be they heard some such melody as that which has found its finest expression in Mr. Matthew Arnold's 'Forsaken Merman:'—

Children dear, was it yesterday
(Call yet once) that she went away?
Once she sate with you and me,
On a red gold throne in the heart of the sea,
And the youngest sate on her knee.
She comb'd its bright hair, and she tended it well,
When down swung the sound of the far-off bell.
She sigh'd, she look'd up through the clear green sea;
She said: 'I must go, for my kinsfolk pray
In the little grey church on the shore to-day.
'Twill be Easter-time in the world—ah me!
And I lose my poor soul, Merman, here with thee.'
I said, 'Go up, dear heart, through the waves,
Say thy prayer, and come back to the kind sea-caves.'
She smil'd, she went up through the surf in the bay.
Children dear, was it yesterday?

Perhaps we should find the antecedents of this Merman's lost Margaret, whom he called back in vain, in the Danish ballad of 'The Merman and the Marstig's Daughter,' who, in Goethe's version,

sought the winsome May in church,
thither riding as a gay knight on

horse of the water clear,
The saddle and bridle of sea-sand were.

They went from the church with the bridal train,
They danced in glee, and they danced full fain;
They danced them down to the salt-sea strand,
And they left them standing there, hand in hand.

'Now wait thee, love, with my steed so free,
And the bonniest bark I'll bring for thee.'
And when they passed to the white, white sand,
The ships came sailing on to the land;

But when they were out in the midst of the sound,
Down went they all in the deep profound!
Long, long on the shore, when the winds were high,
They heard from the waters the maiden's cry.

I rede ye, damsels, as best I can—
Tread not the dance with the Water-Man!

According to other legends, however, the realm under-sea was not a place for weeping. Child-eyes beheld all that the Erl-king promised, in Goethe's ballad—

Wilt thou go, bonny boy? wilt thou go with me?
My daughters shall wait on thee daintily;
My daughters around thee in dance shall sweep,
And rock thee and kiss thee, and sing thee to sleep!

Or perhaps child-eyes, lingering in the burning glow of manhood's passion, might see in the peaceful sea some picture of lost love like that so sweetly described in Heine's 'Sea Phantom:'—

But I still leaned o'er the side of the vessel,
Gazing with sad-dreaming glances
Down at the water, clear as a mirror,
Looking yet deeper and deeper,—
Till far in the sea's abysses,
At first like dim wavering vapours,
Then slowly—slowly—deeper in colour,
Domes of churches and towers seemed rising,
And then, as clear as day, a city grand....
Infinite longing, wondrous sorrow,
Steal through my heart,—
My heart as yet scarce healed;
It seems as though its wounds, forgotten,
By loving lips again were kissed,
And once again were bleeding
Drops of burning crimson,
Which long and slowly trickle down
Upon an ancient house below there
In the deep, deep sea-town,
On an ancient, high-roofed, curious house,
Where, lone and melancholy,
Below by the window a maiden sits,
Her head on her arm reclined,—
Like a poor and uncared-for child;
And I know thee, thou poor and long-sorrowing child!
... I meanwhile, my spirit all grief,
Over the whole broad world have sought thee,
And ever have sought thee,
Thou dearly beloved,
Thou long, long lost one,
Thou finally found one,—
At last I have found thee, and now am gazing
Upon thy sweet face,
With earnest, faithful glances,
Still sweetly smiling;
And never will I again on earth leave thee.
I am coming adown to thee,
And with longing, wide-reaching embraces,
Love, I leap down to thy heart!

The temptations of fishermen to secure objects seen at the bottom of transparent lakes, sometimes appearing like boxes or lumps of gold, and even more reflections of objects in the upper world or air, must have been sources of danger; there are many tales of their being so beguiled to destruction. These things were believed treasures of the little folk who live under water, and would not part with them except on payment. In Blumenthal lake, 'tis said, there is an iron-bound yellow coffer which fishermen often have tried to raise, but their cords are cut as it nears the surface. At the bottom of the same lake valuable clothing is seen, and a woman who once tried to secure it was so nearly drowned that it is thought safer to leave it. The legends of sunken towns (as in Lake Paarsteinchen and Lough Neagh), and bells (whose chimes may be heard on certain sacred days), are probably variants of this class of delusions. They are often said to have been sunk by some final vindictive stroke of a magician or witch resolved to destroy the city no longer trusting them. Landslides, engulfing seaside homes, might originate legends like that of King Gradlon's daughter Dahut, whom the Breton peasant sees in rough weather on rocks around Poul-Dahut, where she unlocked the sluice-gates on the city Is in obedience to her fiend-lover.

If it be remembered that less than fifty years ago Dr. Belon [11] thought it desirable to anatomise gold fishes, and prove in various ways that it is a fallacy to suppose they feed on pure gold (as many a peasant near Lyons declares of the laurets sold daily in the market), it will hardly be thought wonderful that perilous visions of precious things were seen by early fishermen in pellucid depths, and that these should at last be regarded as seductive arts of Lorelei, who have given many lakes and rivers the reputation of requiring one or more annual victims.

Possibly it was through accumulation of many dreams about beautiful realms beneath the sea or above the clouds that suicide became among the Norse folk so common. It was a proverb that the worst end was to die in bed, and to die by suicide was to be like Egil, and Omund, and King Hake, like nearly all the heroes who so passed to Valhalla. The Northman had no doubt concerning the paradise to which he was going, and did not wish to reach it enfeebled by age. But the time would come when the earth and human affection must assert their claims, and the watery tribes be pictured as cruel devourers of the living. Even so would the wood-nymphs and mountain-nymphs be degraded, and fearful legends of those lost and wandering in dark forests be repeated to shuddering childhood. The actual dangers would mask themselves in the endless disguises of illusion, the wold and wave be peopled with cruel and treacherous seducers. Thus suicide might gradually lose its charms, and a dismal underworld of heartless gnomes replace the grottoes and fairies.

We may close this chapter with a Scottish legend relating to the 'Shi'ichs,' or Men of Peace, in which there is a strange intimation of a human mind dreaming that it dreams, and so far on its way to waking. A woman was carried away by these shadowy beings in order that she might suckle her child which they had previously stolen. During her retention she once observed the Shi'ichs anointing their eyes from a caldron, and seizing an opportunity, she managed to anoint one of her own eyes with the ointment. With that one eye she now saw the secret abode and all in it 'as they really were.' The deceptive splendour had vanished. The gaudy ornaments of a fairy grot had become the naked walls of a gloomy cavern. When this woman had returned to live among human beings again, her anointed eye saw much that others saw not; among other things she once saw a 'man of peace,' invisible to others, and asked him about her child. Astonished at being recognised, he demanded how she had been able to discover him; and when she had confessed, he spit in her eye and extinguished it for ever.

NOTES
1   Von Spix and Von Martin's 'Travels in Brazil,' p. 243.
2   'Anatomy of Melancholy.' Fifteenth Edition, p. 124.
3   'Les Dieux en Exile.' Heinrich Heine. Revue des Deux Mondes, April, 1853.
4   'Book of Songs.' Translated by Charles E. Leland. New York: Henry Holt & Co. 1874.
5   Dennys.
6   Bleek, 'Hottentot Fables,' p. 58.
7   Baring-Gould, 'Curious Myths,' &c.
8   Ibid., ii. 299.
9   'Shaski,' vi. 48.
10 Hugh Miller, 'Scenes and Legends,' p. 293.
11 'The Mirror,' April 7, 1832

Chapter X
Darkness

Shadows — Night Deities — Kobolds — Walpurgisnacht — Night as Abettor of
Evil-doers — Nightmare — Dreams — Invisible Foes — Jacob and his Phantom
— Nott — The Prince of Darkness — The Brood of Midnight — Second-Sight —
Spectres of Souter Fell — The Moonshine Vampyre — Glamour —
Glam and Grettir — A Story of Dartmoor

FROM THE LITTLE night which clings to man even by day—his own
shadow—to the world's great shade of darkness, innumerable are
the coverts from which have emerged the black procession of phantoms which have haunted the slumbers of the world, and betrayed
the enterprise of man.

How strange to the first man seemed that shadow walking beside
him, from the time when he saw it as a ghost tracking its steps and giving him his name for a ghost, on to the period in which it seemed the
emanation of an occult power, as to them who brought their sick into
the streets to be healed by the passing shadow of Peter; and still on to
the day when Beaumont wrote—

> Our acts our angels are, or good or ill,
> Our fatal shadows that walk by us still;

or that in which Goethe found therein the mystical symbol of
the inward arrest of our moral development, and said 'No man can
jump off of his shadow.' And then from the culture of Europe we pass
to the Feejee-Islanders, and find them believing that every man has

two spirits. One is his shadow, which goes to Hades; the other is his image as reflected in water, and it is supposed to stay near the place where the man dies.[1] But, like the giants of the Brocken, these demons of the Shadow are trembled at long after they are known to be the tremblers themselves mirrored on air. Have we not priests in England still fostering the belief that the baptized child goes attended by a white spirit, the unbaptized by a dark one? Why then need we apologise for the Fijians?

But little need be said here of demons of the Dark, for they are closely related to the phantasms of Delusion, of Winter, and others already described. Yet have they distinctive characters. As many as were the sunbeams were the shadows; every goddess of the Dawn (Ushas) cast her shadow; every Day was swallowed up by Night. This is the cavern where hide the treacherous Panis (fog) in Vedic mythology, they who steal and hide Indra's cows; this is the realm of Hades (the invisible); this is the cavern of the hag Thökk (dark) in Scandinavian mythology,—she who alone of all in the universe refused to weep for Baldur when he was shut up in Helheim, where he had been sent by the dart of his blind brother Hödr (darkness). In the cavern of Night sleep the Seven Sleepers of Ephesus, and Barbarossa, and all slumbering phantoms whose genius is the night-winged raven. Thorr, the Norse Hercules, once tried to lift a cat—as it seemed to him—from the ground; but it was the great mid-earth serpent which encircles the whole earth. Impossible feat as it was for Thorr—who got only one paw of the seeming cat off the ground—in that glassless and gasless era, invention has accomplished much in that direction; but the black Cat is still domiciled securely among idols of the mental cave.

There is an Anglo-Saxon word, *cof-godas* (lit. cove-gods), employed as the equivalent of the Latin *lares* (the Penates, too, are interpreted as *cof-godu, cofa* signifying the inner recess of a house, *penetrale*). The word in German corresponding to this *cofa*, is *koben*; and from this Hildebrand conjectures *kob-old* to be derived. The latter part of the word he supposes to be walt (one who 'presides over,' *e.g.*, Walter); so that the original form would be *kob-walt*.[2] Here, then, in the recesses of the household, among the least enlightened of its members—the menials, who still often neutralise the efforts of rational people to dispel the delusions of their children—the discredited deities and demons of the past found refuge, and through a little baptismal change of names are familiars of millions unto this day. In the words of the ancient Hebrew, 'they lay in their own houses prisoners of darkness, fettered with the bonds of a long night.' 'No power of the fire might give them light, neither could the bright flames of the stars lighten that horrible night.'[3] Well is it added, 'Fear is nothing else but a betraying of the succours which reason offereth,' a truth which finds ample illustration in the Kobolds. These imaginary beings were naturally associated with the dark recesses of mines. There they gave the name to our metal *Cobalt*. The value of Cobalt was not understood until the 17th century, and the metal was first obtained by the Swedish chemist Brandt in 1733. The miners had believed that the silver was stolen away by Kobolds, and these 'worthless' ores left in its place. Nickel had the like history, and is named after Old Nick. So long did those Beauties slumber in the cavern of Ignorance till Science kissed them with its sunbeam, and led them forth to decorate the world!

How passed this (mental) cave-dweller even amid the upper splendours and vastnesses of his unlit world? A Faust guided by his Mephistopheles only amid interminable Hartz labyrinths.

> How sadly rises, incomplete and ruddy,
> The moon's lone disk, with its belated glow,
> And lights so dimly, that, as one advances,
> At every step one strikes a rock or tree!
> Let us then use a Jack-o'-lantern's glances:
> I see one yonder, burning merrily.
> Ho, there! my friend! I'll levy thine attendance:
> Why waste so vainly thy resplendence?
> Be kind enough to light us up the steep!
>
> Tell me, if we still are standing,
> Or if further we're ascending?
> All is turning, whirling, blending,
> Trees and rocks with grinning faces,
> Wandering lights that spin in mazes,
> Still increasing and expanding.[4]

It could only have been at a comparatively late period of social development that Sancho's benediction on the inventor of sleep could have found general response. The Red Indian found its helplessness fatal when the 'Nick of the Woods' was abroad; the Scotch sailor found in it a demon's opiate when the 'Nigg of the Sea' was gathering his storms above the sleeping watchman. It was among the problems of Job, the coöperation of darkness with evil-doers.

> The eye of the adulterer waiteth for the twilight;
> He saith, No eye will see me,
> And putteth a mask upon his face.

In the dark men break into houses;
In the day-time they shut themselves up;
They are strangers to the light.
The morning to them is the shadow of death;
They are familiar with the dark terrors of midnight.

Besides this fact that the night befriends and masks every treacherous foe, it is also to be remembered that man is weakest at night. Not only is he weaker than by day in the veil drawn over his senses, but physiologically also. When the body is wearied out by the toils or combats of the day, and the mind haunted by dreams of danger, there are present all the terrors which Byron portrays around the restless pillow of Sardanapalus. The war-horse of the day becomes a night-mare in the darkness. In the Heimskringla it is recorded: 'Vanland, Svegdir's son, succeeded his father and ruled over the Upsal domain. He was a great warrior, and went far around in different lands. Once he took up his winter abode in Finland with Snio the Old, and got his daughter Drisa in marriage; but in spring he set out leaving Drisa behind, and although he had promised to return within three years he did not come back for ten. Then Drisa sent a message to the witch Hulda; and sent Visbur, her son by Vanland, to Sweden. Drisa bribed the witch-wife Hulda, either that she should bewitch Vanland to return to Finland or kill him. When this witch-work was going on Vanland was at Upsal, and a great desire came over him to go to Finland, but his friends and counsellors advised him against it, and said the witchcraft of the Fin people showed itself in this desire of his to go there. He then became very drowsy, and laid himself down to sleep; but when he had slept but a little while he cried out, saying, 'Mara was treading on him.' His men hastened to help him; but when they took hold of his head she trod on his legs, and when they laid hold of his legs she pressed upon his head; and it was his death."[5]

This witch is, no doubt, Hildur, a Walkyr of the Edda, leading heroes to Walhalla. Indeed, in Westphalia, nightmare is called Wal-riderske. It is a curious fact that 'Mara' should be preserved in the French word for nightmare, *Cauche-mar*, 'cauche' being from Latin *calcare*, to tread. Through Teutonic folklore this Night-demon of many names, having floated from England in a sieve paddled with cow-ribs, rides to the distress of an increasingly unheroic part of the population. Nearly always still the 'Mahrt' is said to be a pretty woman,—sometimes, indeed, a sweetheart is involuntarily trans-formed to one,—every rustic settlement abounding with tales of how the demoness has been captured by stopping the keyhole, calling the ridden sleeper by his baptismal name, and making the sign of the cross; by such process the wicked beauty appears in human form, and is apt to marry the sleeper, with usually evil results. The fondness of cats for getting on the breasts of sleepers, or near their breath, for warmth, has made that animal a common form of the 'Mahrt.' Sometimes it is a black fly with red ring around its neck. This demoness is believed to suffer more pain than it inflicts, and vainly endeavours to destroy herself.

In savage and nomadic times sound sleep being an element of danger, the security which required men to sleep on their arms demanded also that they should sleep as it were with one eye open. Thus there might have arisen both the intense vividness which de-mons acquired by blending subjective and objective impressions, and the curious inability, so frequent among barbarians and not unknown among the men civilised, to distinguish dream from fact. The habit of day-dreaming seems, indeed, more general than is usually supposed. Dreams haunt all the region of our intellectual twilight,—the borderland of mystery, where rise the sources of the occult and the mystical which environ our lives. The daily terrors of barbarous life avail to haunt the nerves of civilised people, now many generations after they have passed away, with special and irrational shudders at certain objects or noises: how then must they have haunted the dreams of humanity when, like the daughter of Nathan the Wise, rescued from flames, it passed the intervals of strife

> With nerves unstrung through fear,
> And fire and flame in all she sees or fancies;
> Her soul awake in sleep, asleep when wide awake?

Among the sources of demoniac beliefs few indeed are more prolific than Dreams. 'The witchcraft of sleep,' says Emerson, 'divides with truth the empire of our lives. This soft enchantress visits two children lying locked in each other's arms, and carries them asunder by wide spans of land and sea, wide intervals of time. 'Tis superfluous to think of the dreams of multitudes; the astonishment remains that one should dream; that we should resign so quietly this deifying reason and become the theatre of delusions, shows, wherein time, space, persons, cities, animals, should dance before us in merry and mad confusion, a delicate creation outdoing the prime and flower of actual nature, antic comedy alternating with horrid spectres. Or we seem busied for hours and days in peregrinations over seas and lands, in earnest dialogues, strenuous actions for nothings and absurdities, cheated by spectral jokes, and waking suddenly with ghostly laughter, to be rebuked by the cold lonely silent midnight, and to rake with confusion in memory among the gibbering nonsense to find the motive of this contemptible cachinnation.'[6]

It has always been the worst of periods of religious excitement that they shape the dreams of old and young, and find there a fearful and distorted, but vivid and realistic, embodiment of their feverish experiences. In the days of witchcraft thousands visited the Witches' Sabbaths, as they believed and danced in the Walpurgis orgies, borne (by hereditary orthodox canon) on their own brooms up their own chimneys; and to-day, by the same morbid imaginations, the victims are able to see themselves or others elongated, levitated, floating through the air. If people only knew how few are ever really wide-awake, these spiritual nightmares would soon reach their termination. The natural terrors before which helpless man once cowered, have been prolonged past all his real victories over his demons by a succession of such nightmares, so that the vulgar religion might be portrayed somewhat as Richard Wagner described his first tragedy, in which, having killed off forty-two of his characters, he had to bring them back as ghosts to carry on the fifth act!

The perils of darkness, as ambush of foes human and animal, concealer of pitfalls, misguider of footsteps, misdirector of aims, were more real than men can well imagine in an age of gaslight plus the policeman. The myth of Joshua commanding the sun to stand still; the cry of Ajax when darkness fell on the combat, 'Grant me but to see!' refer us to the region from which come all childish shudders at going into the dark. The limit of human courage is reached where its foe is beyond the reach of its force. Fighting in the dark may even be suicidal. A German fable of blindfold zeal—the awakened sleeper demolishing his furniture and knocking out his own teeth in the attempt to punish cats—has its tragical illustrations also. But none of these actual dangers have been of more real evil to man than the demonisation of them. This rendered his very skill a blunder, his energy weakness. If it was bad to retreat in the dusk from an innocent bush into an unrecognised well, it was worse to meet the ghost with rune or crucifix and find it an assassin. When man fights with his shadow, he instantly makes it the demon he fears; ghoul-like it preys upon his paralysed strength, vampyre-like it sucks his blood, and he is consigned disarmed to the evil that is no shadow. The Scottish Sinclair marching through Norway, in the 16th century, owes his monument at Wiblungen rather to the magpie believed to precede him as a spy, with night and day upon its wings, than to his own prowess or power.

In a sense all demons, whatever their shapes, are the ancient brood of night. Mental darkness, even more moral darkness within, supply the phantasmagoria in which unknown things shape themselves as demons. Esau is already reconciled, but guilty Jacob must still wrestle with him as a phantom of Fear till daybreak. A work has already been written on 'The Night-side of Nature,' but it would require many volumes to tell the story of what monsters have been conjured out of the kind protecting darkness. How great is the darkness which man makes for himself out of the imagination which should be his light and vision! Much of the so-called 'religion' of our time is but elaborate demoniculture and artificial preservation of mental Walpurgis-nights. Nott (Night) says the Edda rides first on her horse called Hrimfaxi (frost-maned), which every morning as he ends his course bedews the earth with the foam that falls from his bit. Though the horse of Day— Skinfaxi, or Shining-mane—follows hard after her, yet the foam is by no means drunk up by his fires. Foam of the old phantasms still lingers in our mediæval liturgies, and even falls afresh where the daylight is shut out that altar-candles may burn, or for other dark seances are prepared the conditions necessary for whatsoever loves not the light.

What we call the Dark Ages were indeed spiritually a perpetual seance with lights lowered. Nay, human superstition was able to turn the very moon and stars into mere bluish night-tapers, giving just light enough to make the darkness visible in fantastic shapes fluttering around the Prince of Darkness,—or Non-existence in Chief! How much of the theosophic speculation of our time is the mere artificial conservation of that darkness? How much that still flits bat-winged from universities, will, in the future, be read with the same wonder as that with which even the more respectable bats can now read account of the midnight brood which now for the most part sleep tranquilly in such books as Burton's 'Anatomy of Melancholy'? 'There are,' he says, 'certain spirits which Miraldus calls Ambulones, that walk about midnight on great heaths and desert places, which (saith Lavater) draw men out of their way, and lead them all night by a byway, or quite bar them of their way. These have several names in several places. We commonly call them Pucks. In the deserts of Lop, in Asia, such illusions of walking spirits are often perceived, as you may read in M. Paulus, the Venetian, his travels. If one lose his company by chance, these devils will call him by his name, and counterfeit voices of his companions to seduce him. Lavater and Cicogna have a variety of examples of spirits and walking devils in this kind. Sometimes they sit by the wayside to give men falls, and make their horses stumble and start as they ride (according to the narration of that holy man Ketellus in Nubrigensis, that had an especial grace to see devils); and if a man curse and spur his horse for stumbling, they do heartily rejoice at it.'

While observing a spirited and imaginative picture by Macallum of the Siege of Jerusalem, it much interested me to observe the greater or less ease with which other visitors discovered the portents in the air which, following the narrative of Josephus, the artist had vaguely portrayed. The chariots and horsemen said to have been seen before that event were here faintly blent with indefinite outlines of clouds; and while some of the artist's friends saw them with a distinctness greater, perhaps, than that with which they impressed the eye of the artist himself, others could hardly be made to see anything except shapeless vapour, though of course they all agreed that they were there and remarkably fine.

It would seem that thus, in a London studio, there were present all the mental pigments for frescoing the air and sky with those visions of aërial armies or huntsmen which have become so normal in history as to be, in a subjective sense, natural. In the year 1763, an author, styling himself Theophilus Insulanus, published at Edinburgh a book on Second-Sight, in which he related more than a hundred instances of the power he believed to exist of seeing events before they had occurred, and whilst, of course, they did not exist. It is not difficult in reading them to see that they are all substantially one and the same story, and that the sight in operation was indeed second; for man or woman, at once imaginative and illiterate, have a second and supernumerary pair of eyes inherited from the traditional superstitions and ghost stories which fill all the air they breathe from the cradle to the grave. While the mind is in this condition, that same nature whose apparitions and illusions originally evoked and fostered the glamoury, still moves on with her minglings of light and shade, cloud and mirage, giving no word of explanation. There are never wanting the shadowy forms without that cast their shuttles to the dark idols of the mental cave, together weaving subtle spells round the half-waking mind.

In the year 1743 all the North of England and Scotland was in alarm on account of some spectres which were seen on the mountain of Souter Fell in Cumberland. The mountain is about half-a-mile high. On a summer evening a farmer and his servant, looking from Wilton Hall, half a mile off, saw the figures of a man and a dog pursuing some horses along the mountain-side, which is very steep; and on the following morning they repaired to the place, expecting to find dead bodies, but finding none. About one year later a troop of horsemen were seen riding along the same mountain-side by one of the same persons, the servant, who then called others who also saw the aërial troopers. After a year had elapsed the above vision was attested before a magistrate by two of those who saw it. The event occurred on the eve of the Rebellion, when horsemen were exercising, and when also the popular mind along the Border may be supposed to have been in a highly excited condition.

What was seen on this strongly-authenticated occasion? Was anything seen? None can tell. It is open to us to believe that there may have been some play of mirage. As there are purely aërial echoes, so are there aërial reflectors for the eye. On the other hand, the vision so nearly resembles the spectral processions which have passed through the mythology of the world, that we can never be sure that it was not the troop of King Arthur, emerging from Avallon to announce the approaching strife. A few fleecy, strangely-shaped clouds, chasing each other along the hillside in the evening's dusk would have amply sufficed to create the latter vision, and the danger of the time would easily have supplied all the Second-Sight required to reveal it to considerable numbers. In questions of this kind a very small circumstance—a phrase, a name, perhaps—may turn the balance of probabilities. Thus it may be noted that, in the instance just related, the vision was seen on the steep side of Souter Fell. *Fell* means a hill or a steep rock, as in Drachenfels. But as to Souter, although, as Mr. Robert Ferguson says, the word may originally have meant sheep,[7] it is found in Scotland used as 'shoemaker' in connection with the fabulous giants of that region. Sir Thomas Urquhart, in the seventeenth century, relates it as the tradition of the two promontories of Cromarty, called 'Soutars,' that they were the work-stools of two giants who supplied their comrades with shoes and buskins. Possessing but one set of implements, they used to fling these to each other across the opening of the firth, where the promontories are only two miles apart. In process of time the name Soutar, shoemaker, was bequeathed by the craftsmen to their stools. It is not improbable that the name gradually connected itself with other places bearing traditions connecting them with the fabulous race, and that in this way the Souter Fell, from meaning in early times much the same as Giants' Hill, preserved even in 1743–44 enough of the earlier uncanny associations to awaken the awe of Borderers in a time of rebellion. The vision may therefore have been seen by light which had journeyed all the way from the mythologic heavens of ancient India: substantially subjective—such stuff as dreams and dreamers are made of—no doubt there were outer clouds, shapes and afterglows enough, even in the absence of any *fata morgana* to supply canvas and pigment to the cunning artist that hides in the eye.

In an old tale, the often-slain Vampyre-bat only requests, with pathos, that his body may be laid where no sunlight, but only the moonlight, will fall on it—only that! But it is under the moonshine that it always gains new life. No demon requires absolute darkness, but half-darkness, in which to live: enough light to disclose a Somewhat, but not enough to define and reveal its nature, is just what has been required for the bat-eyes of fable and phantasy, which can make vampyre of a sparrow or giant out of a windmill.

Glamour! A marvellous history has this word of the artists and poets,—sometimes meaning the charm with which the eye invests any object; or, in Wordsworth's phrase, 'the light that never was on land or sea.' But no artist or poet ever rose to the full height of the simple term itself, which well illustrates Emerson's saying, 'Words are fossil poetry.' Professor Cowell of Cambridge says: 'Glám, or in the nominative *Glámr*, is also a poetical name for the Moon. It does not actually occur in the ancient literature, but it is given in the glossary in the Prose Edda in the list of the very old words for the

Moon.' Vigfusson in his dictionary says, 'The word is interesting on account of its identity with Scot. *Glamour*, which shows that the tale of *Glam* was common to Scotland and Iceland, and this much older than Grettir (in the year 1014).' The Ghost or Goblin Glam seems evidently to have arisen from a personification of the delusive and treacherous effects of moonlight on the benighted traveller,

Quale per incertam lunam sub luce malignâ,
Est iter in sylvis.

Now, there is a curious old Sanskrit word, *glau* or *gláv*, which is explained in all the old native lexicons as meaning 'the moon.' It might either be taken as 'waning,' or in a casual sense 'obscuring.'

The following lines from an early mediæval poet, Bhása (seventh century), will illustrate the deceptive character of moonlight from a Hindu point of view. The strong and wild Norse imagination delights in what is terrible and gloomy: the Hindu loves to dwell on the milder and quieter aspects of human life.

'The cat laps the moonbeams in the bowl of water, thinking them to be milk: the elephant thinks that the moonbeams, threaded through the intervals of the trees, are the fibres of the lotus-stalk. The woman snatches at the moonbeams as they lie on the bed, taking them for her muslin garment: oh, how the moon, intoxicated with radiance, bewilders all the world!'

A similar passage, no doubt imitated from this, is also quoted:

'The bewildered herdsmen place the pails under the cows, thinking that the milk is flowing; the maidens also put the blue lotus blossom in their ears, thinking that it is the white; the mountaineer's wife snatches up the jujube fruit, avaricious for pearls. Whose mind is not led astray by the thickly clustering moonbeams?'[8]

In the Icelandic legend of the struggle between the hero Grettir, translated by Magnússen and Morris (London, 1869), the saga supplies a scenery as archæological as if the philologists had been consulted. 'Bright moonlight was there without, and the drift was broken, now drawn over the moon, now driven off from her; and even as Glam fell, a cloud was driven from the moon, and Glam glared up against her.' When the hero beheld these glaring eyes of the giant Ghost, he felt some fiendish craft in them, and could not draw his short sword, and 'lay well nigh 'twixt home and hell.' This half-light of the moon, which robs the Strong of half his power, is repeated in Glam's curse: 'Exceedingly eager hast thou sought to meet me, Grettir, but no wonder will it be deemed, though thou gettest no good hap of me; and this I must tell thee, that thou now hast got half the strength and manhood which was thy lot if thou hadst not met me: now I may not take from thee the strength which thou hast got before this; but that may I rule, that thou shalt never be mightier than now thou art ... therefore this weird I lay on thee, ever in those days to see these eyes with thine eyes, and thou wilt find it hard to be alone—and that shalt drag thee unto death.'

The Moon-demon's power is limited to the spell of illusion he can cast. Presently he is laid low; the 'short sword' of a sunbeam pales, decapitates him. But after Glam is burned to cold coals, and his ashes buried in skin of a beast 'where sheep-pastures were fewest, or the ways of men,' the spell lay upon the hero's eyes. 'Grettir said that his temper had been nowise bettered by this, that he was worse to quiet than before, and that he deemed all trouble worse than it was; but that herein he found the greatest change, in that he was become so fearsome a man in the dark, that he durst go nowhither alone after nightfall, for then he seemed to see all kinds of horrors. And that has fallen since into a proverb, that Glam lends eyes, or gives Glamsight to those who see things nowise as they are.'

In reading which one may wonder how this world would look if for a little moment one's eyes could be purged of glamour. Even at the moon's self one tries vainly to look: where Hindu and Zulu see a hare, the Arab sees coils of a serpent, and the Englishman sees a man; and the most intelligent of these several races will find it hard to see in the moon aught save what their primitive ancestors saw. And this small hint of the degree to which the wisest, like Merlin, are bound fast in an air-prison by a Vivien whose spells are spun from themselves, would carry us far could we only venture to follow it out. 'The Moon,' observed Dr. Johnson unconsciously, 'has great influence in vulgar philosophy.' How much lunar theology have we around us, so that many from the cradle to the grave get no clear sight of nature or of themselves! Very closely did Carlyle come to the fable of Glam when speaking of Coleridge's 'prophetic moonshine,' and its effect on poor John Sterling. 'If the bottled moonshine *be* actually substance? Ah, could one but believe in a church while finding it incredible!... The bereaved young lady *has* taken the veil then!... To such lengths can transcendental moonshine, cast by some morbidly radiating Coleridge into the chaos of a fermenting life, act magically there, and produce divulsions and convulsions and diseased developments.' One can almost fancy Carlyle had ringing in his memory the old Scottish ballad of the Rev. Robert Kirk, translator of the Psalms into Gaelic, who, while walking in his night-gown at Aberfoyle, was 'snatched away to the joyless Elfin bower.'

> It was between the night and day
> When the fairy-king has power.

The item of the night-gown might have already prepared us for the couplet; and it has perhaps even a mystical connection with the vestment of the 'black dragoon' which Sterling once saw patrolling in every parish, to whom, however, he surrendered at last.

A story is told of a man wandering on a dark night over Dartmoor, whose feet slipped over the edge of a pit. He caught the branch of a tree suspended over the terrible chasm, but unable to regain the ground, shrieked for help. None came, though he cried out till his voice was gone; and there he remained dangling in agony until the grey light revealed that his feet were only a few inches from the solid ground. Such are the chief demons that bind man till cockcrow. Such are the apprehensions that waste also the moral and intellectual strength of man, and murder his peace as he regards the necessary science of his time to be cutting some frail tenure sustaining him over a bottomless pit, instead of a release from real terror to the solid ground.

NOTES

1 'The Origin of Civilisation,' &c. By Sir John Lubbock.
2 Hildebrand in Grimm's 'Wörterbuch.'
3 Wisdom of Solomon, xvii. What this impressive chapter says of the delusions of the guilty are equally true of those of ignorance. 'They sleeping the same sleep that night ... were partly vexed with monstrous apparitions, and partly fainted, their heart failing them ... whosoever there fell down was straitly kept, shut up in a prison without iron bars.... Whether it were a whistling wind, or a melodious noise of birds among the spreading branches, or a pleasing fall of water running violently, or a terrible sound of stones cast down, or a running that could not be seen of skipping beasts, or a roaring voice of most savage wild beasts, or a rebounding echo from the hollow mountains: these things made them to swoon for fear. The whole world shined with clear light ... over them only was spread a heavy night, an image of that darkness which should afterward receive them: but yet were they to themselves more grievous than that darkness.'
4 Bayard Taylor's 'Faust.' Walpurgis-night.
5 i. 228.
6 North American Review. March 1877.
7 In his very valuable work, 'Northmen in Cumberland and Westmoreland.' Longmans. 1856.
8 'Journal of Philology,' vi. No. II. On the Word Glamour and the Legend of Glam, by Professor Cowell.

Disease

A FAMILIAR FABLE in the East tells of one who met a fearful phantom, which in reply to his questioning answered—'I am Plague: I have come from yon city where ten thousand lie dead: one thousand were slain by me, the rest by Fear.' Perhaps even this story does not fully report the alliance between the plague and fear; for it is hardly doubtful that epidemics retain their power in the East largely because they have gained personification through fear as demons whose fatal power man can neither prevent nor cure, before which he can only cower and pray.

In the missionary school at Canterbury the young men prepare themselves to help the 'heathen' medically, and so they go forth with materia medica in one hand, and in the other an infallible revelation from heaven reporting plagues as the inflictions of Jehovah, or the destroying angel, or Satan, and the healing of disease the jealously reserved monopoly of God.[1]

The demonisation of diseases is not wonderful. To thoughtful minds not even science has dispelled the mystery which surrounds many of the ailments that afflict mankind, especially the normal diseases besetting children, hereditary complaints, and the strange liabilities to infection and contagion. A genuine, however partial, observation would suggest to primitive man some connection between the symptoms of many diseases and the mysterious universe of which he could not yet recognise himself an epitome. There were indications that certain troubles of this kind were related to the seasons, consequently to the celestial rulers of the seasons,—to the sun that smote by day, and the moon at night. Professor Monier Williams, describing the Devil-dances of Southern India, says that there seems to be an idea among them that when pestilences are rife exceptional measures must be taken to draw off the malignant spirits, supposed to cause them, by tempting them to enter into these wild dancers, and so become dissipated. He witnessed in Ceylon a dance performed by three men who personated the forms and phases of typhus fever.[2] These dances probably belong to the same class of ideas as those of the dervishes in Persia, whose manifold contortions are supposed to repeat the movements of planets. They are invocations of the souls of good stars, and propitiations of such as are evil. Belief in such stellar and planetary influences has pervaded every part of the world, and gave rise to astrological dances. 'Gebelin says that the minuet was the *danse oblique* of the ancient priests of Apollo, performed in their temples. The diagonal line and the two parallels described in this dance were intended to be symbolical of the zodiac, and the twelve steps of which it is composed were meant for the twelve signs and the months of the year. The dance round the Maypole and the Cotillon has the same origin. Diodorus tells us that Apollo was adored with dances, and in the island of Iona the god danced all night. The Christians of St. Thomas till a very late day celebrated their worship with dances and songs. Calmet says there were dancing-girls in the temple at Jerusalem.'[3]

The influence of the Moon upon tides, the sleeplessness it causes, the restlessness of the insane under its occasional light, and such treacheries of moonshine as we have already considered, have populated our uninhabited satellite with demons. Lunar legends have decorated some well-founded suspicions of moonlight. The mother draws the curtain between the moonshine and her little Endymion, though not because she sees in the waning moon a pining Selene whose kiss may waste away the beauty of youth. A mere survival is the 'bowing to the new moon:' a euphonism traceable to many myths about 'lunacy,' among them, as I think, to Delilah ('languishing'), in whose lap the solar Samson is shorn of his locks, leaving him only the blind destructive strength of the 'moonstruck.'

In the purely Semitic theories of the Jews we find diseases ascribed to the wrath of Jehovah, and their cure to his merciful mood. 'Jehovah will make thy plagues wonderful, and the plagues of thy seed; ... he will bring upon thee all the diseases of Egypt whereof thou wast afraid.'[4] The emerods which smote the worshippers of Dagon were ascribed directly to the hand of Jehovah.[5] In that vague degree of natural dualistic development which preceded the full Iranian influence upon the Jews, the infliction of diseases was delegated to an angel of Jehovah, as in the narratives of smiting the firstborn of Egypt, wasting the army of Sennacherib, and the pestilence sent upon Israel for David's sin. In the progress of this angel to be a demon of disease we find a phase of ambiguity, as shown in the hypochondria of Saul. 'The spirit of Jehovah departed from Saul, and an evil spirit from Jehovah troubled him.'[6]

All such ambiguities disappeared under the influence of Iranian dualism. In the Book of Job we find the infliction of diseases and plagues completely transferred to a powerful spirit, a fully formed opposing potentate. The 'sons of God,' who in the first chapter of Job are said to have presented themselves before Jehovah, may be identified in the thirty-eighth as the stars which shouted for joy at the creation. Satan is the wandering or malign planet which leads in the Ahrimanic side of the Persian planisphere. In the cosmographical theology of that country Ormuzd was to reign for six thousand years, and then Ahriman was to reign for a similar period. The moral associations of this speculation are discussed elsewhere; it is necessary here only to point out the bearing of the planispheric conception upon the ills that flesh is heir to. Ahriman is the 'star-serpent' of the Zendavasta. 'When the pâris rendered this world desolate, and overran the universe; when the star-serpent made a path for himself between heaven and earth,' &c.; 'when Ahriman rambles on the earth, let him who takes the form of a serpent glide on the earth; let him who takes the form of the wolf run on the earth, and let the violent north wind bring weakness.'[7]

The dawn of Ormuzd corresponds with April. The sun returns from winter's death by sign of the lamb (our Aries), and thenceforth every month corresponds with a thousand years of the reign of the Beneficent. September is denoted by the Virgin and Child. To the dark domain of Ahriman the prefecture of the universe passes by Libra,—the same balances which appear in the hand of Satan.

The star-serpent prevails over the Virgin and Child. Then follow the months of the scorpion, the centaur, goat, &c., every month corresponding to a thousand years of the reign of Ahriman.

While this scheme corresponds in one direction with the demons of cold, and in another with the entrance and reign of moral evil in the world, beginnings of disease on earth were also ascribed to this seventh thousand of years when the Golden Age had passed. The depth of winter is reached in domicile of the goat, or of Sirius, Seth, Saturn, Satan—according to the many variants. And these, under their several names, make the great 'infortune' of astrology, wherein old Culpepper amply instructed our fathers. 'In the general, consider that *Saturn* is an old worn-out planet, weary, and of little estimation in this world; he causeth long and tedious sicknesses, abundance of sadness, and a Cartload of doubts and fears; his nature is cold, and dry, and melancholy. And take special notice of this, that when Saturn is Lord of an Eclipse (as he is one of the Lords of this), he governs all the rest of the planets, but none can govern him. *Melancholy is made of all the humors in the body of man, but no humor of melancholy.* He is envious, and keeps his anger long, and speaks but few words, but when he speaks he speaks to purpose. A man of deep cogitations; he will plot mischief when men are asleep; he hath an admirable memory, and remembers to this day how *William*the Bastard abused him; he cannot endure to be a slave; he is poor with the poor, fearful with the fearful; he plots mischief against the Superiours, with them that plot mischief against them; have a care of him, KINGS and MAGISTRATES of Europe; he will show you what he can do in the effects of this Eclipse; he is old, and therefore hath large experience, and will give perilous counsel; he moves but slowly, and therefore doth the more mischief; all the planets contribute their natures and strength to him, and when he sets on doing mischief he will do it to purpose; he doth not regard the company of the rest of the Planets, neither do any of the rest of the Planets regard his; he is a barren Planet, and therefore delights not in women; he brings the Pestilence; he is destructive to the fruits of the earth; he receives his light from the Sun, and yet he hates the Sun that gives it him.'[8]

Many ages anterior to this began in India the dread of Ketu, astronomically the ninth planet, mythologically the tail of the demon Rahu, cut in twain as already told (p. 46), supposed to be the prolific source of comets, meteors, and falling stars, also of diseases. From this Ketu or dragon's tail were born the Arunah Ketavah (Red Ketus or apparitions), and Ketu has become almost another word for disease.[9]

Strongly influenced as were the Jews by the exact division of the duodecimal period between Good and Evil, affirmed by the Persians, they never lost sight of the ultimate supremacy of Jehovah. Though Satan had gradually become a voluntary genius of evil, he still had to receive permission to afflict, as in the case of Job, and during the lifetime of Paul appears to have been still denied that 'power of death' which is first asserted by the unknown author of the Epistle to the Hebrews.[10] Satan's especial office was regarded as the infliction of disease. Paul delivers the incestuous Corinthian to Satan 'for the destruction of the flesh,' and he also attributed the sickness and death of many to their communicating unworthily.[11] He also recognises his own 'thorn in the flesh' as 'an angel from Satan,' though meant for his moral advantage.[12]

A penitential Psalm (Assyrian) reads as follows:—

> O my Lord! my sins are many, my trespasses are great; and the
> wrath of the gods has plagued me with disease, and with sickness
> and sorrow.
> I fainted, but no one stretched forth his hand!
> I groaned, but no one drew nigh!
> I cried aloud, but no one heard!
> O Lord, do not abandon thy servant!
> In the waters of the great storm seize his hand!
> The sins which he has committed turn them to righteousness.[13]

This Psalm would hardly be out of place in the English burial-service, which deplores death as a visitation of divine wrath. Wherever such an idea prevails, the natural outcome of it is a belief in demons of disease. In ancient Egypt—following the belief in Ra the Sun, from whose eyes all pleasing things proceeded, and Set, from whose eyes came all noxious things,—from the baleful light of Set's eyes were born the Seven Hathors, or Fates, whose names are recorded in the Book of the Dead. Mr. Fox Talbot has translated 'the Song of the Seven Spirits:'—

> They are seven! they are seven!
> In the depths of ocean they are seven!
> In the heights of heaven they are seven!
> In the ocean-stream in a palace they were born!
> Male they are not: female they are not!
> Wives they have not: children are not born to them!
> Rule they have not: government they know not!
> Prayers they hear not!
> They are seven! they are seven! twice over they are seven! [14]

These demons have a way of herding together; the Assyrian tablets abundantly show that their occupation was manifested by diseases, physical and mental. One prescription runs thus:—

> The god (...) shall stand by his bedside:
> Those seven evil spirits he shall root out, and shall expel them
> from his body:
> And those seven shall never return to the sick man again!

It is hardly doubtful that these were the seven said to have been cast out of Mary Magdalen; for their father Set is *Shedîm* (devils) of Deut. xxxii. 17, and *Shaddai* (God) of Gen. xvi. 1. But the fatal Seven turn to the seven fruits that charm away evil influences at parturition in Persia, also the Seven Wise Women of the same country traditionally present on holy occasions. When Ardá Viráf was sent to Paradise by a sacred narcotic to obtain intelligence of the true faith, seven fires were kept burning for seven days around him, and the seven wise women chanted hymns of the Avesta.[15]

The entrance of the seven evil powers into a dwelling was believed by the Assyrians to be preventible by setting in the doorway small images, such as those of the sun-god (Hea) and the moon-goddess, but especially of Marduk, corresponding to Serapis the Egyptian Esculapius. These powers were reinforced by writing holy texts over and on each side of the threshold. 'In the night time bind around the sick man's head a sentence taken from a good book.' The phylacteries of the Jews were originally worn for the same purpose. They were called Tefila, and were related to *teraphim,* the little idols [16] used by the Jews to keep out demons—such as those of Laban, which his daughter Rachel stole.

The resemblance of teraphim to the Tarasca (connected by some with G. τέρας, a monster) of Spain may be noted,—the serpent figures carried about in Corpus Christi processions. The latter word is known in the south of France also, and gave its name to the town Tarascon. The legend is that an amphibious monster haunted the Rhone, preventing navigation and committing terrible ravages, until sixteen of the boldest inhabitants of the district resolved to encounter it. Eight lost their lives, but the others, having destroyed the monster, founded the town of Tarascon, where the 'Fête de la tarasque' is still kept up.[17] Calmet, Sedley, and others, however, believe that *teraphim* is merely a modification of seraphim, and the Tefila, or phylacteries, of the same origin.

The phylactery was tied into a knot. Justin Martyr says that the Jewish exorcists used 'magic ties or knots.' The origin of this custom among the Jews and Babylonians may be found in the Assyrian Talismans preserved in the British Museum, of which the following has been translated by Mr. Fox Talbot:—

> Hea says: Go, my son!
> Take a woman's kerchief,
> Bind it round thy right hand, loose it from the left hand!
> Knot it with seven knots: do so twice:
> Sprinkle it with bright wine:
> Bind it round the head of the sick man:
> Bind it round his hands and feet, like manacles and fetters.
> Sit down on his bed:
> Sprinkle holy water over him.
> He shall hear the voice of Hea,
> Darkness shall protect him!
> And Marduk, eldest son of Heaven, shall find him a happy
> habitation. [18]

The number seven holds an equally high degree of potency in Singhalese demonolatry, which is mainly occupied with diseases.

The Capuas or conjurors of that island enumerate 240,000 magic spells, of which all except one are for evil, which implies a tolerably large preponderance of the emergencies in which their countervailing efforts are required by their neighbours. That of course can be easily appreciated by those who have been taught that all human beings are included under a primal curse. The words of Micah, 'Thou wilt cast all their sins into the depths of the sea,'[19] are recalled by the legend of these evil spells of Ceylon. The king of Oude came to marry one of seven princesses, all possessing præternatural powers, and questioned each as to her art. Each declared her skill in doing harm, except one who asserted her power to heal all ills which the others could inflict. The king having chosen this one as his bride, the rest were angry, and for revenge collected all the charms in the world, enclosed them in a pumpkin—the only thing that can contain spells without being reduced to ashes—and sent this infernal machine to their sister. It would consume everything for sixteen hundred miles round; but the messenger dropped it in the sea. A god picked it up and presented it to the King of Ceylon, and these, with the healing charm known to his own Queen, make the 240,000 spells known to the Capuas of that island, who have no doubt deified the rescuer of the spells on the same principle that inspires some seaside populations to worship Providence more devoutly on the Sunday after a valuable wreck in their neighbourhood.

The astrological origin of the evils ascribed to the Yakseyo (Demons) of Ceylon, and the horoscope which is a necessary preliminary to any dealing with their influences; the constant recurrence of the number seven, denoting origin with races holding the seven-planet theories of the universe; and the fact that all demons are said, on every Saturday evening, to attend an assemblage called *Yaksa Sabawa* (Witches' Sabbath), are facts that may well engage the attention of Comparative Mythologists.[20] In Dardistan the evil spirits are called *Yatsh*; they dwell 'in the regions of snow,' and the overthrow of their reign over the country is celebrated at the new moon of Daykio, the month preceding winter.

The largest proportion of the Disease Demons of Ceylon are descended from its Hunger Demons. The Preta there is much the same phantom as in Siam, only they are not quite so tall.[21] They range from two to four hundred feet in height, and are so numerous that a Pali Buddhist book exhorts people not to throw stones, lest they should harm one of these harmless starveling ghosts, who die many times of hunger, and revive to suffer on in expiation of their sins in a previous existence. They are harmless in one sense, but filthy; and bad smells are personified in them. The great mass of demons resemble the Pretraya, in that their king (Wessamony) has forbidden them to satisfy themselves directly upon their victims, but by inflicting diseases they are supposed to receive an imaginative satisfaction somewhat like that of eating people.

Reeri is the Demon of Blood-disease. His form is that of a man with face of a monkey; he is fiery red, rides on a red bull, and all hemorrhages and diseases of the blood are attributed to him. Reeri has eighteen different disguises or avatars. One of these recalls his earlier position as a demon of death, before Vishnu revealed to Cap-uas the means of binding him: he is now supposed to be present at every death-bed in the form of a delighted pigmy, one span and six inches high. On such occasions he bears a cock in one hand, a club in the other, and in his mouth a corpse. In the same country Maha Sohon is the 'great graveyard demon.' He resides in a hill where he is supposed to surround himself with carcases. He is 122 feet high, has four hands and three eyes, and a red skin. He has the head of a bear; the legend being that while quarrelling with another giant his head was knocked off, and the god Senasura was gracious enough to tear off the head of a bear and clap it on the decapitated giant. His capua threatens him with a repetition of this catastrophe if he does not spare any threatened victim who has called in his priest-ly aid. Except for this timidity about his head, Maha is formidable, being chief of 30,000 demons. But curiously enough he is said to choose for his steeds the more innocent animals,—goat, deer, horse, elephant, and hog.

One of the demons most dreaded in Ceylon is the 'Foreign Demon' Morotoo, said to have come from the coast of Malabar, and from his residence in a tree disseminated diseases which could not be cured until, the queen being afflicted, one capua was found able to master him. Seven-eighths of the charms used in restraining the disease-demons of Ceylon, of which I have mentioned but a few, are in the Tamil tongue. In various parts of India are found very nearly the same systematic demonolatry and 'devil-dancing;' for example in Travancore, to whose superstitions of this character the Rev. Samuel Mateer has devoted two chapters in his work 'The Land of Charity.'

The great demon of diseases in Ceylon is entitled Maha Cola Sanni Yakseya. His father, a king, ordered his queen to be put to death in the belief that she had been faithless to him. Her body was to be cut in two pieces, one of which was to be hung upon a tree (*Ukberiya*), the other to be thrown at its foot to the dogs. The queen before her execution said, 'If this charge be false, may the child in my womb be born this instant a demon, and may that demon destroy the whole of this city and its unjust king.' So soon as the executioners had finished their work, the two severed parts of the queen's body reunited, a child was born who completely devoured his mother, and then repaired to the graveyard (Sohon), where for a time he fattened on corpses. Then he proceeded to inflict mortal diseases upon the city, and had nearly depopulated it when the gods Iswara and Sekkra interfered, descending to subdue him in the disguise of mendicants. Possibly the great Maha Sohon mentioned above, and the Sohon (graveyard) from which Sanni dealt out deadliness, may be best understood by the statement of the learned writer from whom these facts are quoted, that, 'excepting the Buddhist priests, and the aristocrats of the land, whose bodies were burnt in regular funeral-piles after death, the corpses of the rest of the people were neither burned nor buried, but thrown into a place called *Sohona*, which was an open piece of ground in the jungle, generally a hollow among the hills, at the distance of three or four miles from any inhabited place, where they were left in the open air to be decomposed or devoured by dogs and wild beasts.'[22] There would appear to be even more ground for the dread of the Great Graveyard Demon in many parts of Christendom, where, through desire to preserve corpses for a happy resurrection, they are made to steal through the water-veins of the earth, and find their resurrection as fell diseases. Iswara and

Sekkra were probably two reformers who persuaded the citizens to bury the poor deep in the earth; had they been wise enough to place the dead where nature would give them speedy resurrection and life in grass and flowers, it would not have been further recorded that 'they ordered him (the demon) to abstain from eating men, but gave him Wurrun or permission to inflict disease on mankind, and to obtain offerings.' This is very much the same as the privilege given our Western funeral agencies and cemeteries also; and when the Modliar adds that Sanni 'has eighteen principal attendants,' one can hardly help thinking of the mummers, gravediggers, chaplains, all engaged unconsciously in the work of making the earth less habitable.

The first of the attendants of this formidable avenger of his mother's wrongs is named Bhoota Sanni Yakseya, Demon of Madness. The whole demonolatry and devil-dancing of that island are so insane that one is not surprised that this Bhoota had but little special development. It is amid clear senses we might naturally look for full horror of madness, and there indeed do we find it. One of the most horrible forms of the disease-demon was the personification of madness among the Greeks, as Mania.[23] In the *Hercules Furens* of Euripides, where Madness, 'the unwedded daughter of black Night,' and sprung of 'the blood of Cœlus,' is evoked from Tartarus for the express purpose of imbreeding in Hercules 'child-slaying disturbances of reason,' there is a suggestion of the hereditary nature of insanity. Obedient to the vindictive order of Juno, 'in her chariot hath gone forth the marble-visaged, all-mournful Madness, the Gorgon of Night, and with the hissing of hundred heads of snakes, she gives the goad to her chariot, on mischief bent.' We may plainly see that the religion which embodied such a form was itself ending in madness. Already ancient were the words μαντική (prophecy) and μανική (madness) when Plato cited their identity to prove one kind of madness the special gift of Heaven:[24] the notion lingers in Dryden's line, 'Great wits to madness sure are near allied;' and survive in regions where deference is paid to lunatics and idiots. Other diseases preserve in their names indications of similar association: *e.g.*, Nympholepsy, St. Vitus's Dance, St. Anthony's Fire. Wesley attributes still epilepsy to 'possession.' This was in pursuance of ancient beliefs. Typhus, a name anciently given to every malady accompanied with stupor (τῦφος), seemed the breath of feverish Typhon. Max Müller connects the word *quinsy* with Sanskrit *amh*, 'to throttle,' and Ahi the throttling serpent, its medium being *angina*; and this again is κυνάγχη, dog-throttling, the Greek for quinsy.[25]

The genius of William Blake, steeped in Hebraism, never showed greater power than in his picture of Plague. A gigantic hideous form, pale-green, with the slime of stagnant pools, reeking with vegetable decays and gangrene, the face livid with the motley tints of pallor and putrescence, strides onward with extended arms like a sower sowing his seeds, only in this case the germs of his horrible harvest are not cast from the hands, but emanate from the fingers as being of their essence. Such, to the savage mind, was the embodiment of malaria, sultriness, rottenness, the putrid Pretraya, invisible, but smelt and felt. Such, to the ignorant imagination, is the Destroying Angel to which rationalistic artists and poets have tried to add wings and majesty; but which in the popular mind was no doubt pictured more like this form found at Ostia (fig. 16), and now passing in the Vatican for a Satan,—probably a demon of the Pontine Marshes, and of the fever that still has victims of its fatal cup (p. 291). In these fearful forms the poor savage believed with such an intensity that he was able to shape the brain of man to his phantasy; bringing about the anomaly that the great reformer, Luther, should affirm, even while fighting superstition, that a Christian ought to know that he lives in the midst of devils, and that the devil is nearer to him than his coat or his shirt. The devils, he tells us, are all around us, and are at every moment seeking to ensnare our lives, salvation, and happiness. There are many of them in the woods, waters, deserts, and in damp muddy places, for the purpose of doing folk a mischief. They also house in the dense black clouds, and send storms, hail, thunder and lightning, and poison the air with their infernal stench. In one place, Luther tells us that the devil has more vessels and boxes full of poison, with which he kills people, than all the apothecaries in the whole world. He sends all plagues and diseases among men. We may be sure that when any one dies of the pestilence, is drowned, or drops suddenly dead, the devil does it.

Fig. 16.—Demon found at Ostia

Knowing nothing of Zoology, the primitive man easily falls into the belief that his cattle—the means of life—may be the subjects of sorcery. Jesus sending devils into a herd of swine may have become by artificial process a divine benefactor in the eye of Christendom, but the myth makes Him bear an exact resemblance to the dangerous sorcerer that fills the savage mind with dread. It is probable that the covetous eye denounced in the decalogue means the evil eye, which was supposed to blight an object intensely desired but not to be obtained.

Gopolu, already referred to (p. 136) as the Singhalese demon of hydrophobia, bears the general name of the 'Cattle Demon.' He is said to have been the twin of the demigod Mangara by a queen on the Coromandel coast. The mother died, and a cow suckled the twins, but afterwards they quarrelled, and Gopolu being slain was transformed into a demon. He repaired to Arangodde, and fixed his abode in a Banyan where there is a large bee-hive, whence proceed many evils. The population around this Banyan for many miles being prostrated by diseases, the demigod Mangara and Pattini (goddess of chastity) admonished the villagers to sacrifice a cow regularly, and thus they were all resuscitated. Gopolu now sends all cattle diseases. India is full of the like superstitions. The people of Travancore especially dread the demon Madan, 'he who is like a cow,' believed to strike oxen with sudden illness,—sometimes men also.

In Russia we find superstition sometimes modified by common sense. Though the peasant hopes that Zegory (St. George) will defend his cattle, he begins to see the chief foes of his cattle. As in the folk-song—

> We have gone around the field,
> We have called Zegory....
> O thou, our brave Zegory,
> Save our cattle,
> In the field and beyond the field,
> In the forest and beyond the forest,
> Under the bright moon,
> Under the red sun,
> From the rapacious wolf,
> From the cruel bear,
> From the cunning beast.[26]

Nevertheless when a cattle plague occurs many villages relapse into a normally extinct state of mind. Thus, a few years ago, in a village near Moscow, all the women, having warned the men away, stripped themselves entirely naked and drew a plough so as to make a furrow entirely around the village. At the point of juncture in this circle they buried alive a cock, a cat, and a dog. Then they filled the air with lamentations, crying—'Cattle Plague! Cattle Plague! spare our cattle! Behold, we offer thee cock, cat, and dog!' The dog is a demonic character in Russia, while the cat is sacred; for once when the devil tried to get into Paradise in the form of a mouse, the dog allowed him to pass, but the cat pounced on him—the two animals being set on guard at the door. The offering of both seems to represent a desire to conciliate both sides. The nudity of the women may have been to represent to the hungry gods their utter poverty, and inability to give more; but it was told me in Moscow, where I happened to be staying at the time, that it would be dangerous for any man to draw near during the performance.

In Altmark [27] the demons who bewitch cattle are called 'Bihlweisen,' and are believed to bury certain diabolical charms under thresholds over which the animals are to pass, causing them to wither away, the milk to cease, etc. The prevention is to wash the cattle with a lotion of sea cabbage boiled with infusion of wine. In the same province it is related that once there appeared in a harvest-field at one time fifteen, at another twelve men (apparently), the latter headless. They all laboured with scythes, but though the rustling could be heard no grain fell. When questioned they said nothing, and when the people tried to seize them they ran away, cutting fruitlessly as they ran. The priests found in this a presage of the coming cattle plague. The Russian superstition of the plough, above mentioned, is found in fragmentary survivals in Altmark. Thus, it is said that to plough around a village and then sit under the plough (placed upright), will enable any one to see the witches; and in some villages, some bit of a plough is hung up over a doorway through which cattle pass, as no devil can then approach them. The demons have a natural horror of honest work, and especially the culture of the earth. Goethe, as we have seen, notes their fear of roses: perhaps he remembered the legend of Aspasia, who, being disfigured by a tumour on the chin, was warned by a dove-maiden to dismiss her physicians and try a rose from the garland of Venus; so she recovered health and beauty.

NOTES

1   2 Chron. xvi. 12; 2 Kings xx.; Mark v. 26; James v. 14; &c., &c. The Catholic Church follows the prescription by St. James of prayer and holy anointing for the sick only after medical aid—of which Asa died when he preferred it to the Lord—has failed; i.e. extreme unction. Castelar remarks that the Conclave which elected Pius IX. sat in the Quirinal rather than the Vatican, 'because, while it hoped for the inspirations of the Holy Spirit in every place, it feared that in the palace par excellence divine inspirations would not sufficiently counteract the effluvias of the fever.' The legal prosecutions of the 'Peculiar People' for obeying the New Testament command in case of sickness supply a notable example of the equal hypocrisy of the protestant age. England has distributed the Bible as a divine revelation in 150 different languages; and in London it punishes a sect for obedience to one of its plainest directions.

2   London 'Times,' June 11, 1877.

3   'Mankind: their Origin and Destiny' (Longmans, 1872), p. 91. See also Voltaire's Dictionary for an account of the sacred dances in the Catholic Churches of Spain.

4   Deut. xxviii. 60.

5   1 Sam. v. 6.

6 1 Sam. xvi. 14. In chap. xviii. 10, this evil spirit is said to have proceeded from Elohim, a difference indicating a further step in that evolution of Jehovah into a moral ruler which is fully traced in our chapter on 'Elohim and Jehovah.'

7 Boundesch, ii. pp. 158, 188. For an exhaustive treatment of the astrological theories and pictures of the planispheres, see 'Mankind: their Origin and Destiny' (Longmans, 1872).

8 'Catastrophe Magnatum: or the Fall of Monarchie. A Caveat to Magistrates, deduced from the Eclipse of the Sunne, March 29, 1652. With a probable Conjecture of the Determination of the Effects.' By Nich. Culpeper, Gent., Stud. in Astrol. and Phys. Dan. ii. 21, 22: He changeth the times and the seasons: he removeth Kings, and setteth up Kings: he giveth wisdome to the Wise, and knowledge to them that know understanding: he revealeth the deep and secret things, he knoweth what is in the darkness, and the light dwelleth with him. London: Printed for T. Vere and Nath. Brooke, in the Old Baily, and at the Angel in Cornhil, 1652.'

9 See the Dictionary of Böhtlingk and Roth.

10 Heb. ii. 14.

11 1 Cor. v. 5; xi. 30.

12 2 Cor. xii. 7.

13 'Records of the Past,' iii. p. 136. Tr. by Mr. Fox Talbot.

14 Ibid., iii. p. 143. The refrain recalls the lines of Edgar A. Poe:—
They are neither man nor woman,
They are neither brute nor human,
They are ghouls!

15 The Pahlavi Text has been prepared by Destur Jamaspji Asa, and translated by Haug and West. Trübner, 1872.

16 Cf. fig. 9.

17 Larousse's 'Dict. Universel.'

18 'Records,' &c., iii. p. 141. Marduk is the Chaldæan Hercules.

19 Micah vii. 19.

20 See the excellent article in the Journal of the Ceylon Branch of the R.A.S., by Dundris De Silva Gooneratnee Modliar (1865–66). With regard to this sanctity of the number seven it may be remarked that it has spread through the world with Christianity,—seven churches, seven gifts of the Spirit, seven sins and virtues. It is easy therefore to mistake orthodox doctrines for survivals. In the London 'Times' of June 24, 1875, there was reported an inquest at Corsham, Wiltshire, on the body of Miriam Woodham, who died under the prescriptions of William Bigwood, herbalist. It was shown that he used pills made of seven herbs. This was only shown to be a 'pagan survival' when Bigwood stated that the herbs were 'governed by the sun.'

21 See p. 44.

22 'Jour. Ceylon R. A. Soc.,' 1865–66.

23 This demoness is not to be connected with the Italian Mania, probably of Etruscan origin, with which nurses frightened children. This Mania, from an old word manussignifying 'good,' was, from the relation of her name to Manes, supposed to be mother of the Lares, whose revisitations of the earth were generally of ill omen. According to an oracle which said heads should be offered for the sake of heads, children were sacrificed to this household fiend up to the time of Junius Brutus, who substituted poppy-heads.

24 Phædrus, i. 549. Cf. Ger. selig and silly.

25 'Lect. on Language,' i. 435.

26 Ralston's 'Songs of the Russian People,' p. 230.

27 'Sagen der Altmark.' Von A. Kuhn. Berlin, 1843.

Chapter XII
Death

The Vendetta of Death — Teoyaomiqui — Demon of Serpents — Death on the
Pale Horse — Kali — War-gods — Satan as Death — Death-beds — Thanatos
— Yama — Yimi — Towers of Silence — Alcestis — Hercules, Christ, and Death
— Hel — Salt — Azraël — Death and the Cobbler — Dance of Death —
Death as Foe, and as Friend

SAVAGE RACES BELIEVE that no man dies except by sorcery.
Therefore every death must be avenged. The Actas of the Philip-
pines regard the 'Indians' as the cause of the deaths among them;
and when one of them loses a relative, he lurks and watches until he
has spied an 'Indian' and killed him.[1] It is a progress from this when
primitive man advances to the belief that the fatal sorcerer is an
invisible man—a demon. When this doctrine is taught in the form of
a belief that death entered the world through the machinations of
Satan, and was not in the original scheme of creation, it is civilised;
but when it is inculcated under a set of African or other non-christian
names, it is barbarian.

The following sketch, by Mr. Gideon Lang, will show the intensity
of this conviction among the natives of New South Wales:—

'While at Nanima I constantly saw one of these, named Jemmy,
a remarkably fine man, about twenty-eight years of age, who was
the 'model Christian' of the missionaries, and who had been over and
over again described in their reports as a living proof that, taken in

infancy, the natives were as capable of being truly christianised as a people who had had eighteen centuries of civilisation. I confess that I strongly doubted, but still there was no disputing the apparent facts. Jemmy was not only familiar with the Bible, which he could read remarkably well, but he was even better acquainted with the more abstruse tenets of christianity; and so far as the whites could see, his behaviour was in accordance with his religious acquirements. One Sunday morning I walked down to the black fellows' camp, to have a talk with Jemmy, as usual. I found him sitting in his gunyah, overlooking a valley of the Macquarrie, whose waters glanced bright- ly in the sunshine of the delicious spring morning. He was sitting in a state of nudity, excepting his waistcloth, very earnestly reading the Bible, which indeed was his constant practice; and I could see that he was perusing the Sermon on the Mount. I seated myself, and waited till he concluded the chapter, when he laid down the Bible, folded his hands, and sat with his eyes fixed abstractedly on his fire. I bade him 'good morning,' which he acknowledgedwithout looking up. I then said, 'Jemmy, what is the meaning of your spears being stuck in a circle round you?' He looked me steadily in the eyes, and said solemnly and with suppressed fierceness, 'Mother's dead!' I said that I was very sorry to hear it; 'but what had her death to do with the spears being stuck around so?' 'Bogan black-fellow killed her!' was the fierce and gloomy reply. 'Killed by a Bogan black!' I exclaimed: 'why, your mother has been dying a fortnight, and Dr. Curtis did not expect her to outlive last night, which you know as well as I do.' His only reply was a dogged repetition of the words: 'A Bogan black-fellow killed her!' I appealed to him as a Christian—to the Sermon on the Mount, that he had just been reading; but he absolutely refused to promise that he would not avenge his mother's death. In the afternoon of that day we were startled by a yell which can never be mistaken by any person who has once heard the wild war-whoop of the blacks when in battle array. On marching out we saw all the black fellows of the neighbourhood formed into a line, and following Jemmy in an imaginary attack upon an enemy. Jemmy himself disappeared that evening. On the following Wednesday morning I found him sitting complacently in his gunyah, plaiting a rope of human hair, which I at once knew to be that of his victim. Neither of us spoke; I stood for some time watching him as he worked with a look of mocking defiance of the anger he knew I felt. I pointed to a hole in the middle of his fire, and said, 'Jemmy, the proper place for your Bible is there.' He looked up with his eyes flashing as I turned away, and I never saw him again. I afterwards learned that he had gone to the district of the Bogan tribe, where the first black he met happened to be an old friend and companion of his own. This man had just made the first cut in the bark of a tree, which he was about to climb for an opossum; but on hearing footsteps he leaped down and faced round, as all blacks do, and whites also, when blacks are in question. Seeing that it was only Jemmy, however, he resumed his occupation, but had no sooner set to work than Jemmy sent a spear through his back and nailed him to the tree.[2]

Perhaps if Jemmy could have been cross-examined by the non-missionary mind, he might have replied with some effect to Mr. Lang's suggestion that he ought to part with his Bible. Surely he must have found in that volume a sufficient number of instances to justify his faith in the power of demons over human health and life. Might he not have pondered the command, 'thou shalt not suffer a witch to live,' and imagined that he was impaling another Manasseh, who 'used enchantments, and used witchcraft, and dealt with a familiar spirit, and with wizards (and) wrought much evil in the sight of the Lord to provoke Him to anger.'[3] Those who hope that the Bible may carry light into the dark places of superstition and habitations of cruelty might, one would say, reflect upon the long contest which European science had with bibliolators in trying to relieve the popular mind from the terrors of witchcraft, whose genuineness it was (justly) declared contrary to the Scriptures to deny. There are districts in Great Britain and America, and many more on the continent of Europe, where the spells that waste and destroy are still believed in; where effigies of wax or even onions are labelled with some hated name, and stuck over with pins, and set near fires to be melted or dried up, in full belief that some subject of the charm will be consumed by disease along with the object used. Under every roof where such coarse superstitions dwell the Bible dwells beside them, and experience proves that the infallibility of all such talismans diminishes *pari passu*.

Fig. 17.—Teoyaomiqui

What the savage is really trying to slay when he goes forth to avenge his relative's death on the first alien he finds may be seen in the accompanying figure (17), which represents the Mexican goddess of death—Teoyaomiqui. The image is nine feet high, and is kept in a museum in the city of Mexico. Mr. Edward B. Tylor, from whose excellent book of travels in that country the figure is copied, says of it:—'The stone known as the statue of the war-goddess is a huge block of basalt covered with sculptures. The antiquaries think that the figures on it stand for different personages, and that it is three gods—Huitzilopochtli, the god of war; Teoyaomiqui, his wife; and

311

Mictlanteuctli, the god of hell. It has necklaces of alternate hearts and dead men's hands, with death's heads for a central ornament. At the bottom of the block is a strange sprawling figure, which one cannot see now, for it is the base which rests on the ground; but there are two shoulders projecting from the idol, which show plainly that it did not stand on the ground, but was supported aloft on the tops of two pillars. The figure carved upon the bottom represents a monster holding a skull in each hand, while others hang from his knees and elbows. His mouth is a mere oval ring, a common feature of Mexican idols, and four tusks project just above it. The new moon laid down like a bridge forms his forehead, and a star is placed on each side of it. This is thought to have been the conventional representation of Mictlanteuctli (Lord of the Land of the Dead), the god of hell, which was a place of utter and eternal darkness. Probably each victim as he was led to the altar could look up between the two pillars and see the hideous god of hell staring down upon him from above. There is little doubt that this is the famous war-idol which stood on the great teocalli of Mexico, and before which so many thousands of human beings were sacrificed. It lay undisturbed under ground in the great square, close to the very site of the teocalli, until sixty years ago. For many years after that it was kept buried, lest the sight of one of their old deities might be too exciting for the Indians, who, as I have mentioned before, had certainly not forgotten it, and secretly orna-mented it with garlands of flowers while it remained above ground.'

If my reader will now turn to the (fig. 11) portrait of the Demon of Serpents, he will find a conception fundamentally similar to the Mexican demoness of death or slaughter, but one that is not shut up in a museum of antiquities; it still haunts and terrifies a vast number of the people born in Ceylon. He is the principal demon invoked in Ceylon by the malignant sorcerers in performing the 84,000 different charms that afflict evils (*Hooniyan*). His general title is Oddy Cumara Hooniyan Dewatawa; but he has a special name for each of his six several apparitions, the chief of these being Cali Oddisey, or demon of incurable diseases, therefore of death, and Naga Oddisey, demon of serpents—deadliest of animals. Beneath him is the Pale Horse which has had its career so long and far,—even to the White Mare on which, in some regions, Christ is believed to revisit the earth every Christmas; and also the White Mare of Yorkshire Folklore which bore its rider from Whitestone Cliff to hell. This Singhalese form also, albeit now associated by Capuas with fatal disease, was probably at first, like the Mexican, a war goddess and god combined, as is shown by the uplifted sword, and reeking hand uplifted in triumph. Equally a god of war is our 'Death on the Pale Horse,' which christian art, following the so-called Apocalypse, has made so familiar. 'I looked, and behold a pale horse: and his name that sat on him was Death, and Hell followed with him. And power was given to him over the fourth part of the earth, to kill with sword, and with hunger, and with death, and with the beasts of the earth.' This is but a travesty of the Greek Ares, the Roman Mars, or god of War. In the original Greek-form Ares was not solely the god of war, but of destruction generally. In the Œdipus Tyrannus of Sophocles we have the popular conception of him as one to whom the deadly plague is ascribed. He is named as the 'god unhonoured among gods,' and it is said:—'The city is wildly tossing, and no more can lift up her head from the waves of death; withering the ripening grain in the husks, withering the kine in their pastures; blighted are the babes through the failing labours of women; the fire-bearing god, horrid Pestilence, having darted down, ravages the city; by him the house of Cadmus is empty, and dark Hades enriched with groans and lamentations.'

Mother of the deadliest 'Calas' of Singhalese demonolatry, sister of the Scandinavian Hel in name and nature, is Kali. Although the Hindu writers repudiate the idea that there is any devil among their three hundred and thirty millions of deities, it is difficult to deny Kali that distinction. Her wild dance of delight over bodies of the slain would indicate pleasure taken in destruction for its own sake, so fulfilling the definition of a devil; but, on the other hand, there is a Deccan legend that reports her as devouring the dead, and this would make her a hunger-demon. We may give her the benefit of the doubt, and class her among the demons—or beings whose evil is not gratuitous—all the more because the mysteriously protruding tongue, as in the figure of Typhon (p. 185), probably suggests thirst. Hindu legend does, indeed, give another interpretation, and say that when she was dancing for joy at having slain a hundred-headed giant demigod, the shaking of the earth was so formidable that Siva threw himself among the slain, whom she was crushing at every step, hoping to induce her to pause; but when, unheeding, she trod upon the body of her husband, she paused and thrust out her tongue from surprise and shame. The Vedic description of Agni as an *ugra* (ogre), with 'tongue of flame,' may better interpret Kali's tongue. It is said Kali is pleased for a hundred years by the blood of a tiger; for a thousand by that of a man; for a hundred thousand by the blood of three men.

*Fig. 18.—*Kali

How are we to understand this dance of Death, and the further legend of her tossing dead bodies into the air for amusement? Such a figure found among a people who shudder at taking life even from the lowest animals is hardly to be explained by the destructiveness of nature personified in her spouse Siva. Her looks and legends alike represent slaughter by human violence. May it not be that Kali represents some period when the abhorrence of taking life among a vegetarian people—a people, too, believing in transmigration—might have become a public danger? When Krishna appeared it was, according to the Bhágavat Gita, as charioteer inciting Arjoon to war. There must have been various periods when a peaceful people must fall victims to more savage neighbours unless they could be stimulated to enter on the work of destruction with a light heart. There may have been periods when the human Kalis of India might stimulate their husbands and sons to war with such songs as the women of Dardistan sing at the Feast of Fire (p. 91). The amour of the Greek goddess of Beauty with the god of War, leaving her lawful spouse the Smith, is full of meaning. The Assyrian Venus, Istar, appeared in a vision, with wings and halo, bearing a bow and arrow for Assurbanipal. The Thug appears to have taken some such view of Kali, regarding her as patroness of their plan for reducing population. They are said to have claimed that Kali left them one of her teeth for a pickaxe, her rib for a knife, her garment's hem for a noose, and wholesale murder for a religion. The uplifted right hand of the demoness has been interpreted as intimating a divine purpose in the havoc around her, and it is possible that some such euphemism attached to the attitude before the Thug accepted it as his own benediction from this highly decorated personage of human cruelty.

The ancient reverence for Kali has gradually passed to her mitigated form—Durgá. Around her too are visible the symbols of destruction; but she is supposed to be satisfied with pumpkin-animals, and the weapons in her ten hands are believed to be directed against the enemies of the gods, especially against the giant king Muheshu. She is mother of the beautiful boy Kartik, and of the elephant-headed inspirer of knowledge Ganesa. She is reverenced now as female energy, the bestower of beauty and fruitfulness on women.

The identity of war-gods and death-demons, in the most frightful conceptions which have haunted the human imagination, is of profound significance. These forms do not represent peaceful and natural death, not death by old age,—of which, alas, those who cowered before them knew but little,—but death amid cruelty and agony, and the cutting down of men in the vigour of life. That indeed was terrible,—even more than these rude images could describe.

But there are other details in these hideous forms. The priest has added to the horse and sword of war the adored serpent, and hideous symbols of the 'Land of the Dead.' For it is not by terror of death, but of what he can persuade men lies beyond, that the priest has reigned over mankind. When Isabel (in 'Measure for Measure') is trying to persuade her brother that the sense of death lies most in apprehension, the sentenced youth still finds death 'a fearful thing.'

> Ay, but to die, and go we know not where;
> To lie in cold obstruction and to rot;
> This sensible warm motion to become
> A kneaded clod; and the delighted spirit
> To bathe in fiery floods, or to reside
> In thrilling region of thick-ribbed ice;
> To be imprisoned in the viewless winds,
> And blown with violence round about
> The pendent world; or to be worse than worst
> Of these, that lawless and incertain thoughts
> Imagine howling!—'tis too horrible!
> The weariest and most loathed worldly life
> That age, ache, penury, and imprisonment
> Can lay on nature, is a paradise
> To what we fear of death.

In all these apprehensions of Claudio there is no thought of annihilation. What if he had seen death as an eternal sleep? Let Hamlet answer:—

> To die,—to sleep;—
> No more;—and, by a sleep, to say we end
> The heartache, and the thousand natural shocks
> That flesh is heir to,—'tis a consummation
> Devoutly to be wished.

The greater part of the human race still belong to religions which, in their origin, promised eternal repose as the supreme final bliss. Had death in itself possessed horrors for the human mind, the priest need not have conjured up beyond it those tortures that haunted Hamlet with the dreams of possible evils beyond which make even the wretched rather bear the ills they have than fly to others they know not of. It would have been sufficient sanction to promise immortality only to the pious. But as in Claudio's shuddering lines every hell is reflected—whether of ice, fire, or brutalisation—so are the same mixed with the very blood and brain of mankind, even where literally outgrown. Christianity superadded to the horrors by importing the idea that death came by human sin, and so by gradual development ascribing to Satan the power of death; thereby forming a new devil who bore in him the power to make death a punishment. How the matter stood in the mediæval belief may be seen in figure 19, copied from a Russian Bible of the (early) seventeenth century. Lazarus smiles to see the nondescript soul of Dives torn from him by a devil with a hook, while another drowns the groans with a drum. Satan squirts an infernal baptism on the departing soul, and the earnest co-operation of the archangel justifies the satisfaction of Lazarus and Abraham. This degraded belief is still found in the almost gleeful pulpit-picturings of physical agonies as especially attending the death-beds of 'infidels,'—as Voltaire and Paine,—and its fearful result is found in the degree to which priesthoods are still able to paralyse the common sense and heart of the masses by the barbaric ceremonials with which they are permitted to surround death, and the arrogant line drawn between unorthodox goats and credulous sheep by 'consecrated' ground.

Fig. 19.—Dives and Lazarus (Russian; 17th cent.)

Mr. Keary, in his interesting volume on 'The Dawn of History,'[4] says that it has been suggested that the youthful winged figure on the drum of a column from the temple of Diana at Ephesus to the British Museum, may be a representation of Thanatos, Death. It would be agreeable to believe that the only important representation of Death left by Greek art is that exquisite figure, whose high tribute is that it was at first thought to be Love! The figure is somewhat like the tender Eros of preraphaelite art, and with the same look of gentle melancholy. Such a sweet and simple form of Death would be worthy of the race which, amid all the fiery or cold rivers of the underworld which had gathered about their religion, still saw running there the soft-flowing stream of forgetfulness. Let one study this Ephesian Thanatos reverently—no engraving or photograph can do it even partial justice—and then in its light read those myths of Death which seem to bear us back beyond the savagery of war and the artifices of priests to the simpler conceptions of humanity. In its serene light we may especially read both Vedic and Iranian hymns and legends of Yama.

The first man to die became the powerful Yama of the Hindus, the monarch of the dead; and he became invested with metaphors of the sun that had set.[5] In a solemn and pathetic hymn of the Vedas he is said to have crossed the rapid waters, to have shown the way to many, to have first known the path on which our fathers crossed over.[6] But in the splendours of sunset human hope found its prophetic pictures of a heaven beyond. The Vedic Yama is ever the friend. It is one of the most picturesque facts of mythology that, after Yama had become in India another name for Death, the same name reappeared in Persia, and in the *Avesta*, as a type at once of the Golden Age in the past and of paradise in the future.

Such was the Iranian Yima. He was that 'flos regum' whose reign represented 'the ideal of human happiness, when there was neither illness nor death, neither heat nor cold,' and who has never died. 'According to the earlier traditions of the *Avesta*,' says Spiegel, 'Jima does not die, but when evil and misery began to prevail on earth, retires to a smaller space, a kind of garden or Eden, where he continues his happy life with those who remained true to him.' Such have been the antecedents of our many beautiful myths which ascribe even an earthly immortality to the great,—to Barbarossa, Arthur, and even to the heroes of humbler races as Hiawatha and Glooscap of North American tribes,—who are or were long believed to have 'sailed into the fiery sunset,' or sought some fair island, or to slumber in a hidden grotto, until the world shall have grown up to their stature and requires their return.

In Japan the (Sintoo) god of Hell is now named Amma, and one may suspect that it is some imitation of Yama by reason of the majesty he still retains in the popular conception. He is pictured as a grave man, wearing a judicial cap, and no cruelties seem to be attributed to him personally, but only to the *oni* or demons of whom he is lord.

The kindly characteristics of the Hindu Yama seem in Persia to have been replaced by the bitterness of Ahriman, or Anra-mainyu, the genius of evil. Haug interprets Anra-mainyu as 'Death-darting.' The word is the counterpart of Speñta-mainyu, and means originally the 'throttling spirit;' being thus from *anh*, philologically the root of all evil, as we shall see when we consider its dragon brood. Professor

Whitney translates the name 'Malevolent.' But, whatever may be the meaning of the word, there is little doubt that the Twins of Vedic Mythology—Yama and Yami—parted into genii of Day and Night, and were ultimately spiritualised in the Spirit of Light and Spirit of Darkness which have made the basis of all popular theology from the time of Zoroaster until this day.

Nothing can be more remarkable than the extreme difference between the ancient Hindu and the Persian view of death. As to the former it was the happy introduction to Yama, to the latter it was the visible seal of Ahriman's equality with Ormuzd. They held it in absolute horror. The Towers of Silence stand in India to-day as monuments of this darkest phase of the Parsî belief. The dead body belonged to Ahriman, and was left to be devoured by wild creatures; and although the raising of towers for the exposure of the corpse, so limiting its consumption to birds, has probably resulted from a gradual rationalism which has from time to time suggested that by such means souls of the good may wing their way to Ormuzd, yet the Parsî horror of death is strong enough to give rise to such terrible suspicions, even if they were unfounded, as those which surround-ed the Tower (Khao's Dokhma) in June 1877. The strange behaviour of the corpse-bearers in leaving one tower, going to another, and afterwards (as was said) secretly repairing to the first, excited the belief that a man had been found alive in the first and was afterwards murdered. The story seems to have begun with certain young Parsîs themselves, and, whether it be true or not, they have undoubtedly interpreted rightly the ancient feeling of that sect with regard to all that had been within the kingdom of the King of Terrors. 'As sickness and death,' says Professor Whitney, 'were supposed to be the work of the malignant powers, the dead body itself was regarded with superstitious horror. It had been gotten by the demons into their own peculiar possession, and became a chief medium through which they exercised their defiling action upon the living. Everything that came into its neighbourhood was unclean, and to a certain extent exposed to the influences of the malevolent spirits, until purified by the ceremonies which the law prescribed.'[7] It is to be feared this notion has crept in among the Brahmans; the *Indian Mirror* (May 26, 1878) states that a Chandernagore lady, thrown into the Ganges, but afterwards found to be alive, was believed to be possessed by Dano (an evil spirit), and but for interference would have found a watery grave. The Jews also were influenced by this belief, and to this day it is forbidden a Cohen, or descendant of the priesthood, to touch a dead body.

The audience at the Crystal Palace which recently witnessed the performance of Euripides' *Alcestis* could hardly, it is to be feared, have realised the relation of the drama to their own religion. Apollo induces the Fates to consent that Admetus shall not die provided he can find a substitute for him. The pure Alcestis steps forward and devotes herself to death to save her husband. Apollo tries to persuade Death to give back Alcestis, but Death declares her fate demanded by justice. While Alcestis is dying, Admetus bids her entreat the gods for pity; but Alcestis says it is a god who has brought on the necessity, and adds, 'Be it so!' She sees the hall of the dead, with 'the winged Pluto staring from beneath his black eyebrows.' She reminds her husband of the palace and regal sway she might have enjoyed in Thessaly had she not left it for him. Bitterly does Pheres reproach Admetus for accepting life through the vicarious suffering and death of another. Then comes Hercules; he vanquishes Death; he leads forth Alcestis from 'beneath into the light.' With her he comes into the presence of Admetus, who is still in grief. Admetus cannot recognise her; but when he recognises her with joy, Hercules warns him that it is not lawful for Alcestis to address him 'until she is unbound from her consecration to the gods beneath, and *the third day come.*'

It only requires a change of names to make Alcestis a Passion-play. The unappeasable Justice which is as a Fate binding the deity, though it may be satisfied vicariously; 'the last enemy, Death;' the atonement by sacrifice of a saintly human being, who from a father's palace is brought by love freely to submit to death; the son of a god (Zeus) by a human mother (Alcmene),—the god-man Herakles,—commissioned to destroy earthly evils by twelve great labours,—descending to conquer Death and deliver one of the 'spirits in prison,' the risen spirit not recognised at first, as Jesus was not by Mary; still bearing the consecration of the grave until the third day, which forbade intercourse with the living ('Touch me not, for I am not yet ascended to my Father'),—all these enable us to recognise in the theologic edifices around us the fragments of a crumbled superstition as they lay around Euripides.

From the old pictures of Christ's triumphal pilgrimage on earth parallels for the chief Labours of Herakles may be found; he is shown treading on the lion, asp, dragon, and Satan; but the myths converge in the Descent into Hades and the conquest of Death. It is remarkable that in the old pictures of Christ delivering souls from Hades he is generally represented closely followed by Eve, whose form so emerging would once have been to the greater part of Europe already familiar as that of either Alcestis, Eurydice, or Persephone. One of the earliest examples of the familiar subject, Christ conquering Death, is that in the ancient (tenth century) Missal of Worms,—that city whose very name preserves the record of the same combat under the guise of Siegfried and the Worm, or Dragon. The cross is now the sword thrust near the monster's mouth. The picture illustrates the chant of Holy Week: 'De manu Mortis liberabo eos, de Morte redimam eos. Ero Mors tua, O Mors; morsus tuus ero, inferne.' From the pierced mouth of Death are vomited flames, which remind us of his ethnical origin; but it is not likely that to the christianised pagans of Worms the picture could ever have conveyed an impression so weirdly horrible as that of their own goddess of Death, Hel. 'Her hall is called Elvidnir, realm of the cold storm: Hunger is her table; Starvation, her knife; Delay, her man; Slowness, her maid; Precipice, her threshold; Care, her bed; burning Anguish, the hangings of her apartments. One half of her body is livid, the other half the colour of human flesh.'

With the Scandinavian picture of the Abode of Death may be compared the description of the Abode of Nin-ki-gal, the Assyrian Queen of Death, from a tablet in the British Museum, translated by Mr. Fox Talbot: [8]—

To the House men enter—but cannot depart from:
To the Road men go—but cannot return.
The abode of darkness and famine
Where Earth is their food: their nourishment Clay:
Light is not seen; in darkness they dwell:
Ghosts, like birds, flutter their wings there;
On the door and the gate-posts the dust lies undisturbed.

The Semitic tribes, undisturbed, like the importers of their theology into the age of science, by the strata in which so many perished animal kingdoms are entombed, attributed all death, even that of animals, to the forbidden fruit. The Rabbins say that not only Adam and Eve, but the animals in Eden, partook of that fruit, and came under the power of Sammaël the Violent, and of his agent Azraël, the demon of Death. The Phœnix, having refused this food, preserved the power of renovating itself.

It is an example of the completeness and consistency with which a theory may organise its myth, that the fatal demons are generally represented as abhorring salt—the preserving agent and foe of decay. The 'Covenant of Salt' among the ancient Jews probably had this significance, and the care with which Job salted his sacrifice is considered elsewhere. Aubrey says, 'Toads (Saturnine animals) are killed by putting salt upon them. I have seen the experiment.' The devil, as heir of death-demons, appears in all European folklore as a hater of salt. A legend, told by Heine, relates that a knight, wandering in a wood in Italy, came upon a ruin, and in it a wondrous statue of the goddess of Beauty. Completely fascinated, the knight haunted the spot day after day, until one evening he was met by a servant who invited him to enter a villa which he had not before remarked.

What was his surprise to be ushered into the presence of the living image of his adored statue! Amid splendour and flowers the enraptured knight is presently seated with his charmer at a banquet. Every luxury of the world is there; but there is no salt! When he hints this want a cloud passes over the face of his Beauty. Presently he asks the servant to bring the salt; the servant does so, shuddering; the knight helps himself to it. The next sip of wine he takes elicits a cry from him: it is liquid fire. Madness seizes upon him; caresses, burning kisses follow, until he falls asleep on the bosom of his goddess. But what visions! Now he sees her as a wrinkled crone, next a great bat bearing a torch as it flutters around him, and again as a frightful monster, whose head he cuts off in an agony of terror. When the knight awakes it is in his own villa. He hastens to his ruin, and to the beloved statue; he finds her fallen from the pedestal, and the beautiful head cut from the neck lying at her feet.

The Semitic Angel of Death is a figure very different from any that we have considered. He is known in theology only in the degradation which he suffered at the hands of the Rabbins, but originally was an awful but by no means evil genius. The Persians probably imported him, under the name of Asuman, for we do not find him mentioned in their earlier books, and the name has a resemblance to the Hebrew *shamad*, to exterminate, which would connect it with the biblical 'destroyer' Abaddon. This is rendered more probable because the Zoroastrians believed in an earlier demon, Vizaresha, who carried souls after death to the region of Deva-worshippers (India). The Chaldaic Angel of Death, Malk-ad Mousa, may have derived his name from the legend of his having approached Moses with the object of forcing his soul out of his body, but, being struck by the glory of Moses' face, and by virtue of the divine name on his rod, was compelled to retire. The legend is not so ancient as the name, and was possibly a Saga suggested by the name; it is obviously the origin of the tradition of the struggle between Michael and Satan for the body of Moses (Jude 9.). This personification had thus declined among the Jews into being evil enough to be identified with Samaël,—who, in the Book of the Assumption of Moses, is named as his assailant,—and subsequently with Satan himself, named in connection with the New Testament version. It was on account of this degradation of a being described in the earlier books of the Bible as the commissioner of Jehovah that there was gradually developed among the Jews two Angels of Death, one (Samaël, or his agent Azraël) for those who died out of the land of Israel, and the other (Gabriel) for those who had the happier lot of dying in their own country.

This relegation of Samaël to the wandering Jews—who if they died abroad were not supposed to reach Paradise with facility, if at all—is significant. For Samaël is pretty certainly a conception borrowed from outlying Semitic tribes. What that conception was we find in Job xviii. 18, where he is 'the king of Terrors,' and still more in the Arabic Azraël. The legend of this typical Angel of Death is that he was promoted to his high office for special service. When Allah was about to create man he sent the angels Gabriel, Michael, and Israfil to the earth to bring clay of different colours for that purpose; but the Earth warned them that the being about to be formed would rebel against his creator and draw down a curse upon her (the Earth), and they returned without bringing the clay. Then Azraël was sent by Allah, and he executed his commission without fear; and for this he was appointed the angel to separate souls from bodies. Azraël had subordinate angels under him, and these are alluded to in the opening lines of the Sura 79 of the Koran:

By the angels who tear forth the souls of some with violence;
And by those who draw forth the souls of others with gentleness.

The souls of the righteous are drawn forth with gentleness, those of the wicked torn from them in the way shown in the Russian picture (Fig. 19), which is indeed an illustration of the same mythology.

These terrible tasks were indeed such as were only too likely to bring Azraël into the evil repute of an executioner in the course of time; but no degradation of him seems to have been developed among the Moslems. He seems to have been associated in their minds with Fate, and similar stories were told of him. Thus it is related that once when Azraël was passing by Solomon he gazed intently upon a man with whom Solomon was conversing. Solomon told his companion that it was the Angel of Death who was looking at him, and the man replied, 'He seems to want me: order the wind to carry me from hence into India;' when this was done Azraël approached Solomon and said, 'I looked earnestly at that man from wonder, for I was commanded to take his soul in India.'[9]

Azraël was often represented as presenting to the lips a cup of poison. It is probable that this image arose from the ancient ordeal by poison, whereby draughts, however manipulated beforehand with reference to the results, were popularly held to be divinely mingled for retributive or beneficent effects. 'Cup' thus became among Semitic tribes a symbol of Fate. The 'cup of consolation,' 'cup of wrath,' 'cup of trembling,' which we read of in the Old Testament; the 'cup of blessing,' and 'cup of devils,' spoken of by Paul, have this significance. The cup of Nestor, ornamented with the dove (Iliad, xi. 632), was probably a 'cup of blessing,' and Mr. Schliemann has found several of the same kind at Mycenæ. The symbol was repeatedly used by Christ,—'Let this cup pass from me,' 'The cup that my Father hath given me to drink shall I not drink it,' 'Are ye able to drink of the cup that I drink of,'—and the familiar association of Azraël's cup is expressed in the phrase 'taste of death.'

One of the most pleasing modifications of the belief in the Angel of Death is that found by Lepsius [10] among the Mohammedan negroes of Kordofan. Osraîn (Azraël), it is said, receives the souls of the dead, and leads the good to their reward, the bad to punishment. 'He lives in a tree, el segerat mohana (the tree of fulfilling), which has as many leaves as there are inhabitants in the world. On each leaf is a name, and when a child is born a new one grows. If any one becomes ill his leaf fades, and should he be destined to die, Osraîn breaks it off. Formerly he used to come visibly to those whom he was going to carry away, and thus put them in great terror. Since the prophet's time, however, he has become invisible; for when he came to fetch Mohammed's soul he told him that it was not good that by his visible appearance he should frighten mankind. They might then easily die of terror, before praying; for he himself, although a courageous and spirited man, was somewhat perturbed at his appearance. Therefore the prophet begged God to make Osraîn invisible, which prayer was granted.' Mr. Mackenzie adds on this that, among the Moravian Jews, at new moon a branch is held in its light, and the name of a person pronounced: his face will appear between the horns of the moon, and should he be destined to die the leaves will fade.

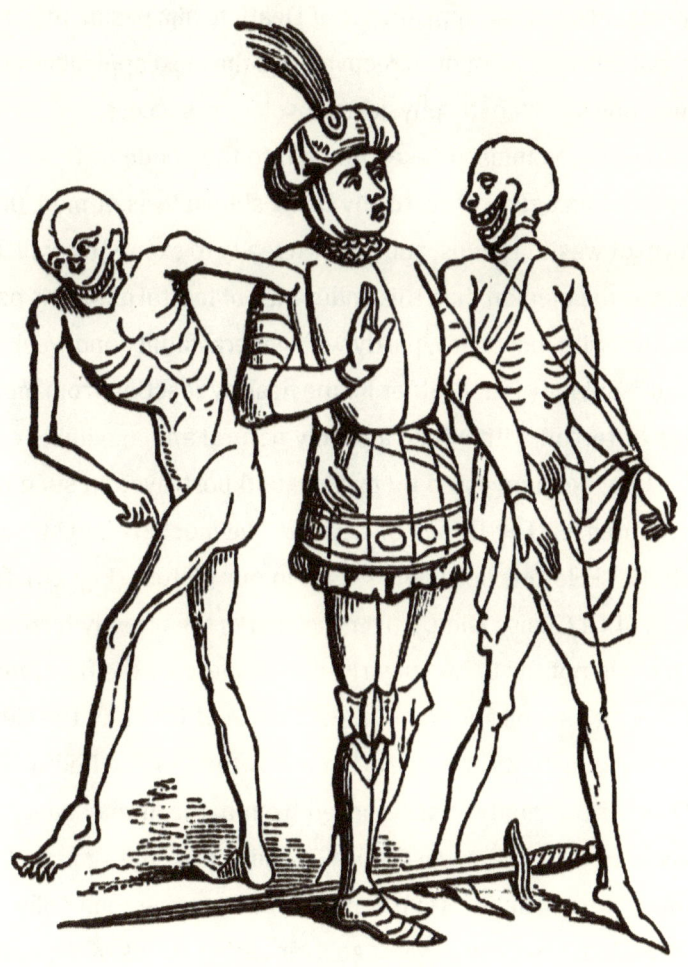

Fig. 20.—The Knight and Death

Mr. John Ruskin has been very severe upon the Italians for the humour with which they introduce Death as a person of their masque. 'When I was in Venice in 1850,' he says, 'the most popular piece of the *comic* opera was "Death and the Cobbler," in which the point of the plot was the success of a village cobbler as a physician, in consequence of the appearance of Death to him beside the bed of every patient who was not to recover; and the most applauded scene in it was one in which the physician, insolent in success, and swollen with luxury, was himself taken down into the abode of Death, and thrown into an agony of terror by being shown lives of men, under the form of wasting lamps, and his own ready to expire.' On which he expresses the opinion that 'this endurance of fearful images is partly associated with indecency, partly with general fatuity and weakness of mind.'[11] But may it not rather be the healthy reaction from morbid images of terror, with which a purely natural and inevitable event has so long been invested by priests, and portrayed in such popular pictures as 'The Dance of Death?' The mocking laughter with which the skeletons beset the knight in our picture (Fig. 20), from the wall of La Chaise Dieu, Auvergne, marks the priestly terrorism, which could not fail to be vulgarised even more by the frivolous. In 1424 there was a masquerade of the Dance of Death in the Cemetery of the Innocents at Paris, attended by the Duke of Bedford and the Duke of Burgundy, just returned from battle. It may have been the last outcome in the west of Kali's dance over the slain; but it is fortunate when Fanaticism has no worse outcome than Folly. The Skeleton Death has the advantage over earlier forms of suggesting the naturalness of death. It is more scientific. The gradual discovery by the people that death is not caused by sin has largely dissipated its horrors in regions where the ignorance and impostures of priest-craft are of daily observation; and although the reaction may not be expressed with good taste, there would seem to be in it a certain vigour of nature, reasserting itself in simplicity.

In the northern world we are all too sombre in the matter. It is the ages of superstition which have moulded our brains, and too generally given to our natural love of life the unnatural counterpart of a terror of death. What has been artificially bred into us can be cultivated out of us. There are indeed deaths corresponding to the two Angels—the death that comes by lingering disease and pain, and that which comes by old age. There are indeed Azraëls in our cities who poison the food and drink of the people, and mingle death in the cup of water; and of them there should be increasing horror until the gentler angel abides with us, and death by old age becomes normal. The departure from life being a natural condition of entering upon it, it is melancholy indeed that it should be ideally confused with the pains and sorrows often attending it. It is fabled that Menippus the Cynic, travelling through Hades, knew which were the kings there by their howling louder than the rest. They howled loudest because they had parted from most pleasures on earth. But all the happy and young have more reason to lament untimely death than kings. The only tragedy of Death is the ruin of living Love. Mr. Watts, in his great picture of Love and Death (Grosvenor Gallery, 1877), revealed the real horror. Not that skeleton which has its right time and place, not the winged demon (called angel), who has no right time or place, is here, but a huge, hard, heartless form, as of man half-blocked out of marble; a terrible emblem of the remorseless force that embodies the incompleteness and ignorance of mankind—a force that steadily crushes hearts where intellects are devoting their energies to alien worlds. Poor Love has little enough science; his puny arm stretched out to resist the colossal form is weak as the prayers of agonised parents and lovers directed against never-swerving laws; he is almost exhausted; his lustrous wings are broken and torn in the struggle; the dove at his feet crouches mateless; the rose that climbed on his door is prostrate; over his shoulder the beam-like arm has set the stony hand against the door where the rose of joy must fall.

The aged when they die do but follow the treasures that have gone before. One by one the old friends have left them, the sweet ties parted, and the powers to enjoy and help become feeble. When of the garden that once bloomed around them memory alone is left, friendly is death to scatter also the leaves of that last rose where the loved ones are sleeping. This is the real office of death. Nay, even when it comes to the young and happy it is not Death but Disease that is the real enemy; in disease there is almost no compensation at all but learning its art of war; but Death is Nature's pity for helpless pain; where love and knowledge can do no more it comes as a release from sufferings which were sheer torture if prolonged. The presence of death is recognised oftenest by the cessation of pain. Superstition has done few heavier wrongs to humanity than by the mysterious terrors with which it has invested that change which, to the simpler ages, was pictured as the gentle river Lethe, flowing from the abode of sleep, from which the shades drank oblivion alike of their woes and of the joys from which they were torn.

NOTES

1   Wake's 'Evolution of Morality,' i. 107.
2   'The Aborigines of Australia' (1865), p. 15.
3   2 Chron. xxxiii. 6.
4   Published by Mozley and Smith, 1878.
5   Max Müller. 'Lectures on Language,' ii. p. 562, et seq.
6   See the beautifully translated funereal hymn of the Veda in Professor Whitney's 'Oriental and Linguistic Studies,' p. 52, etc.
7   'The Avesta.' 'Oriental and Linguistic Studies,' p. 196.
8   'Records of the Past,' i. 143.
9   Sale's 'Koran' (ed. 1836). See pp. 4, 339, 475.
10 'Discoveries,' &c., p. 223.
11 'Modern Painters,' Part V. xix.

Part lll
The Dragon

Chapter I
Decline of Demons

The Holy Tree of Travancore — The growth of Demons in India and their decline
— The Nepaul Iconoclast — Moral Man and unmoral Nature — Man's physical
and mental migrations — Heine's 'Gods in Exile' — The Goban Saor —
Master Smith — A Greek caricature of the Gods — The Carpenter v. Deity and
Devil — Extermination of the Werewolf — Refuges of Demons —
The Giants reduced to Little People — Deities and Demons returning to nature

HAVING INDICATED, NECESSARILY in mere outline and by selected examples, the chief obstacles encountered by primitive man, and
his apprehensions, which he personified as demons, it becomes my
next task to show how and why many of these demons declined from
their terrible proportions and made way for more general forms,
expressing comparatively abstract conceptions of physical evil. This
will involve some review of the processes through which man's necessary adaptation to his earthly environment brought him to the era
of Combat with multiform obstruction.

There was, until within a few recent years, in a mountain of
Travancore, India, an ancient, gigantic Tree, regarded by the natives
as the residence of a powerful and dangerous deity who reigned
over the mountains and the wild beasts.[1] Sacrifices were offered to
this tree, sermons preached before it, and it seems to have been the
ancient cathedral of the district. Its trunk was so large that four men
with outstretched arms could not compass it.

This tree in its early growth may symbolise the upspringing
of natural religion. Its first green leaves may be regarded as cor-

responding to the first crude imaginations of man as written, for instance, on leaves of the Vedas. Perceiving in nature, as we have seen, a power of contrivance like his own, a might far superior to his own, man naturally considered that all things had been created and were controlled by invisible giants; and bowing helplessly beneath them sang thus his hymns and supplications.

'This earth belongs to Varuna, the king, and the wide sky, with its ends far apart: the two seas (sky and ocean) are Varuna's loins; he is also contained in this drop of water. He who would flee far beyond the sky even he would not be rid of Varuna. His spies proceed from heaven towards this earth.'

'Through want of strength, thou ever strong and bright god, have I gone wrong: have mercy, have mercy!'

'However we break thy laws from day to day, men as we are, O god Varuna, do not deliver us to death!'

'Was it an old sin, Varuna, that thou wished to destroy the friend who always praises thee!'

'O Indra, have mercy, give me my daily bread! Raise up wealth to the worshipper, thou mighty Dawn!'

'Thou art the giver of horses, Indra, thou art the giver of cows, the giver of corn, the strong lord of wealth: the old guide of man disappointing no desires: to him we address this song. All this wealth around here is known to be thine alone: take from it conqueror, bring it hither!'

In these characteristic sentences from various hymns we behold man making his first contract with the ruling powers of nature: so much adoration and flattery on his part for so much benefit on theirs. But even in these earliest hymns there are intimations that the gods were not fulfilling their side of the engagement. 'Why is it,' pleads the worshipper, 'that you wish to destroy one who always praises you? Was it an old sin?' The simple words unconsciously report how faithfully man was performing his part of the contract. Having omitted no accent of the prayer, praise, or ritual, he supposes the continued indifference of the gods must be due to an old sin, one he has forgotten, or perhaps one committed by some ancestor.

In this state of mind the suggestion would easily take root that words alone were too cheap to be satisfactory to the gods. There must be offerings. Like earthly kings they must have their revenues. We thus advance to the phase of sacrifices. But still neither in answer to prayer, flattery, or sacrifice did the masses receive health or wealth. Poverty, famine, death, still continued their remorseless course with the silent machinery of sun, moon, and star.

But why, then, should man have gone on fulfilling his part of the contract—believing and worshipping deities, who when he begged for corn gave him famine, and when he asked for fish gave him a serpent? The priest intervened with ready explanation. And here we may consult the holy Tree of Travancore again? Why should that particular Tree—of a species common in the district and not usually very large—have grown so huge? 'Because it is holy,' said the priest. 'Because it was believed holy,' says the fact. For ages the blood and ashes of victims fed its roots and swelled its trunk; until, by an argument not confined to India, the dimensions of the superstition were assumed to prove its truth. When the people complained that all their offerings and worship did not bring any returns the priest replied, You stint the gods and they stint you. The people offered the fattest of their flocks and fruits: More yet! said the priest. They built fine altars and temples for the gods: More yet! said the priest. They built fine houses for the priests, and taxed themselves to support them. And when thus, fed by popular sacrifices and toils, the religion had grown to vast power, the priest was able to call to his side the theologian for further explanation. The theologian and the priest said—'Of course there must be good reasons why the gods do not answer all your prayers (if they did not answer some you would be utterly consumed); mere mortals must not dare to inquire into their mysteries; but that there are gods, and that they do attend to human affairs, is made perfectly plain by this magnificent array of temples, and by the care with which they have supplied all the wants of us, their particular friends, whose cheeks, as you see, hang down with fatness.'

If, after this explanation, any scepticism or rebellion arose among the less favoured, the priest might easily add—'Furthermore, we and our temples are now institutions; we are so strong and influential that it is evident that the gods have appointed us to be their representatives on earth, the dispensers of their favours. Also, of their disfavours. We are able to make up for the seeming indifference of the gods, rewarding you if you give us honour and wealth, but ruining you if you turn heretical.'

So grew the holy Tree. But strong as it was there was something stronger. Some few years ago a missionary from London went to Travancore, and desired to build a chapel near the same tree, no doubt to be in the way of its worshippers and to borrow some of the immemorial sanctity of the spot. This missionary fixed a hungry eye upon that holy timber, and reflected how much holier it would be if ending its career in the beams of a christian chapel. So one day— English authorities being conveniently near—he and his workmen began to cut down the sacred Tree. The natives gradually gathered around, and looked on with horror. While the cutting proceeded a tiger drew near, but shouts drove him off: the natives breathed freer; the demon had come and looked on, but could not protect the Tree from the Englishman. They still shuddered, however, at the sacrilege, and when at last the Holy Tree of Travancore fell, its crash was mingled with the cries and screams of its former worshippers. The victorious missionary may be pointing out in his chapel the cut-up planks which reveal the impotence of the deity so long feared by the natives; and perhaps he is telling them of the bigness of *his* Tree, and claiming its flourishing condition in Europe as proof of its supernatural character. Possibly he may omit to mention the blood and ashes which have fattened the root and enlarged the trunk of *his* Holy Tree!

That Tree in Travancore could never have been so destroyed if the primitive natural religion in which lay its deeper root had not previously withered. The gods, the natural forces, which through so many ages had not heeded man's daily martyrdoms, had now for a long time been shown quite as impotent to protect their own shrines, images, holy trees, and other interests. The priests as vainly invoked those gods to save their own country from subjugation by other nations with foreign gods, as the masses had invoked their personal aid. For a long time the gods in some parts of India have received only a formal service, coextensive with their association with a lingering order, or as part of princely establishments; but they topple down from time to time, as the masses realise their freedom to abandon them with impunity. They are at the mercy of any strong heretic who arises. The following narrative, quoted by Mr. Herbert Spencer, presents a striking example of what some Hindoos had been doing before the missionary cut down the Tree at Travancore:—

'A Nepaul king, Rum Bahâdur, whose beautiful queen, finding her lovely face had been disfigured by smallpox, poisoned herself, cursed his kingdom, her doctors, and the gods of Nepaul, vowing vengeance on all. Having ordered the doctors to be flogged, and the right ear and nose of each to be cut off, he then wreaked his vengeance on the gods of Nepaul, and after abusing them in the most gross way, he accused them of having obtained from him 12,000 goats, some hundred-weights of sweetmeats, 2000 gallons of milk, &c., under false pretences. He then ordered all the artillery, varying from three to twelve-pounders, to be brought in front of the palace. All the guns were then loaded to the muzzle, and down he marched to the headquarters of the Nepaul deities. All the guns were drawn up in front of the several deities, honouring the most sacred with the heaviest metal. When the order to fire was given, many of the chiefs and soldiers ran away panic-stricken, and others hesitated to obey the sacrilegious order; and not till several gunners had been cut down were the guns opened. Down came the gods and the goddesses from their hitherto sacred positions; and after six hours' heavy cannonading, not a vestige of the deities remained.'

However panic-stricken the Nepaulese may have been at this ferocious manifestation, it was but a storm bred out of a more general mental and moral condition. Rum Bahâdur only laid low in a few moments images of gods who, passing from the popular interest, had been successively laid to sleep on the innumerable shelves of Hindu mythology. The early Dualism was developed into Moral Man on one side, and Unmoral Nature on the other. Man had discovered that moral order in nature was represented solely by his own power: by his culture or neglect the plant or animal grew or withered, and where his control did not extend, there sprang the noxious weed or beast. So far as good gods had been imagined they were respected now only as incarnate in men. But the active powers of evil still remained, hurtful and hateful to man, and the pessimist view of nature became inevitable. To man engaged in his life-and-death struggle with nature many a beauty which now nourishes the theist's optimism was lost. The fragrant flower was a weed to the man hungry for bread, and he viewed many an idle treasure with the disappointment of Sâdi when, travelling in the desert, he found a bag in which he hoped to discover grain, but found only pearls. Fatal to every deity not anthropomorphic was the long pessimistic phase of human faith. Each became more purely a demon, and passed on the road to become a devil.

Many particular demons man conquered as he progressively carried order amid the ruggedness and wildness of his planet. Every new weapon or implement he invented punctured a thousand phantoms. Only in the realms he could not yet conquer remained the hostile forces to which he ascribed præternatural potency, because not able to pierce them and see through them. Nevertheless, the early demonic forms had to give way, for man had discovered that they were not his masters. He could cut down the Upas and root up the nightshade; he had bruised many a serpent's head and slain many a wolf. In detail innumerable enemies had been proved his inferiors in strength and intelligence. Important migrations took place: man passes, geographically, away from the region of some of his worst enemies, inhabits countries more fruitful, less malarious, his habitat exceeding that of his animal foe in range; and, still better, he passes by mental migration out of the stone age, out of other helpless ages, to the age of metal and the skill to fashion and use it. He has made the fire-fiend his friend. No longer henceforth a naked savage, with bit of stone or bone only to meet the crushing powers of the world and win its reluctant supplies!

There is a sense far profounder than its charming play of fancy in Heine's account of the 'Gods in Exile,' an essay which Mr. Pater well describes as 'full of that strange blending of sentiment which is characteristic of the traditions of the Middle Age concerning the Pagan religions.'[2] Heine writes: 'Let me briefly remind the reader how the gods of the older world, at the time of the definite triumph of Christianity, that is, in the third century, fell into painful embar-rassments, which greatly resembled certain tragical situations of their earlier life. They now found themselves exposed to the same troublesome necessities to which they had once before been exposed during the primitive ages, in that revolutionary epoch when the Titans broke out of the custody of Orcus, and, piling Pelion on Ossa, scaled Olympus. Unfortunate gods! They had, then, to take flight ignominiously, and hide themselves among us here on earth under all sorts of disguises. Most of them betook themselves to Egypt, where for greater security they assumed the form of animals, as is generally known. Just in the same way they had to take flight again, and seek entertainment in remote hiding-places, when those iconoclastic zealots, the black brood of monks, broke down all the temples, and pursued the gods with fire and curses. Many of these unfortunate emigrants, entirely deprived of shelter and ambrosia, had now to take to vulgar handicrafts as a means of earning their bread. In these circumstances, many, whose sacred groves had been confiscated, let themselves out for hire as wood-cutters in Germany, and had to drink beer instead of nectar. Apollo seems to have been content to take service under graziers, and as he had once kept the cows of Admetus, so he lived now as a shepherd in Lower Austria. Here, however, having become suspected, on account of his beautiful singing, he was recognised by a learned monk as one of the old pagan gods, and handed over to the spiritual tribunal. On the rack he confessed that he was the god Apollo; and before his execution he begged that he might be suffered to play once more upon the lyre and to sing a song. And he played so touchingly, and sang with such magic, and was withal so beautiful in form and feature that all the women wept, and many of them were so deeply impressed that they shortly afterwards fell sick. And some time afterwards the people wished to drag him from the grave again, that a stake might be driven through his body, in the belief that he had been a vampire, and that the sick women would by this means recover. But they found the grave empty.'

Naturally: it is hard to bury Apollo. The next time he appeared was, no doubt, as musical director in the nearest cathedral. The young singers and artists discovered by such severe lessons that it was dangerous to sing Pagan ballads too realistically; that a cowl is capable of a high degree of decoration; that Pan's pipe sounds well evolved into an organ; that Cupids look just as well if called Cherubs. It is odd that it should have required Robert Browning three centuries away to detect the real form and face beneath the vestment of the Bishop who orders his tomb at Saint Praxed's Church:—

> The bas-relief in bronze ye promised me,
> Those Pans and Nymphs ye wot of, and perchance
> Some tripod, thyrsus, with a vase or so,
> The Saviour at his sermon on the mount,
> Saint Praxed in a glory, and one Pan
> Ready to twitch the Nymph's last garment off,
> And Moses with the tables....

So in one direction grew the hermitage to the Vatican; so Zeus regained his throne by exchanging his thunderbolts for Peter's keys, and Mars regained his steed as St. George, and Hercules as Christ wrestles with Death once more. But while these artificial restorations were going on in one direction, in another some of the gods were passing through many countries, outwitting and demolishing their former selves as lowered to demons. There are many legends which report this strange phase of development, one of the finest being that of The Goban Saor, told by Mr. Kennedy. The King of

Munster sent for this wonderful craftsman to build him a castle. The Goban could fashion a spear with three strokes of his hammer—St. Patrick, who found the Trinity in the shamrock, may have determined the number of strokes,—and when he wished to drive in nails high up, had only to throw his hammer at them. On his way to work for the King, Goban, accompanied by his son, passed the night at the house of a farmer, whose daughters—one dark and industrious, the other fair and idle—received from him (Goban) three bits of advice: 'Always have the head of an old woman by the hob; warm yourselves with your work in the morning; and some time before I come back take the skin of a newly-killed sheep to the market, and bring itself and the price of it home again.' As Goban, with his son, journeyed on, they found a poor man vainly trying to roof his house with three joists and mud; and by simply making one end of each joist rest on the middle of another, the other ends being on the wall, the structure was perfect. He relieved puzzled carpenters by putting up for them the pegless and nailless bridge described in Cæsar's Commentaries. Having done various great things, Goban returns to the homestead of the girls who had received his three bits of advice. The idle one had, of course, blundered at each point, and been ridiculed in the market for her proposition to bring back the sheep's skin and its price. The other, by kindly taking in an aged female relative, by working till she was warm, and by plucking and selling the wool of the sheep's skin and bringing home the latter, had obeyed the Goban's advice, and was selected as his daughter-in-law—the prince attending the wedding. Now, as to building the castle, Goban knew that the King had employed on previous castles four architects and then slain them, so that they should never build another palace equal to his. He therefore says he has left at home a necessary implement which his wife will only give to himself or one of royal blood. The King sends his son, who is kept as hostage till the husband's safe return.

This is the Master Smith of Norse fable, who has a chair from which none can rise, and who therein binds the devil; which again is the story of Hephaistos, and the chair in which he entrapped Hera until she revealed the secret of his birth. The 'devil' whom the Master Smith entraps is, in Norse mythology, simply Loki: and as Loki is a degraded Hephaistos, fire in its demonic forms, we have in all these legends the fire-fiend fought with fire.

This re-dualisation of the gods into demonic and saintly forms had a long preparation. The forces that brought it about may be seen already beginning in Hesiod's representations of the gods, in their presentation on the stage by Euripides, in a manner certain to demonise them to the vulgar, and to subject them to such laughter among scholars as still rings across the ages in the divine dialogues of Lucian. What the gods had become to the Lucians before they reached the Heines may be gathered from the accompanying caricature (Fig. 21).[3] Nothing can be more curious than the encounters of the gods with their dead selves, their Manes. What unconscious ingenuity in the combinations! St. Martin on his grey steed divides with the beggar the cloud-cloak of Wodan on his black horse, treading down just such paupers in his wild hunt; as saint he now shelters those whom as storm-demon he chilled; but the identity of Junker Martin is preserved in both titles and myths, and the Martinhorns (cakes), twisted after fashion of the horns of goat or buck pursued by Wodan, are deemed potent like horse-shoes to defend house or stable from the outlawed god.[4]

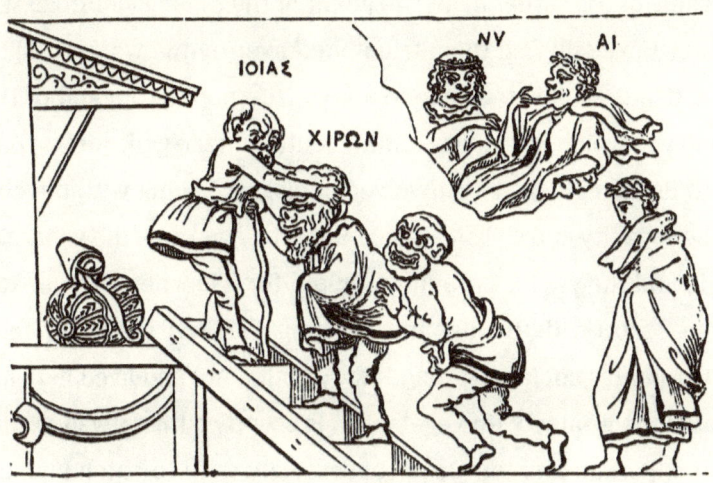

Fig. 21.—Greek Caricature of the Gods

The more impressive and attractive myths transferred to christian saints—as the flowers sacred to Freyja became Our Lady's-glove, or slipper, or smock—there remained to the old gods, in their own name, only the repulsive and puerile, and by this means they were doomed at once to become unmitigated knaves and fools. If Titans, Jötunn or Jinni, they were giant humbugs, whom any small Hans or Jack might outwit and behead. Our Fairy lore is full of stories which show that in the North as well as in Latin countries there had already been a long preparation for the contempt poured by Christianity upon the Norse deities. Many of the stories, as they now stand in Folktales, speak of the vanquished demon or giant as the devil, but it is perfectly easy to detach the being meant from the name so indiscriminately bestowed by christian priests upon most of the outlawed deities. In Lithuania, where survived too much reverence for some of the earlier deities to admit of their being identified with the devil, we still find them triumphed over by the wit and skill of the artisan. Such is the case in a favourite popular legend of that country in which Perkunas—the ancient Thunder-god, corresponding to Perun in Russia—is involved in disgrace along with the devil by the sagacity and skill of a carpenter. The aged god, the venerable Devil, and the young Carpenter, united for a journey. Perkun kept the beasts off with thunder and lightning, the Devil hunted up food, the Carpenter cooked. At length they built a hut and lived in it, and planted the ground with vegetables. Presently a thief invaded their garden. Perkun and the Devil successively tried to catch him, but were well thrashed; whereas the Carpenter by playing the fiddle fascinated the thief, who was a witch, a hag whose hand the fiddler managed to get into a split tree (under pretence of giving her a music lesson), holding her there till she gave up her iron waggon and the whip which she had used on his comrades. After this the three, having decided to separate, disputed as to which should have the hut; and they finally agreed that it should be the possession of him who should succeed in frightening the two others. The Devil raised a storm which frightened Perkun, and Perkun with his thunder and lightning frightened the Devil; but the Carpenter held out bravely, and, in the middle of the night, came in with the witch's waggon, and, cracking her whip, the Devil and Perkun both took flight, leaving the Carpenter in possession of the hut.[5]

So far as Perkun is concerned, and may be regarded as representative of the gods, the hut may be symbol of Europe, and the Carpenter type of the power which conquered all that was left of them after their fair or noble associations had been transferred to christian forms. Somewhat later, the devil was involved in a like fate, as we shall have to consider in a future chapter.

The most horrible superstitions, if tracked in their popular development, reveal with special impressiveness the progressive emancipation of man from the phantasms of ferocity which represented his primal helplessness. The universal werewolf superstition, for instance, drew its unspeakable horrors from deep and wide-spreading roots. Originating, probably, in occasional relapses to cannibalism among tribes or villages which found themselves amid circumstances as urgent as those which sometimes lead a wrecked crew to draw lots which shall die to support the rest, it would necessarily become demonised by the necessity of surrounding cannibalism with dangers worse than starvation. But it would seem that individuals are always liable, by arrest of development which usually takes the form of disease or insanity, to be dragged back to the savage condition of their race. In the course of this dark history, we note first an increasing tendency to show the means of the transformation difficult. In the *Volsunga Saga* it is by simply putting on a 'wolf-shirt' (wolfskin) that a man may become a wolf. Then it is said it is done by a belt made of the skin of a man who has been hung—all executed persons being sacred to Wodan (because not dying a natural death), to whom also the wolf was sacred. Then it is added, that the belt must be marked with the signs of the zodiac, and have a buckle with seven teeth. Then it is said that 'only a seventh son' is possessed of this diabolical power; or others say one whose brows meet over his nose. The means of detecting werewolves and retransforming them to human shape multiplied as those of transformation diminished in number, and such remedies reflected the advance of human skill. The werewolf could be restored by crossing his path with a knife or polished steel; by a sword laid on the ground with point towards him; by a silver ball. Human skill was too much for him. In Posen mothers had discovered that one who had bread in his or her mouth could by even such means discover werewolves; and fathers, to this hint about keeping 'the wolf from the door,' added that no one could be attacked by any such monster if he were in a cornfield. The Slav levelled a plough at him. Thus by one prescription and another, and each representing a part of man's victory over chaos, the werewolf was driven out of all but a few 'unlucky' days in the year, and especially found his last refuge in Twelfth Night. But even on that night the werewolf might be generally escaped by the simple device of not speaking of him. If a wolf had to be spoken of he was then called Vermin, and Dr. Wuttke mentions a parish priest named Wolf in East Prussia who on Twelfth Night was addressed as Mr. Vermin! The actual wolf being already out of the forests in most places by art of the builder and the architect; the phantasmal wolf driven out of fear for most of the year by man's recognition of his own superiority to this exterminated beast; even the proverbial 'ears' of the vanishing werewolf ceased to be visible when on his particular fest-night his name was not mentioned.

The last execution of a man for being an occasional werewolf was, I believe, in 1589, near Cologne, there being some evidence of cannibalism. But nine years later, in France, where the belief in the *Loup-garou* had been intense, a man so accused was simply shut up in a mad-house. It is an indication of the revolution which has occurred, that when next governments paid attention to werewolves it was because certain vagabonds went about professing to be able to transform themselves into wolves, in order to extort money from the more weak-minded and ignorant peasants.[6] There could hardly be conceived a more significant history: the werewolf leaves where he entered. Of ignorance and weakness trying, too often in vain, 'to keep the wolf from the door,' was born this voracious phantom; with the beggar and vagabond, survivals of helplessness become inveterate, he wanders thin and crafty. He keeps out of the way of all culture, whether of field or mind. So is it indeed with all demons in decline—of which I can here only adduce a few characteristic examples. So runs the rune—

When the barley there is,
Then the devils whistle;
When the barley is threshed,
Then the devils whine;
When the barley is ground,
Then the devils roar;
When the flour is produced,
Then the devils perish.

The old Scottish custom, mentioned by Sir Walter Scott, of leaving around each cultivated field an untilled fringe, called the *Gude Man's Croft*, is derived from the ancient belief that unless some wild place is left to the sylvan spirits they will injure the grain

355

and vegetables; and, no doubt, some such notion leads the farmers of Thurgau still to graft mistletoe upon their fruit-trees. Many who can smile at such customs do yet preserve in their own minds, or those of their servants or neighbours, crofts which the ploughshare of science is forbidden to touch, and where the præternatural troops still hide their shrivelled forms. But this wild girdle becomes ever narrower, and the images within it tend to blend with rustling leaf and straw, and the insects, and to be otherwise invisible, save to that second sight which is received from Glam. As in some shadow-pantomime, the deities and demons pursue each other in endless procession, dropping down as awe-inspiring Titans, vanishing as grotesque pigmies—vanishing beyond the lamp into Nothingness!

So came most of the monsters we have been describing—Animals, Volcanoes, Icebergs, Deserts, though they might be—by growing culture and mastery of nature to be called 'the little people;' and perhaps it is rather through pity than euphemism when they were so often called, as in Ireland (*Duine Matha*), 'the good little people.'[7] At every step in time or space back of the era of mechanic arts the little fairy gains in physical proportions. The house-spirits (Domovoi) of Russia are full-sized, shaggy human-shaped beings. In Lithuania the corresponding phantoms (Kaukas) average only a foot in height. The Krosnyata, believed in by the Slavs on the Baltic coast, are similarly small; and by way of the kobolds, elves, fays, travelling westward, we find the size of such shapes diminishing, until warnings are given that the teeth must never be picked with a straw, that slender tube being a favourite residence of the elf! In Bavaria a little red chafer with seven spots (*Coccinella septempunctata*) is able to hold Thor with his lightnings, and in other regions is a form of the goddess of Love![8] Our English name for the tiny beetle 'Lady-bug' is derived from the latter notion; and Mr. Karl Blind has expressed the opinion that our children's rune—

> Lady-bug, lady-bug, fly away home,
> Thy house is on fire, thy children will roam—

is last echo of the Eddaic prophecies of the destruction of the universe by the fire-fiend Loki![9] Such reductions of the ancient gods, demons, and terrors to tiny dimensions would, of course, be only an indirect result of the general cause stated. They were driven from the great world, and sought the small world: they survived in the hut and were adapted to the nerves of the nursery. So alone can Tithonos live on: beyond the age for which he is born he shrinks to a grasshopper; and it is now by only careful listening that in the chirpings of the multitudinous immortals, of which Tithonos is type, may be distinguished the thunders and roarings of deities and demons that once made the earth to tremble.

NOTES

1 The history of this tree which I use for a parable is told in the Rev. Samuel Mateer's 'Land of Charity.' London: John Snow & Co. 1871.

2 'Studies in the History of the Renaissance.' Macmillan & Co. 1873.

3 Concerning which Mr. Wright says: 'It is taken from an oxybaphon which was brought from the Continent to England, where it passed into the collection of Mr. William Hope.... The Hyperborean Apollo himself appears as a quack-doctor, on his temporary stage, covered by a sort of roof, and approached by wooden steps. On the stage lies Apollo's luggage, consisting of a bag, a bow, and his Scythian cap. Chiron (ΧΙΡΩΝ) is represented as labouring under the effects of age and blindness, and supporting himself by the aid of a crooked staff, as he repairs to the Delphian quack-doctor for relief. The figure of the centaur is made to ascend by the aid of a companion, both being furnished with the masks and other attributes of the comic performers. Above are the mountains, and on them the nymphs of Parnassus (ΝΥΜΦΑΙ), who, like all the other actors in the scene, are disguised with masks, and those of a very gross character.... Even a pun is employed to heighten the drollery of the scene, for instead of ΠΥΘΙΑΣ, the Pythian, placed over the head of the burlesque Apollo, it seems evident that the artist had written ΠΕΙΘΙΑΣ, the consoler.'—'History of Caricature,' p. 18. But who is the leaf-crowned figure, without mask, on the right hand? Was it some early Offenbach, who found such representation of the gods welcome at Athens where the attempt to produce our modern Offenbach's Belle Hélène recently caused a theatrical riot?

4 Wuttke. 'Volksaberglaube,' 18.

5 Schleicher, 'Litauische Märchen,' 141–145. Mr. Ralston's translation abridged.

6 Of this latter kind of hungry werewolf a specimen still occasionally revisits the glimpses of the moonshine which, for too many minds, still replaces daylight. So recently as January 17, 1878, one Kate Bedwell, a 'pedlar, was sentenced in the Marylebone Police Court, London, to three months' hard labour for obtaining various sums of money, amounting to 9s. 10d., by terrorism, from Eliza Rolf, a cook. The pedlar came to the plaintiff's place of work and asked her if she would like to have her fortune told. Eliza replied, 'No, I know it; it is hard work or starving.' The fortune-teller asked her next time if she would have her planet ruled; the other still said no; but her nerves yielded when the 'Drud' told her 'she lived under three stars, one good the others bad, and that she could disfigure her or turn her into something else.' 'Thank God, she did not!' exclaimed the poor woman in court. However, she seemed to have trusted rather in her money than in any other providence for her immunity from an unhappy transformation. But even into this rare depth of ignorance enough light had penetrated to enable Eliza to cope with her werewolf in the civilised way of haling her before a magistrate. When Fenris gets three months with hard labour, he no doubt realises that he has exceeded his mental habitat, and that the invisible cords have bound him at last.

7 Elf has, indeed, been referred by some to the Sanskrit alpa=little; but the balance of authority is in favour of the derivation given in a former chapter.

8 Mannhardt, 'Götter,' 287.

9 Freia-Holda, the Teutonic goddess of Love. 'Cornhill Magazine,' May, 1872.

Chapter II
Generalisation of Demons

The Demons' bequest to their conquerors — Nondescripts — Exaggerations
of tradition — Saurian Theory of Dragons — The Dragon not primitive in
Mythology — Monsters of Egyptian, Iranian, Vedic, and Jewish Mythologies —
Turner's Dragon — Della Bella — The Conventional Dragon

AFTER ALL THOSE brave victories of man over the first chaos, organic and inorganic, whose effect upon his phantasms has been indicated; after fire had slain its thousands, and iron its tens of thousands of his demons, and the rough artisan become a Nemesis with his rudder and wheel pursuing the hosts of darkness back into Night and Invisibility; still stood the grim fact of manyformed pain and evil in the world, still defying the ascending purposes of mankind. Moreover, confronting these, he is by no means so different mentally from that man he was before conquering many foes in detail, and laying their phantoms, as he was morally. More courage man had gained, and more defiance; and, intellectually, a step had been taken, if only one: he had learned that his evils are related to each other. Hunger is of many heads and forms. Its yawning throat may be seen in the brilliant sky that lasts till it is as brass, in the deluge, the earthquake, in claw and fang; and then these together do but relate the hunger-brood to Fire and Ferocity; the summer sunbeam may be venomous as a serpent, and the end of them all is Death. Some tendency to these more general conceptions of an opposing principle and power in the world seems to be represented in that phase of development at which nondescript forms arise. These were the conquered demons' bequest.

It is, of course, impossible to measure the various forces which combined to produce the complex symbolical forms of physical evil. Tradition is not always a good draughtsman, and in portraying for a distant generation in Germany a big snake killed in India might not be exact as to the number of its heads or other details. Heroes before Falstaff were liable to overstate their foes in buckram. The less measurable a thing by fact, the more immense in fancy: werewolves of especial magnitude haunted regions where there had not been actual wolves for centuries; huge serpents play a large part in the annals of Ireland, where not even the smallest have been found. But after all natural influences have been considered, one can hardly look upon the sphynx, the chimæra, or on a conventional dragon, without perceiving that he is in presence of a higher creation than a demonic bear or a giant ruffian. The fundamental difference between the two classes is that one is natural, the other præternatural. Of course a werewolf is as præternatural as a gryphon to the eye of science, but as original expressions of human imagination the former could hardly have been a more miraculous monster than the Siamese twins to intelligent people to-day. The demonic forms are generally natural, albeit caricatured or exaggerated. And this effort at a præternatural conception is, in this early form, by no means mere superstition; rather is it poetic and artistic,—a kind of crude effort at *allgemeinheit*, at realisation of the types of evil—the claw-principle, fang-principle in the universe, the physiognomies of venom and pain detached from forms to which they are accidental.

Some of the particular forms we have been considering are, indeed, by no means of the prosaic type. Such conceptions as Ráhu, Cerberus, and several others, are transitional between the natural and mystical conceptions; while the sphynx, however complete a combination of ideal forms, is not all demonic. In this Part III. are included those forms whose combination is not found in objective nature, but which are yet travesties of nature and genuine fauna of the human mind.

Perhaps it may be thought somewhat arbitrary that I should describe all these intermediate forms between demon and devil by the term DRAGON; but I believe there is no other fabulous form which includes so many individual types of transition, or whose evolution may be so satisfactorily traced from the point where it is linked with the demon to that where it bequeathes its characters to the devil. While, however, this term is used as the best that suggests itself, it cannot be accepted as limiting our inquiry or excluding other abstract forms which ideally correspond to the dragon,—the generalised expression for an active, powerful, and intelligent enemy to mankind, a being who is antagonism organised, and able to command every weapon in nature for an antihuman purpose.

The opinion has steadily gained that the conventional dragon is the traditional form of some huge Saurian. It has been suggested that some of those extinct forms may have been contemporaneous with the earliest men, and that the traditions of conflicts with them, transmitted orally and pictorially, have resulted in preserving their forms in fable (proximately). The restorations of Saurians on their islet at the Crystal Palace show how much common sense there is in this theory. The discoveries of Professor Marsh of Yale College have proved that the general form of the dragon is startlingly prefigured in nature; and Mr. Alfred Tylor, in an able paper read before the Anthropological Society, has shown that we are very apt to be on the safe side in sticking to the theory of an 'object-origin' for most things.

Concerning this theory, it may be said that the earliest descriptions, both written and pictorial, which have been discovered of the reptilian monsters around which grew the germs of our dragon-myths, are crocodiles or serpents, and not dragons of any conventional kind,—with a few doubtful exceptions. In an Egyptian papyrus there is a hieroglyphic picture of San-nu Hut-ur, 'plunger of the sea;' it is a marine, dolphin-like monster, with four feet, and a tail ending in a serpent's head.[1] With wings, this might approach the dragon-form. Again, Amen-Ra slew*Naka*, and this serpent 'saved his feet.' Possibly the phrase is ironical, and means that the serpent saved nothing; but apart from that, the poem is too highly metaphorical—the victorious god himself being described in it as a 'beautiful bull'—for the phrase to be important. On Egyptian monuments are pictured serpents with human heads and members, and the serpent Nahab-ka is pictured on amulets with two perfect human legs and feet.[2] Winged serpents are found on Egyptian monuments, but almost as frequently with the incredible number of four as with the conceivable two wings of the pterodactyl. The forms of the serpents thus portrayed with anthropomorphic legs and slight wings are, in their main shapes, of ordinary species. In the Iranian tradition of the temptation of the first man and woman, Meschia and Meschiane, by the 'two-footed serpent of lies.' And it is possible that out of this myth of the 'two-footed' serpent grew the puzzling legend of Genesis that the serpent of Eden was sentenced thereafter to crawl on his belly. The snake's lack of feet, however, might with equal probability have given rise to the explanation given in mussulman and rabbinical stories of his feet being cut off by the avenging angel. But the antiquity of the Iranian myth is doubtful; while the superior antiquity of the Hindu fable of Ráhu, to which it seems related, suggests that the two legs of the Ahriman serpent, like the four arms of serpent-tailed Ráhu, is an anthropomorphic addition. In the ancient planispheres we find the 'crooked serpent' mentioned in the Book of Job, but no dragon.

The two great monsters of Vedic mythology, Vritra and Ahi, are not so distinguishable from each other in the Vedas as in more recent fables. Vritra is very frequently called Vritra Ahi—Ahi being explained in the St. Petersburg Dictionary as 'the Serpent of the Heavens, the demon Vritra.' Ahi literally means 'serpent,' answering to the Greek ἐχι-ς, ἐχι-δνα; and when anything is added it appears to be anthropomorphic—heads, arms, eyes—as in the case of the Egyptian serpent-monsters. The Vedic demon Urana is described as having three heads, six eyes, and ninety-nine arms.

There would appear to be as little reason for ascribing to the *Tannin* of the Old Testament the significance of dragon, though it is generally so translated. It is used under circumstances which show it to mean whale, serpent, and various other beasts. Jeremiah (xiv. 6) compares them to wild asses snuffing the wind, and Micah (i. 8) describes their 'wailing.' The fiery serpents said to have afflicted

Israel in the wilderness are called *seraphim*, but neither in their natural or mythological forms do they anticipate our conventional dragon beyond the fiery character that is blended with the serpent character. Nor do the descriptions of Behemoth and Leviathan comport with the dragon-form.

The serpent as an animal is a consummate development. Its feet, so far from having been amputated, as the fables say, in punishment of its sin, have been withdrawn beneath the skin as crutches used in a feebler period. It is found as a tertiary fossil. Since, therefore, the dragon form *ex hypothesi* is a reminiscence of the huge, now fossil, Saurians which preceded the serpent in time, the early mythologies could hardly have so regularly described great serpents instead of dragons. If the realistic theory we are discussing were true, the earliest combats—those of Indra, for instance—ought to have been with dragons, and the serpent enemies would have multiplied as time went on; but the reverse is the case—the (alleged) extinct forms being comparatively modern in heroic legend.

Mr. John Ruskin once remarked upon Turner's picture of the Dragon guarding the Hesperides, that this conception so early as 1806, when no Saurian skeleton was within the artist's reach, presented a singular instance of the scientific imagination. As a coincidence with such extinct forms Turner's dragon is surpassed by the monster on which a witch rides in one of the engravings of Della Bella, published in 1637.

Fig. 22.—A Witch Mounted (Della Bella)

In that year, on the occasion of the marriage of the grand duke Ferdinand II. in Florence, there was a masque *d'Inferno*, whose representations were engraved by Della Bella, of which this is one, so that it may be rather to some scenic artist than to the distinguished imitator of Callot that we owe this grotesque form, which the late Mr. Wright said 'might have been borrowed from some distant geological period.' If so, the fact would present a curious coincidence with the true history of Turner's Dragon; for after Mr. Ruskin had published his remark about the scientific imagination represented in it, an old friend of the artist declared that Turner himself had told him that he copied that dragon from a Christmas spectacle in Drury Lane theatre. But Turner had shown the truest scientific instinct in repairing to the fossil-beds of human imagination, and drawing thence the conventional form which never had existence save as the structure of cumulative tradition.

NOTES

1 'Records of the Past,' vi. 124.
2 See Cooper's 'Serpent-Myths of Ancient Egypt,' figs. 109 and 112. Serapis as a human-headed serpent is shown in the same essay (from Sharpe), fig. 119.

Chapter III
The Serpent

IN THE ACCOMPANYING picture, a medal of the ancient city of Tyre, two of the most beautiful forms of nature are brought together,—the Serpent and the Egg. Mr. D. R. Hay has shown the endless extent to which the oval arches have been reproduced in the ceramic arts of antiquity; and the same sense of symmetry which made the Greek vase a combination of Eggs prevails in the charm which the same graceful outline possesses wherever suggested,—as in curves of the swan, crescent of the moon, the elongated shell,—on which Aphrodite may well be poised, since the same contours find their consummate expression in the flowing lines attaining their repose in the perfect form of woman. The Serpent— model of the 'line of grace and beauty'—has had an even larger fascination for the eye of the artist and the poet. It is the one active form in nature which cannot be ungraceful, and to estimate the extent of its use in decoration is impossible, because all undulating and coiling lines are necessarily serpent forms. But in addition to the perfections of this form—which fulfil all the ascent of forms in Swedenborg's mystical morphology, circular, spiral, perpetual-circular, vortical, celestial—the Serpent bears on it, as it were, gems of the underworld that seem to find their counterpart in galaxies.

Fig. 23.—Serpent and Egg (Tyre)

One must conclude that Serpent-worship is mainly founded in fear. The sacrifices offered to that animal are alone sufficient to prove this. But as it is certain that the Serpent appears in symbolism and poetry in many ways which have little or no relation to its terrors, we may well doubt whether it may not have had a career in the human imagination previous to either of the results of its reign of terror,—worship and execration. It is the theory of Pestalozzi that every child is born an artist, and through its pictorial sense must be led on its first steps of education. The infant world displayed also in its selection of sacred trees and animals a profound appreciation of beauty. The myths in which the Serpent is represented as kakodemon refer rather to its natural history than to its appearance; and even when its natural history came to be observed, there was—there now is—such a wide discrepancy between its physiology and its functions, also between its intrinsic characters and their relation to man, that we can only accept its various aspects in mythology without attempting to trace their relative precedence in time.

The past may in this case be best interpreted by the present. How different now to wise and observant men are the suggestions of this exceptional form in nature!

Let us read a passage concerning it from Ralph Waldo Emerson:—

'In the old aphorism, *nature is always self-similar*. In the plant, the eye or germinative point opens to a leaf, then to another leaf, with a power of transforming the leaf into radicle, stamen, pistil, petal, bract, sepal, or seed. The whole art of the plant is still to repeat leaf on leaf without end, the more or less of heat, light, moisture, and food, determining the form it shall assume. In the animal, nature makes a vertebra, or a spine of vertebræ, and helps herself still by a new spine, with a limited power of modifying its form,—spine on spine, to the end of the world. A poetic anatomist, in our own day, teaches that a snake being a horizontal line, and man being an erect line, constitute a right angle; and between the lines of this mystical quadrant, all animated beings find their place: and he assumes the hair-worm, the span-worm, or the snake, as the type or prediction of the spine. Manifestly, at the end of the spine, nature puts out smaller spines, as arms; at the end of the arms, new spines, as hands; at the other end she repeats the process, as legs and feet. At the top of the column she puts out another spine, which doubles or loops itself over, as a span-worm, into a ball, and forms the skull, with extremities again: the hands being now the upper jaw, the feet the lower jaw, the fingers and toes being represented this time by upper and lower teeth. This new spine is destined to high uses. It is a new man on the shoulders of the last."[1]

As one reads this it might be asked, How could its idealism be more profoundly pictured for the eye than in the Serpent coiled round the egg,—the seed out of which all these spines must branch out for their protean variations? What refrains of ancient themes subtly sound between the lines,—from the Serpent doomed to crawl on its belly in the dust, to the Serpent that is lifted up!

Now let us turn to the page of Jules Michelet, and read what the Serpent signified to one mood of his sympathetic nature.

'It was one of my saddest hours when, seeking in nature a refuge from thoughts of the age, I for the first time encountered the head of the viper. This occurred in a valuable museum of anatomical imitations.

The head marvellously imitated and enormously enlarged, so as to remind one of the tiger's and the jaguar's, exposed in its horrible form a something still more horrible. You seized at once the delicate, infinite, fearfully prescient precautions by which the deadly machine is so potently armed. Not only is it provided with numerous keen-edged teeth, not only are these teeth supplied with an ingenious reservoir of poison which slays immediately, but their extreme fineness which renders them liable to fracture is compensated by an advantage that perhaps no other animal possesses, namely, a magazine of supernumerary teeth, to supply at need the place of any accidentally broken. Oh, what provisions for killing! What precautions that the victim shall not escape! What love for this horrible creature! I stood by it *scandalised*, if I may so speak, and with a sick soul. Nature, the great mother, by whose side I had taken refuge, shocked me with a maternity so cruelly impartial. Gloomily I walked away, bearing on my heart a darker shadow than rested on the day itself, one of the sternest in winter. I had come forth like a child; I returned home like an orphan, feeling the notion of a Providence dying away within me.'[2]

Many have so gone forth and so returned; some to say, 'There is no God;' a few to say (as is reported of a living poet), 'I believe in God, but am against him;' but some also to discern in the viper's head Nature's ironclad, armed with her best science to defend the advance of form to humanity along narrow passes.

The primitive man was the child that went forth when his world was also a child, and when the Serpent was still doing its part towards making him and it a man. It was a long way from him to the dragon-slayer; but it is much that he did not merely cower; he watched and observed, and there is not one trait belonging to his deadly crawling contemporaries that he did not note and spiritualise in such science as was possible to him.

The last-discovered of the topes in India represents Serpent-worshippers gathered around their deity, holding their tongues with finger and thumb. No living form in nature could be so fitly regarded in that attitude. Not only is the Serpent normally silent, but in its action it has 'the quiet of perfect motion.' The maximum of force is shown in it, relatively to its size, along with the minimum of friction and visible effort. Footless, wingless, as a star, its swift gliding and darting is sometimes like the lightning whose forked tongue it seemed to incarnate. The least touch of its ingenious tooth is more destructive than the lion's jaw. What mystery in its longevity, in its self-subsistence, in its self-renovation! Out of the dark it comes arrayed in jewels, a crawling magazine of death in its ire, in its unknown purposes able to renew its youth, and fable for man imperishable life! Wonderful also are its mimicries. It sometimes borrows colours of the earth on which it reposes, the trees on which it hangs, now seems covered with eyes, and the 'spectacled snake' appeared to have artificially added to its vision. Altogether it is unique among natural forms, and its vast history in religious speculation and mythology does credit to the observation of primitive man.

Recent experiments have shown the monkeys stand in the greatest terror of snakes. Such terror is more and more recognised as a survival in the European man. The Serpent is almost the only animal which can follow a monkey up a tree and there attack its young. Our arboreal anthropoid progenitors could best have been developed in some place naturally enclosed and fortified, as by precipices which quadrupeds could not scale, but which apes might reach by swinging and leaping from trees. But there could be no seclusion where the Serpent could not follow. I am informed by the King of

Bonny that in his region of Africa the only serpent whose worship is fully maintained is the *Nomboh*(Leaper), a small snake, white and glistening, whose bite is fatal, and which, climbing into trees, springs thence upon its prey beneath, and can travel far by leaping from branch to branch. The first arboreal man who added a little to the natural defences of any situation might stand in tradition as a god planting a garden; but even he would not be supposed able to devise any absolute means of defence against the subtlest of all the beasts. Among the three things Solomon found too wonderful for him was 'the way of a serpent upon a rock' (Prov. xxx. 19). This comparative superiority of the Serpent to any and all devices and contrivances known to primitive men—whose proverbs must have made most of Solomon's wisdom—would necessarily have its effect upon the animal and mental nerves of our race in early times, and the Serpent would find in his sanctity a condition favourable to survival and multiplication. It is this fatal power of superstition to change fancies into realities which we find still protecting the Serpent in various countries. From being venerated as the arbiter of life and death, it might thus actually become such in large districts of country. In Dubufe's picture of the Fall of Man, the wrath of Jehovah is represented by the lightning, which has shattered the tree beneath which the offending pair are now crouching; beyond it Satan is seen in human shape raising his arm in proud defiance against the blackened sky. So would the Serpent appear. His victims were counted by many thousands where the lightning laid low one. Transmitted along the shuddering nerves of many generations came the confession of the Son of Sirach, 'There is no head above the head of a serpent.'

NOTES

1 'Representative Men,' American edition of 1850, p. 108.
2 'L'Oiseau,' par Jules Michelet.

Chapter IV
The Worm

An African Serpent-drama in America — The Veiled Serpent — The Ark of the
Covenant — Aaron's Rod — The Worm — An Episode on the Dii Involuti —
The Serapes — The Bambino at Rome — Serpent-transformations

ON THE EVE of January 1, 1863,—that historic New Year's Day on
which President Lincoln proclaimed freedom to American slaves,—I
was present at a Watchnight held by negroes in a city of that country. In opening the meeting the preacher said,—though in words
whose eloquent shortcomings I cannot reproduce:—'Brethren and
sisters, the President of the United States has promised that, if the
Confederates do not lay down their arms, he will free all their slaves
to-morrow. They have not laid down their arms. To-morrow will be
the day of liberty to the oppressed. But we all know that evil powers
are around the President. While we sit here they are trying to make
him break his word. But we have come together to watch, and see
that he does not break his word. Brethren, the bad influences around
the President to-night are stronger than any Copperheads.[1] The Old
Serpent is abroad to-night, with all his emissaries, in great power.
His wrath is great, because he knows his hour is near. He will be in
this church this evening. As midnight comes on we shall hear his
rage. But, brethren and sisters, don't be alarmed. Our prayers will
prevail. His head will be bruised. His back will be broken. He will go

raging to hell, and God Almighty's New Year will make the United States a true land of freedom.'

The sensation caused among the hundreds of negroes present by these words was profound; they were frequently interrupted by cries of 'Glory!' and there were tears of joy. But the scene and excitement which followed were indescribable. A few moments before midnight the congregation were requested to kneel, which they did, and prayer succeeded prayer with increasing fervour. Presently a loud, prolonged hiss was heard. There were cries—'He's here! he's here!' Then came a volley of hisses; they seemed to proceed from every part of the room, hisses so entirely like those of huge serpents that the strongest nerves were shaken; above them rose the preacher's prayer that had become a wild incantation, and ecstatic ejaculations became so universal that it was a marvel what voices were left to make the hisses. Finally, from a neighbouring steeple the twelve strokes of midnight sounded on the frosty air, and immediately the hisses diminished, and presently died away altogether, and the New Year that brought freedom to four millions of slaves was ushered in by the jubilant chorus of all present singing a hymn of victory.

Far had come those hisses and that song of victory, terminating the dragon-drama of America. In them was the burden of Ezekiel: 'Son of man, set thy face against Pharaoh, king of Egypt, and prophesy against him and against all Egypt, saying, Thus saith the Lord Jehovah: Behold I am against thee, Pharaoh king of Egypt, the great dragon that lieth in the midst of the rivers ... I will put a hook in thy jaws.' In them was the burden of Isaiah: 'In that day Jehovah with his sore and great and strong sword shall punish Leviathan the piercing serpent, even Leviathan that crooked serpent: he shall slay the dragon that is in the sea.' In it was the cry of Zophar: 'His meat in his bowels is turned, it is the gall of asps within him. He hath swallowed down riches, and he shall vomit them up again: God shall cast them out of his belly.' And these Hebrew utterances, again, were but the distant echoes of far earlier voices of those African slaves still seen pictured with their chains on the ruined walls of Egypt,— voices that gathered courage at last to announce the never-ending struggle of man with Oppression, as that combat between god and serpent which never had a nobler event than when the dying hiss of Slavery was heard in America, and the victorious Sun rose upon a New World of free and equal men.

The Serpent thus exalted in America to a type of oppression is very different from any snake that may this day be found worshipped as a deity by the African in his native land. The swarthy snake-worshipper in his migration took his god along with him in his chest or basket—at once ark and altar—and in that hiding-place it underwent transformations. He emerged as the protean emblem of both good and evil. In a mythologic sense the serpent certainly held its tail in its mouth. No civilisation has reached the end of its typical supremacy.

Concerning the accompanying Eleusinian form (Fig. 24), Calmet says:—'The mysterious trunk, coffer, or basket, may be justly reckoned among the most remarkable and sacred instruments of worship, which formed part of the processional ceremonies in the heathen world.

Fig. 24.—*Serpent and Ark (from a Greek coin)*

This was held so sacred that it was not publicly exposed to view, or publicly opened, but was reserved for the inspection of the initiated, the fully initiated only. Completely to explain this symbol would require a dissertation; and, indeed, it has been considered, more or less, by those who have written on the nature of the Ark of the testimony among the Hebrews. Declining the inquiry at present, we merely call the attention of the reader to what this mystical coffer was supposed to contain—a serpent!' The French Benedictine who wrote this passage, though his usual candour shames the casuistry of our own time, found it necessary to conceal the Hebrew Ark: it was precisely so that the occupant of the Ark was originally concealed; and though St. John exorcised it from the Chalice its genius lingers in the Pyx, before whose Host 'lifted up' the eyes of worshippers are lowered.

The writer of the Epistle to the Hebrews (chap. ix.), describing the Tabernacle, says: 'After the second veil, the tabernacle which is called the Holiest of all; which had the golden censer, and the ark of the covenant overlaid round about with gold, wherein was the golden pot that had manna, and Aaron's rod that budded, and the tables of the covenant.' But this rod of Aaron, which, by budding, had swallowed up all rival pretensions to the tribal priesthood, was the same rod which had been changed to a serpent, and swallowed up the rod-serpents of the sorcerers in Pharaoh's presence. So soft and subtle is 'the way of a serpent upon a rock!'

This veiling of the Serpent, significant of a great deal, is characteristic even of the words used to name it. Of these I have selected one to head this chapter, because it is one of the innumerable veils which shielded this reptile's transformation from a particular external danger to a demonic type. This general description of things that wind about or turn (*vermes*, traced by some to the Sanskrit root *hvar*, 'curved'), gradually came into use to express the demon serpents. Dante and Milton call Satan a worm. No doubt among the two hundred names for the Serpent, said to be mentioned in an Arabic work, we should find parallels to this old adaptation of the word 'worm.' In countries—as Germany and England—where no large serpents are found, the popular imagination could not be impressed by merely saying that Siegfried or Lambton had slain a snake. The tortuous character of the snake was preserved, but, by that unconscious dexterity which so often appears in the making of myths, it was expanded so as to include a power of supernatural transformation. The Lambton worm comes out of the well very small, but it afterwards coils in nine huge folds around its hill. The hag-ridden daughter of the King of Northumberland, who

> crept into a hole a worm
> And out stept a fair ladye,

did but follow the legendary rule of the demonic serpent tribe.

Why was the Serpent slipped into the Ark or coffer and hid behind veils? To answer this will require here an episode.

In the Etruscan theology and ceremonial the supreme power was lodged with certain deities that were never seen. They were called the *Dii Involuti*, the veiled gods. Not even the priests ever looked upon them. When any dire calamity occurred, it was said these mysterious deities had spoken their word in the council of the gods,—a word always final and fatal.

There have been fine theories on the subject, and the Etruscans have been complimented for having high transcendental views of the invisible nature of the Divine Being. But a more prosaic theory is probably true. These gods were wrapped up because they were not fit to be seen. The rude carvings of some savage tribe, they had been seen and adored at first: temples had been built for them, and their priesthood had grown powerful; but as art advanced and beautiful statues arose, these rude designs could not bear the contrast, and the only way of preserving reverence for them, and the institutions grown up around them, was to hide them out of sight altogether. Then it could be said they were so divinely beautiful that the senses would be overpowered by them.

There have been many veiled deities, and though their veils have been rationalised, they are easily pierced. The inscription on the temple of Isis at Sais was: 'I am that which has been, which is, and which shall be, and no one has yet lifted the veil that hides me.' Isis at this time had probably become a negro Madonna, like that still worshipped in Spain as holiest of images, and called by the same title, 'Our Immaculate Lady.' As the fair race and the dark mingled in Egypt, the primitive Nubian complexion and features of Isis could not inspire such reverence as more anciently, and before her also a curtain was hung. The Ark of Moses carried this veil into the wilderness, and concealed objects not attractive to look at—probably two scrawled stones, some bones said to be those of Joseph, a pot of so-called manna, and the staff said to have once been a serpent and afterwards blossomed. Fashioned by a rude tribe, the Ark was a fit thing to hide, and hidden it has been to this day. When the veil of the Temple was rent,—allegorically at the death of Christ, actually by Titus,—nothing of the kind was found; and it would seem that the Jews must long have been worshipping before a veil with emptiness behind it. Paul discovered that the veil said to have covered the face of Moses when he descended from Sinai was a myth; it meant that the people should not see to the end of what was nevertheless transient. 'Their minds were blinded; for unto this day, when Moses is read, that veil is on their heart.'

Kircher says the Seraphs of Egypt were images without any eminency of limbs, rolled as it were in swaddling clothes, partly made of stone, partly of metal, wood, or shell. Similar images, he says, were called by the Romans 'secret gods.' As an age of scepticism advanced, it was sometimes necessary that these 'involuti' should be slightly revealed, lest it should be said there was no god there at all. Such is the case with the famous *bambino* of Aracœli Church in

Rome. This effigy, said to have been carved by a pilgrim out of a tree on the Mount of Olives, and painted by St. Luke while the pilgrim was sleeping, is now kept in its ark, and visitors are allowed to see part of its painted face. When the writer of this requested a sight of the whole form, or of the head at any rate, the exhibiting priest was astounded at the suggestion. No doubt he was right: the only wonder is that the face is not hid also, for a more ingeniously ugly thing than the flat, blackened, and rouged visage of the bambino it were difficult to conceive. But it wears a very cunning veil nevertheless. The face is set in marvellous brilliants, but these are of less effect in hiding its ugliness than the vesture of mythology around it. The adjacent walls are covered with pictures of the miracles it has performed, and which have attracted to it such faith that it is said at one time to have received more medical fees than all the physicians in Rome together. Priests have discovered that a veil over the mind is thicker than a veil on the god. Such is the popular veneration for the bambino, that, in 1849, the Republicans thought it politic to present the monks with the Pope's state coach to carry the idol about. In the end it was proved that the Pope was securely seated beside the bambino, and he presently emerged from behind his veil also.

There came, then, a period when the Serpent crept behind the veil, or lid of the ark, or into a chalice,—a very small worm, but yet able to gnaw the staff of Solomon. No wisdom could be permitted to rise above fear itself, though its special sources might be here and there reduced or vanquished. The snake had taught man at last its arts of war. Man had summoned to his aid the pig, and the ibis made havoc among the reptiles; and some of that terror which is the parent of that kind of devotion passed away. When it next emerged, it was in twofold guise,—as Agathodemon and Kakodemon,—but in both forms as the familiar of some higher being. It was as the genius of Minerva, of Esculapius, of St. Euphemia. We have already seen him (Fig. 13) as the genius of the Eleans, the Sosopolis, where also we see the Serpent hurrying into his cavern, leaving the mother and child to be worshipped in the temple of Lucina. In Christian symbolism the Seraphim—'burning (*sáraf*) serpents'—veiled their faces and forms beneath their huge wings, crossed in front, and so have been able to become 'the eminent,' and to join in the praises of modern communities at being delivered from just such imaginary fiery worms as themselves!

NOTE

1   A deadly Southern snake, coloured like the soil on which it lurks, had become the current name for politicians who, while professing loyalty to the Union, aided those who sought to overthrow it.

Chapter V
Apophis

THE CONSIDERATIONS ADVANCED in the previous chapter enable us to dismiss with facility many of the rationalistic interpretations which have been advanced to explain the monstrous serpents of sacred books by reference to imaginary species supposed to be now extinct. Flying serpents, snakes many-headed, rain-bringing, woman-hating, &c., may be suffered to survive as the fauna of bibliolatrous imaginations. Such forms, however, are of such mythologic importance that it is necessary to watch carefully against this method of realistic interpretation, especially as there are many actual characteristics of serpents sufficiently mysterious to conspire with it. A recent instance of this literalism may here be noticed.

Mr. W. R. Cooper [1] supposes the evil serpent of Egyptian Mythology to have a real basis in 'a large and unidentified species of coluber, of great strength and hideous longitude,' which 'was, even from the earliest ages, associated as the representative of spiritual, and occasionally physical evil, and was named Hof, Rehof, or Apophis,' the '*destroyer*, the *enemy of the gods*, and the *devourer* of the souls of men.' That such a creature, he adds, 'once inhabited the

Libyan desert, we have the testimony of both Hanno the Carthaginian and Lucan the Roman, and if it is now no longer an inhabitant of that region, it is probably owing to the advance of civilisation having driven it farther south.'

Apart from the extreme improbability that African exploration should have brought no rumours of such a monster if it existed, it may be said concerning Mr. Cooper's theory: (1.) If, indeed, the references cited were to a reptile now unknown, we might be led by mythologic analogy to expect that it would have been revered beyond either the Asp or the Cobra. In proportion to the fear has generally been the exaltation of its objects. Primitive peoples have generally gathered courage to pour invective upon evil monsters when—either from their non-existence or rarity—there was least danger of its being practically resented as a personal affront. (2.) The regular folds of Apophis on the sarcophagus of Seti I. and elsewhere are so evidently mystical and conventional that, apparently, they refer to a serpent-form only as the guilloche on a wall may refer to sea-waves. Apophis (or Apap) would have been a decorative artist to fold himself in such order.

These impossible labyrinthine coils suggest Time, as the serpent with its tail in its mouth signifies Eternity,—an evolution of the same idea. This was the interpretation given by a careful scholar, the late William Hickson,[2] to the procession of nine persons depicted on the sarcophagus mentioned as bearing a serpent, each holding a fold, all being regular enough for a frieze. 'The scene,' says this author, 'appears to relate to the Last Judgment, for Osiris is seen on his throne, passing sentence on a crowd before him; and in the same tableaux are depicted the river that divides the living from the dead, and the bridge of life. The death of the serpent may possibly be intended to symbolise the end of time.' This idea of long duration might be a general one relating to all time, or it might refer to the duration of individual life; it involved naturally the evils and agonies of life; but the fundamental conception is more simple, and also more poetic, than even these implications, and it means eternal waste and decay. One has need only to sit before a clock to see Apophis: there coil upon coil winds the ever-moving monster, whose tooth is remorseless, devouring little by little the strength and majesty of man, and reducing his grandest achievements—even his universe—to dust. Time is the undying Worm.

> God having made me worm, I make you—smoke.
> Though safe your nameless essence from my stroke,
> Yet do I gnaw no less
> Love in the heart, stars in the livid space,—
> God jealous,—making vacant thus your place,—
> And steal your witnesses.
>
> Since the star flames, man would be wrong to teach
> That the grave's worm cannot such glory reach;
> Naught real is save me.
> Within the blue, as 'neath the marble slab I lie,
> I bite at once the star within the sky,
> The apple on the tree.
> To gnaw yon star is not more tough to me
> Than hanging grapes on vines of Sicily;
> I clip the rays that fall;
> Eternity yields not to splendours brave.
> Fly, ant, all creatures die, and nought can save
> The constellations all.
> The starry ship, high in the ether sea,
> Must split and wreck in the end: this thing shall be:

The broad-ringed Saturn toss
To ruin: Sirius, touched by me, decay,
As the small boat from Ithaca away
That steers to Kalymnos.³

The natural history of Apophis, so far as he has any, is probably suggested in the following passage cited by Mr. Cooper from Wilkinson:—'Ælian relates many strange stories of the asp, and the respect paid to it by the Egyptians; but we may suppose that in his sixteen species of asps other snakes were included. He also speaks of a dragon which was sacred in the Egyptian Melite, and another kind of snake called Paries or Paruas, dedicated to Æsculapius. The serpent of Melite had priests and ministers, a table and bowl. It was kept in a tower, and fed by the priests with cakes made of flour and honey, which they placed there in a bowl. Having done this they retired. The next day, on returning to the apartment, the food was found to be eaten, and the same quantity was again put into the bowl, for it was not lawful for any one to see the sacred reptile.'⁴

It was in this concealment from the outward eye that the Serpent was able to assume such monstrous proportions to the eye of imagination; and, indeed, it is not beyond conjecture that this serpent of Melite, coming in conflict with Osirian worship, was degraded and demonised into that evil monster (Apophis) whom Horus slew to avenge his destruction of Osiris (for he was often identified with Typhon).

Though Horus cursed and slew this terrible demon-serpent, he reappears in all Egyptian Mythology with undiminished strength, and all evil powers were the brood of himself or Typhon, who were sometimes described as brothers and sometimes as the same beings. From the 'Ritual of the Dead' we learn that it was the high privilege and task of the heroic dead to be reconstructed and go forth to encounter and subdue the agents of Apophis, who sent out to engage them the crocodiles Seb, Hem, and Shui, and other crocodiles from north, south, east, and west; the hero having conquered these, acquires their might, and next prevails over the walking viper Ru; and so on with other demons called 'precursors of Apophis,' until their prince himself is encountered and slain, all the hero's guardian deities attending to fix a knife in each of the monster's folds. These are the Vanquishers of Time,—the immortal.

In Apophis we find the Serpent fairly developed to a principle of evil. He is an 'accuser of the sun;' the twelve gateways into Hades are surmounted by his representatives, which the Sun must pass—twelve hours of night. He is at once the 'Nachash beriach' and 'Nachash aktalon'—the 'Cross-bar serpent' and the 'Tortuous serpent'—which we meet with in Isa. xxvii. 1: 'In that day the Lord with his sore and great and strong sword shall punish leviathan the piercing serpent, even leviathan that crooked serpent.' The marginal translation in the English version is 'crossing like a bar,' instead of piercing, and the Vulgate has *serpens vectis*. This refers to the moral function of the serpent, as barring the way, or guarding the door. No doubt this is the 'crooked serpent' of Job xxvi. 13, for the astrological sense of it does not invalidate the terrestrial significance. Imagination could only project into the heavens what it had learned on earth. Bochart in identifying 'Nachash-beriach' as 'the flying Serpent,' is quite right: the Seraph, or winged Serpent, which barred the way to the tree of life in Eden, and in some traditions was the treacherous guard at the gate of the garden, and which bit Israel in the wilderness, was this same protean Apophis. For such tasks, and to soar into the celestial planisphere, the Serpent must needs have wings; and thus it is already far on its way to become the flying Dragon. But in one form, as the betrayer of man, it must lose its wings and crawl upon the ground for ever. The Serpent is thus not so much agathodemon and kakodemon in one form, as a principle of destructiveness which is sometimes employed by the deity to punish his enemies, as Horus employs fiery Kheti, but sometimes requires to be himself punished.

There have been doubts whether the familiar derivation of ὄφις, serpent, from ὄψ, the eye, shall continue. Some connect the Greek word with ἔχις, but Curtius maintains that the old derivation from ὄψ is correct.[5] Even were this not the etymology, the popularity of it would equally suggest the fact that this reptile was of old supposed to kill with its glance; and it was also generally regarded as gifted with præternatural vision. By a similar process to that which developed avenging Furies out of the detective dawn—Erinyes from Saranyu, Satan from Lucifer [6]—this subtle Spy might have become also a retributive and finally a malignant power. The Furies were portrayed bearing serpents in their hands, and each of these might carry ideally the terrors of Apophis: Time also is a detective, and the guilty heard it saying, 'Your sin will find you out.'

Through many associations of this kind the Serpent became at an early period an agent of ordeal. Any one handling it with impunity was regarded as in league with it, or specially hedged about by the deity whose 'hands formed the crooked serpent.' It may have been as snake-charmers that Moses and Aaron appeared before Pharaoh and influenced his imagination; or, if the story be a myth, its existence still shows that serpent performances would then have been regarded as credentials of divine authentication. So when Paul was shipwrecked on Malta, where a viper is said to have fastened on his hand, the barbarians, having at first inferred that he was a murderer, 'whom though he hath escaped the sea, yet Vengeance suffereth not to live,' concluded he was a god when they found him unharmed. Innumerable traditions preceded the words ascribed to Christ (Luke x. 19), 'Behold, I give unto you power to tread on serpents and scorpions, and over all the power of the enemy, and nothing shall by any means hurt you.' It is instructive to compare this sentence attributed to Christ with the notion of the barbarians concerning Paul's adventure, whatever it may have been. Paul's familiarity with the Serpent seems to them proof that he is a god. Such also is the idea represented in Isa. xi. 8, 'The sucking child shall play on the hole of the asp.' But the idea of treading on serpents marks a period more nearly corresponding to that of the infant Hercules strangling the serpents. Yet though these two conceptions—serpent-treading, and serpent-slaying—approach each other, they are very different in source and significance, both morally and historically. The word used in Luke, πατεῖν, conveys the idea of walking over something in majesty, not in hostility; it must be interpreted by the next sentence (x. 20), 'Notwithstanding, in this rejoice not, that the spirits are subject unto you (τα πνεύματα ὑποτάσσεται).' The serpent-slayer or dragon-slayer is not of Semitic origin. The awful supremacy of Jehovah held all the powers of destruction chained to his hand; and to ask man if he could draw out Leviathan with a hook was only another form of reminding him of his own inferiority to the creator and lord of Leviathan. How true the Semitic ideas running through the Bible, and especially represented in the legend of Paul in Malta, are to the barbarian nature is illustrated by an incident related in Mr. Brinton's 'Myths of the New World.' The pious founder of the Moravian Brotherhood, Count Zinzendorf, was visiting a missionary station among the Shawnees in the Wyoming Valley, America. Recent quarrels with the white people had so irritated the red men that they resolved to make him their victim. After he had retired to his hut several of the braves softly peered in. Count Zinzendorf was seated before a fire, lost in perusal of the Scriptures; and while the red men gazed they saw what he did not—a huge rattlesnake trailing across his feet to gather itself in a coil before the comfortable warmth of the fire. Immediately they forsook their murderous purpose, and retired noiselessly, convinced that this was indeed a divine man.

NOTES
1   See his learned and valuable treatise, 'The Serpent Myths of Ancient Egypt.' Hardwicke, 1873.
2   'Time and Faith,' i. 204. Groombridge, 1857.
3   'The Epic of the Worm,' by Victor Hugo. Translated by Bayard Taylor from 'La Légende des Siècles.'
4   Bruce relates of the Abyssinians that a serpent is commonly kept in their houses to consult for an augury of good or evil. Butter and honey are placed before it, of which if it partake, the omen is good; if the serpent refuse to eat, some misfortune is sure to happen. This custom seems to throw a light on the passage—'Butter and honey shall he eat, that he may know to refuse the evil and choose the good' (Isa. vii. 15).—Time and Faith, i. 60.
    Compare the apocryphal tale of Bel and the Dragon. Bel was a healing god of the Babylonians, and the Dragon whom he slew may have been regarded in later times as his familiar
5   'Principles of Greek Etymology,' ii. 63. English translation.
6   See pp. 8 and 20.

The Serpent in India

THAT SERPENT-WORSHIP in India was developed by euphemism seems sufficiently shown in the famous Vedic hymn called *Kankato na*, recited as an antidote against all venom, of which the following is a translation:—

'1. Some creature of little venom; some creature of great venom; or some venomous aquatic reptile; creatures of two kinds, both destructive of life, or poisonous, unseen creatures, have anointed me with their poison.

'2. The antidote coming to the bitten person destroys the unseen venomous creatures; departing it destroys them; deprived of substance it destroys them by its odour; being ground it pulverises them.

'3. Blades of *sara* grass, of *kusara*, of *darhba*, of *sairya*, of *munja*, of *virana*, all the haunt of unseen venomous creatures, have together anointed me with their venom.

'4. The cows had lain down in their stalls; the wild beasts had retreated to their lairs; the senses of men were at rest; when the unseen venomous creatures anointed me with their venom.

'5. Or they may be discovered in the dark, as thieves in the dusk of evening; for although they be unseen yet all are seen by them; therefore, men be vigilant.

'6. Heaven, serpents, is your father; Earth, your mother; Soma, your brother; Aditi, your sister; unseen, all-seeing, abide in your holes; enjoy your own good pleasure.

'7. Those who move with their shoulders, those who move with their bodies, those who sting with sharp fangs, those who are virulently venomous; what do ye here, ye unseen, depart together far from us.

'8. The all-seeing Sun rises in the East, the destroyer of the unseen, driving away all the unseen venomous creatures, and all evil spirits.

'9. The Sun has risen on high, destroying all the many poisons; Aditya, the all-seeing, the destroyer of the unseen, rises for the good of living beings.

'10. I deposit the poison in the solar orb, like a leathern bottle in the house of a vendor of spirits; verily that adorable Sun never dies; nor through his favour shall we die of the venom; for, though afar off, yet drawn by his coursers he will overtake the poison: the science of antidotes converted thee, Poison, to ambrosia.

'11. That insignificant little bird has swallowed thy venom; she does not die; nor shall we die; for although afar off, yet, drawn by his coursers, the Sun will overtake the poison: the science of antidotes has converted thee, Poison, to ambrosia.

'12. May the thrice-seven sparks of Agni consume the influence of the venom; they verily do not perish; nor shall we die; for although afar off, the Sun, drawn by his coursers, will overtake the poison: the science of antidotes has converted thee, Poison, to ambrosia.

'13. I recite the names of ninety and nine rivers, the destroyers of poison: although afar off, the Sun, drawn by his coursers, will overtake the poison: the science of antidotes will convert thee, Poison, to ambrosia.

'14. May the thrice-seven peahens, the seven-sister rivers, carry off, O Body, thy poison, as maidens with pitchers carry away water.

'15. May the insignificant mungoose carry off thy venom, Poison: if not, I will crush the vile creature with a stone: so may the poison depart from my body, and go to distant regions.

'16. Hastening forth at the command of Agastya, thus spake the mungoose: The venom of the scorpion is innocuous; Scorpion, thy venom is innocuous.' [1]

Though, in the sixth verse of this hymn, the serpents are said to be born of Heaven and Earth, the context does not warrant the idea that any homage to them is intended; they are associated with the evil Rakshasas, the Sun and Agni being represented as their haters and destroyers. The seven-sister rivers (streams of the sacred Ganges) supply an antidote to their venom, and certain animals, the partridge and the mungoose, are said, though insignificant, to be their superiors. The science of antidotes alluded to is that which Indra taught to Dadhyanch, who lost his head for communicating it to the Aswins. It is notable, however, that in the Vedic period there is nothing which represents the serpent as medicinal, unless by a roundabout process we connect the expression in the Rig-Veda that the wrath of the Maruts, or storm-gods, is 'as the ire of serpents,' with the fact that their chief, Rudra, is celebrated as the bestower of 'healing herbs,' and they themselves solicited for 'medicaments.' This would be stretching the sense of the hymns too far. It is quite possible, however, that at a later day, when serpent-worship was fully developed in India, what is said in the sixth verse of the hymn may have been adduced to confirm the superstition.

It seems clear, then, that at the time the *Kankato na* was written, the serpent was regarded with simple abhorrence. And we may remember, also, that even now, when the Indian cobra is revered as a Brahman of the highest caste, there is a reminiscence of his previous ill repute preserved in the common Hindu belief that a certain mark on his head was left there by the heel of Vishnu, Lord of Life, who trod on it when, in one of his avatars, he first stepped upon the earth. Although in the later mythology we find Vishnu, in the intervals between his avatars or incarnations, reposing on a serpent (*Sesha*), this might originally have signified only his lordship over it, though Sesha is also called *Ananta*, the Infinite. The idea of the Infinite is a late one, however, and the symbolisation of it by Sesha is consistent with a lower significance at first. In Hindu popular fables the snake appears in its simple character. Such is the fable of which so many variants are found, the most familiar in the West being that of Bethgelert, and which is the thirteenth of the 4th Hitopadesa. The Brahman having left his child alone, while he performs a rite to his ancestors, on his return finds a pet mungoose (nakula) smeared with blood. Supposing the mungoose has devoured his child, he slays it, and then discovers that the poor animal had killed a serpent which had crept upon the infant. In the *Kankato na* the word interpreted by Sáyana as mungoose (*Viverra Mungo*, or ichneumon) is not the same (*nakula*), but it evidently means some animal sufficiently un-important to cast contempt upon the Serpent.

The universality of the Serpent as emblem of the healing art—found as such among the Egyptians, Greeks, Germans, Aztecs, and natives of Brazil—suggests that its longevity and power of casting its old skin, apparently renewing its youth, may have been the basis of this reputation. No doubt, also, they would have been men of scientific tendencies and of close observation who first learned the snake's susceptibilities to music, and how its poison might be drawn, or even its fangs, and who so gained reputation as partakers of its supposed powers. Through such primitive rationalism the Serpent might gain an important alliance and climb to make the asp-crown of Isis as goddess of health (the Thermuthis), to twine round the staff of Esculapius, to be emblem of Hippocrates, and ultimately survive to be the sign of the European leech, twining at last as a red stripe round the barber's pole. The primitive zoologist and snake-charmer would not only, in all likelihood, be a man cunning in the secrets of nature, but he would study to meet as far as he could the popular demand for palliatives and antidotes against snake-bites; all who escaped death after such wounds would increase his credit as a practitioner; and even were his mitigations necessarily few, his knowledge of the Serpent's habits and of its varieties might be the source of valuable precautions.

Such probable facts as these must, of course, be referred to a period long anterior to the poetic serpent-symbolism of Egypt, and the elaborate Serpent mythology of Greece and Scandinavia. How simple ideas, having once gained popular prestige, may be caught up by theologians, poets, metaphysicians, and quacks, and modified into manifold forms, requires no proof in an age when we are witnessing the rationalistic interpretations by which the cross, the sacraments, and the other plain symbols are invested with all manner of philosophical meanings. The Serpent having been adopted as the sign-post of Egyptian and Assyrian doctors—and it may have been something of that kind that was set up by Moses in the wilderness—would naturally become the symbol of life, and after that it would do duty in any capacity whatever.

An ingenious anthropologist, Mr. C. Staniland Wake,[2] supposes the Serpent in India to have been there also the symbol of præternatural and occult knowledge. Possibly this may have been so to a limited extent, and in post-Vedic times, but to me the accent of Hindu serpent-mythology appears to be emphatically in the homage paid to it as the guardian of the treasures. I may mention here also the theory propounded by Miss A. W. Buckland in a paper submitted to the Anthropological Institute in London, March 10, 1874, on 'The Serpent in connection with Primitive Metallurgy.' In this learned monograph the writer maintains that a connection may be observed between the early serpent-worship and a knowledge of metals, and indeed that the Serpent was the sign of Turanian metallurgists in the same way as I have suggested that in Egypt and Assyria it was the sign of physicians. She believes that the Serpent must have played some part in the original discovery of the metals and precious stones by man, in recognition of which that animal was first assumed as a totem and thence became an emblem. She states that traditional and ornamentational evidences show that the Turanian races were the first workers in metals, and that they migrated westward, probably from India to Egypt and Chaldæa, and thence to Europe, and even to America, bearing their art and its sign; and that they fled before the Aryans, who had the further art of smelting, and that the Aryan myths of serpent-slaying record the overthrow of the Turanian serpent-worshippers.

I cannot think that Miss Buckland has made out a case for crediting nomadic Turanians with being the original metallurgists; though it is not impossible that it may have been a Scythian tribe in Southern India who gave its fame to 'the gold of Ophir,' which Max Müller has shown to have been probably an Indian region.[3] But that these early jewellers may have had the Serpent as their sign or emblem is highly probable, and in explanation of it there seems little reason to resort to the hypothesis of aid having been given by the Serpent to man in his discovery of metals. Surely the jewelled decoration of the serpent would in itself have been an obvious suggestion of it as the emblem of gems. Where a reptile for some reasons associated with the snake—the toad—had not the like bright spots, the cognate superstition might arise that its jewel is concealed in its head. And, finally, when these reptiles had been connected with gems, the eye of either would easily receive added rays from manifold eye-beams of superstition.

We might also credit the primitive people with sufficient logical power to understand why they should infer that an animal so wonderfully and elaborately provided with deadliness as the Serpent should have tasks of corresponding importance. The medicine which healed man (therefore possibly gods), the treasures valued most by men (therefore by anthropomorphic deities), the fruit of immortality (which the gods might wish to monopolise),—might seem the supreme things of value, which the supreme perfection of the serpent's fang might be created to guard. This might be so in the heavens as well as in the world or the underworld. The rainbow was called the 'Celestial Serpent' in Persia, and the old notion that there is a bag of gold at the end of it is known to many an English and American child.

Whatever may have been the nature of the original suggestion, there are definite reasons why, when the Serpent was caught up to be part of combinations representing a Principle of Evil, his character as guardian of treasures should become of great importance. Wealth is the characteristic of the gods of the Hades, or unseen world beneath the surface of the earth.

In the vast Sinhalese demonology we find the highest class of demons (dewatawas) described as resident in golden palaces, glittering with gems, themselves with skins of golden hue, wearing cobras as ornaments, their king, Wessamony seated on a gem-throne and wielding a golden sword. Pluto is from the word for wealth (πλοῦτος), as also is his Latin name Dis (*dives*). For such are lords of all beneath the sod, or the sea's surface. Therefore, it is important to observe, they own all the seeds in the earth so long as they remain seeds. So soon as they spring to flower, grain, fruitage, they belong not to the gods of Hades but to man: an idea which originated the myth of Persephone, and seems to survive in a school of extreme vegetarians, who refuse to eat vegetables not ripened in the sun.

These considerations may enable us the better to apprehend the earlier characters of Ahi, the Throttler, and Vritra, the Coverer. As guardians of such hidden treasures as metals and drugs the Serpent might be baroneted and invoked to bestow favours; but those particular serpents which by hiding away the cloud-cows withheld the rain, or choked the rivers with drought, all to keep under-world garners fat and those of the upper world lean, were to be combated. Against them man invoked the celestial deities, reminding them that their own altars must lack offerings if they did not vanquish these thievish Binders and Concealers.

The Serpent with its jewelled raiment, its self-renovating power, and its matchless accomplishments for lurking, hiding, fatally striking, was gradually associated with undulations of rivers and sea-waves on the earth, with the Milky-way, with 'coverers' of the sky—night and cloud—above all, with the darting, crooked, fork-tongued lightning. It may have been the lightning that was the Amrita churned out of the azure sea in the myth of the 'Mahábhárata,' when the gods and demons turned the mountain with a huge serpent for cord (p. 59), meaning the descent of fire, or its discovery; but other fair and fruitful things emerged also,—the goddess of wine, the cow of plenty, the tree of heaven. The inhabitants of Burmah still have a custom of pulling at a rope to produce rain. A rain party and a drought party tug against each other, the rain party being allowed the victory, which, in the popular notion is generally followed by rain. I have often seen snakes hung up after being killed to bring rain, in the State of Virginia. For there also rain means wealth. It is there believed also that, however much it may be crushed, a snake will not die entirely until it thunders. These are distant echoes of the Vedic sentences. 'Friend Vishnu,' says Indra, 'stride vastly; sky give room for the thunderbolt to strike; let us slay Vritra and let loose the waters.' 'When, Thunderer, thou didst by thy might slay Vritra, who stopped up the streams, then thy dear steeds grew.'

Vritra, though from the same root as Varuna (the sky), means at first a coverer of the sky—cloud or darkness; hence eventually he becomes the hider, the thief, who steals and conceals the bounties of heaven—a rainless cloud, a suffocating night; and eventually Vritra coalesces with the most fearful phantasm of the Aryan mind—the serpent Ahi.

The Greek word for Adder, ἔχις, is a modification of Ahi. Perhaps there exists no more wonderful example of the unconscious idealism of human nature than the history of the name of the great Throttler, as it has been traced by Professor Max Müller. The Serpent was also called *ahi* in Sanskrit, in Greece *echis* or *echidna*, in Latin *anguis*. The root is *ah* in Sanskrit, or *amh*, which means to press together, to choke, to throttle. It is a curious root this *amh*, and it still lives in several modern words, In Latin it appears as *ango, anxi, anctum*, to strangle; in *angina*, quinsy; in *angor*, suffocation. But *angor* meant not only quinsy or compression of the neck: it assumed a moral import, and signifies anguish or anxiety. The two adjectives *angustus*, narrow, and *anxius*, uneasy, both came from the same root. In Greek the root retained its natural and material meaning; in *eggys*, near, and *echis*, serpent, throttler. But in Sanskrit it was chosen with great truth as the proper name of sin. Evil no doubt presented itself under various aspects to the human mind, and its names are many; but none so expressive as those derived from our root *amh*, to throttle. *Amhas* in Sanskrit means sin, but it does so only because it meant originally throttling—the consciousness of sin being like the grasp of the assassin on the throat of the victim. All who have seen and contemplated the statue of Laokoon and his sons, with the serpent coiled around them from head to foot, may realise what those ancients felt and saw when they called sin *amhas*, or the throttler. This *amhas* is the same as the Greek *agos*, sin. In Gothic the same root has produced *agis*, in the sense of fear, and from the same source we have *awe*, in *awful, i.e.*, fearful, and *ug* in *ugly*. The English *anguish* is from the French *angoise*, a corruption of the Latin *angustitæ*, a strait.[4] In this wonderful history of a word, whose biography, as Max Müller in his Hibbert Lectures said of *Deva*, might fill a volume, may also be included our *ogre*, and also the German *unke*, which means a 'frog' or 'toad,' but originally a 'snake'—especially the little house-snake which plays a large part in Teutonic folklore, and was supposed to bring good luck.[5]

This euphemistic variant is, however, the only exception I can find to the baleful branches into which the root *ah* has grown through the world; one of its fearful fruits being the accompanying figure, copied from one of the ornamental bosses of Wells Cathedral.

Fig. 25.—Anguish

The Adder demon has been universal. Herodotus relates that from a monster, half-woman, half-serpent, sprang the Scythians, and the fable has often been remembered in the history of the Turks. The

'Zohák' of Firdusi is the Iranian form of Ahi. The name is the Arabi-cised form of the 'Azhi Daháka' of the Avesta, the 'baneful serpent' vanquished by Thraêtaono (Traitana of the Vedas), and this Iranian name again (Dásaka) is Ahi. The name reappears in the Median Ast-yages.[6] Zohák is represented as having two serpents growing out of his shoulders, which the late Professor Wilson supposed might have been suggested by a phrase in the *Kankato na* (ye ansyá ye angyáh) which he translates, 'Those who move with their shoulders, those who move with their bodies,' which, however, may mean 'those pro-duced on the shoulders, biting with them,' and 'might furnish those who seek for analogies between Iranian and Indian legends with a parallel in the story of Zohák.' The legend alluded to is a favourite one in Persia, where it is used to point a moral, as in the instruction of the learned Saib to the Prince, his pupil. Saib related to the boy the story of King Zohák, to whom a magician came, and, breathing on him, caused two serpents to come forth from the region of his breast, and told him they would bring him great glory and pleasure, provided he would feed these serpents with the poorest of his sub-jects. This Zohák did; and he had great pleasure and wealth until his subjects revolted and shut the King up in a cavern where he became himself a prey to the two serpents. The young Prince to whom this legend was related was filled with horror, and begged Saib to tell him a pleasanter one. The teacher then related that a young Sultan placed his confidence in an artful courtier who filled his mind with false notions of greatness and happiness, and introduced into his heart Pride and Voluptuousness. To those two passions the young Sultan sacrificed the interests of his kingdom, until his subjects banished him; but his Pride and Voluptuousness remained in him, and, unable to gratify them in his exile, he died of rage and despair. The prince-pupil said, 'I like this story better than the other.' 'And yet,' said Saib, 'it is the same.'

It is curious that this old Persian fable should have survived in the witch-lore of America, and at last supplied Nathaniel Hawthorne with the theme of one of his beautiful allegorical romances,—that, namely, of the man with a snake in his bosom which ever threatened to throttle him if he did not feed it. It came to the American fabulist through many a mythical skin, so to say. One of the most beautiful it has worn is a story which is still told by mothers to their children in some districts of Germany. It relates that a little boy and girl went into the fields to gather strawberries. After they had gathered they met an aged woman, who asked for some of the fruit. The little girl emptied her basket into the old woman's lap; but the boy clutched his, and said he wanted his berries for himself. When they had passed on the old woman called them back, and presented to each a little box. The girl opened hers, and found in it two white caterpillars which speedily became butterflies, then grew to be angels with golden wings, and bore her away to Paradise. The boy opened his box, and from it issued two tiny black worms; these swiftly swelled to huge serpents, which, twining all about the boy's limbs, drew him away into the dark forest; where this Teutonic Laokoon still remains to illustrate in his helplessness the mighty power of little faults to grow into bad habits and bind the whole man.

NOTES

1 'Rig-veda,' v. (Wilson).
2 In a paper on the 'Origin of Serpent-worship,' read before the Anthropological Institute in London, December 17, 1872.
3 'Science of Language,' i. 230.
4 'Lectures on Language,' i. 435.
5 Grimm's 'Mythology,' p. 650 ff. Simrock, p. 440.
6 Roth, in the 'Journal of the German Oriental Society,' vol. ii. p. 216 ff., has elucidated the whole myth.

Chapter VII
The Basilisk

The Serpent's gem — The Basilisk's eye — Basiliscus mitratus — House-snakes in Russia and Germany — King-snakes — Heraldic dragon — Henry III — Melusina — The Laidley Worm — Victorious dragons — Pendragon — Merlin and Vortigern — Medicinal dragons

A DRAGOON ONCE presented himself before Frederick the Great and offered the king a small pebble, which, he said, had been cut from the head of a king-snake, and would no doubt preserve the throne. Frederick probably trusted more to dragoons than dragons, but he kept the little curiosity, little knowing, perhaps, that it would be as prolific of legends as the cock's egg, to which it is popularly traceable, in cockatrices (whose name may have given rise to the cock-fables) or basilisks. It has now taken its place in German folklore that Frederick owed his greatness to a familiar kept near him in the form of a basilisk. But there are few parts of the world where similar legends might not spring up and coil round any famous reputation. An Indian newspaper, the *Lawrence Gazette*, having mentioned that the ex-king of Oudh is a collector of snakes, adds—'Perhaps he wishes to become possessed of the precious jewel which some serpents are said to contain, or of that species of snake by whose means, it is said, a person can fly in the air.' Dr. Dennys, in whose work on Chinese Folklore this is quoted, finds the same notion in China. In one story a foreigner repeatedly tries to purchase a butcher's bench, but the butcher refuses to sell it, suspecting there must be some hidden value in the article; for this reason he puts the bench by, and when the foreigner returns a year afterwards, learns from him that lodged in the bench was a snake, kept alive by the blood soaking through it, which held a precious gem in its mouth—quite worthless after the snake was dead. Cursing his stupidity at having put the bench out of use, the butcher cut it open and found the serpent dead, holding in its mouth something like the eye of a dried fish.

Here we have two items which may only be accidental, and yet, on the other hand, possibly possess significance. The superior knowledge about the serpent attributed to a 'foreigner' may indicate that such stories in China are traditionally alien, imported with the Buddhists; and the comparison of the dead gem to an eye may add a little to the probabilities that this magical jewel, whether in head of toad or serpent, is the reptile's eye as seen by the glamour of human eyes. The eye of the basilisk is at once its wealth-producing, its fascinating, and its paralysing talisman, though all these beliefs have their various sources and their several representations in mythology. That it was seen as a gem was due, as I think, to the jewelled skin of most serpents, which gradually made them symbols of riches; that it was believed able to fascinate may be attributed to the general principles of illusion already considered; but its paralysing power, its evil eye, connects it with a notion, found alike in Egypt and India, that the serpent kills with its eye. Among Sanskrit words for serpent are 'drig-visha' and 'drishti-visha'—literally 'having poison in the eye.'

While all serpents were lords and guardians of wealth, certain of them were crested, or had small horns, which conveyed the idea of a crowned and imperial snake, the βασιλίσκος. Naturalists have recognised this origin of the name by giving the same (*Basiliscus mitratus*) to a genus of Iguanidæ, remarkable for a membranous crest not only on the occiput but also along the back, which this lizard can raise and depress at pleasure. But folklore, the science of the ignorant, had established the same connection by alleging that the basilisk is hatched from the egg of a black cock,—which was the peasant's explanation of the word cockatrice. De Plancy traces one part of the belief to a disease which causes the cock to produce a small egg-like substance; but the resemblance between its comb and the crests of serpent and frog [1] was the probable link between them; while the ancient eminence of the cock as the bird of dawn relegated the origin of the basilisk to a very exceptional member of the family—a black cock in its seventh year. The useful fowl would seem, however, to have suffered even so slightly mainly through a phonetic misconception. The word 'cockatrice' is 'crocodile' transformed. We have it in the Old French 'cocatrix,' which again is from the Spanish 'cocotriz,' meaning 'crocodile,'—κροκοδειλος; which Herodotus, by the way, uses to denote a kind of lizard, and whose sanctity has extended from the Nile to the Danube, where folklore declares that the skeleton of the lizard presents an image of the passion of Christ, and it must never be harmed. Thus 'cockatrice' has nothing to do with 'cock' or 'coq,' though possibly the coincidence of the sound has marred the ancient fame of the 'Bird of Dawn.' Indeed black cocks have been so generally slain on this account that they were for a long time rare, and so the basilisks had a chance of becoming extinct. There were fabulous creatures enough, however, to perpetuate the basilisk's imaginary powers, some of which will be hereafter considered. We may devote the remainder of this chapter to the consideration of a variant of dragon-mythology, which must be cleared out of our way in apprehending the Dragon. This is the agathodemonic or heraldic Dragon, which has inherited the euphemistic characters of the treasure-guarding and crowned serpent.

In Slavonic legend the king-serpent plays a large part, and innumerable stories relate the glories of some peasant child that, managing to secure a tiny gem from his crown, while the reptilian monarch was bathing, found the jewel daily surrounded with new treasures. This is the same serpent which, gathering up the myths of lightning and of comets, flies through many German legends as the red Drake, Kolbuk, Alp, or Alberflecke, dropping gold when it is red, corn if blue, and yielding vast services and powers to those who can magically master it. The harmless serpents of Germany were universally invested with agathodemonic functions, though they still bear the name that relates them to Ahi, viz., *unken*. Of these household-snakes Grimm and Simrock give much information. It is said that in fields and houses they approach solitary children and drink milk from the dish with them. On their heads they wear golden crowns, which they lay down before drinking, and sometimes forget when they retire. They watch over children in the cradle, and point out to their favourites where treasures are hidden. To kill them brings misfortune. If the parents surprise the snake with the child and kill it, the child wastes away. Once the snake crept into the mouth of a pregnant woman, and when the child was born the snake was found closely coiled around its neck, and could only be untwined by a milk-bath; but it never left the child's side, ate and slept with it, and never did it harm. If such serpents left a house or farm, prosperity went with them. In some regions it is said a male and female snake appear whenever the master or mistress of the house is about to die, and the legends of the *Unken* sometimes relapse into the original fear out of which they grew. Indeed, their vengeance is everywhere much dreaded, while their gratitude, especially for milk, is as imperishable as might be expected from their ancestor's quarrel with Indra about the stolen cows. In the *Gesta Romanorum* it is related that a milk-maid was regularly approached at milking-time by a large snake to which she gave milk. The maid having left her place, her successor found on the milking-stool a golden crown, on which was inscribed 'In Gratitude.' The crown was sent to the milkmaid who had gone, but from that time the snake was never seen again.[2]

In England serpents were mastered by the vows of a saintly Christian. The Knight Bran in the Isle of Wight is said to have picked up the cockatrice egg, to have been pursued by the serpents, which he escaped by vowing to build St. Lawrence Church in that island,— the egg having afterwards brought him endless wealth and uniform success in combat. With the manifold fables concerning the royal dragon would seem to blend traditions of the astrological, celestial, and lightning serpents. But these would coincide with a develop-ment arising from the terrestrial worms and their heroic slayers. The demonic dragon with his terrible eye might discern from afar the advent of his predestined destroyer. It might seek to devour him in infancy. As the comet might be deemed a portent of some powerful prince born on earth, so it might be a compliment to a royal family, on the birth of a prince, to report that a dragon had been seen. Nor would it be a long step from this office of the dragon as the herald of greatness to placing that monster on banners. From these banners would grow sagas of dragons encountered and slain. The devices might thus multiply. Some process of this kind would account for the entirely good reputation of the dragon in China and Japan, where it is the emblem of all national grandeur. It would also appear to underlie the proud titles of the Pythian Apollo and Bellerophon, gained from the monsters they were said to have slain. The city of Worms takes its name from the serpent instead of its slayer.[3] Pendragon, in the past—and even our dragoon of the present—are names in which the horrors of the monster become transformed in the hero's fame. The dragon, says Mr. Hardwicke, was the standard of the West Saxons, and of the English previous to the Norman Conquest. It formed one of the supporters of the royal arms borne by all the Tudor monarchs, with the exception of Queen Mary, who substituted the eagle. Several of the Plantagenet kings and princes inscribed a figure of the dragon on their banners and shields. Peter Langtoffe says, at the battle of Lewis, fought in 1264, 'The king schewed forth his schild, his dragon full austere.' Another authority says the said king (Henry III.) ordered to be made 'a dragon in the manner of a banner, of a certain red silk embroidered with gold; its tongue like a flaming fire must always seem to be moving; its eyes must be made of sapphire, or of some other stone suitable for that purpose.'[4]

It will thus be seen that an influence has been introduced into dragon-lore which has no relation whatever to the demon itself. This will explain those variants of the legend of Melusina—the famous woman-serpent—which invest her with romance. Melusina, whose indiscreet husband glanced at her in forbidden hours, when she was in her serpent shape, was long the glory of the Chateau de Lusignan, where her cries announced the approaching death of her descendants. There is a peasant family still dwelling in Fontaineb-leau Forest who claim to be descended from Melusina; and possibly some instance of this kind may have dropped like a seed into the memory of the author of 'Elsie Venner' to reappear in one of the finest novels of our generation. The corresponding sentiment is found surrounding the dragon in the familiar British legend of the Laidley [5] Worm. The king of Northumberland brought home a new Queen, who was also a sorceress, and being envious of the beauty of her step-daughter, changed that poor princess into the worm which devastated all Spindleton Heugh. For seven miles every green thing was blighted by its venom, and seven cows had to yield their daily supplies of milk. Meanwhile the king and his son mourned the disappearance of the princess. The young prince fitted out a ship to go and slay the dragon. The wicked Queen tries unsuccessfully to prevent the expedition. The prince leaps from his ship into the shallow sea, and wades to the rock around which the worm lay coiled. But as he drew near the monster said to him:

> Oh, quit thy sword, and bend thy bow,
> And give me kisses three;
> If I'm not won ere the sun goes down,
> Won I shall never be.
> He quitted his sword and bent his bow,
> He gave her kisses three;
> She crept into a hole a worm,
> But out stept a ladye.

In the end the prince managed to have the wicked Queen transformed into a toad, which in memory thereof, as every Northumbrian boy knows, spits fire to this day: but it is notable that the sorceress was *not* transformed into a dragon, as the story would probably have run if the dragon form had not already been detached from its original character, and by many noble associations been rendered an honourable though fearful shape for maidens like this princess and like Melusina.

In the same direction point the legends which show dragons as sometimes victorious over their heroic assailants. Geoffrey of Monmouth so relates of King Morvidus of Northumbria, who encountered a dragon that came from the Irish Sea, and was last seen disappearing in the monster's jaws 'like a small fish.' A more famous instance is that of Beowulf, whose Anglo-Saxon saga is summed up by Professor Morley as follows:—'Afterward the broad land came under the sway of Beowulf. He held it well for fifty winters, until in the dark night a dragon, which in a stone mound watched a hoard of gold and cups, won mastery. It was a hoard heaped up in sin, its lords were long since dead; the last earl before dying hid it in the earth-cave, and for three hundred winters the great scather held the cave, until some man, finding by chance a rich cup, took it to his lord. Then the den was searched while the worm slept; again and again when the dragon awoke there had been theft. He found not the man but wasted the whole land with fire; nightly the fiendish air-flyer made fire grow hateful to the sight of men. Then it was told to Beowulf.... He sought out the dragon's den and fought with him in awful strife. One wound the poison-worm struck in the flesh of

Beowulf.' Whereof Beowulf died.

Equally significant is the legend that when King Arthur had embarked at Southampton on his expedition against Rome, about midnight he saw in a dream 'a bear flying in the air, at the noise of which all the shores trembled; also a terrible dragon, flying from the west, which enlightened the country with the brightness of its eyes. When these two met they had a dreadful fight, but the dragon with its fiery breath burned the bear which assaulted him, and threw him down scorched to the earth.' This vision was taken to augur Arthur's victory. The father of Arthur had already in a manner consecrated the symbol, being named Uther Pendragon (dragon's head). On the death of his brother Aurelius, it was told 'there appeared a star of wonderful magnitude and brightness,' darting forth a ray, at the end of which was a globe of fire, in form of a dragon, out of whose mouth issued two rays, one of which seemed to stretch out itself towards the Irish Sea, and ended in seven lesser rays.' Merlin interpreted this phenomenon to mean that Uther would be made king and conquer various regions; and after his first victory Uther had two golden dragons made, one of which he presented to Winchester Cathedral, retaining the other to attend him in his wars.

In the legend of Merlin and Vortigern we find the Dragon so completely developed into a merely warrior-like symbol that its moral character has to be determined by its colour. As in the two armies of serpents seen by Zoroaster, in Persian legends, which fought in the air, the victory of the white over the black foreshowing the triumph of Ormuzd over Ahriman, the tyranny of Vortigern is represented by a red dragon, while Aurelius and Uther are the two heads of a white dragon. Merlin, about to be buried alive, in pursuance of the astrologer's declaration to Vortigern that so only would his ever-falling wall stand firm, had revealed that the recurring disaster was caused by the struggle of these two dragons underground. When the monsters were unearthed they fought terribly, until the white one

> Hent the red with all his might,
> And to the ground he him cast,
> And, with the fire of his blast,
> Altogether brent the red,
> That never of him was founden shred;
> But dust upon the ground he lay.

The white dragon vanished and was seen no more; but the tyrant Vortigern fulfilled the fate of the red dragon, being burnt in his castle near Salisbury. These two dragons met again, however, as red and white roses.

Many developments corresponding to these might be cited. One indeed bears a startling resemblance to our English legends. Of King Nuat Meiamoun, whose conquest of Egypt is placed by G. Maspero about B.C. 664–654, the Ethiopian 'Stele of the Dream' relates:—'His Majesty beheld a dream in the night, two snakes, one to his right, the other to his left, (and) when His Majesty awoke ... he said: 'Explain these things to me on the moment,' and lo! they explained it to him, saying: 'Thou wilt have the Southern lands, and seize the Northern, and the two crowns will be put on thy head, (for) there is given unto thee the earth in all its width and its breadth.' These two snakes were probably suggested by the *uræi* of the Egyptian diadem.

Beyond the glory reflected upon a monster from his conqueror, there would be reason why the alchemist and the wizard should encourage that aspect of the dragon. The more perilous that Gorgon whose blood Esculapius used, the more costly such medicament; while, that the remedy may be advantageous, the monster must not be wholly destructive. This is so with the now destructive now preservative forces of nature, and how they may blend in the theories, and subserve the interests, of pretenders is well shown in a German work on Alchemy (1625) quoted by Mr. Hardwicke. 'There is a dragon lives in the forest, who has no want of poison; when he sees the sun or fire he spits venom, which flies about fearfully. No living animal can be cured of it; even the basilisk does not equal him. He who can properly kill this serpent has overcome all his danger. His colours increase in death; physic is produced from his poison, which he entirely consumes, and eats his own venomous tail. This must be accomplished by him, in order to produce the noblest balm. Such great virtue as we will point out herein that all the learned shall rejoice.'

It will be readily understood that these traditions and fables would combine to 'hedge about a king' by ascribing to him familiarity with a monster so formidable to common people, and even investing him with its attributes. The dragon's name, δράκῶν, derived from the Sanskrit word for serpent (dṛig-visha), came to mean 'the thing that sees.' While this gave rise to many legends of præternatural powers of vision gained by tasting or bathing in a dragon's blood, as in the poem of Siegfried; or from waters it guarded, as 'Eye Well,' in which Guy's dragon dipped its tail to recover from wounds; the

Sanskrit sense of eye-poisoning was preserved in legends of occult and dangerous powers possessed by kings,—one of the latest being the potent evil eye popularly ascribed in Italy to the late Pius IX. But these stories are endless; the legends adduced will show the sense of all those which, if unexplained, might interfere with our clear insight into the dragon itself, whose further analysis will prove it to be wholly bad,—the concentrated terrors of nature.

NOTES
1   I have in my possession a specimen of the horned frog of America, and it is sufficiently curious.
2   Gesta Rom., cap. 68. Grimm's Myth., 650 ff. Simrock, p. 400.
3   Others derive the name from the ancient Borbetomagus.
4   Traditions, p. 44.
5   Loathely.

Chapter VIII

The Dragon's Eye

The Eye of Evil — Turner's Dragons — Cloud-phantoms — Paradise and the
Snake — Prometheus and Jove — Art and Nature — Dragon forms: Anglo-Saxon,
Italian, Egyptian, Greek, German — The modern conventional Dragon

THE ETYMOLOGIES OF the words Dragon and Ophis given in the
preceding chapter, ideally the same, both refer to powers of the
serpent which it does not possess in nature,—the præternatural
vision and the glance that kills. The real nature of the snake is thus
overlaid; we have now to deal with the creation of another world.

There are various conventionalised types of the Dragon, but
through them all one feature is constant,—the idealised serpent. Its presence is the demonic or supernatural sign. The heroic dragon-slayer must
not be supposed to have wrestled with mere flesh and blood, in whatever
powerful form. The combat which immortalises him is waged with all
the pains and terrors of earth and heaven concentrated and combined
in one fearful form.

Impossible and phantasmal as was this form in nature, its
mystical meaning in the human mind was terribly real. It was this
Eye of anti-human nature which filled man with dismay, and conjured
up the typical phantom. It was this Pain, purposed and purposing,
the Agony of far-searching vision, subtlest skill, silently creeping,
winged, adapted to meet his every device with a cleverer device,

which gradually impressed mankind with belief in a general principle of antagonism to human happiness.

It is only as a combination that any dragon form is miraculous. Every constituent feature and factor of it is in nature, but here they are rolled together in one pandemonic expression and terror. Yet no such form loses its relations with nature: it is lightning and tempest, fever-bearing malaria and fire, venom and fang, slime and jungle, all the ferocities of the earth, air, and heavens, gathering to their fatal artistic force, and waylaying man at every step in his advance. In Turner's picture of Apollo slaying the Python there is a marvellous suggestion of the natural conceptions from which the dragon was evolved. The fearful folds of the monster, undulating with mound and rock on which he lies, at points almost blend with tangle of bushes and the jagged chaos amid which he stretches. The hard, wild, cruel aspects of inanimate nature seem here and there rankly swelling to horrible life, as yet but half-distinguishable from the stony-hearted matrix; the crag begins to coil and quiver, the jungle puts forth in claws; but above all appear the monstrous EYES, in which the forces of pain, hardship, obstacle have at last acquired purpose and direction. The god confronts them with eyes yet keener; his arrow, feathered with eyebeams, has reached its mark, straight between the monster's eyes; but there is no more anger in his face than might mar the calm strength of a gardener clearing away the stone and thicket that make the constituent parts of Python.

If we turn now to the neighbouring picture in the National Gallery by the same artist, the Hesperian Gardens and their Guard, we behold the Dragon on his high crag outlining and vitalising not only the edge of rock but also the sky it meets. His breath steams up into cloud. The heavens also have their terrors, which take on eyes and coils. On the line of the horizon were hung the pictures of the primitive art-gallery. Imagination painted them with brush dipped now in blackness of the storm, now in fires of the lightning or the sunset, but the forms were born of experience, of earthly struggle, defeat, and victory.

As I write these words, I lay aside my pen to look across a little lake amid the lonely hills of Wales to a sunset which is flooding the sky with glory. Through the almost greenish sky the wind is bearing fantastic clouds, that sometimes take the shape of chariots, in which cloud-veiled forms are seated, and now great birds with variegated plumage, all hastening as it were to some gathering-place of aerial gods. Beneath a long bar of maroon-tint stretches a sea of yellow light, on the hither side of which is set a garden of fleecy trees touched with golden fruit. Amid them plays a fountain of changing colours. On the left has stood, fast as a mountain range, a mass of dark-blue cloud with uneven peaks; suddenly a pink faint glow shines from behind that leaden mass, and next appears, sinuous with its long indented top, the mighty folds of a fiery serpent. Nay, its head is seen, its yawning lacertine jaws, its tinted crest. It is sleepless Ladon on his high barrier keeping watch and ward over the Hesperian garden.

Juno set him there, but he is the son of Ge,—the earth. The tints of heaven invest and transform, and in a sense create him; but he would never have been born mythologically had it not been that in this world stings hover near all sweetness, danger environs beauty, and, as Plato said, 'Good things come hard.' The grace and lustre of the serpent with his fatal fang preceded him, and all the perils that lurk beneath things fair and fascinating. So far there is nothing essentially moral or unmoral about him. This dragon is a shape designed by primitive meteorology and metaphysics together. Man has asked what is so, and this is the answer: he has not yet asked why it is so, whether it ought to be so, and whether it may not be otherwise. The challenge has not yet been given, the era of combat not yet arrived. The panoplied guard and ally of gods as unmoral as himself has yet to be transformed under the touch of the religious sentiment, and expelled from the heaven of nobler deities as a dragon cast down, deformed, and degraded for ever.

As thought goes on, such allies compromise their employers; the creator's work reflects the creator's character; and after many timorous ages we find the dragon-guarded deities going down with their cruel defenders. It is not without significance that in the Sanskrit dictionary the most ancient of all words for god, *Asura*, has for its primary meaning 'demon' or 'devil:' the gods and dragons united to churn the ocean for their own wealth, and in the end they were tarred with one brush. I have already described in the beginning of this work the degradation of deities, and need here barely recall to the reader's memory the forces which operated to that result. The bearing of that force upon the celestial or paradise-guarding Serpent is summed up in one quatrain of Omar Khayyám:—

> O Thou who man of baser earth didst make,
> And e'en in Paradise devised the Snake;
> For all the sin wherewith the face of man
> Is blackened, man's forgiveness give—and take!

The heart of humanity anticipated its logic by many ages, and, long before the daring genius of the Persian poet wrote this immortal epitaph on the divine allies of the Serpent, heroes had given battle to the whole fraternity. Nay, in their place had arisen a new race of gods, whose theoretical omnipotence was gladly surrendered in the interest of their righteousness; and there was now war in heaven; the dragon and his allies were cast down, and man was now free to fight them as enemies of the gods as well as himself. Woe henceforth to any gods suspected of taking sides with the dragon in this man's life-and-death struggle with the ferocities of nature, and with his own terrors reflected from them! The legend of Prometheus was their unconsciously-given 'notice to quit,' though it waited many centuries for its great interpreter. It is Goethe who alone has seen how pale and weak grow Jove's fireworks before the thought-thunderbolts of the artist, launched far beyond the limitations that chain him in nature. Gods are even yet going down in many lands before the sublime sentence of Prometheus:—

> Curtain thy heavens, thou Jove, with clouds and mist,
> And, like a boy that moweth thistles down,
> Unloose thy spleen on oaks and mountain-tops;
> Yet canst thou not deprive me of my earth,
> Nor of my hut, the which thou didst not build,
> Nor of my hearth, whose little cheerful flame
> Thou enviest me!
>
> I know not aught within the universe
> More slight, more pitiful than you, ye gods!
> Who nurse your majesty with scant supplies
> Of offerings wrung from fear, and muttered prayers,
> And needs must starve, were't not that babes and beggars
> Are hope-besotted fools!

When I was yet a child, and knew not whence
My being came, nor where to turn its powers,
Up to the sun I bent my wildered eye,
As though above, within its glorious orb,
There dwelt an ear to listen to my plaint,
A heart, like mine, to pity the oppressed.

Who gave me succour
Against the Titans in their tyrannous might?
Who rescued me from death—from slavery?
Thou!—thou, my soul, burning with hallowed fire,
Thou hast thyself alone achieved it all!
Yet didst thou, in thy young simplicity,
Glow with misguided thankfulness to him
That slumbers on in idlenesse there above!

I reverence thee?
Wherefore? Hast thou ever
Lightened the sorrows of the heavy laden?
Thou ever stretch thy hand to still the tears
Of the perplexed in spirit?
Was it not
Almighty Time, and ever-during Fate—
My lords and thine—that shaped and fashioned me
Into the MAN I am?

Belike it was thy dream
That I should hate life—fly to wastes and wilds,
For that the buds of visionary thought
Did not all ripen into goodly flowers?

Here do I sit and mould
Men after mine own image—
A race that may be like unto myself,
To suffer, weep; to enjoy, and to rejoice;
And, like myself, unheeding all of thee!

The myth of Prometheus reveals the very dam of all drag-

ons,—the mere terrorism of nature which paralysed the energies of man. Man's first combat was to be with his own quailing heart. Apollo driving back the Argives to their ships with the image of the Gorgon's head on Jove's shield is Homer's picture of the fears that unnerved heroes:—

> Phœbus himself the rushing battle led;
> A veil of clouds involved his radiant head:
> High held before him, Jove's enormous shield
> Portentous shone, and shaded all the field:
> Vulcan to Jove th' immortal gift consigned,
> To scatter hosts, and terrify mankind....
> Deep horror seizes ev'ry Grecian breast,
> Their force is humbled, and their fear confest.
> So flies a herd of oxen, scattered wide,
> No swain to guard them, and no day to guide,
> When two fell lions from the mountain come,
> And spread the carnage thro' the shady gloom....
> The Grecians gaze around with wild despair,
> Confused, and weary all their pow'rs with prayer. [1]

A generation whose fathers remembered the time when men educated in universities regarded Franklin with his lightning-rod as 'heaven-defying,' can readily understand the legend of Vulcan—type of the untamed force of fire—being sent to bind Prometheus, master of fire.[2] How much fear of the forces of nature, as personified by superstition, levelled against the first creative minds and hands the epithets which Franklin heard, and which still fall upon the heads of some scientific investigators! Storm, lightning, rock, ocean, vulture,—these blend together with the intelligent cruelty of Jove in the end; and behold, the Dragon! The terrors of nature, which drive cowards to their knees, raise heroes to their height. Then it is a flame of genius matched against mad thunderbolts. Whether the jealous nature-god be Jehovah forbidding sculpture, demanding an altar of unhewn stone, and refusing the fruits of Cain's garden, or Zeus jealous of the artificer's flame, they are thrown into the Opposition by the artist; and when the two next meet, he of the thunderbolt with all his mob will be the Dragon, and Prometheus will be the god, sending to its heart his arrow of light.

Fig. 26.—Swan-Dragon (French)

The dragon forms which have become familiar to us through mediæval and modern iconography are of comparatively little importance as illustrating the social or spiritual conditions out of which they grew, and of which they became emblems. They long ago ceased to be descriptive, and in the rude periods or places a very few scratches were sometimes enough to indicate the dragon; such mere suggestions in the end allowing large freedom to subsequent designers in varying original types.

Fig. 27—Anglo-Saxon Dragons (Cædmon M.S., tenth century)

Fig. 28.—From the Fresco at Arezzo

As to external form, the various shapes of the more primitive dragons have been largely determined by the mythologic currents amid which they have fallen, though their original basis in nature may generally be traced. In the far North, where the legends of swan-maidens, pigeon-maidens, and vampyres were paramount in the Middle Ages, we find the bird-shaped dragon very common. Sometimes the serpent-characteristics are pronounced, as in this ancient French Swan-Dragon (Fig. 26); but, again, and especially in regions where serpents are rare and comparatively innocuous, the serpent tail is often conventionalised away, as in this initial V from the Cædmon Manuscript, tenth century (Fig. 27), a fair example of the ornamental Anglo-Saxon dragon. The cuttlefish seems to have suggested the animalised form of the Hydra, which in turn helped to shape the Dragon of the Apocalypse. Yet the Hydra in pictorial representation appears to have been influenced by Assyrian ideas; for although the monster had nine heads, it is often given seven (number of the Hathors, or Fates) by the engravers, as in Fig. 6. The conflicts of Hercules with the Hydra repeated that of Bel with Tiamat ('the Deep'), and had no doubt its counterpart in that of Michael with the Dragon,—the finest representation of which, perhaps, is the great fresco by Spinello (fourteenth century) at Arezzo, a group from which is presented in Fig. 28. In this case the wings represent those always attributed in Semitic mythology to the Destroying Angel. The Egyptian Dragon, of which the crocodile is the basis, at an early period entered into christian symbolism, and gradually effaced most of the pagan monsters. The crocodile and the alligator, besides being susceptible of many horrible variations in pictorial treatment, were particularly acceptable to the Christian propaganda, because of the sanctity attached to them by African tribes,—a sanctity which continues to this day in many parts of that country, where to kill one of these reptiles is believed to superinduce dangerous inundations. In Semitic traditions, also, Leviathan was generally identified as a demonic crocodile, and the feat of destroying him was calculated to impress the imaginations of all varieties of people in the Southern countries for which Christianity struggled so long. This form contributed some of its characters to the lacertine dragons which were so often painted in the Middle Ages, with what effect may be gathered from the accompanying design by Albert Durer (Fig.

29). In this loathsome creature, which seeks to prevent deliverance of 'the spirits in prison,' we may remark the sly and cruel eye: the præternatural vision of such monsters was still strong in the traditions of the sixteenth century. In looking at this lizard-guard at the mouth of hell we may realise that it has been by some principle of psychological selection that the reptilian kingdom gradually gained supremacy in these portrayals of the repulsive. If we compare with Fig. 29 the well-known form of the Chimæra (Fig. 30), most of us will be conscious of a sense of relief; for though the reptilian form is present in the latter, it is but an appendage—almost an ornament—to the lion. It is impossible to feel any loathing towards this spirited Trisomatos, and one may recognise in it a different animus from that which depicted the christian dragon. One was meant to attest the boldness of the hero who dared to assail it; the other was meant, in addition to that, to excite hatred and horror of the monster assailed. We may, therefore, find a very distinct line drawn between such forms as the Chimæra and such as the Hydra, or our conventional Dragon. The hairy inhabitants of Lycia, human or bestial, whom Bellerophon conquered,[3] were not meant to be such an abstract expression of the evil principle in nature as the Dragon, and while they are generalised, the elements included are also limited. But the Dragon, with its claws, wings, scales, barbed and coiling tail, its fiery breath, forked tongue, and frequent horns, includes the organic, inorganic, the terrestrial and atmospheric, and is the combination of harmful contrivances in nature.

Fig. 29.—From Albert Durer's 'Passion'

Nearly all of the Dragon forms, whatever their original types and their region, are represented in the conventional monster of the European stage, which meets the popular conception. This Dragon is a masterpiece of the popular imagination, and it required many generations to give it artistic shape. Every Christmas he appears in some London pantomime, with aspect similar to that which he has worn for many ages. His body is partly green, with memories of the sea and of slime, and partly brown or dark, with lingering shadow of storm-clouds. The lightning flames still in his red eyes, and flashes from his fire-breathing mouth. The thunderbolt of Jove, the spear of Wodan, are in the barbed point of his tail. His huge wings—batlike, spiked—sum up all the mythical life of extinct Harpies and Vampyres. Spine of crocodile is on his neck, tail of the serpent, and all the jagged ridges of rocks and sharp thorns of jungles bristle around him, while the ice of glaciers and brassy glitter of sunstrokes are in his scales. He is ideal of all that is hard, obstructive, perilous, loathsome, horrible in nature: every detail of him has been seen through and vanquished by man, here or there, but in selection and combination they rise again as principles, and conspire to form one great generalisation of the forms of Pain—the sum of every creature's worst.

Fig. 30.—Chimæra

NOTES
1 Pope's 'Homer,' Book xv.
2 See p. 59.
3 See p. 154.

Chapter IX

The Combat

The pre-Munchausenite world — The Colonial Dragon — Io's journey — Medusa — British Dragons — The Communal Dragon — Savage Saviours — A Mimac helper — The Brutal Dragon — Woman protected — The Saint of the Mikados

THE REALM OF the Unknown has now, by exploration of our planet and by science, been pretty well pressed into annexation with the Unknowable. In early periods, however, unexplored lands and seas existed only in the human imagination, and men appear to have included them within the laws of analogy as slowly as their descendants so included the planets. The monstrous forms with which superstition now peoples regions of space that cannot be visited could then dwell securely in parts of the world where their existence or non-existence could not be verified. Science had not yet shown the simplicity and unity underlying the superficial varieties of nature; and though Rudolf Raspe appeared many times, and related the adventures of his Baron Munchausen in many languages, it was only a hundred years ago that he managed to raise a laugh over them. It has taken nearly another hundred to reveal the humour of Munchausenisms that relate to invisible and future worlds.

The Dragon which now haunts the imagination of a few compulsory voyagers beyond the grave originated in speculations concerning the unseen shores of equally mythical realms, whose burning zones and frozen seas had not yet been detached from this planet to make the Inferno of another. In our section on Demonology we have considered many of these imaginary forms in detail, limiting ourselves generally to the more realistic embodiments of special obstacles. Just above that formation comes the stratum in which we find the separate features of the previous demonic fauna combining to forms which indicate the new creative power which, as we have seen, makes nature over again in its own image.

Beginning thus on the physical plane, with a view of passing to the social, political, and metaphysical arenas where man has successively met his Dragons, we may first consider the combination of terrors and perils, real and imaginary, which were confronted by the early colonist. I will venture to call this the COLONIAL DRAGON.

This form may be represented by any of those forms against which the Prometheus of Æschylus cautions Io on her way to the realm which should be called Ionia. 'When thou shalt have crossed the stream that bounds the continents to the rosy realms of the morning where the sun sets forth, ... thou shalt reach beyond the roaring sea Cisthene's Gorgonian plains, where dwell the Phorkides, ... and hard by are their three winged sisters, the Snake-haired Gorgons, by mortals abhorred, on whom none of human race can look and live.... Be on thy guard against the Gryphons, sharp-fanged hounds of Jove that never bark, and against the cavalry host of one-eyed Arimaspians, dwelling on the gold-gushing fount, the stream of Pluto. Thou wilt reach a distant land, a dark tribe, near to the fount of the sun, where runs the river Æthiops.'[1]

One who has looked upon Leonardo da Vinci's Medusa at Flor-

433

ence—one of the finest interpretations of a mythologic subject ever painted—may comprehend what to the early explorer and colonist were the fascinations of those rumoured regions where nature was fair but girt round with terrors. The Gorgon's head alone is given, with its fearful tangle of serpent tresses; her face, even in its pain, possesses the beauty that may veil a fatal power; from her mouth is exhaled a vapour which in its outline has brought into life vampyre, newt, toad, and loathsome nondescript creatures. Here is the malaria of undrained coasts, the vermin of noxious nature. The source of these must be destroyed before man can found his city; it is the fiery poisonous breath of the Colonial Dragon.

Fig. 31.—Bellerophon and Chimæra (Corinthian)

Most of the Dragon-myths of Great Britain appear to have been importations of the Colonial monsters. Perhaps the most famous of these in all Europe was the Chimæra, which came westward upon coins, Bellerophon having become a national hero at Corinth—almost superseding the god of war himself—and his effigy spread with many migrations. Our conventional figure of St. George is still Bellerophon, though the Dragon has been substituted for Chimæra,—a change which christian tradition and national respect for the lion rendered necessary (Fig. 31). Corresponding to this change in outward representation, the monster-myths of Great Britain have been gradually pressed into service as moral and religious lessons. The Lambton Worm illustrates the duty of attending mass and sanctity of the sabbath; the demon serpents of Ireland and Cornwall prove the potency of holy exorcism; and this process of moralisation has extended, in the case of the Boar, whose head graces the Christmas table at Queen's College, Oxford, to an illustration of the value of Aristotelian philosophy. It was with a volume of Aristotle that the monster was slain, the mythologic affinities of the legend being quaintly preserved in the item that it was thrust down the boar's throat.

But these modifications are very transparent, the British legends being mainly variants of one or two original myths which appear to have grown out of the heraldic devices imported by ancient families. These probably acquired realistic statement through the prowess and energy of chieftains, and were exaggerated by their descendants, perhaps also connected with some benefit to the community, in order to strengthen the family tenure of its estates. For this kind of duty the Colonial Dragon was the one usually imported by the family romancer or poet. The multiplication of these fables is, indeed, sufficiently curious. It looks as if there were some primitive agrarian sentiment which had to be encountered by aid of appeals to exceptional warrant. The family which could trace its title to an estate to an ancestor who rescued the whole district, was careful to preserve some memorial of the feat. On account of the interests concerned in old times we should be guarded in receiving the rationalised interpretations of such myths, which have become traditional in some localities. The barbaric achievements of knights did not lose in the ballads of minstrels any marvellous splendours, but gained many; and most of these came from the south and east. The Dragon which Guy of Warwick slew still retained traces of Chimæra; it had 'paws as a lion.' Sir William Dugdale thought that this was a romanticised version of a real combat which Guy fought with a Danish chief, A.C. 926. Similarly the Dragon of Wantley has been reduced to a fraudulent barrister.

The most characteristic of this class of legends is that of Sockburn. Soon after the Norman conquest the Conyers family received that manor by episcopal grant, the tradition being that it was because Sir John Conyers, Knight, slew a huge Worm which had devoured many people. The falchion with which this feat was achieved is still preserved, and I believe it is still the custom, when a new bishop visits that diocese, for the lord of Sockburn to present this sword. The lord of the manor meets the bishop in the middle of the river Tees, and says:—'My Lord Bishop, I here present you with the falchion wherewith the Champion Conyers slew the Worm, Dragon, or fiery flying Serpent, which destroyed man, woman, and child, in memory of which the king then reigning gave him the manor of Sockburn to hold by this tenure,—that upon the first entrance of every bishop into the country this falchion should be presented.' The bishop returns the sword and wishes the lord long enjoyment of the tenure, which has been thus held since the year 1396. The family tradition is that the Dragon was a Scotch intruder named Comyn, whom Conyers compelled to kneel before the episcopal throne. The Conyers family of Sockburn seem to have been at last overtaken by a Dragon which was too much for them: the last knight was taken from a workhouse barely in time not to die there.

In the 'Memoirs of the Somervilles' we read that one of that family acquired a parish by slaying a 'hydeous monster in forme of a worme.'[2]

> The wode Laird of Laristone
> Slew the Worme of Worme's Glen,
> And wan all Linton parochine.

It was 'in lenth 3 Scots yards, and somewhat bigger than an ordinary man's leg, with a hede more proportionable to its lenth than its greatness; its forme and collour (like) to our common muir adders.'

This was a very moderate dragon compared with others, by slaying which many knights won their spurs: this, for example, which Sir Dygore killed in the fourteenth century—

> ——A Dragon great and grymme,
> Full of fyre, and also of venymme:
> With a wide throte and tuskes grete,
> Uppon that knight fast gan he bete;

And as a Lionn then was his fete,
His tayle was long and ful unmete;
Between his hede and his tayle
Was xxii. fote withouten fayle;
His body was like a wine tonne,
He shone full bright ageynst the sunne;
His eyes were bright as any glasse,
His scales were hard as any brasse.

The familiar story of St. Patrick clearing the snakes out of Ireland, and the Cornish version of it, in which the exorcist is St. Petrox, presents some features which relate it to the colonist's combat with his dragon, though it is more interesting in other aspects. The Colonial Dragon includes the diseases, the wild beasts, the savages, and all manner of obstructions which environ a new country. But when these difficulties have been surmounted, the young settlement has still its foes to contend with,—war-like invaders from without, ambitious members within. We then find the Dragon taking on the form of a public enemy, and his alleged slayer is representative of the commune,—possibly in the end to transmit its more real devourer. Most of the British Dragon-myths have expanded beyond the stage in which they represent merely the struggles of immigrants with wild nature, and include the further stage where they represent the formation of the community. The growth of patriotism at length is measured by its shadow. The Colonial is transformed to the Communal Dragon. Many Dragon-myths are adaptations of the ancient symbolism to *hostes communes*: such are the monsters described as desolating villages and districts, until they are encountered by antagonists animated by public spirit. Such antagonists are distinguishable from the heroes that go forth to rescue the maiden in distress: their chief representative in mythology is Herakles, most of whose labours reveal the man of self-devotion redressing public wrongs, and raising the standard of humanity as well as civilisation.

The age of chivalry has its legend in the Centaurs and Cheiron. The Hippo-centaurs are mounted savages: Cheiron is the true knight, withstanding monsters in his own shape, saving Peleus from them, and giving hospitality to the Argonauts. The mounted man was dragon to the man on foot until he became the chevalier; then the demonic character passed to the strategist who had no horse. It is curious enough to find existing among the Mormons a murderous order calling themselves Danites, or Destroying Angels, after the text of Gen. xlix. 17, 'Dan shall be a serpent by the way, an adder in the path, that biteth the horse's heel that his rider shall fall backward.' The Ritter, however, so far as his Dragon was concerned, was as one winged, and every horse a Pegasus when it bore him to decide the day between the adder and its victim. It is remarkable that the Mormons should have carried from the East a cruel superstition to find even among the Red Men, who are disappearing before the western march of Saxon strength, more gentle fables.

Among the Mimacs, the aborigines of Nova Scotia, there is a legend of a young hero named Keekwajoo, who, in seeking for a wife, is befriended by a good sage named Glooscap, who warns him against a powerful magician disguised as a beaver, and two demon sisters, who will waylay him in the disguise of large weasels. The youth is admonished to beat a certain drum as his canoe passes them, and he is saved as Orpheus in passing Cerberus and Ulysses in sailing past the Syrens. The weasels, hearing the music, aspire to wed the stars, but find themselves in an indescribable nest at the top of a tall white pine.[3]

The chevalier encounters also the Brutal Dragon, whose victim is Woman. From immemorial time man's captive, unable to hold her own against brute force, she is at the mercy of all who are insensible to the refined and passive powers. The rock-bound Andromeda, the pursued Leto, or whatever fair maid it may be that the Dragon-slayer rescues, may have begun mythologically as emblem of the Dawn, whose swallower is the Night Cloud; but in the end she symbolises a brighter dawn,—that of civility and magnanimity among men.

It is a notable fact that far away in Japan we should find a Dragon-myth which would appear to represent, with rare beauty, the social evolution we have been considering. Their great mythological Serpent, Yamati-no-orochi, that is, the serpent of eight heads and tails, stretching over eight valleys, would pretty certainly represent a river annually overflowing its banks. One is reminded by this monster of the accounts given by Mencius of the difficulties with streams which the Chinese had to surmount before they could make the Middle States habitable. But this Colonial Dragon, in the further evolution of the country, reappears as the *Brutal Dragon*. The admirable legend relates that, while the rest of the world were using stone implements, there came into the possession of Sosa-no-o-no-Mikoto (the Prince of Sosano) a piece of iron which was wrought into a sword. That maiden-sword of the world was fleshed to save a maiden from the jaws of a monster. The prince descended from heaven to a bank of the river Hino Kawa, and the country around seemed uninhabited; but presently he saw a chopped stick floating down the stream, and concluded that there must be beings dwelling farther up; so he travelled until he came to a spot where he beheld an aged man and his wife (Asinaduti and Tenaduti), with their beautiful daughter, Himé of Inada. The three were weeping bitterly, and the prince was informed that Himé was the last of their daughters, seven of whom had been devoured by a terrible serpent. This serpent had eight heads, and the condition on which it had ceased to desolate the district was that one of these eight maidens should be brought annually to this spot to satisfy his voracity. The last had now been brought to complete the dreadful compact. The Japanese are careful to distinguish this serpent from a dragon, with them an agathodemon. It had no feet, and its heads branched by as many necks from a single body, this body being so large that it stretched over eight valleys. It was covered with trees and moss, and its belly was red as blood. The prince doubted if even with his sword he could encounter such a monster, so he resorted to stratagem; he obtained eight vast bowls, filled them with eight different kinds of wine, and, having built a fence with the same number of openings, set a bowl in each. The result may be imagined: the eight heads in passing over the bowls paused, drank deep, and were soon in a state of beastly intoxication. In this condition the heads were severed from their neck, and the maiden saved to wed the first Mikado Prince.

NOTES
1   Æsch. Prom. 790, &c.
2   Vol. i. p. 38.
3   'North American Review,' January 1871.

Chapter X
The Dragon-slayer

Demigods — Alcestis — Herakles — The Ghilghit Fiend — Incarnate deliverer
of Ghilghit — A Dardistan Madonna — The religion of Atheism — Resuscitation
of Dragons — St. George and his Dragon — Emerson and Ruskin on George —
Saintly allies of the Dragon

THEOLOGY HAS PRONOUNCED Incarnation a mystery, but nothing is simpler. The demigod is man's appeal from the gods. It may also be, as Emerson says, that 'when the half-gods go the gods arrive,' but it is equally true that their coming signals the departure of deities which man had long invoked in vain. The great Heraklean myth presents us the ideal of godlike force united to human sympathy. Ra (the Sun) passing the twelve gates (Hours) of Hades (Night)[1] is humanised in Herakles and his Twelve Labours. He is Son of Zeus by a human mother—Alcmene—and his labours for human welfare, as well as his miraculous conception, influenced Christianity. The divine Man assailing the monsters of divine creation represents human recognition of the fact that moral order in nature is co-extensive with the control of mankind. One expression of this perception is the Alcestis of Euripides, whose significance in relation to death we have considered.[2]

'Alcestis,' as I have written in another work, 'is one of the few ancient Greek melodramas. The majority of dramas left us by the poets of Greece turn upon religious themes, and usually they are tragedies. It is evident that to them the popular religion around them was itself a tragedy. Their heroes and heroines—such as Prometheus and Macaria—were generally victims of the jealousy or caprice of the gods; and though the poets display in their dramas the irresistible power of the gods, they do so without reverence for that power, and generally show the human victims to be more honourable than the gods. But the 'Alcestis' of Euripides is not a tragedy; it ends happily, and in the rescue of one of those victims of the gods. It stands as about the first notice served on the gods that the human heart had got tired of their high-handed proceedings, and they might prepare to quit the thrones of a universe unless they could exhibit more humanity.... Knowing that neither he nor any other deity can legally resist the decree of another deity, Apollo is reduced to hope for help from man. Human justice may save when divine justice sacrifices. He prophesies to Death that although he may seize Alcestis, a man will come who will conquer him, and deliver that woman from the infernal realm.... Then Hercules comes on the scene. He has been slaying lion and dragon, and he now resolves to conquer Death and deliver Alcestis. This he does.'[3]

In this pre-christian yet christian Passion Play, the part played by the heart of woman is equally heroic with that which represents the honour of man. So in the religion which followed there was an effort to set beside the incarnate vanquisher of infernal powers the pierced heart of Mary. But among all the legends of this character it were difficult to find one more impressive than that which Dr. Leitner found in Dardistan, and one which, despite its length, will repay a careful perusal. This legend of the origin of the Ghilghit tribe and

443

government was told by a native.

'Once upon a time there lived a race at Ghilghit whose origin is uncertain. Whether they sprung from the soil or had immigrated from a distant region is doubtful; so much is believed that they were Gayupí, *i.e.*, spontaneous, aborigines, unknown. Over them ruled a monarch who was a descendant of the evil spirits, the Yatsh, who terrorised over the world. His name was Shiribadatt, and he resided at a castle in front of which was a course for the performance of the manly game of Polo. His tastes were capricious, and in every one of his actions his fiendish origin could be discerned. The natives bore his rule with resignation, for what could they effect against a monarch at whose command even magic aids were placed? However, the country was rendered fertile, and round the capital bloomed attractive. The heavens, or rather the virtuous Peris, at last grew tired of his tyranny, for he had crowned his iniquities by indulging in a propensity for cannibalism. This taste had been developed by an accident. One day his cook brought him some mutton broth the like of which he had never tasted. After much inquiry as to the nature of the food on which the sheep had been brought up, it was eventually traced to an old woman, its first owner. She stated that her child and the sheep were born on the same day, and losing the former, she had consoled herself by suckling the latter. This was a revelation to the tyrant. He had discovered the secret of the palatability of the broth, and was determined to have a never-ending supply of it. So he ordered that his kitchen should be regularly provided with children of a tender age, whose flesh, when converted into broth, would remind him of the exquisite dish he had once so much relished. This cruel order was carried out. The people of the country were dismayed at such a state of things, and sought slightly to improve it by sacrificing, in the first place, all orphans and children of neighbouring tribes. The tyrant, however, was insatiable, and soon was his cruelty felt by many families at Ghilghit, who were compelled to give up their children to slaughter.

'Relief came at last. At the top of the mountain Ko, which it takes a day to ascend, and which overlooks the village of Doyur, below Ghilghit, on the other side of the river, appeared three figures. They looked like men, but much more strong and handsome. In their arms they carried bows and arrows, and turning their eyes in the direction of Doyur, they perceived innumerable flocks of sheep and cattle grazing on a prairie between that village and the foot of the mountain. The three strangers were brothers, and none of them had been born at the same time. It was their intention to make Azru Shemsher, the youngest, Rajah of Ghilghit, and, in order to achieve their purpose, they hit upon the following plan. On the already no-ticed prairie, which is called Didingé, a sportive calf was gambolling towards and away from its mother. It was the pride of its owner, and its brilliant red colour could be seen from a distance. 'Let us see who is the best marksman,' exclaimed the eldest, and, saying this, he shot an arrow in the direction of the calf, but missed his aim. The second brother also tried to hit it, but also failed. At last, Azru Shemsher, who took a deep interest in the sport, shot his arrow, which pierced the poor animal from side to side and killed it. The brothers, whilst de-scending, congratulated Azru on his sportsmanship, and on arriving at the spot where the calf was lying, proceeded to cut its throat and to take out from its body *the titbits, namely, the kidneys and the liver.*

'They then roasted these delicacies, and invited Azru to partake of them first. He respectfully declined, on the ground of his youth, but they urged him to do so, 'in order,' they said, 'to reward you for such an excellent shot.' Scarcely had the meat touched the lips of Azru than the brothers got up, and, vanishing into the air, called out, 'Brother! you have touched impure food, which Peris never should eat, and we have made use of your ignorance of this law, because we want to make you a human being [4] who shall rule over Ghilghit; remain, therefore, at Doyur.' Azru, in deep grief at the separation, cried, 'Why remain at Doyur, unless it be to grind corn?' 'Then,' said the brothers, 'go to Ghilghit.' 'Why,' was the reply, 'go to Ghilghit, unless it be to work in the gardens?' 'No, no,' was the last and consoling rejoinder; 'you will assuredly become the king of this country, and deliver it from its merciless oppressor!' No more was heard of the departing fairies, and Azru remained by himself, endeavouring to gather consolation from the great mission which had been bestowed on him. A villager met him, and, struck by his appearance, offered him shelter in his house. Next morning he went on the roof of his host's house, and calling out to him to come up, pointed to the Ko mountain, on which, he said, he plainly discerned a wild goat. The incredulous villager began to fear he had harboured a maniac, if no worse character; but Azru shot off his arrow, and, accompanied by the villager (who had assembled some friends for protection, as he was afraid his young guest might be an associate of robbers, and lead him into a trap), went in the direction of the mountain. There, to be sure, at the very spot that was pointed out, though many miles distant, was lying the wild goat, with Azru's arrow transfixing its body. The astonished peasants at once hailed him as their leader, but he exacted an oath of secrecy from them, for he had come to deliver them from their tyrant, and would keep his incognito till such time as his plans for the destruction of the monster would be matured.

'He then took leave of the hospitable people of Doyur, and went to Ghilghit. On reaching this place, which is scarcely four miles distant from Doyur, he amused himself by prowling about in the gardens adjoining the royal residence. There he met one of the female companions of Shiribadatt's daughter fetching water for the princess. This lady was remarkably handsome, and of a sweet disposition. The companion rushed back, and told the young lady to look from over the ramparts of the castle at a wonderfully handsome young man whom she had just met. The princess placed herself in a place from which she could observe any one approaching the fort. Her maid then returned, and induced Azru to come with her in the Polo ground, in front of the castle; the princess was smitten with his beauty, and at once fell in love with him. She then sent word to the young prince to come and see her. When he was admitted into her presence he for a long time denied being anything more than a common labourer. At last he confessed to being a fairy's child, and the overjoyed princess offered him her heart and hand. It may be mentioned here that the tyrant Shiribadatt had a wonderful horse, which could cross a mile at every jump, and which its rider had accustomed to jump both into and out of the fort, over its walls. So regular were the leaps which this famous animal could take that he invariably alighted at the distance of a mile from the fort, and at the same place. On that very day on which the princess had admitted young Azru into the fort King Shiribadatt was out hunting, of which he was desperately fond, and to which he used sometimes to devote a week or two at a time.

'We must now return to Azru, whom we left conversing with the princess. Azru remained silent when the lady confessed her love. Urged to declare his sentiments, he said that he would not marry her unless she bound herself to him by the most stringent oath; this she did, and they became in the sight of God as if they were wedded man and wife. He then announced that he had come to destroy her father, and asked her to kill him herself. This she refused; but as she had sworn to aid him in every way she could, he finally induced her to promise that she would ask her father *where his soul was*. 'Refuse food,' said Azru, 'for three or four days, and your father, who is devotedly fond of you, will ask for the reason of your strange conduct; then say, 'Father, you are often staying away from me for several days at a time, and I am getting distressed lest something should happen to you; do reassure me by letting me know where your soul is, and let me feel certain that your life is safe.' This the princess promised to do, and when her father returned refused food for several days. The anxious Shiribadatt made inquiries, to which she replied by making the already named request. The tyrant was for a few moments thrown into mute astonishment, and finally refused compliance with her preposterous demand. The love-smitten lady went on starving herself, till at last her father, fearful for his daughter's life, told her not to fret herself about him as *his soul was of snow, in the snows*, and that he could only perish by fire. The princess communicated this information to her lover. Azru went back to Doyur and the villages around, and assembled his faithful peasants. Them he asked to take twigs of the fir-tree, bind them together, and light them; then to proceed in a body with torches to the castle in a circle, keep close together, and surround it on every side. He then went and dug out a very deep hole, as deep as a well, in the place where Shiribadatt's horse used to alight, and covered it with green boughs. The next day he received information that the torches were ready. He at once ordered the villagers gradually to draw near the fort in the manner which he had already indicated.

King Shiribadatt was then sitting in his castle; near him his treacherous daughter, who was so soon to lose her parent. All at once he exclaimed, 'I feel very close; go out, dearest, and see what has happened.' The girl went out, and saw torches approaching from a distance; but fancying it to be something connected with the plans of her husband, she went back and said it was nothing. The torches came nearer and nearer, and the tyrant became exceedingly restless. 'Air, air,' he cried, 'I feel very ill; do see, daughter, what is the matter.' The dutiful lady went, and returned with the same answer as before. At last the torch-bearers had fairly surrounded the fort, and Shiribadatt, with a presentiment of impending danger, rushed out of the room, saying, 'that he felt he was dying.' He then ran to the stables and mounted his favourite charger, and with one blow of the whip made him jump over the wall of the castle. Faithful to its habit the noble animal alighted at the same place, but, alas! only to find itself engulfed in a treacherous pit. Before the king had time to extricate himself the villagers had run up with their torches. 'Throw them upon him,' cried Azru. With one accord all the blazing wood was thrown upon Shiribadatt, who miserably perished.'

Azru was then most enthusiastically proclaimed king, celebrated his nuptials with the fair traitor, and, as sole tribute, exacted the offering of one sheep annually, instead of the human child, from every one of the natives.

When Azru had safely ascended the throne he ordered the tyrant's place to be levelled to the ground. The willing peasants, manufacturing spades of iron, flocked to accomplish a grateful task, and sang whilst demolishing his castle:—

'My nature is of a hard metal,' said Shiri and Badatt. 'Why hard? I, Koto, the son of the peasant Dem Singh, am alone hardy; with this iron spade I raze to the ground thy kingly house. Behold now, although thou art of race accursed, of Shatsho Malika, I, Dem Singh's son, am of a hard metal; for with this iron spade I level thy very palace; look out! look out!'[5]

An account of the Feast of Torches, instituted as a memorial of this tradition, has already been given in another connection.[6] The legend, the festival, and the song just quoted constitute a noble human epic. That startling defiance of the icy-hearted god by the human-hearted peasant, that brave cry of the long cowering wretch who at last holds in his spade an iron weapon to wield against the hardness of nature, are the sublime pæan of the Dragon-slayer. Look out, ye snow-gods! Man's heart is there, and woman's heart; their courage, plus the spade, can level your palaces; their love will melt you, their arts and sciences kill you: so fatal may be torches!

All great religions were born in this grand atheism. As the worship of Herakles meant the downfall of Zeus, the worship of Christ meant the overthrow of both Jove and Jehovah. Every race adores the epoch when their fathers grew ashamed of their gods and identified them as dragons—the supreme cruelties of nature—welcoming the man who first rose from his knees and defied them. But in the end the Priests of the Dragon manage to secure a compromise, and by labelling him with the name of his slayer, manage to resuscitate and re-enthrone him. For, as we shall presently see, the Dragon never really dies.

Christianity did not fail to avail itself of the Dragon-slayer's prestige, which had preceded it in Europe and in Africa. It could not afford to offer for popular reverence saints less heroic than pagan warriors and demigods. The old Dragon-myths, especially those which made the fame of Herakles, were appropriated to invest saintly forms. St. Michael, St. Andrew, St. Margaret, and many another, were pictured subduing or treading on Dragons. Christ was shown crushing the serpent Sin, spearing the dragon Death, or even issuing from its impotent jaws, like Jason from the Dragon.[7] But in this competition for the laurels of dead Dragon-slayers, and fierce hostility to dragons already slain, the real Dragon was left to revive and flourish in security, and in the end even inherited the mantle and the palm of his own former conqueror.

The miscarriage of canonisation in the case of St. George is a small and merely curious thing in itself; but it is almost mystical in its coincidence with the great miscarriage which brought the cross of Christ to authorise the crucifixions of the men most like him for a thousand years.

Mr. John Ruskin has sharply challenged Ralph Waldo Emerson's penetrating touch on the effigy that decorates the escutcheons of England and Russia. 'George of Cappadocia,' says Emerson, 'born at Epiphania in Cilicia, was a low parasite, who got a lucrative contract to supply the army with bacon. A rogue and an informer, he got rich and was forced to run from justice. He saved his money, embraced Arianism, collected a library, and got promoted by a faction to the episcopal throne of Alexandria. When Julian came, A.D. 361, George was dragged to prison. The prison was burst open by the mob, and George was lynched as he deserved. And this precious knave became in good time Saint George of England, patron of chivalry, emblem of victory and civility, and the pride of the best blood of the modern world.' Whereon Emerson further remarks that 'nature trips us up when we strut.'

It is certainly rather hard for the founder of the St. George Association to be told that his patron was no Dragon-slayer at all, but the Dragon's ally. Mr. Ruskin may be right in contending that whatever may have been the facts, they who made George patron saint of England still meant their homage for a hero, or at any rate not for a rogue; but he is unsatisfactory in his argument that our St. George was another who died for his faith seventy years before the bacon-contractor. Even if the Ruskin St. George, said to have suffered under Diocletian, could be shown historical, his was a very commonplace martyrdom compared with that of a bishop torn in pieces by a 'pagan' mob. The distant christian nations would never have listened to the pagan version of the story even had it reached them. A bishop so martyred would have been the very man to give their armies a watchword. The martyr was portrayed as a Dragon-slayer only as a title might be added to the name of one knighted, or the badge of an order set upon his breast; the heraldic device grew into a variant of the common legend which suggests the origin of the mythical George. 'The magician Athanasius, successively an opponent of Christianity, a convert, and a martyr, is his chief antagonist; and the city of Alexandria appears as the Empress Alexandria, the wife of Diocletian, and herself a convert and a martyr.' This sentence from Smith's 'Dictionary of Greek and Roman Biography' tells more than Professor Ruskin's seventeenth-century authority. The Dragon is the same Athanasius whose creed sends forth its anathemas in churches dedicated to the Arian canonised for having slain him!

Though it be granted that they who made George of Cappadocia the ideal hero of England really intended their homage for a martyr and hero, it must equally be acknowledged that his halo was clearly drawn from Dragon-fire. He was a man who had taken to the sword, and by it perished; so much was known and announced in his canonisation. He was honoured as 'the Victor' among the Greeks, therefore to-day patron of Russia; as protector of Crusaders, therefore now patron of England; thus is he saint of a war waged by the strong against the weak, in interest of a church and priesthood against human freedom; therefore George was taking the side of the Dragon against Christ, restoring the priestly power he had assailed, and delivering up his brave brothers in all history to be nailed to Christianity as a cross.

Let George remain! Whether naming fashionable temples or

engraved on gold coins, the fictitious Dragon-slayer will remain the right saint in the right place so long as the real Dragon-slayer is made to name every power he hated, and to consecrate every lie in whose mouth he darted his spear.

NOTES
1   'Records of the Past,' x. 79.
2   Page 285.
3   'Alcestis in England.' Printed by the South Place Society, Finsbury, London. 1877.
4   Eating meat was the process of incarnation.
5   'Results of a Tour in Dardistan, Kashmir,' &c., by Chevalier Dr. G. W. Leitner, Lahore, vol. i. part iii. Trübner & Co.
6   Page 91.
7   In the Etruscan Museum at Rome there is a fine representation of this. The old belief was that a dragon could only be attacked successfully inside.

Chapter XI

The Dragon's Breath

Medusa — Phenomena of recurrence — The Brood of Echidna and their survival — Behemoth and Leviathan — The Mouth of Hell — The Lambton Worm — Ragnar — The Lambton Doom — The Worm's Orthodoxy — The Serpent, Superstition, and Science

ASURA HAS ALREADY been mentioned as the most ancient Aryan name for deity. The meaning of it is, the Breather. It has also been remarked that in the course of time the word came to signify both the good and the evil spirit. What this evil breath meant in nature is told in Leonardo da Vinci's picture of the expiring Medusa, referred to on p. 386, from whose breath noxious creatures are produced. It may have been that the artist meant only to interpret the Gorgon as a personification of the malarious vapours of nature and their organic kindred; if so, he painted better than he knew, and has suggested that fatal vitality of the evil power which raised it to its throne as a principle coeternal with good.

The phenomena of recurrence in things evil made for man the mystery of iniquity. The darkness may be dispersed, but it returns; the storm may clear away, but it gathers again; inundations, sickly seasons, dog-days, Cain-winds, they go and return; the cancer is cut out and grows again; the tyrant may be slain, tyranny survives. The serpent slipping from one skin to another coils steadily into the symbol of endlessness. In another expression it is the poisonous breath of the Dragon. It is this breath that cannot be killed; the special incarnations of it, any temporary brood of it, may be destroyed, but the principle in nature which produces them cannot be exterminated.

Dragon fables have this undertone to their brave strain. In the Rig Veda (v. 32) it is said that when Indra slew Ahi, 'another more powerful was generated.' Isaiah (xiv. 29) cries, 'Rejoice not thou, whole Palestina, because the rod of him that smote thee is broken: for out of the serpent's root shall come forth a cockatrice, and his fruit shall be a fiery flying serpent.' Herakles struggles with the giant robber, Antæus, only to find the demon's strength restored by contact with the earth. He kills one head of the Hydra only to see two grow in its place; and even when he has managed to burn away these, the central head is found to be immortal, and he can only hide it under a rock. That one is the self-multiplying principle of evil. The vast brood of Echidna in mythology expresses the brood of evil in nature. Echidna, daughter of Ge and Tartarus, Earth and Hell—phonetic reappearance of Ahi—is half-serpent, half-woman, with black eyes, fearful and bloodthirsty. She becomes the mother of fire-breathing Typhon, buried beneath the earth by Jove's lightning when he aspired to scale Olympus; of the Dragon that guarded the Hesperian garden; of the Sphinx which puzzled and devoured; of three-headed Cerberus; of the eagle that preyed on rock-bound Prometheus; of the Nemæan lion which Herakles slew; of Chimæra; and of Scylla the monster whom Homer describes sitting between two large rocks waylaying mariners on the way from Italy to Sicily,—possessing twelve feet, six long necks and mouths, each with three rows of rushing teeth.

The Dragon that Cadmus slew also had terrible teeth; and it will be remembered that when these teeth were sown they sprang up as armed men. Like them, the ancient Dragon-myths were also sown, broadcast, in the mental and moral fields, cleared and ploughed by a new theology, and they sprang up as dogmas more hard and cruel than the ferocious forces of nature which gave birth to their ancestral monsters.

What the superstitious method of interpreting nature, forced as it is to personify its painful as well as its pleasant phenomena, inevitably results in, finds illustration in the two great lines of tradition—the Aryan and the Semitic—which have converged to form the christian mythology.

The Hebrew personification, Jehovah, originating in a rude period, became invested with many savage and immoral traditions; but when his worshippers had reached a higher moral culture, national sentiment had become too deeply involved with the sovereign majesty of their deity for his alleged actions to be criticised, or his absolute supremacy and omnipotence to be questioned, even to save his moral character. Thus, the Rabbins appear to have been at their wits' end to account for the existence of the two great monsters which had got into their sacred records—from an early mythology—Behemoth and Leviathan. Unwilling to admit that Jehovah had created foes to his own kingdom, or that creatures which had become foes to it were beyond his power to control, they worked out a theory that Behemoth and Leviathan were made and preserved by special order of Jehovah to execute his decrees at the Messianic Day of Judgment. They probably corresponded at an earlier period with the gryphon, or grabber, and the serpent which bit, guardians at the gate of paradise; but the need of such guards, biters, and spies by the all-powerful all-seeing Shaddai having been recognised, the monsters had to be rationalised into accord with his character as a retributive ruler. Hence Behemoth and Leviathan are represented as being fattened with the wicked, who die in order to be the food of the righteous during the unsettled times that follow the revelation of the Messiah! Behemoth is Jehovah's 'cattle on a thousand hills' (Ps. i. 10). In Pireque de Rabbi Eliezur he is described as feeding daily upon a thousand mountains on which the grass grows again every night; and the Jordan supplies him with drink, as it is said in Job (xl. 23), 'he trusteth that he can draw up Jordan into his mouth.' In the Talmud these monsters are divided into two pairs, but are said to have been made barren lest their progeny should destroy the earth. They are kept in the wilderness of Dendain, the mythical abode of the descendants of Cain, east of Eden, for the unique purpose mentioned.

But now we may remark the steady progress of these monsters to the bounds of their mythological habitat. There came a time when Behemoth and Leviathan were hardly more presentable than other personified horrors. They too must 'take the veil,'—a period in the history of mythical, corresponding to extinction in that of actual, monsters. The following passage in the Book of Enoch is believed by Professor Drummond to be a later insertion, probably from the Book of Noah, and as early as the middle of the first century:—'In that day two monsters shall be divided; a female monster named Leviathan, to dwell in the abyss of the sea, above the sources of the waters; but the male is called Behemoth, which occupies with its breast a desolate wilderness named Dendain, on the east of the garden where the elect and righteous dwell, where my grandfather (Enoch) was taken up, being the seventh from Adam, the first man whom the Lord of the spirits created. And I asked that other angel to show me the might of these monsters, how they were separated in one day, and one was set in the depth of the sea, the other on the firm land of the wilderness. And he spoke to me, 'Thou son of man, thou desirest in this to know what has been concealed.' And the other angel who went with me, and showed me what is in concealment, spake, ... 'These two monsters are prepared conformably to the greatness of God to be fed, in order that the penal judgment of God may not be in vain.'[1]

We may thus see that there were antecedents to the sentiment of Aquinas,—'Beati in regno cœlesti videbunt pœnas damnatorum, ut beatitudo illis magis complaceat.' Or, perhaps, one might say rather to the logic of Aquinas; for though he saw that it would be necessary for souls in bliss to be happy at vision of the damned or else deficient in bliss, it is said he could hardly be happy from thinking of the irreversible doom of Satan himself. It would appear that only the followers of the Genevan who anticipated his god's hell for Servetus managed to adapt their hearts to such logic, and glory in the endless tortures of their fellow-creatures.

An eloquent minister in New York, Octavius B. Frothingham, being requested to write out his views on the 'question' of everlasting damnation, began with the remark that he felt somewhat as a sportsman suddenly called upon to hunt the Iguanodon. Really it is Behemoth and Leviathan he was called to deal with. Leviathan transmitted from Jonah to the Middle Ages the idea of 'the belly of Hell,' and Behemoth's jaws expanded in the 'mouth of Hell' of the Miracle-plays; and their utility, as described in the Book of Enoch, perhaps originated the doctrine of souls tasting heavenly joys from the agonies of others. The dogma of Hell has followed the course of its prototype with precision. It has arrived at just that period when, as in the case of Enoch's inquiring, the investigator finds it has taken the veil. Theologians shake their heads, call it a terrible question, write about free-will and sin, but only a few, of the fatuous sort, confess belief in the old-fashioned Hell where the worm dieth not and the fire is not quenched.

Let us now take under consideration the outcome of the Aryan Dragon, which has travelled far to meet Behemoth in the west. And it is probable that we could not, with much seeking, find an example so pregnant with instruction for our present inquiry as our little Durham folk-tale of the Lambton Worm.

This Worm is said to have been slain by Sir Lambton, crusader, and ancestor of the Earls of Durham. This young Lambton was a wild fellow; he was fond of fishing in the river Wear, which runs near Durham Castle, and he had an especial taste for fishing there on Sunday mornings. He was profane, and on Sundays, when the people were all going to mass, they were often shocked by hearing the loud oaths which Lambton uttered whenever he had no rise. One Sunday morning something got hold of his hook, pulled strong, and he made sure of a good trout; what was his disappointment when instead thereof he found at the end of his line a tiny black worm. He tore it off with fierce imprecations and threw it in a well near by.

However, soon after this the young man joined the crusaders and went off to the Holy Land, where he distinguished himself by slaying many Saracens.

But while he was off there things were going on badly around Durham Castle. Some peasant passing that well into which the youth had cast the tiny black worm looked into it, and beheld a creature that made him shudder,—a diabolical big snake with nine ferocious eyes. A little time only had elapsed before this creature had grown too large for the well to hold it, and it came out and crawled on, making a path of desolation, breakfasting on a village, until it came to a small hill. Around that hill it coiled with nine coils, each weighty enough to make a separate terrace. One may still see this hill with its nine terraces, and be assured of the circumstances by peasants residing near. Having taken up its headquarters on this hill, the nine-eyed monster was in the habit of sallying forth every day and satisfying his hunger by devouring the plumpest family he could find, until at length the people consulted an oracle—some say a witch, others again a priest—and were told that the monster would be satisfied if it were given each day the milk of nine cows. So nine cows were got together, and a plucky dairymaid was found to milk the cows and carry it to the dragon. If a single gill of the milk was missing the monster took a dire revenge upon the nearest village. This was the unpleasant situation which young Lambton found when he returned home from the crusades. He was now an altered man. He was no longer given to fishing and profanity. He felt keenly that by raising the demon out of the river Wear he had brought woe upon his neighbours, and he resolved to engage the Worm in single combat. But he learned that it had already been fought by several knights, and had slain them, while no wounds received by itself availed anything, since, if it were cut in twain, the pieces grew together again. The knight then consulted the oracle, witch or priest, and was told that he could prevail in the combat on certain conditions. He must provide himself with special armour, all over which must be large razor-blades. He must manage to entice the worm into the middle of the river Wear, in whose waters the combat must take place. And, finally, he must vow to slay as a sacrifice the first living thing he should meet after his victory. These conditions having been fulfilled, the knight entered the stream. The dragon, not having received his milk as usual that morning, crawled from his hill seeking whom he might devour, and seeing the knight in the river, went at him. Quickly he coiled around the armour, but its big razors cut him into many sections; and these sections could not piece themselves together again because the current of the river washed them swiftly away.

Now, observe how this dragon was pieced together mythologically. He is a storm cloud. He begins smaller than a man's hand and swells to huge dimensions; that characteristic of the howling storm was represented in the howling wolf Fenris of Norse Mythology, who was a little pet, a sort of lapdog for the gods at first, but when full grown broke the chains that tied him to mountains, and was only fettered at last by the thread finer than cobweb, which was really the sunbeam conquering winter. Then, when this worm was cut in two, the parts came together again. This feature of recurrence is especially characteristic of Hydras. In the Egyptian 'Tale of Setnau,' Ptah-nefer-ka saw the river-snake twice resume its form after he had killed it with his sword,—he succeeded the third time by placing sand between the two parts; and what returning floods taught the ancient scribe remained to characterise the dragon encountered by Guy of Warwick, which recovered from every wound by dipping its tail in the well it had guarded. The Lernean Hydra had nine heads, the Lambton Worm nine eyes and nine folds, and drank nine cows' milk. His fondness for the milk of cows connects him straightly with the dragon Vritra, whom Indra slew because he stole Indra's cows (that is, the good clouds, whose milk is gentle rain, and do no harm), and shut them up in a cavern to enjoy their milk himself. That is the oldest Dragon fable on record, and it is said in the Rig-Veda that beneath Indra's thunderbolt the monster broke up into pieces, and was washed away in a current of water. Finally, in being destroyed at last by razor blades, the dragon is connected with that slain by Ragnar, in whose armour the sun-darts of Apollo had turned to icicles. In the 'Death-Song of Ragnar Lodbrach,' preserved by Olaus Wormius, it is said that King Ella of Northumberland having captured that terror of the North (8th cent.), ordered him to be thrown into a pit of serpents. His surname, Lodbrach, or Hair Breeches, had been given because of his method of slaying a Worm which devastated Gothland, whose king had promised his daughter to the man who should slay the same. Ragnar dressed himself in hairy skins, and threw water over the hair, which, freezing, encased him in an armour of ice. The Worm, unable to bite through this, was impaled by Ragnar. Another version is that Ragnar killed two serpents which the King of Gothland had set to guard his daughter, but which had grown to such size that they terrified the country. It may be observed that the

Lambton story christianises the Ragnar legend, showing that to be done in atonement for sin which in the other was done for love. The Cornish legend of St. Petrox has also taken a hint from Ragnar, and announces the rescue of christians from the serpent-pit in which the pagan hero perished. The icicles reappear on the slayer of the dragon of Wantley, represented by long spikes bristling from his armour.

The Knight Lambton, remembering his vow to slay as a sacrifice the first living thing he might meet after the combat, had arranged that a dog should be placed where it would attract his eye. But it turned out that his own father came rushing to him. As he could not kill his father, he consulted the oracle again to know what would be the penalty of non-fulfilment of his vow. It was that no representative of the family should die in his bed for nine generations. The notion is still found in that neighbourhood that no Earl of Durham has since then died in his bed. The nine generations have long passed since any crusading Lambton lived, but several peasants of the district closed their narrative with, 'Strange to say, no Earl of Durham has died in his bed!' At the castle I talked with a servant on the estate while looking at the old statues of the knight, worm, and dairymaid, all kept there, and he told me he had heard that the late Earl, as death drew nigh, asked to sit up—insisted—and died in a chair. If there be any truth in this, it would show that the family itself has some morbid feeling about the legend which has been so long told them with pride. The old well from which the little worm emerged a monster is now much overgrown, but I was told that it was for a long time a wishing-well, and the pins cast in by rustics may still be seen at the bottom of it.

Pins are the last offerings at the Worm's Well; 'wishes' its last prayers; but where go now the coins and the prayers? To propitiate a power and commute a doom resting upon much the same principles as those represented in the Lambton legend. A community desolated because one man is sinful miniatures a world's doom for Adam's sin. The demand of a human sacrifice is more clear in the Sockburn story, where Conyers offered up his only son to the Holy Ghost in the parish church before engaging the Dragon, that being a condition of success prescribed by the 'Oracle' or 'Sybil.' This claim of the infernal powers represented by the Worm—many-eyed, all-seeing—cannot be set aside; Lambton's filial love may resist it only to have it pass as the hereditary doom of his family, representing an imputed sin. 'For I, the Lord thy God, am a jealous God, and visit the sins of the fathers on the children unto the third and fourth generation.'

There are processes of this kind in nature, hereditary evils, transmitted diseases and disgraces, and afflictions of many through the offences of one. But a fearful Nemesis follows the deification and adoration of them. 'How can I be happy in heaven,' said a tender-hearted lady to her clerical adviser, 'when I must see others in hell?' 'You will be made to see that it is all for the best.' 'If I am to be made so heartless, I prefer to go to hell.' This genuine conversation reports the doom of all deities whose extension is in dragons. Hell implies a Dragon as its representative and ruler. Theology may induce the abject and cowardly to subject their human hearts to the process of induration required for loyalty to such powers, but in the end it makes atheism the only salvation of brave, pure, and loving natures. The Dragons' breath has clouded the ancient heavens and blighted the old gods; but the starry ideals they pursue in vain. Behemoth has supplied sirloins to many priesthoods for a long time, but he has at last become too tough even for their teeth, and they feed him less carefully every year. Nay, he is encountered now and then by his professional feeders, and has found even in Westminster Abbey his Guy of Warwick.

> Nor could this desp'rate champion daunt
> A Dun Cow bigger than elephant;
> But he, to prove his courage sterling,
> Cut from her enormous side a sirloin.

Fig. 32.—From the Temptation of St. Anthony (Callot)

The Worms—whether Semitic Leviathan or Aryan Dragon—are nearly fossilised as to their ancient form. The sacrifice of Jephtha's daughter to the one, and of young Conyers to the other, found commutation in the case of man's rescue from Satan by Christ's descent to Hades, and in the substitution of nine uneasy deaths for the demanded parricide in the Lambton case; and the most direct 'survival' of these may be found in any country lad trying to cure his warts by providing a weed for them to adhere to. Their end in Art was in such forms as this starveling creature of Callot's (Fig. 32), whose thin, spectacled rider, tilting at St. Anthony, denotes as well the doom of all powers, however lofty, whose majesty requires *tali auxilio et istis defensoribus*. The Dragon passes and leaves a roar of laughter behind him, in which even St. Anthony could now join. But Leviathan and Lambton Worm have combined and merged their life in a Dogma; it is a Dogma as remorseless and voracious as its prototype, and requires to be fed with all the milk of human kindness, or it at once begins to gnaw the foundations of Christendom itself. Christianity rests upon the past work of the Worm in Paradise, and its present work in Hell. It makes no real difference whether man's belief in a universe enmeshed in serpent-coils be expressed in the Hindu's cowering adoration of the venomous potentate, or the christian's imprecation upon it: fundamentally it is serpent-worship in each case. Vishnu reposes on his celestial Serpent; the god of Dogma maintains his government by support of the infernal Serpent. Fear beheld him appearing in Durham to vindicate the mass and the Sabbath; but the same fear still sees him in the fiery world punishing Sabbath-breakers and blasphemers against his Creator and chief. That fear built every cathedral in Christendom, and they must crumble with the phantasm evoked for their creation.

The Serpent in itself is a perfect type of all evil in nature. It is irreconcilable with the reign of a perfectly good and omnipotent man over the universe. No amount of casuistry can explain its co-existence with anthropomorphic Love and Wisdom, as all acknowledge when a parallel casuistry attempts to defend any other god than their own from deeds that are, humanly considered, evil. It is just as easy to defend the jealousy and cruelty of Jove, on the ground that his ways are not as our ways, as it is to defend similar tempers in Jehovah. The monster sent by one to devour Prometheus is ethically atwin with the snake created by the other to bite the heel of man.

Man is saved from the superstitious evolution of the venomous Serpent into a Dragon by recognising its real evolution as seen by the eye of Science. Science alone can tell the true story of the Serpent, and justify its place in nature. It forbids man his superstitious method of making a god in his own image, and his egotistic method of judging nature according to his private likes and dislikes, his convenience or inconvenience. Taught by Science man may, with a freedom the barbarian cannot feel, exterminate the Serpent; with a freedom the christian cannot know, he may see in that reptile the perfection of that economy in nature which has ever defended the advancing forms of life. It judges the good and evil of every form with reference to its adaptation to its own purposes. Thus Science alone wields the spear of Ithuriel, and beneath its touch every Dragon shrinks instantly to its little shape in nature to be dealt with according to what it is.

NOTES
1   'The Jewish Messiah,' &c. By James Drummond, B.A. Longmans & Co. (1877). See in this valuable work chapter xxi.

Chapter XII
Fate

Dorè's 'Love and Fate' — Moira and Moiræ — The 'Fates' of Æschylus —
Divine absolutism surrendered — Jove and Typhon — Commutation of the
Demon's share — Popular fatalism — Theological fatalism — Fate and Necessity
— Deification of Will — Metaphysics, past and present

GUSTAVE DORÈ HAS painted a picture of 'Love and Fate,' in which
the terrible hag is portrayed towering above the tender Eros, and
while the latter is extending the thread as far as he can, the wrinkled hands of Destiny are the boundaries of his power, and the fatal
shears close upon the joy he has stretched to its inevitable limit. To
the ancient mind these two forms made the two great realms of the
universe, their powers meeting in the fruit with a worm at its core, in
seeds of death germinating amid the play of life, in all the limitations
of man. They are projected in myths of Elysium and Hades, Eden and
the Serpent, Heaven and Hell, and their manifold variants.

Perhaps there is no one line of mythological development
which more clearly and impressively illustrates the forces under
which grew the idea of an evil principle, than the changes which
the personification of Fate underwent in Greece and Rome. The
Moira, or Fate with Homer, is only a secondary cause, if that, and
simply carries out the decrees of her father, Zeus. Zeus is the real
Fate. Nevertheless, while this is the Homeric theory or theology,
there are intimations (see chap. xxvii. part 4) that the real awe of

men was already transferred from Zeus to the Erinnyes. This fore-shadows a change of government. With Hesiod we find, instead of one, three Moiræ. They are no longer offspring of Zeus, but, as it were, his Cabinet. They do not act independently of him, but when, in pursuance of their just counsels, Zeus issues decrees, the Moiræ administer them. Next we find the Moiræ of Hesiod developed by other writers into final Recorders; they write the decrees of Zeus on certain indestructible tablets, after which they are irrevocable and inevitable. With Æschylus we find the Moiræ developed into independent and supreme powers, above Zeus himself. The chained Prometheus looks not to Zeus but to Fate for his final liberation.

> *Chorus.* Who, then, is the guide of Necessity?
> *Prometheus.* The tri-form Fates and the unforgetting Furies.
> *Cho.* Is Zeus, then, less powerful than they?
> *Prom.* At least 'tis certain he cannot escape his own doom.
> *Cho.* And what can be Zeus' doom but everlasting rule?
> *Prom.* This ye may not learn; press it not.
> *Cho.* Surely some solemn mystery thou hidest.
> *Prom.* Turn to some other theme: for this disclosure time has not ripened: it must be veiled in deep mystery, for by the keeping of this secret shall come my liberty from base chains and misery.

These great landmarks represent successive revolutions in the Olympian government. Absolutism became burthensome: as ir-responsible monarch, Zeus became responsible for the woes of the world, and his priests were satisfied to have an increasing share of that responsibility allotted to his counsellors, until finally the whole of it is transferred. From that time the countenance of Zeus, or Jupi-ter, shines out unclouded by responsibility for human misfortunes and earthly evils; and, on the other hand, the once beautiful Fates are proportionately blackened, and they become hideous hags, the aged and lame crones of popular belief in Greece and Rome, every line of whose ugliness would have disfigured the face of Zeus had he not been subordinated to them.

Moira means 'share,' and originally, perhaps, meant simply the power that meted out to each his share of life, and of the pains and pleasures woven in it till the term be reached. But as the Fates gained more definite personality they began to be regarded as having also a 'share' of their own. They came to typify all the dark and formidable powers as to their inevitableness. No divine power could set them aside, or more than temporarily subdue them. Fate measured out her share to the remorseless Gorgon as well as to the fairest god. But where destructive power was exercised in a way friendly to man, the Fates are put somewhat in the background, and the feat is claimed for some god. Such, in the 'Prometheus' of Æschylus, is the spirit of the wonderful passage concerning Typhon, rendered with tragic depth by Theodore Buckley:—'I commiserated too,' says the rock-bound Prometheus, 'when I beheld the earth-born inmate of the Cilician caverns, a tremendous prodigy, the hundred-headed impetuous Typhon, overpowered by force; who withstood all the gods, hissing slaughter from his hungry jaws, and from his eyes there flashed a hideous glare as if he would perforce overthrow the sovereignty of Jove. But the sleepless shaft of Jupiter came upon him, the descending thunderbolt breathing forth flame which scared him out of his presumptuous bravadoes; for having been smitten to his very soul he was crumbled to a cinder, and thunder-blasted in his prowess. And now, a hapless and paralysed form, is he lying hard by a narrow frith, pressed down beneath the roots of Ætna. And, seated on the topmost peaks, Vulcan forges the molten masses whence there shall burst forth floods, devouring with full jaws the level fields of fruitful Sicily; with rage such as this shall Typhon boil over in hot artillery of a never glutted fire-breathing storm; albeit he hath been reduced to ashes by the thunderbolt of Jupiter.'

In this passage we see Jove invested with the glory of defeating a great demon; but we also recognise the demon still under the protection of Fate. Destiny must bear that burthen. So was it said in the Apocalypse Satan should be loosed after being bound in the Pit a thousand years; and so Mohammed declared Gog and Magog should break loose with terror and destruction from the mountain-prison in which Allah had cast them. The destructive Principle had its 'share' as well as the creative and preservative Principles, and could not be permanently deprived of it. Gradually the Fates of various regions and names were identified with the deities, whose interests, gardens, or treasures they guarded; and when some of these deities were degraded their retainers were still more degraded, while in other cases deities were enabled to maintain fair fame by fables of their being betrayed and their good intentions frustrated by such subordinates. Thus we find a certain notion of technical and official power investing such figures as Satan, Ahriman, Iblis, and the Dragon, as if the upper gods could not disown or reverse altogether the bad deeds done by these commissioners.

But the large though limited degree of control necessarily claimed for the greatest and best gods had to be represented theologically. Hence there was devised a system of Commutation. The

Demon or Dragon, though abusing his power, could not have it violently withdrawn, but might be compelled to accept some sacrifice in lieu of the precise object sought by his voracity. These substitutions are found in every theological system, and to apply them to individuals constitutes the *raison d'être* of every priesthood. In the progress towards civilisation the substitutes diminish in value, and finally they become merely nominal and ceremonial,—an effigy of a man instead of the man, or wine instead of blood. At first the commutation was often in the substitution of persons of lower for others of higher rank, as when slaves or wives were, or are, sacrificed to assure paradise to the master or husband. Thus, Death is allowed to take Alcestis instead of Admetus. A higher degree of civilisation substitutes animals for human victims. In keeping with this is the legend of Christ's sending demons out of two men into a herd of swine:[1] which, again, is referable to the same class of ideas as the legend that followed concerning Jesus himself as a vicarious offering; mankind in this case being the herd, as compared with the son of a god, and the transfer of the Satanic power from the human race to himself, for even a little time, being accepted in theology as an equivalent, on account of the divine dignity of the being who descended into hell. It was some time, however, before theology worked out this theory as it now stands, the candid fathers having rejoiced in the belief that the contract for commutation on its face implied that Christ was to remain for ever in hell, Satan being outwitted in this.

The ancient Babylonian charms often end with the refrain:—'May the enchantment go forth and to its own dwelling-place betake itself,' Every evil spirit was supposed to have an appropriate dwelling, as in the case of Judas, into whom Satan entered,[2] and of whom it is said he 'by transgression fell, that he might go to his own place.[3] Very ingenious are some of the ancient speculations concerning the habitations and congenial resorts of demons. In some regions the colour of a disease on the skin is supposed to indicate the tastes of the demon causing it; and the spells of exorcism end by assigning him to something of the same hue. The demon of jaundice is generally consigned to the yellow parrots, and inflammation to the red or scarlet weeds. Their colours are respected. Humanity is little considered in the Eastern formulas of this kind, and it is pretty generally the case that in praying against plague or famine, populations are often found selecting a tribe to which their trouble is adjured to betake itself. 'May Nin-cigal,' says a Babylonian exorcism, 'turn her face towards another place; may the noxious spirit go forth and seize another; may the female cherub and the female demon settle upon his body; may the king of heaven preserve, may the king of earth preserve!'

So is it in regions and times which we generally think of as semi-barbarous. But every now and then communities which fancy themselves civilised and enlightened are brought face to face with the popular fatalism in its pagan form, and are shocked thereat, not remembering that it is equally the dogma of vicarious satisfaction or atonement. A lady residing in the neighbourhood of the Traunsee, Austria, informs me that recently two men were nearly drowned in that lake, being rescued at the last moment and brought to life with great difficulty. But this incident, instead of causing joy among the neighbours of the men, excited their displeasure; and this not because the rescued were at all unpopular, but because of a wide-spread notion that the Destinies required two lives, that they would have to be presently satisfied with two others, and that since the agonies of the drowning men had passed into unconsciousness, it would have been better to surrender the selected victims to their fate. At Elsinore, in Denmark, when the sea moans it is said to 'want somebody,' and it is generally the case that some story of a person just drowned circulates afterwards.

While the early mythological forms of the Fates diminish and pass away as curious superstitions, they return in metaphysical disguises. They gather their kindred in primitive sciences and cosmogonies, and finding their old home swept free of pagan demons, and, garnished with philosophic phrases, they enter as grave theories; but their subtlety and their sting is with them, and the last state of the house they occupy is worse than the first.

Yes, worse: for all that man ever won of courage or moral freedom, by conquering his dragons in detail, he surrenders again to the phantom-forces they typified when he gives up his mind to belief in a power not himself that makes for evil. The terrible conclusion that Evil is a positive and imperishable Principle in the universe carries in it the poisonous breath of every Dragon. It lurks in all theology which represents the universe as an arena of struggle between good and evil Principles, and human life as a war of the soul against the flesh. It animates all the pious horrors which identify Materialism with wickedness. It nestles in the mind which imagines a personal deity opposed by any part of nature. It coils around every heart which adores absolute sovereign Will, however apotheosised.

All of these notions, most of all belief in a supreme arbitrary Will, are modern disguises of Fate; and belief in Fate is the one thing fatal to human culture and energy. The notion of Fate (*fatum*, the word spoken) carries in it the conception of arbitrariness in the universe, of power deliberately exerted without necessary reference to the nature of things; and it is precisely opposed to that idea of Necessity taught by Science, which is another name for the supremacy of Law. Happily the notion of a universe held at the mercy of a personal decree is suicidal in a world full of sorrows and agonies, which, on such a theory, can only be traced to some individual caprice or malevolence. However long abject fear may silence the lips of the suffering, rebellion is in their hearts. Every blow inflicted, directly or permissively, by mere Will, however omnipotent, every agony that is consciously detached from universal organic necessity, in order that it may be called 'providential,' can arouse no natural feeling in man nobler than indignation. The feeling of a suitor in a court of law, who knows that the adverse judgment that ruins him has no root in the facts or the law, but proceeds from the prejudice or whim of the judge, can be nowise different from that of a mother who sees her son stricken down by death, and hears at his grave that he was consumed by the wrath of a god who might have yielded to her prayer, but refused it. The heart's protest may be throttled for a time by the lingering coil of terror, but it is there, and christian theologians will be as anxious to protect their deity from it, at whatever cost to his sovereignty, as their predecessors who invented the Cabinet of Women to relieve Jove from responsibility.

Metaphysics—which appear to have developed into the art

of making things look true in words when their untruth in fact has been detected—have indeed already set about the task just predicted. Eminent divines are found writing about matter and spirit, freedom and natural law, as solemnly as if all this discussion were new, and had never been carried out to its inevitable results. They can only put in christian or modern phraseology conclusions which have been reached again and again in the history of human speculation. The various schools of Buddhist and Vedantist philosophy have come by every conceivable route to their fundamental unity of belief in God, Soul, and Matter; in a pessimist visible nature, an ideal invisible nature, and a human soul held in matter like a frog in a snake's mouth, but able by certain mysterious, mostly metaphysical or verbal, tactics, to gain release, and pass into a corresponding situation in the deity.

'As a king, whose son had strayed away from him and lived in ignorance of his father among the Veddahs (wild men), will, on discovering his son, exclaim, 'Come to me, my darling son!' and make him a participator of the happiness he himself enjoys, even so will the Supreme God present himself before the soul when in distress—the soul enmeshed in the net of the five Veddahs (senses), and, severing that soul from Pâsam (Matter), assimilate it to himself, and bless it at his holy feet.'

It is too late for man to be interested in an 'omnipotent' Personality, whose power is mysteriously limited at the precise point when it is needed, and whose moral government is another name for man's own control of nature. Nevertheless, this Oriental pessimism is the Pauline theory of Matter, and it is the speculative protoplasm out of which has been evolved, in many shapes, that personification which remains for our consideration—the Devil.

VAMzzz Publishing

Paper books

VAMzzz Publishing is located in the very centre of old Amsterdam, in The Netherlands. Our publishing company creates high quality revised editions of five star occult, witchcraft, Gothic and esoteric classics, mostly written in the Fin de siècle-period and early 20th century.

As a publisher, we deeply respect the writer of any book we choose, so we join our forces (top level graphic design & thirty years of occult studies) to produce enchanting volumes which maximize the reading pleasure and inform, often with extra added information. In contrast to the current trend of digital screen addiction, we think, this variety of literature needs to be presented on paper. *No e-books, but real books!*

Apart from republications of valuable but forgotten books, we are also in the preparation of new publications on topics such as self-healing, magic, new astrology and more.

VAMzzz Publishing
P.O. Box 3340
1001 AC Amsterdam
The Netherlands
contactvamzzz@gmail.com
www.vamzzz.com

Previews of all books including a complete table of contents can be viewed on www.vamzzz.com. More books will be added to the list. *VAMzzz Publishing* strives to publish new volumes every month. Please visit our website regularly for the latest updates.

Recommended

*Demonology
and Devil-Lore 2*
Author:
Moncure Daniel Conway
518 pages, paperback
ISBN 978-94-92355-16-4

Demonology and Devil Lore 1 & 2, by Moncure Daniel Conway, were both published in 1897. Within the demonology scope, this rare and mostly forgotten, almost 1000 pages thick masterpiece, remains unsurpassed in quality and completeness. Even in the 21st century the works offer fascinating missing links for both the academic and student of occult traditions.

Volume 2 deals primarily with the diabolic and with the Devil himself, his ethnic history and connected topics. Themes like Ahriman and Ormuzd, women and the Star-Serpent in Persia, Lilith, Samael, Kali, Satan, Tiamat, Bohu, Ra and Apophis, Typhon, Gnostic theories, exorcism, Black Art Schools, the blood covenant, the witches Sabbath, the goat and cat, the Wild Hunt, Faust and Mephistopheles, magic seals, The Raven Book, Papal sorcery and a lot more.

Taboo, Magic, Spirits
A study of primitive elements in Roman religion
by Eli Edward Burriss
200 pages, Paperback, ISBN 9789492355034

In Ancient Rome Mana was the term used for a mysterious, magical medium, which could be helpful or harmful (Taboo). Just like the Chinese qi, it could empower the positive and the negative. Contents: Mana, Magic and Animism – Positive and Negative Mana (Taboo) – Miscellaneous Taboos – Magic Acts: The General Principles – Removing Evils by - Magic Acts – Incantation and Prayer– Naturalism and Animism.

Chaldean Magic
It's Origin and Development
by François Lenormant
454 pages, Paperback, ISBN 9789492355027

The essentials of magic in Chaldea are presented inside a context of comparison or contrast to Egyptian, Median, Turanian, Finno-Tartarian and Akkadian magic, mythologies, religion and speech. Interesting is the Chaldean demonology, with its incubus, succubus, vampire, nightmare and many Elemental spirits, most of them coalesced with the primal powers of nature.

Unicorn
A mythological investigation
by Robert Brown Jr.
124 pages, Paperback, ISBN 9789492355072

Brown Jr. believes the unicorn to be a lunar symbol, and draws on mythology from a wide range of sources all over the world to build his case. The author discusses the heraldic use of the unicorn, relates the creature to ancient goddesses like Astarte, Hecate en the Gorgon Medusa, and provides the reader with lost esoteric Moon-lore.

Là-Bas
A Journey into the Self
by Joris-Karl Huysmans
378 pages, Paperback, ISBN 9789492355058

The plot of *Là-Bas* concerns the novelist Durtal, who is disgusted by the emptiness and vulgarity of the modern world. He seeks relief by turning to the study of the Middle Ages. Through his contacts in Paris, Durtal discovers that Satanism is not a thing of the past but alive and kicking in turn of the century France. The novel culminates with a description of a black mass.

Devil-worship in France
Or The Question of Lucifer
by Arthur Edward Waite
240 pages, Paperback, ISBN 9789492355065

In *Devil-Worship in France,* Waite attempts to discern what is genuine from what is fake in the evidence of 19th century Satanism. To get the answers he spends a great deal of time investigating the French Masonic echelon, debunking a "conspiracy of falsehood" and determining what should be understood by Satanism and what not. Huysmans' diabolical novel *Là-Bas* (1891) inspired Waite to write this sceptical analysis.

Testament of Solomon
A First Century AD Grimoire
76 pages, Paperback, ISBN 9789492355041

A first century AD grimoire, and therefore the oldest, and least known, of all grimoires (magical instruction books) in the occult tradition. The book describes health inflicting demons of zodiacal decans, summoned by King Solomon, and how he controlled them to use their forces to build his temple and more. Translated by F. C. Conybeare, appeared first in the *Jewish Quarterly Review* of October, 1898.

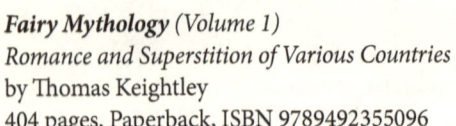

Fairy Mythology *(Volume 1)*
Romance and Superstition of Various Countries 1
by Thomas Keightley
404 pages, Paperback, ISBN 9789492355096

Fairy Mythology *(Volume 2)*
Romance and Superstition of Various Countries 2
by Thomas Keightley
404 pages, Paperback, ISBN 9789492355102

The term Fairy covers all kinds of nature spirits, not just the tiny sugar sweet creatures hovering around flowers. A unique and impressive book on this subject, published in a revised 2 volume-edition. No wiccan or pagan can afford to leave these books unopened. About Elves, Dwarfs, Kobolds, Trolls, Changelings, Meremaids, Nisses, Fairies, Brownies, Puck and other Elemental spirits all over the world.

Etruscan Magic & Occult Remedies
(Two volumes in one book)
by Charles Godfrey Leland
628 pages, Paperback, ISBN 9789492355003

Part One of the book offers complete and detailed insight in the Etruscan and Roman rooted pantheon of the Tuscan Streghe (witches). Part Two describes many of their spells, incantations, sorcery and several lost divination methods. Much information in this book, Leland received first hand from the Tuscan witches Maddalena and Marietta.

Amazons *- Two publications in one book -*
I. The Amazons by Guy Cadogan Rothery
II. Religious Cults Associated With the Amazons
   by Florence Mary Bennett
328 pages, Paperback, ISBN 9789492355089

Contents I: The Amazons of Antiquity – Amazons
in Far Asia – Modern Amazons of the Caucasus –
Amazons of Europe – Amazons of Africa – Amazons of
America – The Amazon Stones.
Contents II: The Amazons in Greek legend – The Great
Mother – Ephesian Artemis – Artemis Astrateia and
Apollo Amazonius – Ares.

Ophiolatreia
Rites and Mysteries of Serpent Worship
by Hargrave Jennings
186 pages, Paperback, ISBN 9789492355126

An account of the rites and mysteries connected with
the origin, rise and development of serpent worship in
various parts of the world, enriched with interesting
traditions, and a full description of the celebrated
serpent mounds & temples, the whole forming an
exposition of one of the phases of phallic, or sex
worship.

Voodoos and Obeahs
Phases of West India Witchcraft
by Joseph J. Williams
374 pages, Paperback, ISBN 9789492355119

This work goes into great depth concerning the New
World-African connection and is highly recommended if
you want a deep understanding of the dramatic historical
background of Haitian and Jamaican magic and witchcraft,
and the profound influence of imperialism, slavery and
racism on its development. Williams includes numerous
quotations from rare documents and books on the topic.

Aradia
Gospel of the Witches
by Charles Godfrey Leland
174 pages, Paperback, ISBN 9789492355010

This wonderful book describes the creation according to Italian witch-lore. We also read about the witch-meeting or sabbath (treguenda) and the book contains many original magical recipes, like spells for love and good fortune. Diana is further connected to the Moon and the fairy world.

www.ingramcontent.com/pod-product-compliance
Lightning Source LLC
Chambersburg PA
CBHW030349130626
46549CB00004B/1417